Advertising in Developing and Emerging Countries

Advertising in Developing and Emerging Countries

The Economic, Political and Social Context

The Economic, Political and Social Context

Edited by
EMMANUEL C. ALOZIE

GOWER

Published by
Gower Publishing Limited
Wey Court East
Union Road
Farnham
Surrey
GU9 7PT
England

Gower Publishing Company
Suite 420
101 Cherry Street
Burlington
VT 05401-4405
USA

www.gowerpublishing.com

Gower Applied Business Research
Our programme provides leaders, practitioners, scholars and researchers with thought provoking, cutting edge books that combine conceptual insights, interdisciplinary rigour and practical relevance in key areas of business and management.

Emmanuel C. Alozie has asserted his moral right under the Copyright, Designs and Patents Act, 1988, to be identified as the editor of this work.

British Library Cataloguing in Publication Data
Advertising in developing and emerging countries : the
   economic, political and social context.
   1. Advertising--Developing countries.
   I. Alozie, Emmanuel C.
   659.1'091724-dc22

Library of Congress Cataloging-in-Publication Data
Advertising in developing and emerging countries : the economic, political and social context / [edited by] Emmanuel C. Alozie.
      p. cm.
   Includes index.
   ISBN 978-0-566-09174-2 (hbk.) -- ISBN 978-0-566-09175-9
(ebook) 1. Advertising--Developing countries. I. Alozie, Emmanuel C.

   HF5813.D44A38 2011
   659.109172'4--dc22

                                                         2011009183

ISBN   978-0-566-09174-2 (hbk)
ISBN   978-0-566-09175-9 (ebk)

MIX
Paper from
responsible sources
FSC® C018575

Printed and bound in Great Britain by the
MPG Books Group, UK

Contents

List of Figures

List of Tables

Contributor Biographies

Emmanuel C. Alozie (PhD, University of Southern Mississippi) has worked professionally in public relations, advertising and journalism and has taught mass communication for two decades. His research interests are in international/intercultural communications, advertising/publication relations (strategic communication), journalism and new media, with an emphasis on the role of mass media and new technologies in nation building, international relations/policies, reconciliation and national development. A former assistant editor with *Democratic Communiqué*, Alozie published *Marketing in Developing Countries: Nigerian Advertising in a Global and Technological Economy* (2009, Routledge), *Cultural Reflections and the Role of Advertising in the Socio-Economic and National Development of Nigeria* (2005, Edwin Mellen), and co-edited, *Toward the Common Good: Perspectives in International Public Relations* (2004, Allyn and Bacon). Alozie serves on the editorial boards of the *International Journal of Information and Communication Technology in Research and Development in Africa (IJICTRDA)*. Alozie has published several refereed articles in journals, conference proceedings and book chapters, and has presented at academic conferences. He has refereed and reviewed scholarly works for various journals, publishers, academic organizations and conferences and sits on a number of editorial boards. An award winning teacher and researcher, Alozie has received fellowships from the Freedom Forum, the American Press Institute, Cap-Cities/ABC, Inland Press Association, Dow Jones Newspaper Fund and the Poynther Institute.

Jennifer Argo is an Assistant Professor in the department of Marketing, Business Economics, and Law at the University of Alberta in Edmonton, Alberta. Her research interests are primarily focused on understanding the role of social influences in consumption situations. In addition she is also interested in advertising in international contexts. Her work has appeared in the *Journal of Consumer Research*, the *Journal of Public Policy and Marketing* and the *International Journal of Advertising*.

Olugbenga C. Ayeni (PhD, University of Southern Mississippi) teaches a broad range of Advertising and Public Relations courses at Eastern Connecticut State University, Willimantic, Connecticut. Dr Ayeni worked for many years in Nigeria's national newspaper, *The Daily Times*, rising to executive position, while he served as Senior Correspondent to the international news journal, *West Africa*. He also had a short stint in the advertising industry as Account Executive. His research interests are in comparative studies in international mass media and cross cultural communications. He is the author of "A Comparative Study of the Political Communication Styles of Bill Clinton and Tony Blair" (2005, Edwin Mellen), and has published book chapters, research articles, and reviews in *Business Research Yearbook, Athens Institute of Education and Research Books Series, Encyclopedia of International Media and Communications, Global Media Journal, Journal of International Media*

Management and *Proceedings of the American Academy of Advertising.* In 2008, he worked as Consultant and Head of Public Awareness Department at SERVICOM, a United Kingdom DFID-funded Nigeria government service delivery reforms agency, coordinating all public information programs. An award winning teacher, Dr Ayeni has presented his scholarly work at national and international conferences, and his students have won grand prizes in state-wide advertising and public relations campaigns competitions.

Mukesh Bhargava (PhD, University of Texas at Austin) is Associate Professor in the Department of Management and Marketing at the Oakland University, Rochester, Michigan. Bhargava's interests include advertising research, strategic market planning and marketing for non-profit organizations. His recent areas of research have examined out-door advertising effectiveness and new techniques (data envelopment analysis) for measuring efficiency in a variety of managerial settings. He has published in the *Journal of Advertising Research, Journal of the Academy of Marketing Sciences, Marketing Letters* and the *Journal of Business Research* among others. His professional experience includes marketing research services for diverse clients such as Nestlé, Goodyear Tires, Union Carbide and the World Bank.

Tej K. Bhatia is Professor of Linguistics at Syracuse University and a Fellow at the Center for the Study of Popular Television at the S.I. Newhouse School of Public Communications, Syracuse University, Syracuse, New York. He has been Director of Linguistic Studies Program and Acting Director of Cognitive Sciences at his university. He has published a number of books and articles in the area of globalization, bilingualism and multiculturalism, language and cognition, media (advertising) discourse, and sociolinguistics, and has been consultant to several academic, administrative and business organizations. His books include, *Advertising in Rural India: Language, Marketing Communication, and Consumerism* (2000, Tokyo Press), *Handbook of Bilingualism* (2003, Blackwell), *Handbook of Child Language Acquisition* (1999, Academic Press) and *Handbook of Second Language Acquisition* (1996, Academic Press).

Thomas G. Brashear (PhD, Georgia State University) is an Associate Professor of Marketing in the Eugene M. Isenberg School of Management at the University of Massachusetts Amherst. His research has appeared in the *Journal of Advertising, Journal of the Academy of Marketing Science, Journal of Business Research* and the *Journal of Business and Industrial Marketing* among other journals and was presented at numerous conferences.

Mary Frances Casper is Assistant Professor in the Department of Communication, Boise State University, Boise, Idaho. Her primary research interests are the media rhetoric used in the marketing of America and American ideologies internationally.

Aliaa Dakroury, PhD, is Assistant Professor at the Department of Communication, University of Ottawa, Canada. She previously taught at the Departments of Communication, Sociology, and Law at Carleton University in Ottawa. She is the managing editor of the *American Journal of Islamic Social Sciences*, and serves on the editorial boards of several academic journals and as an organizing committee member for various international conferences. She is the author of *Communication and Human Rights* (2009), editor of *The Right to Communicate: Historical Hopes, Global Debates and Future Premises* (2009), and co-editor of *Introduction to Communication and Media Studies* (2008). Dr Dakroury has presented numerous papers at Canadian and international conferences of major communication and media associations, such as: the Canadian Communication Association, the Middle East Studies Association, the Association of Muslim Social Scientists, and the Canadian Ethnic Studies Association. Her publications appear in various refereed journals, such as *The International Communication Gazette, The Journal of Intergroup Relations, Culture, Language, and Representation, The Global Media Journal, Reconstruction: Studies in Contemporary Culture, Media Development, Journal of the World Association for Christian Communication, American Journal of Islamic Social Sciences* and *The Journal of International Communication*. Dr Dakroury can be reached at: adakrour@uottawa.ca.

Janez Damjan is Senior Lecturer in Marketing Education Management since 1992 at the Faculty of Economics, University of Ljubljana, Slovenia. He has been a Senior Partner since 2007 of Sartes Ltd., a family consulting and research company specializing in regional food, retail and services firms, President of the Slovenian Marketing Association (1991–2000) and Program Coordinator of the Golden Drum International Ad Festival. Educated at the Scandinavian International Management Institute and Publisher of *Jaz Magazine* (2006), Damjan's research interests are in small business, developing brands and consumer behavior in markets in transition.

Jaime S. Gomez (PhD, University of Utah), is Professor and Chair of the Communication Department at Eastern Connecticut State University, Willimantic, Connecticut, where he teaches media aesthetics and video producing and directing. His research interests include the use of information and communication technologies (ICT) as catalysts for development in Third World countries, media aesthetics and visual communication. Gomez has taught communication courses at San Francisco State University, University of Utah, Universidad del Norte (Northern University), Universidad Autonoma del Caribe (Caribbean Autonomous University) and Universidad del Atlantico in Colombia. He was head researcher for the project *Towards a System of Regional Public Educational Television: A New Model for the Colombian Caribbean Region Based on Technological Convergence*, under a research grant from the Colombian National Television Committee. He is co-author of *Introduction to Video Production: Studio, Field and Beyond* (2006, Allyn and Bacon) and author of *Distance Education: The Challenges of Technology and Communication* (2000, Universidad del Atlántico Press in Colombia). In Barranquilla, Colombia, in 1998, he designed and implemented a teacher's training program through the regional television network. He has presented refereed papers in Cuba, Spain, Colombia and the United States. He received a Simon Bolivar Award, the highest recognition in Colombian television, for Best Documentary 1991.

S.M. Mazharul Haque (PhD, Ohio University) is Professor in Mass Communication at the University of Southern Mississippi where he has been since 1984. Haque has published in a number of journals including *Journalism Quarterly, Asian Journal of Communication, Gazette, Media Asia* and others. His most recent book, co-authored with Dr Ming-May Jessie Chen, is *Representation of the Cultural Revolution in Chinese Films by the Fifth Generation Filmmakers* (2007, Edwin Mellen). Other publications include *What is News in India* (1988, University Press of America) and *Information Societies and the Developing World: A Synthesis of Theories* (1993, University of Georgia).

Joseph P. Helgert (PhD, Union Institute and University, Cincinnati) is an Associate Professor of Communications at Grand Valley State University in Allendale, Michigan. He has published in business and communications journals and maintains an interest in international advertising and East Asian Studies. In 1997 he was awarded a Sasakawa Fellowship at San Diego State University.

Amir Hetsroni (PhD, The Hebrew University of Jerusalem) is an Associate Professor in the School of Communication at Ariel University Center, Israel. His research interests include applications of cultivation theory and the study of sex and violence in advertising and in popular TV programming and cultivation theory. His articles have appeared in the *Journal of Communication*, *Journal of Advertising*, *Mass Communication and Society*, *Communication Monographs*, *Sex Roles*, *Social Science Quarterly* and other outlets. He is also a co-author of the book *Sex Differences: Summarizing more than a Century of Scientific Research* (2008, Routledge) and editor of the books *Reality TV: Merging the Global and the Local* (2011, Nova Science) and the forthcoming *Advertising and Reality: A Global Study of Representation and Content* (2012, Continuum).

Bruce A. Huhmann (PhD, University of Alabama) is an Associate Professor in the Department of Marketing at New Mexico State University, Las Cruces, New Mexico. His primary stream of research focuses on verbal and visual appeals and processing in advertising. His work on international advertising has focused on Africa, Asia and Canada. He has published articles in the *Journal of Consumer Research*, *Journal of Advertising*, *Journal of the Academy of Marketing Science*, *International Journal of Advertising*, *Journal of Public Policy and Marketing*, *Psychology and Marketing* and other journals and has presented his research at many national and international conferences.

Elzbieta Lepkowska-White (PhD, University of Massachusetts, Amherst) is an Associate Professor of Marketing at Skidmore College, Saratoga Springs, New York. Her research interests focus on international advertising, the Internet and public policy issues. She has published her work in the *Journal of Business Research*, *Journal of Advertising*, *Journal of Global Marketing*, *Journal of Consumer Affairs*, *Journal of Consumer Marketing*, *Journal of Internet Commerce* and *Journal of Marketing Management*, among other journals, and has presented her studies at national and international conferences.

Michael H. McBride is Professor Emeritus of Mass Communication at Texas State University-San Marcos, Texas. He was a Fulbright Scholar in the Republic of Moldova during 2005 and in Bulgaria during 1994–95. A member of the American Academy of Advertising and the Association for Education in Journalism and Mass Communication, McBride served on the board of editors for three marketing journals, authored or co-authored more than 80 referred and invited papers, book chapters, publications and presentations representing advertising, marketing, public relations and mass media, and was a panelist, moderator and discussant at academic conferences. He has received several research grants and was recognized for outstanding teaching and research.

Amy O'Connor (PhD, Purdue University) is an Assistant Professor in communication at North Dakota State University, Fargo, North Dakota. Her research interests include corporate advocacy advertising and its influence on public behavior. Recent published work investigates Philip Morris values advocacy messages and the ability of the messages to influence jury verdicts. She is currently working on research examining corporate social responsibility and the relationships between corporations and NGOs.

Emmanuel Onyedike (PhD, University of Iowa), Professor in the Department of Mass Communications at Virginia Union University, has more than 25 years of experience teaching journalism and mass communication at the college level. He has been an administrator for seven of those years. He has served as chair of the Minorities and Communications Division of AEJMC. Professionally, he has written and edited news stories for the *Oakland Tribune* in Oakland, California and has been a newspaper columnist for the *Weekly Star* in Enugu, Nigeria. He has also served as an information officer. His scholarly publications include: "Coverage of Africa by the African-American Press: Perceptions of African-American Newspaper Editors," "Re-Positioning Africa: The Role of African-American Leaders in Changing Media Treatment of Africa," "Cultural and Communication Problems in American Nursing," "Origins and Interpretation of Nigerian Press Laws," "Journalism Education in Nigeria: Balancing Theory and Practice," and "Government–Press Relations in Nigeria: Effects of the Press Laws." Onyedike received all his graduate degrees (PhD Education, MA Public Affairs and MA Journalism) from the University of Iowa, Iowa City. He received his baccalaureate degree in mass communications from the University of Nigeria, Nsukka.

Jan Quarles (PhD, University of Tennessee) is a Professor in the Department of Electronic Media Communication in the College of Mass Communication at Middle Tennessee State University, Murfreesboro, Tennessee. Since joining MTSU in 1994, Quarles has also served as chair of the Department of Journalism, Associate Dean of the College and Assistant Dean for Accreditation and Internationalization. She now teaches international communication and new media courses and formerly taught journalism, public relations and advertising in her various university posts in the United States and abroad. She served as Director of the Public Relations program at the Royal Melbourne Institute of Technology in Australia from 1989 to 1993 and worked to develop public relations accreditation in Australia. She is co-author, with Bill Rowlings, of *Practicing Public Relations: A Case Study Approach* (1993, Longman Australia) for students in Australia and Southeast Asia. Quarles held a Senior Specialist Fulbright to Cambodia in 2003 to develop a public relations and advertising curriculum at the Royal University of Phnom Penh and a postdoctoral research Fulbright to Australia in 1988. She has traveled extensively for consulting and teaching in Asia and Europe. She spent several summers in St Petersburg, Russia working with colleagues there. She is a Salzburg Fellow and an AEJMC Leadership in Diversity Fellow. Quarles is currently working on a research project on world trade, UNESCO and cultural industries. She completed both her BA in Philosophy and her doctoral degree at the University of Tennessee at Knoxville. She also attended the University of North Carolina at Chapel Hill.

Amos Owen Thomas is Professor of international business at the Harold Pupkewitz Graduate School of Business of the Polytechnic of Namibia. His research interests include the political economy of media, globalization strategies, comparative management and business ethics, on which he has published journal articles, chapters and a couple of books. Prior to his academic career at universities across three continents, he worked for a decade and a half in MNCs (mostly advertising agencies), NGOs and government around the Asia-Pacific region.

Gladys Torres-Baumgarten (PhD, Rutgers University) is Associate Professor in International Business at Ramapo College of New Jersey, Mahwah, New Jersey. She earned her MBA in marketing from Columbia University and a BA from the University of Pennsylvania. Her research interests focus on international business issues in emerging markets, including international marketing and foreign direct investment patterns.

Anuradha Venkateswaran (PhD, MBA, Virginia Polytechnic Institute and State University), is Associate Professor of Marketing at Wilberforce University, Ohio. A member of the American Marketing Association and a professionally certified marketer (PCM), her research interests include strategic marketing and management, multi-cultural marketing, branding, promotion—advertising and public relations, and consumer behavior. Additionally, she has an interest in emerging interdisciplinary areas spanning business and engineering/physical sciences such as disaster management and risk analysis. Dr Venkateswaran has published over 30 papers, in wide-ranging areas, in refereed journals, books and conference proceedings. Prior to her appointment at Wilberforce University she held positions as a design engineer at Media One (now Time Warner), a National Research Council Associate at the Wright Patterson Air Force Base, Dayton, Ohio and a Post-doctoral Fellow and Instructor at Virginia Polytechnic Institute and State University.

Fei Xue is an Assistant Professor in the School of Mass Communication and Journalism at the University of Southern Mississippi, Hattiesburg, Mississippi. He received his PhD in Mass Communication from the University of Alabama, and his MA in Mass Communication and BA in Journalism from Huazhong University of Science and Technology in China. His research interests involve advertising and consumer psychology, international advertising and the social effects of advertising. He has published in a variety of marketing and advertising journals, such as the *Journal of Advertising, Advances in International Marketing* and the *International Journal of Internet Marketing and Advertising*.

Anne Zahradnik (PhD, Western Michigan University) is Assistant Professor, Health Care Administration at Marist College, Poughkeepsie, New York. She has worked as a marketing consultant for companies in the software and healthcare industries. She has published and presented on measuring healthcare marketing return on investment and has an ongoing research interest in cost-effectively providing healthcare to uninsured adults.

Introduction:
Global Advertising and Values

S.M. MAZHARUL HAQUE

Advertising within a nation in today's world may contain certain distinctive values and features, yet it has to be understood in the context of the larger ongoing process of globalization. This is a phenomenon that has given rise to fairly heated discussion and debate among laypeople, scholars, politicians, workers and business people of different stripes during recent decades. Globalization can be seen as a historical process of interaction and integration of people representing a variety of commercial, noncommercial, government and nongovernmental institutions throughout the world, facilitated in the latest phase by the emergence of a global digital information network.

Globalization as a phenomenon has been associated with free market-based classical liberal economic policies pursued by developing and transitional societies of the world, that have embraced Western, more precisely, American values and modes of doing things not only in the realms of economics and politics but more visibly in the production, consumption and circulation of popular culture products, manifested in a pervasive process of commodification through advertising. Some social theorists seem to have pointed out that at its core globalization is a process of fundamental changes in which spatial and temporal features in human existence and their activities undergo dramatic transformation as distance between geographic locations is compressed or annihilated leading to a new sense or perception of space and temporality (http://plato.stanford.edu/entries/globalization/).

We have known, as Marshall McLuhan (1964) pointed out, that new communication systems devised by humans throughout history have not only extended human senses and opened up incredible opportunities for communication but they profoundly shaped the human psyche in unanticipated ways. For example, development of print technology in the fifteenth century undoubtedly gave us a vast array of reading materials but it also reinforced a linear, rational and logical way of thinking and developing arguments that on the surface would seem to be totally unrelated to the technology itself. We shape technology to meet our needs but it often ends up shaping us. Globalization in the contemporary phase through digital revolution has the potential of integrating disparate human groups to a point that national and local boundaries and the traditional concept of a community rooted in a geographic area may lose their meaning. Globalization in today's world clearly has implications for every conceivable arena of human endeavor, especially for cultural products and commodities where they are accessible to people as part of a global market. Therefore, marketers and multinational advertisers are concerned about strategies as how best to market products: through standardized, uniform advertising through an emphasis on universal brand identity or glocalization where the emphasis would be on identifying and making use of idiosyncratic local values and conditions in the market?

Even though the term globalization has gained particular currency since the 1970s there have been numerous allusions to and discussions of it in the literature since the nineteenth century. The changes in the compression of space made possible by high-speed modes of transportation and communication (such as rail, aircraft, telegraph and telephone) since the emergence of industrial capitalism in the nineteenth and early twentieth centuries have indicated dimensions of globalization. Karl Marx himself was intrigued in the mid-nineteenth century by the "intercourse in every direction" and "universal interdependence of nations," brought about by the bourgeoisie in their own interest of capitalist production. Despite the negative implications of capitalist exploitation, Marx saw in it possibilities of a progressive, cosmopolitan and socialist future the vastly increased range of human interactions across national and other separative barriers and boundaries offered.

Social theorists seem to be developing a consensual view that globalization has given rise to deterritorialization and disintermediation where people are increasingly engaging in electronic commerce across the globe without going through intermediaries, viewing television reports of coups, wars and earthquakes in real time from both neighboring and remote lands, and communicating via cyberspace with a globally dispersed community of people bound by only common ideologies, interests, passions and emotions. Evidently, there is a social interconnectedness among people and the activities conducted through the cyberspace despite intervening geographic or psychological distance. High-speed digital communication technology also leads to an acceleration of social life. In today's world advertising may have a new challenge to overcome in its effort to reach a global, national or local audience.

In globalized politics, it is notable that increasingly larger segments of population within national territories are participating in transnational movements of different kinds particularly in areas of human rights through global digital networks of communication. Social and political activists are using the same high-speed networks to disseminate their political messages nationally and globally, and mobilize the interested publics and stakeholders through persuasively designed advertising messages in political or electoral campaigns. We also note the emergence of supranational forms of lawmaking and regulatory networks in vast continental groupings like the European Union that are often replacing what has traditionally been considered to be an area of activity reserved for national self-government. Similarly, we see the emergence of globalized financial markets beyond the immediate control of national governments where transactions are being made and assets are being transferred on a 24-hour basis by people not territorially identified.

Development of new technologies and new liberal free market policies in trade and investment by governments across the world in recent years have made it possible for many countries to enter into a new phase of economic development that is qualitatively different. Governments and transnational corporations have negotiated agreements to reduce barriers to trade and investment and promote the free flow of goods, services and investment. It has been reported that since 1950 the volume of world trade has gone up 20-fold (http://www.globalization101.org/What is Globalization.html), and UNCTAD reports that foreign direct investment stocks (FDI) alone constitute 20 percent of global gross domestic product. It is in this environment that many multinational advertising corporations from the United States and other Western countries have invested in and created subsidiary operations in many emerging nations in East and Central Europe, Asia and Latin America.

Such a profound and all-encompassing phenomenon as globalization that impacts every facet of life of people in countries of the world that are at varied levels of socio-economic development with different levels of economic insecurities and anxieties are bound to generate controversies. Proponents of globalization argue that this process allows less developed or poor countries to develop economically and raise their living standards by using the global market. Communist China follows a number of Asian countries that provide good examples of what a less developed country can do by using the global market through export-oriented economic policies on the one hand, and by developing a consumption-oriented domestic economy on the other, to achieve phenomenal economic growth and reduction of poverty. China has been able to create a huge middle class for several hundred million people in a few short decades, unprecedented in human history, by creating an industrial system of manufacturing products and marketing them in a globalized market. It goes without saying that the advertising industry historically has played a key role in creating consumerist values and lifestyles in the West that lie behind the creation of a consumption-oriented society like the United States, and it is likely to do so in China and other developing countries as well.

Opponents of globalization point to the negative consequences of this process in which multinational corporations in the West are out to make a buck by outsourcing jobs to poor countries like India where wages are low because poor countries have no ecological standards to maintain, and have no minimum wage requirements for their workers, and where laws against child workers are not enforced. So, globalization in this view not only leads to the loss of jobs for American workers, unskilled or semi-skilled, but it causes the lowering of wages and standard of living even for highly-skilled and trained workers. The threat of outsourcing of jobs has a deep dampening effect on the ability of even the highly-skilled workers to bargain for wages and benefits.

Advertising

It can be argued that advertising as a basic part of popular culture, designed to achieve the goal of persuading an audience is also one of the most influential institutions of socialization in a post-industrial and post-modern society. Jhally (1990) enumerates some of the cultural functions of advertising by pointing out that it structures mass media content, it may play a key role in the construction of gender identity, it deeply influences cultural institutions, such as sports and popular music, and it impacts the relation between children and parents in the mediation and creation of needs and demands for various products, sometimes of questionable value. It is a dominant force in electoral political campaigns at national or local levels. In the United States, advertising messages known as "attack ads" have emerged as a primary strategic or tactical tool in the hands of political partisans to delegitimize opponents, or, at a minimum, implant doubts about the viability of opposition candidates and their platforms in the minds of voters, potentially favorably inclined to them. Through a variety of claims, often bordering on the deceptive, partisans wish to sway public opinion in favor of a candidate for public office or clinch policy debates in their favor. Political advertisements are known to have a decisive role in debates on every major national issue ranging from healthcare reform, to social security policy revisions, or important judicial appointments. In the public health arena, government or nonprofit agencies have launched campaigns to educate citizens by providing basic information about preventable diseases or sensitize them to the need for certain dietary or nutritional habits and exercise as part of a health-conscious, desirable way of living.

As a form of discourse, advertising is concerned about a universal relationship between people, objects, goods, services or commodities. Humans seem to develop a deep psychic relationship with objects or commodities possibly because of the all-pervasive consumer socialization process in capitalist societies, where possession of objects without true value may symbolize perceived superior or inferior social status. Marcuse (1972) says, objectification is not a small part of human experience, it is its deeper foundation. It is through objectification or commodification that we gather distinctive human experience, the mediation of needs through objects.

Many countries of the world, even the emerging nations as have been covered in this book, have government and/or industry regulatory agencies to ensure that unsuspecting consumers are not victimized by unfair, misleading or deceptive advertising. In the United States, it is the responsibility of the Federal Trade Commission (FTC) as the primary government regulator of the advertising industry. This agency defines advertising, as a matter of custom and practice, any action, method or device intended to draw the attention of the public to merchandise, persons and organizations. Trading stamps, contests, freebies, premiums and even product labels are included in this broad definition, in addition to the more common categories of product and service advertising (Pember, 2002). The American Marketing Association defines advertising as any paid form of nonpersonal presentation and promotion of ideas, goods or services by an identified sponsor. But defining advertising also involves defining what is not permissible because of deceptiveness or falsity of the message. So, the FTC defines a deceptive message as one that is a misrepresentation of a product or service, with an omission of material information about it, or a practice that is likely to mislead the consumer, looked at from the perspective of a reasonable consumer. So, this definition would allow puffery or exaggerated claims by advertisers on the assumption that a reasonable or rational consumer would expect an advertiser to make certain degree of superlative claims about a product or service and a rational consumer would not accept them at face value.

However, the FTC has at its disposal a range of tools to fight deceptive or false advertisements, some of which are called guides because they are advisory opinions concerning what the FTC believes to be permissible claims about a product, and when an advertiser is crossing the limits. The FTC may allow voluntary compliance to an advertiser under which it terminates a questionable advertising campaign because the company has had a reasonably good record in the past. The other tools, including consent agreement, litigated orders, substantiation, corrective advertising, injunctions and trade regulation rules, allow the FTC to use varying degrees of legally coercive power to deal with untruthful advertising campaigns. Obviously, countries in different parts of the world use different models of regulation of commercial messages. The United States may be unique in allowing even commercial messages certain constitutional protection of free speech under the First Amendment. For a long time the US legal system simply did not recognize any free-speech related constitutional protection, but since the 1970s, through case law the country has developed a commercial speech doctrine under which the government has fairly broad powers to regulate advertising if it is false or misleading; it can also regulate advertising for unlawful products and services. But when the advertising message is truthful and for a legal product or service the government can regulate it strictly under three conditions: it has a substantial state interest to justify the regulation, the regulation directly advances the interest articulated by the government, and there is a reasonable fit between the state interest and regulation, i.e., the cost of regulation balances out the presumed benefit (Pember, 2002). This doctrine clearly recognizes the value of free expression even in the form of commercial speech because, among other things, consumers are believed to have the paramount constitutional right to receive information, especially about legal products and services.

Values

Values are broad and general cultural principles embodying standards for thinking and behaving (Haque, 2003). Culture manifests itself in the meaning systems observed in the values, ideas and beliefs expressed through the various symbolic forms of representations and artifacts, including advertising (Cheng, 1994; Cheng and Schwitzer, 1996). Rokeach (1973) defines value as a specific mode of conduct or end state of existence being personally preferable to an opposite or a converse mode of conduct or end state of existence. A value system assumes an organization of values according to an implicit evaluation of the enduring beliefs on some scale of relative importance.

Africa and the Middle East

A number of articles included in this book examine values in advertisements. By employing a qualitative method of analysis in the overall context of globalization and the theoretical construct of cultural imperialism, Emmanuel C. Alozie examines Nigerian print advertisements produced by Western multinational corporations to answer some basic questions: What are the values and symbols conveyed in the ads? Do the values, symbols and context conveyed in the ads promote products or services, or do they expose the social conditions of Nigeria? Advertising in Africa has often given rise to pro and con arguments among scholars concerning its benefits and negative effects.

Proponents have argued under a rationalist model that essentially consumers make rational purchase decisions that are consistent with their economic interests without being unduly influenced by sales pitches of advertisers, and this contributes to economic growth and development. Critics argue that multinational advertisers often push unhealthy products like Rothman cigarettes by creating sexual imagery with white models in black countries, along with a sense of high status and pleasure, associated with a product. This undermines traditional social and cultural values. By creating demands for expensive, inessential imported products advertisers may encourage wasteful, extravagant lifestyles among the small local elite which also undermine the local manufacturing capacity, and distort the overall economy through the misallocation of scarce resources. In addition, opponents believe that the majority of advertising messages foster sexism, corruption, class division and a dependency relationship conducive to the promotion of cultural imperialism between core–periphery nations. However, there is a neutralist school as well which takes the middle course by suggesting that advertising ordinarily does not either serve or harm the welfare of a society though it has the potential to do both depending on what uses it is put to.

Alozie, in his analysis, concludes that transnational advertising in Nigeria tends to promote gender and class division as well as white racial superiority. The advertiser's message emphasizing the need for Nigerians to possess luxury goods such as air conditioners, beyond the buying capacity of most citizens, can be socially divisive because it can breed jealousy of the small elite by the masses. A consumer culture emphasizing the acquisition of objects is likely to encourage corruption, abuse of power and a shallow lifestyle among the elite delinked from its African natural roots. The author, however, notes that advertising may be an important vehicle for the manufacturers to reach and expand consumer bases in Nigeria and other African countries. The right pro-development advertising messages could also serve the cause of national development.

In a case study of Nigeria, Olugbenga C. Ayeni examines the advertising market in the country. Despite a history of poor macro-economic management, inadequate infrastructure building, political instability and horrendous corruption by consecutive governments since its independence in 1960 from the British rule, Nigeria as Africa's most populous (estimated population of 135 million) country was still able to produce an over 5 percent annual growth rate and a GDP of 191 billion dollars (in purchase power parity terms) in 2006, backed by its considerable oil sector contributing about 20 percent to its national income. Nigeria naturally is believed to have the potential of developing a significant market.

Before the incursion of Europeans into Africa, in an oral society Nigerian kings and tribal chiefs used gong men to disseminate news in marketplaces, and traders employed magicians and snake charmers to endorse products and footmen to scream the virtues of their products to passersby. With the introduction of printing technology in the nineteenth century, newspapers began to be published which provided a limited vehicle for advertisement of the arrival and departure of European ships. Cinema, billboards, radio and television followed later as advertising outlets. In the 1920s the first ad agency, a subsidiary of a British multinational company, got started, but today there are over 80 agencies in operation generating a total billing of $50 million for the industry. The agencies, however, remain undercapitalized, very small-scale, non-transparent operations that do not follow internationally accepted business practices.

Advertising has been used to establish brands in Nigeria since the early days. In recent years the telecom industry has used ad campaigns to popularize mobile phones, a product that has social benefits, but breweries of alcoholic beverages like beer by increasing their sales have caused social concern. However, creative campaigns have also been used for purposes of social mobilization in family planning, AIDS prevention, childhood immunization and the prevention of female circumcision, among others. Unfortunately, the Nigerian counterparts of the American political parties and politicians are also engaging in opponent-focused, debasing political ads that also appeal to ethnic, religious and other biases that may exacerbate existing divisions.

Aliaa Dakroury in a content analysis of advertisements in social magazines and television shows from Egypt and Saudi Arabia tries to explore Arab taste patterns and popular culture. The researcher follows the French sociologist Pierre Bourdieu, who theorized that corporations not only sell goods and services, they also disseminate through various forms of the media symbols and ideas as new tastemakers and arbiters of a morality and lifestyle which are associated with an art of consuming, spending and enjoyment.

Obviously, Arab tastes have been influenced by their history of being colonized by Europeans, and hence colonization has generally produced acceptance, familiarity and the imitation of Western values and aesthetic standards by Arabs, and this is particularly observed in the consumption patterns of the Arab elite who were educated in the West.

Specifically, Dakroury finds a difference between print and television ads in taste themes. The magazine ads used the Western taste attribute as a superior, elite one, while television paid more attention to traditional, national and local taste. The results also suggest a close relation of Arab taste with the theme of luxury. The words and the imagery in the ads, especially from Saudi Arabia, indicate that costly and luxurious products are symbolic of superior taste. Arab television ads use music extensively and universally and Western music in them seems to represent a high-culture taste. Ads also use expressions like "golden," "outstanding," "unique," "best," "elegant" and "finest." Ads for clothes, electronics and other products used foreign models with blonde hair and light eye color. Ads also used celebrities both foreign and domestic. A notable detergent ad showed a homemaker and a maid from the Far East suggesting a comfortable Arab family lifestyle that requires a foreign maid in the family to do the mundane chores, an indication of conspicuous consumption as a desirable thing.

Amir Hetsroni sketches the evolution of the Israeli advertising industry from the 1930s before the founding of the Jewish state until the present time. In the early stages in the 1930s, ad agencies were one-person operations. The economy was small, with a population of only about half a million, and only print ads and posters were made to glorify Zionist organizations which urged people to engage in altruistic deeds. After the establishment of the state of Israel in 1948, the country was relatively poor with government owning a major share of the economy. Therefore, demand for advertising and production of it were rudimentary.

During the second phase (1960–67) radio and cinema were also available for advertising in addition to print, but skills and creativity for the production of modern advertising were in short supply. However, in 1961 the Israeli Union for Advertising Agencies was formed to represent the industry. It is only during the third phase (1967–80) that modern advertising began in earnest after the Six-Day War. The economy took off, the standard of living improved, multinational companies began to arrive with demands for modern marketing. Young professionals trained in the United States or Europe replaced old operatives and began to respond to these demands. During the fourth phase (1980–93) technological developments like offset printing and digital color separation created new opportunities for ad professionals, yet some restrictive government policies, such as not allowing commercials for goods and services on television, cramped the advertising market. The latest phase began in 1993 with the arrival of commercial television and the Internet along with the growth of the economy to a European level and the influx of Jewish refugees from Eastern Europe. Foreign conglomerates like McCann Erickson and BBDO brought their expertise and worked through local subsidiaries. Many full-service and specialty service agencies began to offer services in a market that had Arabic, Russian and other language-speaking subpopulations that needed target marketing.

Over the early decades, advertisements sometimes used unpaid national leaders like Ben Gurion to promote important causes. Ads also contained more altruistic values, like collectivism and patriotism. But recent studies indicate Western values both hedonistic, such as joy and enjoyment, and pragmatic, such as saving, efficiency and excellence, have become dominant, and traditional values have become less visible.

Asia

Jan Quarles examines advertising in Cambodia as a newly emerging, relatively small Southeast Asian country, with a population of approximately 14 million that has an estimated GDP of $39 billion translating to per capita income of $2,800. The country has a fairly recent history of genocidal bloodletting in the 1970s under the communist Khmer Rouge regime, and it is still trying to recover from the loss of its educated and skilled manpower, almost continuous political instability, corruption and misgovernance. Since it is a largely rural country with a small market, mostly dependent on the export of garments and tourism for foreign exchange earnings, where the media infrastructure is relatively undeveloped, and with a population that has a low income (35 percent of which lives under the poverty line), its demand for goods and services and advertising is also low, compared to that of its much larger neighbors, Thailand and Vietnam. However, since 1999 some multinational companies have come into the market and media spending showed an increase. Advertisers use Khmer and English newspapers, periodicals, television, radio, billboards, leaflets, loudspeakers on trucks and event sponsorship to reach consumers. Advertising activities largely center around services like mobile phone services, travel agents, hotels, and products like pharmaceuticals, alcoholic and non-alcoholic beverages, tobacco and clothing. Even though advertising of alcohol is permitted, health warnings are required, and while tobacco advertising is banned on state-owned television, private stations can sell airtime. Government and some nongovernmental organizations also use media campaigns to raise awareness about public health hazards like AIDS.

Amy O'Connor and Mary Frances Casper in their chapter examine the indirect advertising strategies employed by multinational tobacco companies to legitimize and popularize their products in China, a country in which 2,000 people are estimated to die every day from tobacco-consumption-related diseases. Despite the staggering death figures, China remains the largest consumer and producer country of tobacco products where 66 percent of the male population smokes, and the total number of smokers is expected to rise to 400 million by 2050. Even though only 1 percent of Chinese women currently smoke, it is feared that tobacco companies may target this group to increase their market just as they seem to have done among teens. Western companies are eyeing the emerging markets of the less developed countries as potential areas of growth, since these countries have fewer rules to restrict the marketing of products, and Western governments are consistently trying to delegitimize tobacco products and restrict their marketing efforts through increasingly stringent legal hurdles.

In order to operate in a large country like China a cigarette company needs to establish social legitimacy, which it can do by creating linkages with the society through sponsorships of special events of social significance and making outright financial contributions to causes that would be viewed by the key publics and policy makers as desirable. Three specific strategies have been historically used by corporations to establish legitimacy: linking with charities and other organizations that already enjoy a high degree of legitimacy in the society; using advertising campaigns to influence the overall business environment to make it more congruent with their interests; and altering their behavior, products and services to make them more consistent with social norms and expectations. Multinational tobacco companies have tapped into a deep-seated craving in Asian consumers for things that are Western, even products that can pose health hazards.

So, as Saffer (2000) points out, cigarette advertising does not often provide product-specific information to the consumer, but through the use of appealing symbolism of different kinds, it rather creates a fantasy of sophistication, pleasure and social success. The use of the product promises the aspiring, achievement-oriented consumer to be linked with American or European fantasy lifestyles. Even in China, after an early period of unfettered advertising, the cigarette as a product has come under government scrutiny and advertising has been banned on various media. Cigarette companies, therefore, have had to resort to indirect advertising to keep their brands salient in the public minds. By sponsoring, popular sporting events, television series and musical events companies like Phillip Morris, R.J. Reynolds and British Tobacco Company are accomplishing the basic goal of associating themselves with popular, enjoyable cultural products, such as television shows that are symbolic of clean and healthy activities. They are also conveying a sense to the public that without their sponsorship these cultural products would not be available to them, therefore, these companies are contributing to the creative cultural life of the country by playing the role of good citizens. Obviously, tobacco companies, through the indirect advertising strategy, have found a way to bypass legal restrictions and avoid dealing with questions of the staggering health costs of tobacco-related illness, decreased worker productivity and the premature deaths of smokers leading to family insecurity.

With a diverse, polyglot population of 235 million people, and an estimated GDP of approximately a trillion dollars in purchase power parity, Indonesia is the largest Muslim-majority, archipelagic nation in the world that also has the potential of becoming a significant economic power both in Asia and the world. Market segmentation studies already indicate that the country has a substantial and growing middle class (estimated at over 21 million) with a disposable income for spending on durable and consumable goods and services, as evidenced by over 58 million mobile phone owners, and over 16 million Internet users, along with a yearly rate of growth in credit card users in double digits. It is not surprising that in a vast resource-rich market like Indonesia, with good economic prospects (yearly economic growth rate 5.5 percent) despite the fact that a fairly large segment of the population (17 percent) lives under the poverty line, advertisers are already spending a significant amount of money on advertising ($2.4 billion in 2005).

Anuradha Venkateswaran, in the chapter on Indonesia, provides an assessment of the political, social, economic and cultural influences on advertising in the nation by pointing out that the government has the difficult task of maintaining a fragile balance between preserving the indigenous value system on the one hand, and encouraging economic growth, multi-media convergence and consumerism on the other. Some of the fundamental ideological guiding principles as enunciated in the constitution are encompassed by *Pancasila*, namely belief in one supreme God, humanitarianism, nationalism expressed in the unity of the nation, consultative democracy and social justice for all. Upholding these guiding principles has meant a historical role of the government in controlling and regulating media in Indonesia in the interest of maintaining racial harmony and national integration. Advertising has also not escaped government scrutiny. Television commercials were banned in 1981 for a period of ten years for promoting conspicuous consumption. The Code of Ethics and Practices of Advertising require advertisers not only to conform to the principles of *Pancsila* but more specifically to be truthful, socially responsible, compliant with regulations, not offensive to religious faiths, or violative of racial or cultural traditions. There are also restrictions on advertising products, such as cigarettes or alcoholic beverages, etc. Television commercials are required to be previewed and approved by the government before airing. In general, the Consumer Protection Law specifies that the consumers have a right to obtain accurate, clear and honest information on goods and services, and therefore advertisements must give true and correct information on these.

Venkateswaran in discussing the broader context of Indonesian culture uses a number of widely used cultural dimensions proposed by Hofstede which allow cross-cultural comparisons. These are masculinity versus femininity, power distance, individualism versus collectivism, high context versus low context, uncertainty avoidance, and long-term versus short-term orientation. On the gender dimension in organizations in terms of work goals, men find advancement, earnings, training, up-to-dateness to be more important, while to women a friendly atmosphere, position security, physical conditions and cooperation are more important. Indonesia as a culture falls more on the feminine side of the spectrum (Hofstede, 2001). Power distance refers to the extent to which the less powerful members accept and expect that power is distributed unequally. Malay countries like Indonesia and Malaysia have large power distances, in which subordinates display a heavy dependence on their bosses, and a reluctance to question or contradict their bosses. In individualistic societies, such as the United states, individuals are believed to look out for themselves and their immediate family. In collectivist societies, individuals are expected to be loyal to strong, cohesive in-groups. Indonesia and Malaysia are largely collectivist in their orientation, countries that emphasize collective responsibility and interdependency, where it may be considered impolite to be direct or boastful, and even logic-based comparative ads, commonly encountered in individualistic societies are to be avoided. There is also the high context versus low context dimension. Asian countries in general, including Indonesia, are high-context societies in which they rely more on contextual factors in communication, such as socio-relational, physical and perceptual matters rather than specific, explicit and overt language cues. Tolerance for ambiguity and uncertainty avoidance is another dimension that refers to a culture's level of anxiety in uncertain situations, its need to have predictability and control. Indonesia ranks somewhat low on this index. Asian nations seem to be more inclined to value virtue over truth, they seem to have a long-term orientation for economic development emphasizing thrift, perseverance and respect for social obligations. All these cultural factors have important implications for multinational advertisers. For example, a corporation from the United States, a low-context culture, would have to realize that advertising in a high-context, collectivist society such as Indonesia using nonverbal messages, face-saving tactics and building long-term relationships may be very useful communication tactics to appeal to the consumers and achieve business success.

Bhatia and Bhargava examine advertising in rural India where walls and other structures serve as billboards or a medium of advertising. India offers an enormously interesting example of a pluralistic, multi-ethnic and multi-lingual country of continental proportion to cultural scholars, the second most populous nation with 1.12 billion people who speak 21 different officially recognized major languages and over 1,600 dialects. With a GDP of over four trillion dollars in purchase power parity, it currently ranks fourth in the world in overall size of economy, yet it ranks 118th in per capita income. It is a country of great contrasts that has some of the largest cities in the world while more than 70 percent of the population live in rural areas constituting 600 to 700 million potential rural customers. This demographic picture presents a challenge to the national and multinational advertisers as to how to reach the consumer segments in the rural areas who are often unreachable through the conventional media, and are not part of the organized market, yet comprise a market of their own that constitutes 70 percent of the sales of durables, such as bicycles, portable radios and mechanical wristwatches, and nondurable, consumable products, such as detergents. Moreover, some estimate that this rural market is becoming bigger than the urban market in India.

The researchers in this study of wall advertising examined a sample of 2,000 wall ads, in six languages, collected from villages in five states in three regions of the country. Indian wall ads are somewhat similar to Western banner ads seen in sports arenas. They serve primarily as information-only ads in which advertisers use, to varying degrees, the following components: product name, company name, contact information, taste or other properties, price, invitation to use the product and slogan. The researchers conclude that in order to draw the hard-to-reach masses of rural consumers in this vast country, advertisers in this age of globalization have to rely on a mix of conventional and nontraditional media. Walls provide an effective medium of advertising to draw the attention of the rural consumers, but advertisers can optimize and enhance the appeal of their messages by an imaginative mix of languages and scripts keeping in mind that English is the language of globalization but local language offers the best method of communicating ideas about service or product.

Fei Xue, in his examination of East Asian (China, Japan, South Korea) advertising styles, uses only two of the multiple dimensions (i.e., high-context versus low-context and collectivism versus individualism) propounded by Hofstede and discusses some broad themes, appeals and techniques of presentation in advertising. Since this region of the world has a combined population of nearly 1.5 billion people with a GDP of over 15 trillion dollars (in purchase power parity), which exceeds that of the United States, it has emerged as one of the most economically and culturally vibrant and dynamic areas of the world, calling for scholarly attention. An appeal is a motivational message employed by an advertiser to induce a potential consumer to buy a product or service by drawing his/her attention explicitly or implicitly to a psychic element that touches a responsive chord. Messages embedded with values and norms that are consonant with those of the deeply-held beliefs of the consumers in a culture are likely to have resonance with them. Since Western and East Asian consumers hold cultural beliefs that are different, advertising appeals used in these parts of the world also reflect the differences. Some of the commonly used East-Asian appeals fall into three categories that are related to group consensus, veneration of the elderly or tradition, and status.

Some researchers, such as, Pan et al. (1994), in a comparative analysis of Chinese and American cultural values, note that US culture values individual personality, while traditional Chinese culture places emphasis on a person's duty to family, clan and state. It is not surprising then that comparative analysis of advertising content shows that US commercials use more individualistic appeals than those in Korea or China. In the second category, wisdom of the elderly and the respect for tradition are emphasized. Analysis of comparative advertising messages indicates that despite a fast-changing society in China, veneration of the elderly remains a common theme, along with family, technology and tradition while in the United States dominant themes are of enjoyment, individualism and economy.

In Chinese commercials visual images of the elderly are more frequently used than in the United States along with ancient characters and historical events or ancient sayings. In the category of status appeal, it is interesting to note that a Confucian society can emphasize the value of social status reflected in a person's material possessions and economic achievements leading to upward social mobility. It was found that Japanese ads had a greater tendency to show the importance of social status than American ones. Chinese ads used status appeals by using expressions like power, boss or pictures of people with material possessions or successful careers. Paradoxically, in Asian countries, including the most developed societies like Japan whose products enjoy recognition, acceptance and admiration for their high quality throughout the world, foreign expressions, foreign goods, foreign celebrity endorsements and models seem to enjoy a very high status. In general, in East Asia the advertising techniques used could be labeled as a soft-sell approach in which advertisers make an attempt to convey mood and sentiments through beautiful visual and aural imagery, rather than a hard-sell direct approach in which product qualities and virtues are emphasized. Also, in these high-context Asian cultures, advertising messages often contain less product-specific information cues, they prefer to create brand images in the minds of the consumers for a long-term return.

Europe

With an area of 1.05 million square miles, Kazakhstan is the largest landlocked Central Asian country. It has an economy larger than that of all the other Central Asian countries combined. Kazakhstan had been a Soviet Republic since 1936, but after the dissolution of the Soviet Union in 1991 it declared itself an independent state and made an uneasy transition from communism to capitalism through an initial period of turbulence in which the economy shrank considerably. Amos Owen Thomas examines the advertising practices and improvisations used in the business in this resource-rich, sizable, new economy.

Multinational advertising corporations introduced advertising in the county after the collapse of the Soviet Union and they remained a major force in the market contributing a third of all advertising expenditure. Television and radio stations sold airtime and also provided creative production through their in-house facilities to advertisers. Usually, the agencies received revenue on a commission basis which was set on the percentage of the sales of the previous year. Television rating research is not considered reliable, so, advertisers go with their instincts as to which program is suitable for their products. In general, news has the top rating followed by movies, sports programming and music. Thomas suggests that the state of development of media and advertising in Kazakhstan is closer to those in the developing countries of Asia rather than those in Europe. In most post-communist countries the ruling elite transformed themselves into capitalists, many of whom owned the wealth-producing institutions including the media. The new group of crony capitalists often promote establishment-oriented tabloid news to draw large audiences and also act in a partisan way as did media managers in the communist era.

Michael H. McBride also provides a description of advertising in Moldova, a small East European landlocked country of four million people with a GDP per capita of slightly over $2,500, ranking as the poorest country in the continent. Moldova declared its independence from the Soviet Union in 1991 after its dissolution, and began to adopt macroeconomic reform policies of liberalization and privatization like other former communist countries. After an initial period of production decline, the new policies implemented produced steady economic growth, even though the country still is fairly dependent on agriculture with a high unemployment rate and has a high rate of absolute poverty. Notably, it has also an estimated emigration rate of 25 percent of the working-age population. The emerging economy is trying to use advertising to sell products and services, and television as a medium claims 67 percent of the advertising expenditure, followed by outdoor media with 12 percent, print media with 11 percent and radio with 10 percent. This poor, former socialist European country in its transition to capitalist economy symbolizes the use of advertising and marketing for economic growth.

Ion Macari, known as the father of Moldovan advertising, began an agency in the 1940s with the approval of the Soviet authorities, even though advertising as a business activity remained under suspicion. Others followed in his footsteps, but Western advertising concepts created a conflict of values. However, the introduction of *perestroika* under Mikhail Gorbachev in the 1980s offered opportunities for new initiatives. A combination of factors favored the growth of the ad industry: domestic firms wanted to advertise, mass media needed the revenues advertising would generate for them, and ad agencies were ready to exploit them. Foreign consulting and ad agencies like McCann Erickson and Ogilvy & Mather brought in the expertise to provide a range of services, including strategic media planning, media buying, sales promotion, direct marketing and public relations. Some agencies provided special services, such as, creating designs, holding special events and placing ads in the media. The Moldovan *Yellow Pages* directory indicates that more than a hundred ad agencies ranging from full to specialty service firms are currently in operation. Some of the top categories of products advertised are mobile phones, washing detergents, shampoos, soaps, beer, television, insurance, soft drinks and banks, while among the top advertisers are: Procter & Gamble, Voxtel, Moldcell, Vitanta, Nestlé, Wrigley and Bosch.

Moldova also provides the example of a post-socialist country that allows advertising yet questions its potential effect on the public. Therefore, it has rules limiting political ad time allowed for a candidate during election campaigns, but more notably, it also restricts tobacco ads even though a quarter of Moldovans earned some income from tobacco products, and the government earned a fifth of its revenue from this sector during the 1980s. There are also time limits placed as to when commercials on alcohol, medicine and guns can be aired on television.

In the chapter by Elzbieta Lepkowska-White and Thomas G. Brashear, they examine changes in print advertisements in Poland, a Central European country, after the fall of communism in 1989. She culled ads over a 14-year period with the assumption that during the early stages of evolution messages would be primarily text-based, focused on practical product features, whereas in the later stages, they would be more visually oriented, creating meanings for consumers by linking them with certain lifestyles through the use of symbols. Through content analysis Lepkowska-White and Brashear draw the conclusion that over time the print ads used less texts and more visual images. However, the results indicate that the ads have not become more creative over time, and the use of humor, surprise and celebrity endorsements is quite infrequent. Information about the functional characteristics of products was provided by the ads and was used increasingly over time.

Michael H. McBride and Janez Damjan in their chapter discuss advertising in Slovenia, a small country of two million people in an area of less than 8,000 square miles in south-central Europe that gained independence from Yugoslavia in 1991. Despite its small size, it is an enormously interesting, fairly developed country with a GDP per capita of around $26,000 (on purchase parity basis). The authors refer to a survey that suggests Slovenia has more in common with West European nations than former Yugoslavian countries or post-socialist East European countries regarding values and attitudes towards civil society, family, religion, politics and democracy. Obviously, advertising in the country reflects these values.

Slovenia has a history of advertising that dates back to the late eighteenth century when ads were mostly printed in newspapers. The socialist regime in Yugoslavia did not promote much commercial activity and consequently advertising became almost non-existent. With the advent of television during the 1950s some forms of commercials were developed, and television continued to be the sole producer of commercials until the 1970s when Studio Marketing, the first agency, was established which produced TV commercials and other promotional messages. Since Slovenians had access to Italian and Austrian television and also to foreign print media, the local advertisers had to keep up with the developments in advertisements in advanced capitalist countries. But after 1991, with the privatization of state enterprises, liberalization of the economy and investment by foreign multinational corporations, the economy took off and so did the advertising industry. Gross advertising expenditure in the country was estimated to be 300 million Euros for 2006, of which television received 60 percent, followed by 17 percent for magazines, 11 percent for newspapers, 7 percent for radio and 5 percent for outdoor media. Even though use of the Internet for advertising in the country has not been examined very much, it is known that a third of Slovenians have made purchases through this medium during the recent years. Given the fast growth of broadband connections and almost universal mobile phone subscription, these new media are bound to be used for advertising purposes in the future. Slovenia has extensive advertising regulations that limit commercial time on TV to 15 percent of the broadcast day, require demarcation of advertising from other messages, prohibits prejudicial or discriminatory ad material based on ethnicity or gender, require the protection of children from violent or pornographic material, and generally ban advertising tobacco products from all mass media.

South America

Gladys Torres-Baumgarten provides an historical account of multinational advertising in Latin America. A number of US ad agencies like J. Walter Thompson, N.W. Ayer and McCann Erickson established their operations in Latin America as early as the 1920s. Understandably, the largest and economically most powerful countries like Brazil, Mexico, Argentina and Chile have also provided the most important advertising markets. The four countries have a combined population of approximately 350 million with a GDP of over three trillion dollars in purchase power parity. So, consumer packaged goods companies, automotive companies, telecommunication and oil companies have been spending a considerable amount of money on advertising to reach this large consumer base. These countries also developed a large pool of skilled, creative talents for working in the advertising industry as they have had well-developed television and film industries. On the question of to what extent the multinational ad companies practice standardization and localization in marketing products, research seems to suggest that on strategic activities they seem to use standardized approaches across regions but at the level of copy production, media planning, buying and placement they tend to operate locally. Latin American subsidiary agencies of multinationals operate largely as country-specific, autonomous units because of differences in culture, regulatory requirements and a lack of availability of regional media.

Jaime S. Gomez provides a case study analysis of a Colombian Juan Valdez coffee advertising campaign in the context of the ongoing broad trends in Latin American advertising. Latin America is a vast area of the world, consisting of 20 countries and ten dependencies, with a current population of over half a billion and a combined GDP of $4.5 trillion in purchase power parity. Advertising expenditure in a country clearly reflects its economic strength, growth and development. Advertising expenditure in general in Latin America has been on an upward trajectory during the past decade. This indicates the region's economic growth and ability to draw significant amounts of foreign direct investment in the context of the liberal and free trade policies leading to expansion, diversification and internationalization of the market. Colombia is the third largest country in Latin America with a population of 44 million. Coffee, grown by over half a million families, is an important export item accounting for over 6 percent of the export earnings, and hence global marketing of this product through advertising campaigns has shown notable ingenuity and creativeness.

The fictitious Juan Valdez campaign character was created in 1959 by the New York advertising agency DDB. The campaign, in different versions since its inception, has been very successful because it has been able to create a good image of the product, a perception of superior quality, and in general a psychological association of good coffee with Colombia in much of the coffee-drinking world. In one humorous, award-winning version, for example, speeding planes, trains and cars make 180 degree turns to get Colombian coffee because regardless of where you are, and where you are headed, life would be inconceivable without this coffee. The campaign re-launch in 2006 not only reminds consumers of the positive value of Colombian coffee through Juan Valdez coffee shops, but directs its message to younger coffee drinkers who might be interested in new mixes of the product, thus trying to ensure an expanding share of the future global market.

Cross-Cultural Exploration: North America and Others

Bruce A. Huhmann and Jennifer J. Argo, in their chapter in Part V, examine the depiction of gender roles and social power in advertisements in four categories of popular consumer magazines, including general interest, women's, news and business, printed in eight countries. Of these, two are North African Arab countries, namely Egypt and Morocco (the former a British colony, the latter a French), four are African countries (Kenya, Nigeria, Uganda and South Africa) and the remaining two are the United States and Canada, two North American countries. The findings indicated that in advertisements from both continents males were portrayed more often than females in work settings, professional occupations with masculine products, conversely, females were portrayed more often than males in nonprofessional occupations, with feminine and non-technology-based products. The findings supported the assumption that females would possess superior social power in more ads from Africa than from North America. Gender equality was observed in North American ads while female superiority in social power was observed in African ads. Since an advertiser in its message mirrors a culture's values and enhances their acceptance, it is interesting to note that North American ads showed gender parity in fewer than half of the gender roles examined. In African ads, gender parity was observed in more ads, even though the depiction of male and female superiority is pretty close. The researchers draw the conclusion that there is evidence to suggest that in both continents men act and women appear. But the broader conclusion is that there is a commonality between the North American and African ads in the portrayal of gender roles, yet the superior female social power in African ads runs contrary to the gender stereotypes in the West of African females that advertisers need to be aware of.

Joseph P. Helgart and his co-author, Anne Zahradnik make a comparative analysis of direct-to-consumer advertising strategies used in the United States and New Zealand. The United States and New Zealand are the only two developed countries known to permit the large-scale direct-to-consumer advertising of drugs, a technique used by pharmaceutical companies to bypass the health-care providers to directly influence the patients and consumers. Canada is known to allow this practice on a very limited basis while some other countries like Australia and South Africa considered but decided against it. European Union countries are supposed to be studying the implications of this type of advertising before making a decision on the matter.

Japan presents a different case where historically comparative ads were banned until 1986 as the authorities viewed them often as libelous to a competitor. Japan as a culture placed great value on the importance of harmony in the society, and the need for being considerate to others which comparative or competitive ads potentially threatened. However, American multinational corporations doing business in Japan complained that the ban on comparative ads was a form of trade barrier that made selling products difficult. Hence, comparative ads were legalized as part of market-opening measures. Pepsi pioneered comparative ads in the Japanese market when it positioned itself against Coke. Over the years, comparative ads in Japan stylistically evolved from fact-based to argumentative messages.

In assessing the impact of direct-to-consumer ads on the healthcare market there are different views. One view seems to suggest that this type of advertising adds to the marketing costs of pharmaceutical companies thus raising the costs of drugs to the patients. It is also believed that companies developing the drugs often create an artificial demand by appealing directly to the patients over the head of the doctors, creating pressure on the doctors to prescribe them even when the evidence of benefits to a patient is dubious. This has the potential of creating an unsustainable cost inflation in the healthcare market that government has an obligation to control in the overall public interest. Both in the United States and New Zealand rights of free speech even in the commercial sphere for legal products, including the right to receive and disseminate information, have been used to justify direct-to-consumer advertising. There seems to be a concern that these profit-driven advertising practices devised by American corporations will be exported to other countries as yet another undesirable dimension of globalization.

References

Cheng, H. (1994). Reflection of cultural values: a content analysis of Chinese magazine advertisement from 1982 and 1992. *International Journal of Advertising*, 13: 167–83.

Cheng, H. and J.C. Schwitzer (1996). Cultural values reflected in Chinese and US television commercials. *Journal of Advertising Research*, 36: 27–45.

Haque, M. (2003). Cultural values and mass communications. *Encyclopedia of International Media and Communications*, 1: 369–80.

Hofstede, G. (2001). *Culture's Consequences: Comparing Values, Behaviors, Institutions, and Organizations across Nations*. 2nd ed. Thousand Oaks, CA: Sage.

Jhally, S. (1990). *The Codes of Advertising: Fetishism and the Political Economy of Meaning in the Consumer Society*. New York: Routledge.

Marcuse, H. (1972). *One Dimensional Man*. London: Abacus.

McLuhan, M. (1964). *Understanding Media: The Extensions of Man*. Cambridge, MA: MIT Press.

Pan, Z., H.C. Steven, G.C. Chu and Y. Ju (1994). *To See Ourselves: Comparing Traditional Chinese and American Cultural Values*. Boulder, CO: Westview Press.

Pember, D. (2001–2002). *Mass Media Law*. New York: McGraw Hill.

Rokeach, M. (1973). *The Nature of Human Values*. New York: Free Press.

Saffer, H. (2000). Tobacco advertising and promotion. In P. Jha and F. Chaloupka (eds), *Tobacco Control in Developing Countries* (pp. 215–36). New York: Oxford University Press.

Africa and the Middle East

CHAPTER **1**

Advertising and Globalization: The Transmission of Culture in Nigerian Print Advertising

EMMANUEL C. ALOZIE

Introduction

The past half-century has witnessed a growth in scholarship and course offerings on topics concerning cross-cultural and international communications, the aim of which is to help individuals and businesses to understand and to deal effectively with the challenges of meeting the demands of a multicultural world (Cheng, 1997), "Where space and time have collapsed and the experience of distance imploded" (Sreberny-Mohammadi, 1991, p. 118). Despite this growing trend toward globalization, people continue to inhabit a world where cultural, economic and philosophical differences persist (Giddens, 1990).

Growing interest in this subject can be attributed to the ongoing debate concerning the role of mass communications, including advertising, as a means of cultural transmission and economic modernization. Twitchell (1997) contends that advertising plays a role in driving cultural evolution and has taken on the function of shared cultural memory. He goes on to argue that advertising has now become the bedrock of modern culture, replacing traditional sources of icons like painting, drama, music and museums, even religion.

In this era of globalization, breakthroughs in ICTs (information and communication technologies) have drawn nations closer together and have enabled producers of mass media artifacts rapidly to transmit their messages to a global audience. Such rapid, worldwide audience access is blamed for superimposing the values of developed nations onto developing regions because developing nations are dependent on the developed world for technical support, capital, program content and mass media advertising systems (Schiller, 1969/1992; Sreberny-Mohammadi, 1991; Sussman, 1997).

However, Fortner (1993) contends that the notion of media cultural imperialism and dependency remains questionable because the amount of cultural products (films, books, television programs, newspapers and magazines) exported from the core nations to developing nations is minimal and insignificant, making it difficult for the West to exert a great deal of influence on Third World audiences as critics allege. Fortner cites UNESCO figures that indicate the range of cultural materials (books) flowing from the developed to developing nations range from 6.2 percent to 12.7 percent. He observes that the same could be said of films and television programming and other communication-oriented materials. Yet, it is revealing to note, as Fortner explained, that the UNESCO study "did confirm the almost nonexistent South-to-North trading in media commodities" (p. 202). Despite this observation, Fortner concluded, "it hardly suggested that developed nations were swamping the developing nations with cultural products" (p. 202).

Leibes and Katz (1990) agree. They point out that meaning is not planted in Western programming that flows to the Third World; rather, meaning is created and influenced on the basis of cultural values and philosophical orientations existing in a specific society. They also argue that the flow of capital, equipment and program content from the core to developed nations relates to demands and assistance, and is not achieved through coercion (Sreberny-Mohammadi, 1991).

On the other hand, critics point out that since their introduction mass media outlets and consumers, as well as governments in developing countries, have and are becoming increasingly reliant on Western mass media sources for information, entertainment and advertising (Uche, 1988 and 1994; Schiller, 1969/1992 and 1998). This is especially true in this era of globalization because of structural policies initiated and maintained by core nations through supra-national organizations and international treaties (Schiller, 1998; Uche, 1994; Thussu, 2000; McPhail, 2002). When programming comes from local sources, it is laden with Western values, because Western corporations serve as the source of revenue for the constantly financially strapped mass media in the developing world (Schiller, 1969/1992; Mattelart, 1979 and 1991; Domatob, 1988). It should be noted that Africans have never viewed their cultures as inferior to Western culture (Oladipo, 1995).

Schiller (1991) and Compaine and Gomery (2000) argue that, if advertisers are able to influence the contents and framing of news and other events in a developed nation such as the United States, how much greater must their influence be in countries where an infant and unsophisticated mass media relies on multinational corporations for a large portion of advertising revenue. In the developing world, advertisers exert undue influence on both private and public mass media because of their dependence on them for revenue—this is especially true of multinational corporations that dominate the economic landscape. Domatob (1988) describes that domination as "neo-colonialism" which emanates from the organizational, political, economic, technical and financial superiority of one group over the other. Western corporations as well as mass media organizations, transnational advertising and public relations agencies have been accused of using these superior capabilities to undermine the growth and development of African and other Third World socioeconomic and cultural institutions (Anderson, 1984; Tsao, 1996; Schiller, 1969/1992 and 1998).

Significance of the Study

In spite of this debate, few studies have been conducted to examine the values, messages, and context manifested in advertising in Africa, to see if they reflect the prevailing socioeconomic-and-cultural conditions in Nigeria or other African countries in the current era of globalization (Alozie, 2003a and 2003b; El Kamel, 1991; Kennan and Shoreh, 2000). In view of the neglect of Africa, this study is an attempt to bridge this analytical gap. To achieve this the study makes use of a combination of political economy and textual analysis.

Political economy was used to explore the structural and theoretical arguments surrounding international communications. While Frith's (1997) three-stage qualitative analysis approach was used to examine the messages and values conveyed in numerous transnational consumer advertisements published in Nigerian print media between 1998 through 2000. Western multinational corporations with significant operations in Nigeria and other African countries produced the advertisements under analysis. Frith's three-state approach involves reading the surface meanings, exploring the advertiser's intended and unintended meanings, and finally establishing the ideological values they convey. This study explores the following questions and issues:

- What are the values, symbols and context conveyed in Nigerian advertisements?
- Do the values, symbols and context conveyed in the advertisements tell and promote products and/or services, or do they expose the social condition of Nigeria?

While using the theoretical framework of cultural imperialism, dependency, convergence and globalization, the study will attempt to flesh out the debate regarding their relevance within the current global economic circumstances.

To explore how this analysis of hundreds of Nigerian print advertisements was conducted to extract the messages, values, symbols and implications conveyed in the advertisements using Frith's three-state approach, a detailed deconstruction of two of the advertisements used as exemplars is provided. The author chose these specific consumer advertisements as exemplars because transnational corporations produced them and they convey specific ideological and contextual values. Both advertisements appear frequently in Nigerian mass media, and very likely in other sub-Saharan African nations.

The messages and contexts found in such advertisements remain the subject of intense debate in developing countries. Critics contend transnational advertising represents an ideological vehicle employed to undermine the socioeconomic and cultural development of African nations (Anderson, 1984; Mattelart, 1991; Leiss, Kline and Jhally, 1997; Ewen, 2001). Messages conveyed in both advertisements under analysis are memorable and generate heated controversy among the public. Critics allege that multinational advertisers make false claims and import foreign values that influence consumers in the Third World (Schiller, 1969/1992 and 1998; Sreberny-Mohammadi, 1991 and 1997; Mattelart, 1991; Ewen, 2001). For example, the Sharp advertisement uses white models in a predominantly black society, relying on image, pleasure and sex to promote its electronic products. A Rothman advertisement conveys the message that smoking is a healthy activity to undertake. However, studies have shown that smoking-related diseases affect the economy adversely and can lead to death. Consequently, multinational advertisers and mass media have also been accused of undermining the cultural values of developing nations. They are also accused of distorting Third World economies by using advertising to convince consumers of the need to acquire products produced abroad and imported for sale at very high costs (Anderson, 1984; Mattelart, 1991; Ewen, 2001).

On the other hand, proponents of advertising state that advertising provides information to the public, but does not necessarily mislead or exert undue influence because consumers are rational and make rational decisions. They contend that advertising assists economic growth (Hunt, 1989; Arens, 2004). This analysis assesses the evolution of the concepts of cultural imperialism, dependency and their relationship with convergence and globalization.

THE ECONOMIC AND PRINT MEDIA CONTEXT IN NIGERIA

Economic

Nigeria has a population estimated to be about 120 million with 57 percent of the population literate. Despite the country's abundant natural and human resources, about 45 percent live below the poverty line. Unemployment hovers at more than 30 percent. The real per capita income stands at about 3,000 naira (Nigerian currency—since the late 1980s, the exchange rate has fluctuated between N90 and N130 to US$1). Household income or consumption by percentage share ranges from 1.6 percent for the lowest 10 percent to 40.8 percent for the highest 10 percent. Purchasing power parity in Nigeria is about $900 (Alozie, 2003a and 2003b; Abacci Atlas, 2004; International Trade Administration, US Dept. of Commerce, 2004).

Corruption, poor economic planning, political instability and dependence on oil at the expense of other economic activities are blamed for the nation's economic woes. Despite earning more than $300 billion from oil windfalls over the past three decades, Nigeria's foreign debt is more than $30 billion (Alozie, 2003a and 2003b; Abacci Atlas, 2004; International Trade Administration, US Dept. of Commerce, 2004).

Mass media

The modern printing press arrived in Nigeria in the early 1800s. A lack of systematic studies and poor record keeping on circulation and readership make it difficult to ascertain an accurate number for newspaper circulation and percentage of readership. Estimates of the largest dailies and weeklies range from 50,000 to 70,000 per day. Nigeria has a dynamic press and readership remains wide among the literate because of the multiplier effect where one issue is read by many people and people congregate to listen to radio and television. Thus, both print and broadcast advertisements reach a large segment of elites and the masses. Nigeria has an ample radio and television industry. Most broadcasting outlets are government-owned, but private ownership is growing. Modern avenues of communications such as the Internet and cell phones are growing because of privatization.

Advertisements constitute around 28–35 percent of the newspaper content, with privately-owned newspapers carrying a higher percentage than government-owned newspapers. Nigerian print advertising exists mainly in classified and display forms. Advertising in Nigerian magazines is not as extensive as newspaper advertising. The amount charged for various forms of print advertising is uncertain because most media outlets treat their prices as trade secrets and refuse to disclose their charges.

Advertising: Imperialism and Dependency Debates in the Information Age

European imperialism in Africa began when Magellan's ship concluded the circumnavigation of the earth almost a century after Prince Henry the Navigator of Portugal started and successfully organized a series of African expeditions in 1814. This successful exploration allowed trade to flourish on the high seas instead of via overland routes, which were often subject to robberies, demands for tributes and other uncertainties (Mendelsohn, 1976).

EUROPEAN COLONIZATION OF AFRICA

The success of the Portuguese prompted other Europeans to engage in sea trade. British enterprises arrived in West Africa in the 1600s. Two centuries later, the British began the gradual consolidation and colonization of Nigeria for its commercial benefits and material exploitation at the expense of the political, cultural and economic welfare of the indigenous people. By 1861, formal British administration spread from the Lagos coast to the interior with the introduction of direct rule. Used in other British colonies in other parts of the world, direct rule was a system of government in which the colonizers governed the natives directly. When it was introduced in Nigeria, direct rule was unsuccessful because of the numerical inferiority of British colonial officials. The system of government was also unsuccessful because some ethnic groups in Nigeria have long-established native ruling systems and resisted foreign intervention in their affairs (Fadeiye, 1978).

The resistance compelled the British to employ its military superiority to conquer and bring various parts of Nigeria under submission. Britain completed its creation of Nigeria with the amalgamation of the north and south in 1914. The amalgamation created the Federation of Nigeria, as it exists today, a nation that "has never really been one homogenous country, for its widely differing peoples and tribes are yet to find any basis for true unity" (Madiebo, 1980, p. 3). Rupert described Nigeria and other countries the European masters left behind in Africa as "businesses—colonies meant to profit European governments and traders who controlled them" (1998, p. A18). It could be argued that this marked the beginning of cultural imperialism and economic dependency. Realizing the failure of implementing direct rule, Britain introduced indirect rule in their conquered business estates. Direction allowed the colonial administration to use established African institutions (monarchy, age groups, religious institutions and warrant chiefs) to govern a society. The natives maintained direct leadership and contact with their people, while carrying out the policies of the colonialists (Fadeiye, 1978).

Rodney (1974) argues that Africa's current political upheaval and economic underdevelopment could be traced back to European policies of imposing their political, economic and social values on the continent. He contends that African human and natural resources were exploited for the benefit of European colonial powers. While the colonial masters used cheap African labor to extract African natural resources, most of the raw material resources were bundled out of the continent to the West where they were processed into manufactured goods for world commerce and as exports to Africa at very high prices. The structure produced a neo-colonial relationship in which Western governments and multinationals controlled the means of production and global market, thus producing an unequal association for almost a century (Baran, 1957; Rodney, 1974; Mattelart, 1979; Rupert, 1998). However, Agbango (1997) does not absolve African leaders of their failures. He observes that almost a half century after independence, most African countries suffer from chronic economic stagnation, underdevelopment, poverty, political instability and health deprivation because of the ineptness of African leaders who have failed to improve the social welfare of their people, whilst continuing to blame the imperialistic and dependent structure of their former colonial masters and the international socioeconomic system.

CULTURAL IMPERIALISM

Describing the structural theory of imperialism, Galtung (1971 and 1980) contends that inequality within and between nations exists in every aspect of human activity. The desire to maintain dominance creates resistance to change. This resistance to change evolves from structural violence that permits a special type of dominance system. Galtung and others have identified the four dimensions of achieving structural imperialism as exploitation, penetration, fragmentation and marginalization (Galtung, 1971 and 1980). For example, Great Britain used the kingdom's technical, military and economic superiority to dominate societies in Africa and Asia. Colonial rule enabled the British to penetrate, exploit, marginalize and fragment nations in these parts of the world. Galtung describes this dominance system as imperialism and he points out that structural imperialism usually existed between collectives, especially among nations.

Galtung (1971, p. 81) also states that imperialism is a concept that "splits up collectivities and relates some of the parts to each other in relations of harmony of interest and other parts in relations of disharmony of interest, or conflict of interest." Galtung contends that theories of imperialism and the conflict of interest rear their heads as a result of relationships in which the goals of the parties involved are incompatible. These goals represent the true interests of each party. They include sovereignty, living conditions, quality of life, cultural perversion, human or national subjects for self-preservation and other demographic factors by maintaining some kind of structural control such as international communications (Mosco, 1996). For example, critics of the Western dominance of international communications argue that core nations use the media to promote cultural imperialism and dependency through their technological, capital, trade and professional production dominance and the control of international organizations responsible for regulating communication (Schiller, 1969/1992; Sussman, 1997). That dominance and control gives the West control of most aspects of international communication, including the flow of information, film, television programming and software. As stated earlier, international mechanisms such as supra-national organizations and treaties are also used to maintain the status quo in order to retain their interests and the dominance of their ideological values (Boyd-Barrett, 1977; Golding, 1979; Anderson, 1984).

Given these struggles, nationalists, activists and intellectuals have sought to define imperialism on socio-cultural, socio-political or socio-economic grounds. The concept has been defined as the domination of one group over another group to perpetuate the interests of the more powerful group. Critics contend that imperialism could be spoken of in terms of cultural imperialism, religious imperialism, economic imperialism and political imperialism (Baumgart, 1982). Azikiwe (1969, p. 50) interprets socio-cultural imperialism to mean: "to command, to rule, to govern, to hold in trust, to civilize, to educate, to Christianize."

Economic imperialism may be defined as a system where the center (developed nations) has power over the periphery (developing nations) with regard to factors of production such as capital, technology, communication, distribution and manpower. The center nations use these factors to exploit and dominate states in the periphery. Building on Galtung's (1971 and 1980) works, Anderson (1984, p. 49) describes communication and advertising imperialism as "the way in which advertising exchange between nations is structured internationally with the effect that some nations may dominate other nations and create a disharmony of interest between them." Elaborating on the relationship between a center and periphery nations with regard to advertising, Anderson (1984, p. 50) states:

- The Center exercises domination by imposing a certain advertising structure on the Periphery.
- The Center penetrates the Periphery by creating a center of local, internationalized elites to serve as bridgehead for the Center in its advertising spillover into economics, politics, culture, and other areas within the Periphery society.

Uche (1988 and 1994) and Domatob's (1988) analyses of mass communication, cultural identity and sovereignty support these relationships with regard to Africa. "Neo-colonialism", Domatob states, is an African reality that dominates every aspect of life, including economic, social, political, religious and cultural institutions.

THE DEPENDENCY CONTEXT

At the time of independence, most of the newly emerging states, including Nigeria, did not possess adequate technologies or the financial means to establish viable indigenous broadcasting, print and advertising media agencies (Schiller, 1969/1992 and 1998; Janus, 1986; Hamelink, 1997). Countries that did, possessed either unsophisticated operations, or operations inadequate to compete with Western mass media outlets (Schiller, 1969/1992 and 1998; Janus, 1986). As a result, global corporations operating in these countries depended on Western advertising agencies to promote their products and services. That dependence gave Western Transnational Advertising Agencies (TNAA) a foothold in these countries. It enabled them to use Western-oriented advertising to dominate the market and mass media in developing nations (Anderson, 1984; Janus, 1986).

The relationships between nations (center and periphery) have been explained through a related concept known as dependency (Gunder-Frank, 1969; Golding and Elliot, 1974; Thussu, 2000). Critics of the unequal socio-economic and cultural relationship between developed and developing nations claim that mass communication and advertising promote capitalism and perpetuate the cultural, economic, social and political dependency of Third World countries on the West (Schiller, 1969/1992; Cardoso, 1977; Anderson, 1984; Hamelink, 1997). Over time, residents of the developing nations have attempted to resist aspects of cultural imperialism and dependency by producing and distributing local films and television films and programs that reflect native values (Mohammadi and Sreberny-Mohammadi, 1994). Some governments and activists in developing nations have attempted to fight back by courting and adopting socialism and employing local values and ideologies in their economic policies. They have also attempted to produce and distribute native materials through formal and informal networks (Hamelink, 1997). The results of these efforts have been mixed. However, in recent years local productions have been increasing in Latin America, Asia and Africa. Nigeria produces many videos for national and regional distribution but has been unable to make inroads into markets outside the continent. African music from Nigeria, Ghana and Mali has made strides within and outside the continent through a genre known as world beat, but its impact remains minimal. On the other hand, Western produced cultural materials dominate African and Third World markets.

The dependency model is based on the notion that transnational corporations operating in the Third World take advantage of their technological, financial, managerial, operational, processing and production superiority to impose their values and exploit the mineral and human resources in developing nations (Anderson, 1984; Schiller, 1969/1992 and 1998). The dependency model charges that transnational corporations collude with local elites to institute structures that inhibit progressive social policies, thus denying the upward mobility of the masses (Martins, 1982). Dependency stipulates that Western institutions provide technological hardware, technical training and capital assistance to develop the communication sectors of developing nations, but the relationship remains one of exploitation and domination by the developed nations (Cardoso, 1977), instead of one of equality or one providing true assistance (Anderson, 1984; Uche, 1988 and 1994). Tansey and Hyman (1994) describe the four tenets of the dependency model:

- Center–Periphery: Relationship exists between advanced, developed countries and less developed countries because economic and political power is distributed asymmetrically between the center and the periphery.
- Many of the tenets of classical economics, especially the Theory of Comparative Advantage, do not apply to the economic development of the periphery.
- The center realizes disproportionate gains from trade that favors it.
- Conspicuous consumption by the affluent minority impedes economic development in the periphery by diverting critically needed investment capital (Tansey and Hyman, 1994, p. 28).

Dependency theorists blame advertising and other forms of communication for undermining the cultural values of the developing nations (MacBride et al., 1980; Roncagliolo, 1986). Roncagliolo charges that the Western domination of international communication and the business world promoted the welfare of the transnationals and inculcated alien values without regard for the values and welfare of Third World residents. Freire explains how transglobal advertisements from developed nations affect the culture of peripheral countries, "The invaders penetrate the cultural context of another group, in disrespect of the latter's potentialities; they impose their own view of the world upon those they invade and inhibit the creativity of the invaded by curbing their expression" (Freire, 1993, p. 133). Others have argued that dependency is achieved through training, philosophy, economic orientation and mass media programming and contended that the demise of the Communist bloc gave the West a free hand to capture and overwhelm the developing regions (Domatob, 1988; Uche, 1994).

GLOBALIZATION AND CONVERGENCE

Critics of the theories of cultural imperialism and dependency argue that they suffer from a lack of clear fundamental definitions, an absence of quantifiable data and limited case studies, and that they ignore questions regarding the form and content of media as well as the role of the audience within societal boundaries. They also point out that both theories do not account for how global media texts work within a particular national context ignoring local patterns of media consumption. They argue that the degree to which foreign products exert an influence upon a society is highly contextual (Fortner, 1993; Thussu, 2000; Elasmar, 2003[1]).

Criticism of cultural imperialism and dependency theories has been compounded by recent ethnographic studies that have established a variety of cultural responses ranging from cultural homogeneity to hybridity and glocalization that can be used to explain how societies, communities, cultures and other regional factors contribute to global cultural dispensation (Robertson, 1992; Lull, 1995; Strubhaar, 1997). Others argue that the roles of cultural imperialism and dependency have been taken over by technological innovations and economic forces (Thussu, 2000). For example, they point out that US and Western media outlets have adopted new business strategies by investing in developing nations or forming foreign ventures which give the indigenous partners a greater influence on programming, advertising content, technological acquisition and professional development. However, these new business strategies do not undo cultural imperialism or dependency. Rather, it is the forcing of mass media outlets in the developing world to adopt commercial broadcasting models which allows Western dominance because Third World mass media relies on its Western partners for ideological underpinning, advertising, genre, content, and human and technical support.

Opponents of imperialism and dependency theories contend that the core nations do not covertly lead the peripheral nations to adopt their political economic, social and cultural values. Rather, they argue that the core nations influence the dynamics of socioeconomic development that is then emulated by most developing nations all over the world. Wallerstein (1974/1980, 1979 and 1991) claims that the successful emulation, adoption and economic evolution of semi-peripheral nations in Eastern Europe and parts of Asia contributed to the spread of Western economic, political and social values in the rest of the developing world. Thus, the socioeconomic success of the core nations as well as sustained socioeconomic growth achieved by semi-peripheral nations prompt the less developed nations to clone Western capitalism and values. He calls the gradual process of adoption and eventual spread of Western capitalism world systems theory. He argues that the spread of Western values is not achieved through coercion (Wallerstein, 1974/1980, 1979 and 1991).

Since the end of the Cold War about one and a half decades ago, capitalism has become the dominant economic orientation worldwide. As capitalism spreads, proponents of cultural imperialism and dependency argue that free market structures affect most aspects of socioeconomic life in developing nations, including their media systems as they become reliant on advertising sponsored by multinationals, thus exposing their audiences to Western lifestyles through advertising and other forms of communication.

---

1   This is a collection of essays addressing the debate on international communication and imperialism. The book argues cultural imperialism does not exist.

As residents of the developing societies become exposed to Western values, they cannot resist being integrated into the dominant world capitalist system (Wallerstein, 1974/1980, 1979 and 1991). McPhail (2002, p. 15) describes world systems theory as a concept that states "global economic expansion takes place from a relatively small group of core-zone nation-states out to other zones of nation-states, these being in the semi-peripheral and peripheral zones."

Based on these tendencies and as a result of the increased convergence and globalization of international communication and the global economic and political changes that have occurred over the last decade and a half, cultural imperialism, dependency and related theories have become less prominent. They have drawn increased criticism and have been describe as a-theoretical. Their critics claim the end of the Cold War, convergence and globalization have contributed to increased liberalization, privatization and amalgamation of international communications and economy. Breakthroughs in the speed of delivery, networking, storage and transmission have made it possible for anyone anywhere in the world to access information. This era has ushered in what has been described as the information society—a period in which the global economy is interlocked and the production and transmission of information have become the dominant economic activity. However, these innovations have resulted in the dominance of a few Western supra-national media organizations.

Such dominance is assisting in the implantation of Western values, thereby promoting cultural imperialism and dependency. While Western scholars argue that the theories of cultural imperialism and dependency are outmoded, developing nations have grown increasingly dependent on the West for ICT infrastructure. Audiences in the developing world are inundated with Western produced texts and software. They are also growing increasingly dependent on the West for economic policies, approach and assistance because of Western control of world economic bodies like the World Trade Organization and the World Bank. Third World debt remains high and most of their income is used to service this debt (Alozie, 2003a and 2003b; Abacci Atlas, 2004; International Trade Administration, US Dept. of Commerce, 2004).

Considering these issues as well as the economic and political implications of international communications, this study contends that the need to employ cultural imperialism and dependency theory, as a conceptual framework with which to examine the conduct of international communications, has grown rather than diminished. These theories were influential in shaping international communication policies in the 1970s and 1980s; they will remain relevant in shaping the international communication polices of the global information age (Frith, 1997; Thussu, 2000; McPhail, 2002). For example, the ITU (International Telecommunications Union), which exercises minimal control over the operation of the Internet, organized a meeting in the fall of 2003 at the request of developing nations. The purpose of this meeting was to explore mechanisms by which the union could exercise some degree of control of ICTs for the benefit of developing nations and assist them in developing their capabilities in the context of the growing digital divide that exists between the developed and the developing world and its growing role in international economies.

In view of these concerns, efforts should be made to develop new approaches of conceptualizing recent developments in international communications. For example, electronic colonialism states that "foreign produced, created, or manufactured cultural products have the ability to influence, or possibly displace, indigenous cultural productions, artifacts, and media to the detriment of receiving nations" (McPhail, 2002, p. 243). This concept is regarded as an attempt to build on world systems theory and render a more balanced explanation of the governance and operation of international communications.

Considering current developments where Western media organizations and multinational corporations are growing increasingly influential in the global economy, one could argue that cultural imperialism and dependency theories remain viable tools for explaining the micro and macro issues in international communication. To overcome the criticisms being leveled at these frameworks, it is important for scholars to develop qualitative and empirical case studies that examine the operations of international communications. These criticisms do not call for going back to the drawing board; rather, caution should be taken not to be reductionist or abandon the ideal initiated by Schiller (1969/1992 and 1998) and his cohorts.

Literature Review: The Debate on the Impact of Advertising

Global corporations depend on public relations, marketing and advertising to extend their reach and to encourage their growth and profitability by promoting their goods and services in emerging countries. To achieve these goals, critics allege transnational corporations rely on advertising to create artificial tastes, artificial consumption habits and a market for their mass produced goods and services (Anderson, 1984; Leiss, Kline and Jhally, 1997). That reliance could be attributed to the fact that capitalistic values view advertising as an instrument of industrial growth, mass production and modernization (Marchand, 1986; Kotler, 1987; Lears, 1995; Fox, 1997; Twitchell, 1997).

However, cultural studies on the role of advertising in socioeconomic—and cultural—development have produced three schools of thought. The first, known as "advocates of advertising," claims that advertising is a useful tool for promoting national development. This school contends that advertising can be used to promote national development programs through public service and commercial campaigns (Nwosu, 1990). This concept, known as social marketing, is a variation of traditional commercial advertising (Kotler and Roberto, 1989). In Nigeria and developing countries, public service campaigns are used to address social issues such as drinking and driving, the spread of AIDS, family planning and poverty alleviation programs (El Kamel, 1991). It should be noted that governments, not local or transnational corporations, sponsor the bulk of public service campaigns. Advocates of advertising as a tool for national development credit advertising with educating the public about goods and services available in the marketplace. Advertising, they claim, makes the media available and affordable (Kennan and Shoreh, 2000).

The second school, known as "critics of advertising," contends that advertising hinders social development and that advertising is deceptive, intrusive and immoral. It claims that the majority of advertisements are marketing techniques that endorse sexism, corruption, class division, imperialism and dependency (Langrehr and Caywood, 1980; Anderson, 1984). Commercial advertising rarely engages in promoting useful habits and rather imports foreign values and ideologies (Leiss, Kline and Jhally, 1997).

Advertising is seen as a force that not only pollutes the mind, but also pollutes the social, economic and political environment. Despite the huge amount spent on advertising, the medium has yet to demonstrate how it helps the economy. Advertisements are blamed for commodifying societies and promoting consumerism in capitalist economies (Packard, 1981; Packard and Horowitz, 1995; Branston and Stafford, 1996; Mueller, 1996; Ewen, 2001). Considering their interpretation of the harms of advertising, critics are calling on Third World governments to regulate and censor it because it plays on human emotions, simplifies human situations and exploits human anxieties. They charge that advertising employs techniques of intensive persuasion that amount to manipulation (Packard, 1981; Goldman, 1992; Packard and Horowitz, 1995; Branston and Stafford, 1996; Mueller, 1996; Ewen, 2001).

The third school is known as the "neutralist" school. Neutralists adopt a rational and relative view of advertising. Proponents do not hold a strictly positive or negative view of advertising. Advertising, they say, does not necessarily promote or harm the welfare of a society. Neutralists say advertising is useful if it is used to promote goods and services without making exaggerated and deceptive claims. However, they point out that advertising becomes distasteful if it makes exaggerated claims, exposing a society to harmful consumerism that can distort the nature of the economy (MacBride et al., 1980). They advocate responsible advertising that offers useful goods and services and positive behavior (Kotler, 1987). However, MacBride cautions that, if not utilized responsibly, advertising could produce unintended consequences. He contends that advertising could adversely affect economic development by encouraging wasteful spending through consumerism (Ewen and Ewen, 1992; Twitchell, 2002), imposing alien values (Leiss, Kline and Jhally, 1997), objectifying women (Van Zoonen, 1994), and leading people to cultivate bad habits (Ewen and Ewen, 1992; Fox, 1997; Leiss, Kline and Jhally, 1997; Kilbourne and Pipher, 2000; Twitchell, 2002).

Analysis of Nigerian Print Advertisements

APPROACH

A combination of political economy and textual and ideological analysis were used to analyze an available sample of hundreds of transnational consumer commercials consisting of various products published in Nigerian print media from 1998 through 2000. Two advertisements (an electronic and cigarette promotion) were used as exemplars for detailed deconstruction to explain how the information, messages and values were extracted from numerous advertisements analyzed in order to examine their implications.

Analysis of the advertisements relied on Frith's three-stage approach, which entails an initial reading of the surface meaning, exploring the advertiser's intended and unintended meaning, and establishing the ideological meaning and values it conveys (Frith, 1997) to uncover the values and context in an advertisement. The first stage of the analysis involves exploring the surface meaning of the advertisements by recording every object in the advertisement on the analysis sheet without offering any interpretation. The second stage involves a closer reading and identification of the advertiser's intended meaning by exploring discursive strategies conveyed in the advertisements. Symbols, themes, values, headlines, narrative structure, meanings, tone and omissions are recorded on the analysis sheet. This process allows the analyst to explore the hidden implications of the advertisement and to determine any themes that may be missing. The final stage involves discerning the cultural and/or ideological meaning. To discern the subjective or cultural forms in the texts, the analysis sheet is used as a guide to explore any recurrent patterns and dominant themes, as well as the missing values in order to offer interpretation of the findings within the framework of ideological analysis.

SHARP: ELECTRONIC PRODUCT

The surface meaning

In its advertisement, Sharp, a transnational corporation, uses the portrait of a white family (a husband, wife and their two children—a boy and girl sitting in the comfort of their home and smiling), to promote one of its products—an air conditioner. The father carries his son on his lap while sitting on the right edge of the couch stretched out. The mother is sitting on the left side with her legs crossed. The daughter is sitting on her stool with her hands pressing on her knees. She leans toward her mother. There is a huge air conditioner above them blowing cool air over the family. The father and mother are smiling as their children look on with pride and satisfaction.

The advertiser's intended meaning

This advertisement implies that, in Nigeria, a father is charged with taking care of his family by ensuring family comfort. One way to provide comfort in Nigeria's climate is to purchase an air conditioner. The advertisement points out that, without an air conditioner, life may be uncomfortable and unbearable because of the area's high temperature and humidity. The advertisement implies a family lives stylishly if it uses Sharp products. The advertisement claims Sharp products are durable and enable a family to save money:

Father says "super-durable."

Mother says: "easy to clean."

Everyone agrees, "Life is so much more comfortable with a stylish SHARP air conditioner."

(*This Day*, November 11, 1998, p. 24)

The cultural or ideological meaning

This advertisement uses white models in a predominantly black nation. By using white models, the advertisement may be promoting the superiority of whites. This argument may be called into question by those who argue Sharp is a Japanese company. However, that argument can be countered by pointing out that multinational corporations operate in their own interest and will use any symbol that enhances their profits. By using white models, the advertisement implies that most of the natives cannot afford such comfort and the few who can are enjoying a pleasure and comfort that they have learned from the West. At the same time, they are appealing to elites who tend to emulate Western lifestyle and values. They are telling them that Sharp provides them with the consumer goods to live like their brethren in the West. It demonstrates there are two classes in Nigeria: a class that can afford the comfort of modern living, and a mass that can only aspire to live the superior life.

The advertisement also maintains the ideological position of a male-dominated society as the text reads: Father says "super-durable." Mother says: "easy to clean." This statement implies the father is the breadwinner, while the mother is the homemaker. It portrays women as subordinates. By stating its products are durable and economical, the advertising is implying that electronic goods produced locally are inferior. It implies that those who buy Nigerian-made goods waste their money. This message promotes imperialism and dependency because Nigerians tend to prefer foreign-made goods to those produced in Nigeria, encouraging unemployment and the failure of the Nigerian manufacturing sector.

ROTHMANS: ANALYSIS OF CIGARETTE ADVERTISING

The surface meaning

With a headline proclaiming, "There is Nothing Better," the Rothmans advertisement features four male models in what appears to be a celebration after receiving an award. Three of the male models, two whites and a black, are in the background. Of the three, one seems to be clapping his hands; the second is smiling, while the third intently looks at the model in the foreground. The leading model towers in front with a big smile. He clinches his right palm, while holding a trophy with his left hand. The trophy is placed over an open pack of Rothmans king size cigarettes. Three of the 24 sticks are protruding, indicating that they are ready to be consumed for pleasure. It is not clear from the background whether the advertisement was shot in Nigeria or in a Western setting, but the models are physically like Westerners (the advertisement featured white models). The four models are sporty and dressed in a sophisticated fashion.

The advertiser's intended meaning

The four models in this advertisement are dressed handsomely. They do not look Nigerian, they look Western and they are also young. The cheerful mood and stylish pose of the models imply that smoking is synonymous with big wins, success and good health. In spite of showing the males as healthy and sporty, the advertisement carries a health warning regarding smoking. The pictures and other text used in the advertisement are in color, with the exception of the health warning. The clenched fist signifies the model is a symbol of power. This message, which is contrary to that conveyed by government health education, implies that people who smoke are no more prone to illness than those who do not. Rather, they will become stronger and better able to compete and conquer. By conveying this message, the advertisement is encouraging Nigerian youth not to abandon smoking on health grounds.

The cultural or ideological meaning

Youth culture and image dominate cigarette advertisements in the Nigerian mass media. These values are evident in television and magazine advertisements. The messages conveyed by this and other cigarette commercials are: smoking is a fashionable thing to do, and we do it in the West. Westerners celebrate by smoking and it keeps them healthy. If this is so, you must emulate Westerners. This message is very powerful in the Third World where most young people attempt to clone Western values. Cigarette manufacturers are being deceptive and exploitative when they promote cigarette smoking as a youthful activity that builds friendship among cohorts. They realize they can get away with this kind of promotion because advertising regulations are poorly enforced in Nigeria.

The messages in this and other cigarette advertisements are in sharp contrast to studies finding that smoking causes diseases leading to early death. According to a report in National Radio's news program, Weekend All Things Considered, a study by the World Health Organization found that smoking would be the single leading cause of death in the world in the next 30 years (National Public Radio, May 22, 1999). In many Western countries, cigarette advertising and marketing have been banned. To find new markets, these companies are pushing hard in developing nations where regulation remains lax (*Indian Express*, June 26, 1997).

Discussion of Findings and Conclusion

The end of World War II marked the emergence of many new states in parts of Asia and in most of Africa. The emergence of these new countries created the need to improve the economic and social welfare of the people in these states. Assisted by the political hegemony of the United States, several Western global corporations, including those from Japan, were presented with the opportunity to expand their operations or move into these newly independent states (Solomon, 1978). Transnational corporations rely on advertising as a vehicle to expand and maintain their products and services in Nigeria and other African countries. The purpose of this study is explore the symbols, themes, values, headlines, narrative structure, meanings, tone and omissions conveyed in an available sample of numerous transnational advertisements published in Nigerian print media from 1998 through 2000.

As a tool for national development, some scholars advocate advertising and other activities of multinational corporations as tools to foster the economic well-being of individuals and to promote the economic growth of developing countries (Gainsbrugh, 1960). Detractors charge that transnational corporations use advertising as an imperialistic tool to undermine the socioeconomic and cultural values of developing nations (Anderson, 1984).

Nigeria and many African countries are at a turning point in their development as they move from an era of post-independence authoritarian administrations and state controlled economies to democratic pluralism and market economies. The Nigerian government has embarked on the privatization of public companies and is working hard to attract foreign investment. This turning point provides an opportunity to explore the values and messages conveyed in Nigerian's contemporary mass media advertising in order to discern the values and context they convey. This will contribute to the debate about the role of advertising in the socioeconomic and cultural development of developing nations. They have not yet formed a mature modern ideology of their own, based upon African, rather than Western, values.

Thus, discerning the ideological discourse used in these advertisements and the ways meanings are denoted in their messages is the main goal of this study. It should be noted that the advertisements analyzed contain more and/or other meanings than have been identified here, and that the analysis of meanings in these advertisements should be considered as subjective and dependent on the analyst's philosophical and theoretical viewpoint and understanding of the socioeconomic development of Nigeria and sub-Saharan African nations (Pajnik and Lesjak-Tusek, 2002). On the other hand, one person's interpretation can always be followed by another, what could be called a "circle of meaning" (Derrida, 1981, p. 42 cited in Pajnik and Lesjak-Tusek, 2002)—meanings are constantly produced and reproduced, depending on their cultural contexts and their specific time and place as well as the economic status of a particular society.

Based on textual explorations and extractions of the symbols, themes, values, headlines, narrative structure, meanings, tone and omissions found in numerous transnational commercials published in Nigerian print media from 1998 through 2000 and detailed deconstruction of two of these advertisements, the analyst believes that the study's findings and implications demonstrate that transnational advertisements in Nigerian mass media tend to promote gender and class division as well as racial superiority. They undermine African values and distort national economies (Schiller, 1969/1992). They may also promote unhealthy behavior (Mueller, 1996). They also promote competition and a desire to acquire consumer goods (National Public Radio, May 22, 1999). For example, Sharp used white models in a black society. Using white models in this context promotes white superiority (Oladipo, 1995). Most African societies are tied to nature and their values view nature as a force matter, to be cooperated with, not subjugated (Obeng-Quaido, 1986; Moemeka, 1997). However, the Sharp advertisement stresses that nature (African high tropical temperature and humidity) must be conquered if a family is to have comfort and pleasure. The need to overcome the tropical temperature and humidity exists, thus it must be said that advertising provides a needed message that helps the public. At the same time, it should be noted that only the elites could afford such luxury. This is a move to modernity, presumably to promote socioeconomic development that must be recognized. Yet, it should be noted that most Nigerian homes and work environments are not equipped with air-conditioners. The advertiser's emphasis on the need for parents to provide their families with high-priced consumer goods promotes consumerism. It may distort the economic realities of Nigeria and may inhibit the development of the economy and exacerbate economic and class division in Nigeria. This is because the inability of the masses to acquire these expensive products may be socially divisive and breed jealousy of the elite by the masses. On the part of the elite, an over emphasis of the acquisition of consumer goods encourages shallowness, corruption and abuse of office (Okoro, 2001).

Considering these findings, the analyst argues that different forms of communication including advertising may be used as vehicles that transnational corporations in developing nations use to maintain socioeconomic imperialism and the dependency of peripheral nations because advertising:

1. promotes Western consumer products and services at the expense of locally produced ones (Eyre and Walrave, 2002; Leiss, Kline and Jhally, 1997), thus distorting the economy;
2. sells the ideology of consumption to those who cannot afford it, thus undermining the values and welfare of the masses (Roncagliolo, 1986; Oliveira, 1991);
3. recruits, rewards and justifies the shortcomings of the elites (Martins, 1982; Twitchell, 2002);

4. distorts the economy and widens the gap between developed and underdeveloped nations by compelling Third World consumers to purchase goods from multinationals that may not necessarily reinvest in these countries (Goffman, 1979; Roncagliolo, 1986; Oliveira, 1991);
5. breeds and perpetuates class, gender and social division relations among various groups in developing countries (Goldman, 1992; Van Zoonen, 1994; Twitchell, 2002).

However, it should be noted that these vices of advertising could be reinterpreted as vices of capitalism in general. All techniques applied by advertisers in the Third World are used just as heavily in the First World, except when they are banned by law. Despite explicating these problematic values, it is important to note that advertising remains an important vehicle in a free market system because it offers manufacturers opportunities to reach and expand consumer bases, thus enhancing manufacturing. Consequently, it assists in promoting the socioeconomic welfare of various societies. Leaders in the developing world could find ways of working voluntarily with the manufacturers to develop advertising messages that help with national development.

With increasing reliance on economic globalization, Nigeria and other developing nations must find ways to chart their economic welfare to compete in the global economy and promote the social and economic development of their peoples. Reliance on Western models of development such as the concept of using advertising to promote consumerism should be modified, if not abandoned, because the reliance perpetuates Western values, distortion of the economy, the creation of class division and the promotion of dependency.

To help these nations, there is a need to conduct studies to demystify the ideological and cultural hold of Western mass media artifacts in order to understand the values they convey. This demystification would liberate, emancipate and enlighten Third World consumers. The liberation would help consumers avoid remaining victimized by the forces of mass media, transnationals and dominant elites in these countries. Nigeria and other African nations can only achieve the goals of social modernization when they pursue true development. Proper development will take place when it is "built on national values and starting from national realities" as Senghor (1964, p. 3) contends.

An interesting subject for future exploration is to compare the advertisements published in an African country with those published in the West or other regions of the world.

References

Abacci Atlas (2004, March 8). The Nigerian economy. [Online]. http://www.abacci.com/atlas/economy3.asp?countryID=282 (retrieved March 8, 2004).

Agbango, G. (1997). Political instability and economic development in sub-Saharan Africa. In G. Agbango (ed.), *Society and Politics in Africa—Issues and Trends in Contemporary African Politics: Stability, Development and Democratization* (pp. 13–51). New York: Peter Lang.

Alozie, E.C. (2003a). Reflections of culture: an analysis of Nigerian mass media advertising. *Ecquid Novi*, 24(2): 157–80.

Alozie, E.C. (2003b). Critical analysis of cultural values found in Nigerian mass media advertisements. *SIMILE: Studies in Media and Information Literacy Education*, 3.4. [Online]. http://www.utpress.utoronto.ca/journal./ejournal/simile (retrieved April 1, 2009).

Anderson, M. (1984). *Madison Avenue in Asia: Politics and Transnational Advertising*. Cranbury, NJ: Associated University Press.

Arens, W. (2004). *Contemporary Advertising*. 9th ed. Boston, MA: McGraw Hill.

Azikiwe, N. (1969). *Renascent Africa*. New York: Negro Universities Press.

Baran, P. (1957). *The Political Economy of Growth*. New York: Monthly Review Press.

Baumgart, W. (1982). *Imperialism: The Idea of and Reality of British and French Colonial Expansion, 1880–1914*. London: Oxford University Press.

Boyd-Barrett, O. (1977). Media imperialism: towards an international framework for the analysis of media systems. In J. Curran, M. Gurevitch and J. Woollacott (eds), *Mass Communication and Society* (pp. 116–35). London: Edward Arnold.

Branston, G. and R. Stafford (1996). *The Advertising Handbook*. London and New York: Routledge.

Cardoso, F. (1977). The consumption of dependency theory. *Latin American Review*, 12(3): 7–24.

Cheng, H. (1997). Toward an understanding of cultural values manifest in advertising: a content analysis of Chinese television commercials in 1990 and 1995. *Journalism and Mass Communication Quarterly*, 74(4): 773–96.

Compaine, B. and D. Gomery (2000). *Who Owns the Media? Competition and Concentration in the Mass Media Industry*. 3rd ed. Mahwah, NJ: Lawrence Erlbaum.

Derrida, J. (1981). Positions. In S. Hall (ed.), *Representation, Cultural Representations and Signifying Practices*. London, Sage. Cited in M. Pajnik and P. Lesjak-Tusek (2002) Observing discourses of advertising: Mobitel's interpellation of potential consumers. *Journal Communication Inquiry*, 26(3): 277–99.

Domatob, J. (1988). Sub-Saharan Africa's media and neo-colonialism. *Africa Media Review* 3(1): 149–73.

Elasmar, M. (2003). *The Impact of International Television: A Paradigm Shift*. Mahwah, NJ: Lawrence Erlbaum.

El Kamel, F. (1991). Television advertising for national development. In K. Boafo and N. George (eds), *Communication Processes: Alternative Channels and Strategies for Development Support* (pp. 84–95). Nairobi: African Council for Communication Education.

Ewen, S. (2001). *The Captains of Consciousness: Advertising and the Social Roots of Consumer Culture*. New York: Basic Books.

Ewen, S. and E. Ewen (1992). *Channels of Desire: Mass Images and the Shaping of American Consciousness*. 2nd ed. Minneapolis, MN: University of Minnesota Press.

Eyre, R. and M. Walrave (2002). Advertising and marketing. In C. Newbold, O. Boyd-Barrett and D. Bulck (eds), *The Media Handbook* (pp. 318–37). London: Arnold.

Fadeiye, D. (1978). *Current Affairs Essays on Social Studies: Based on Nigeria and Africa*. Imo Ilesha, Nigeria: Ilesami Press.

Fortner, R. (1993). *International Communication: History, Conflict, and Control of the Global Metropolis*. Belmont, CA: Wadsworth.

Fox, S. (1997). *The Mirror Makers: A History of American Advertising and Its Creators*. Urbana, IL: University of Illinois Press.

Freire, P. (1993). *Pedagogy of the Oppressed*, trans. Myra B. Ramos. New York: Continuum.

Frith, K. (1997). Preface and Undressing the ad: reading culture in advertising. In K. Frith (ed.), *Undressing the Ad: Reading Culture in Advertising* (pp. 1–14). New York: Peter Lang.

Gainsbrugh, M. (1960). Advertising as investment, not cost. In C. Sandage and V. Fryburger (eds), *The Role of Advertising: A Book of Readings* (pp. 74–80). Homewood, IL: Irwin.

Galtung, J. (1971). A structural theory of imperialism. *Journal of Peace Research*, 8: 81–117.

Galtung, J. (1980). *The True Worlds: A Transnational Perspective*. New York: Free Press.

Giddens, A. (1990). *The Consequences of Modernity*. Stanford, CA: Stanford University Press.

Goffman, E. (1979). *Gender Advertisements*. New York: Harper & Row.

Golding, P. (1979). Media professionalism in the Third World: the transfer of an ideology. In J. Curran, M. Gurevitch and J. Woollacott (eds), *Mass Communication and Society* (pp. 291–308). Beverly Hills, CA: Sage.

Golding, P. and P. Elliot (1974). Mass communication and social change: the imagery of development and development imagery. In E. de Kadt and G. Williams (eds), *Sociology and Development* (pp. 229–54). London: Tavistock.

Goldman, R. (1992). *Reading Ads Socially*. London and New York: Routledge.

Gunder-Frank, A. (1969). *Capitalism and Underdevelopment in Latin America*. New York: Monthly Review Press.

Hamelink, C. (1997). MacBride with hindsight. In P. Golding and P. Harris (eds), *Beyond Cultural Imperialism: Globalization, Communication and the New International Order* (pp. 68–92). Thousand Oaks, CA. Sage.

Hunt, D. (1989). *Economic Theories of Development: An Analysis of Competing Paradigms*. Savage, MD: Barnes and Noble.

Indian Express Newspaper (Bombay) Ltd., Reuters and *The Financial Express* (1997, June 26). US cigarette makers in search of new markets. [Online]. http://www.expressindia.com/fe/daily19970626/177555273.html (retrieved June 27, 1997).

International Trade Administration, US Dept. of Commerce (2004). *Country Commercial Guide FY2002: Nigeria*. [Online]. http://www.world-digest.com/Guides/ni/ (retrieved March 10, 2004).

Janus, N. (1986). Transnational advertising: some considerations on the impact of peripheral Societies. In A. Rita and E. McAnany (eds), *Communication and Latin American Society: Trends in Critical Research, 1960–1985* (pp. 127–42). Madison, WI: University of Wisconsin.

Kennan, K. and B. Shoreh (2000). How advertising is covered in the Egyptian press: a longitudinal examination of content. *International Journal of Advertising*, 19(2): 245–58.

Kilbourne, J. and M. Pipher (2000). *Can't Buy My Love: How Advertising Changes the Way We Think and Live*. New York: Touchstone Books.

Kotler, P. (1987). *Strategic Marketing for Nonprofit Organizations*. Englewood Cliffs, NJ: Prentice-Hall.

Kotler, P. and E. Roberto (1989). *Social Marketing*. New York: Free Press.

Langrehr, F. and C. Caywood (1989). An assessment of the "sins" and "virtues" portrayed in advertising. *International Journal of Advertising*, 8: 391–403.

Lears, J. (1995). *Fables of Abundance: A Cultural History of Advertising in America*. New York: Basic Books.

Leibes, T. and E. Katz (1990). *The Export of Meaning: Cross-cultural Readings of Dallas*. New York: Oxford University Press.

Leiss, W., S. Kline and S. Jhally (1997). *Social Communication in Advertising: Persons, Products and Images of Well-being*. 2nd ed. London and New York: Routledge.

Lull, J. (1995). *Media, Communication, Culture: A Global Approach*. Cambridge: Polity Press.

MacBride, S. et al. (1980). *Many Voices, One World: Communication and Society, Today, and Tomorrow*. New York: UNESCO.

McPhail, T. (2002). *Global Communication: Theories, Stakeholders, and Trends*. Boston, MA: Allyn and Bacon.

Madiebo, A. (1980). *The Nigerian Revolution and the Biafran War*. Enugu, Nigeria: Fourth Dimension Press.

Marchand, R. (1986). *Advertising and the American Dream: Making Way for Modernity, 1920–1940*. Berkeley, CA: University of California Press.

Martins, L. (1982). The state-transnational corporation-local entrepreneur joint venture in Brazil: how to relax and enjoy a forced marriage. In H. Makler, A. Martinnelli and N. Smelser (eds), *The New International Economy* (pp. 281–6). Beverly Hills, CA: Sage.

Mattelart, A. (1979). *Multinational Corporations and the Control of Culture*. Atlantic Highlands, NJ: Humanities Press.

Mattelart, A. (1991). *Advertising International: The Privatisation of Public Space*. London: Routledge.

Mendelssohn, K. (1976). *The Secret of Western Domination*. New York: Praeger.

Moemeka, A. (1997). Communalistic societies: community and self-respect as African values. In C. Christians and M. Traber (eds), *Communication Ethics and Universal Values* (pp. 170–93). Thousand Oaks, CA: Sage.

Mohammadi, A. and A. Sreberny-Mohammadi (1994). *Small Media, Big Revolution: Communication, Culture and the Iranian Revolution*. Minneapolis, MN: University of Minnesota Press.

Mosco, V. (1996). *The Political Economy of Communication: Rethinking and Renewal*. London: Sage.

Mueller, B. (1996). *International Advertising: Communicating across Culture*. Belmont, CA: Wadsworth.

National Public Radio (1999, May 22). *New Program: Morning Edition and/or All-Things Considered*.

Nwosu, I. (1990). Public relations and advertising in the process of governance and economic recovery in Nigeria. In I. Nwosu (ed.), *Mass Communication and National Development: Perspectives on the Communication Environments of Development in Nigeria* (pp. 231–42). Aba, Nigeria: Frontiers Publishers.

Obeng-Quaidoo, I. (1986). A proposal for new communication research methodologies in Africa. *Africa Media Review*, 1(1): 89–98.

Okoro, B. (2001, May 23). Nigeria squanders 280bn oil revenue: Anya. *Post Express Wired*. [Online]. http://www.postexpresswired.com/post (retrieved May 24, 2001).

Oladipo, O. (1995). Reason, identity, and the African quest: the problems of self-definition in African philosophy. *Africa Today*, 42(3): 39–64.

Oliveira, O. (1991). Mass media, culture and communication in Brazil: the heritage of dependency. In G. Sussman and J. Lent (eds), *Transnational Communication: Wiring the Third World* (pp. 200–213). London: Sage.

Packard, V. (1981). *The Hidden Persuaders*. Harmondsworth: Penguin.

Packard, V. and D. Horowitz (1995). *American Social Classes in the 1950s: Selections from Vance Packard's the Status Seekers* (The Bedford Series in History and Culture). New York: Bedford/St. Martin's Press.

Pajnik, M. and P. Lesjak-Tusek (2002). Observing discourses of advertising: Mobitel's interpellation of potential consumers. *Journal Communication Inquiry*, 26(3): 277–99.

Robertson, R. (1992). *Globalization: Social Theory and Global Culture*. London: Sage.

Rodney, W. (1974). *How Europe Underdeveloped Africa*. Washington, DC: Howard University Press.

Roncagliolo, R. (1986). Transnational communication and culture. In R. Atwood and E. McAnany (eds), *Communication and Latin American Society: Trends in Critical Research, 1960–1985* (pp. 79–88). Madison, WI: University of Wisconsin Press.

Rupert, J. (1998, Nov. 9). Denied wealth, Nigeria's poor take dire steps. *Washington Post*. Washington Post Foreign Service, A18.

Schiller, H. (1969/1992). *Mass Communications and American Empire*. New York: Augustus M. Kelley. Second revised and updated edition published by Westview Press in 1992.

Schiller, H. (1991). *Culture, Inc.: The Corporate Takeover of Public Expression*. New York: Oxford University Press.

Schiller, H. (1998). Striving for communication dominance: a half-century review. In D. Thussu (ed.), *Electronic Empires* (pp. 17–26). London: Arnold.

Senghor, L. (1964). *On African Socialism*, trans. Mercer Cook. New York: Praeger.

Solomon, I. (1978). *Multinational Corporations and the Emerging World*. Port Washington, NY: Kennikat Press.

Sreberny-Mohammadi, A. (1991). The global and the local in international communications. In J. Curran and M. Gurevitch (eds), *Mass Media and Society* (pp. 118–38). London: Edward Arnold.

Sreberny-Mohammadi, A. (1997). The many cultural faces of imperialism. In P. Golding and P. Harris (eds), *Beyond Cultural Imperialism* (pp. 49–68). London: Sage.

Strubhaar, J. (1997). Distinguishing the global, regional and national levels of world television. In A. Sreberny-Mohammadi, D. Winseck, J. McKenna and O. Boyd-Barrett (eds), *Media in Global Context: A Reader* (pp. 284–98). New York: St. Martin's Press.

Sussman, G. (1997). *Communication, Technology and Politics in the Information Age*. Thousand Oaks, CA: Sage.

Tansey, R. and M. Hyman (1994). Dependency theory and the effects of advertising by foreign based multinational corporations in Latin America. *Journal of Advertising*, 23(1): 27–41.

Thussu, D. (2000). *International Communication: Continuity and Change*. London: Arnold.

Tsao, J. (1996). Advertising in Taiwan: sociopolitical change and multinational impact. In K. Frith (ed.), *Advertising in Asia: Communication, Culture and Consumption* (pp. 103–14). Ames, IA: Iowa State University Press.

Twitchell, J. (1997). *Adcult USA*. New York: Columbia University Press.

Twitchell, J. (2002). *Living It Up*. New York: Columbia University Press.

Uche, L. (1988). Mass communication and cultural identity: the unresolved issue of national sovereignty and cultural autonomy in the wake of new communication technologies. *Africa Media Review*, 3(1): 83–120.

Uche, L. (1994). Some reflections on the dependency theory. *Africa Media Review*, 8(2): 39–55.

Van Zoonen, L. (1994). *Feminist Media Studies*. London: Sage.

Wallerstein, I. (1974/1980). *The Modern World System*. 2 volumes. New York: Academic Press.

Wallerstein, I. (1979). *The Capitalist World-Economy*. Cambridge: Cambridge University Press.

Wallerstein, I. (1991). *Geopolitics and Geoculture: Essays on the Changing World System*. Cambridge: Cambridge University Press.

2 *Advertising in Transition: A Case Study on Nigeria's Burgeoning Market*

OLUGBENGA C. AYENI

Introduction

With a meager per capita income figure of $310 and Gross National Product (GNP) of $38 billion, Nigeria has the potential to be a leading emerging market in Africa. The country boasts of huge but yet-to-be-tapped economic potentials, and a 993,000 square-kilometer stretch of fertile land should place Nigeria in the league of exporting economies of the world. The projected population of nearly 150 million adds further strength to other variables that make the country an enormous reservoir of human and natural resources, and a fertile ground for trade and investment.

This dense population pales significantly in comparison to the robust oil revenue that has served as the lifeline for the economic growth of Africa's most populous nation. The World Bank estimates that oil revenue, with the attendant upsurge in prices over the summer, is likely to be well over $6 billion in the year 2004. Nigeria's huge market potential is a haven for companies seeking not just new swathes of profitable consumer bases but also an open arena of opportunities to wrest market control from manufacturing companies that currently produce crudely manufactured products.

In the past few years, since the return of a democratically elected government, things have been looking up for Nigeria's economy. Having had its share of unwelcome military dictatorships that slowed down development and brought about years of pillage by corrupt leaders and smart practices in business, vigorous effort is being put in place to sanitize the corrupt practices in high and low realms with a view to creating a clement environment for foreign investments. This is all good news for the marketing communications sector of the economy, one of the major victims of these crippling economic activities that plagued Nigeria in the earlier part of the 1990s.

With a new democracy in place Nigeria is sending the message that it is back in business and that the doors are wide open for those who may want to invest in the country's market. The government is opening up the economy to direct foreign investment and is divesting itself of most of the burdensome infrastructural sectors of the economy through privatization. In the last few years, the government has encouraged foreign investment in the telecommunications, oil and agro-related industries to tap into the new political and economic environment.

Businesses are being resurrected from years of crippling trade to an environment open to the embrace of joint enterprises. For example, telecom companies parading the Global System for Mobile Communication (GSM) technology paid $285 million for an operating license to compete with the government-owned moribund Nigeria Telecommunications Limited (NITEL). Moreover, in 2010 the performance of Nigeria's stock market exceeded all expectations, especially when compared to other emerging markets. It rallied more than "20% in January, with average daily volumes up 76% against a year ago on trading of about US$20 million dollars" (*How We Made It in Africa*, 2011).

In this environment, all of the portents for the marketing communications industry are good. Having languished during the long military rule when the economy was near comatose, the advertising and marketing industry is bracing for the challenging tasks ahead. Generally criticized for many social ills, advertising and marketing communications are not just about pervasive or invasive audience manipulation. Advertising can be made to play a significant role in providing the necessary impetus to encourage consumer patronage and enable companies to realize their return on investments (ROI), as well as play key roles in development efforts that lend strength to the country's nascent democracy.

The aim of this case study is, therefore, to provide a descriptive analysis of the advertising industry in Nigeria, one of the areas of mass communication about which very little is said in existing literature on Nigeria. This is with a view to identifying the problems and prospects faced by industry practitioners, clients and consumers. A synopsis that presents the state of affairs in the industry has its merit in being both reflective and predictive in scope, and it can provide a starting point for deeper and more specific issue-related studies that focus on content, effects, impact, regulations and other associated issue-focused research on advertising in Nigeria. The case analysis is broad in scope and takes a bird's-eye view of the environment as presented by key industry personnel over the past few years. The study begins by reviewing the evolution and growth of advertising as an industry, the areas of contribution, problems and prospects.

Nigeria and other African countries have not fully tapped into the phenomenal growth trend witnessed in the advertising industry over the last ten years. In the area of press advertising, which holds the best promise of growth in most of Africa, advertising spending figures are still unimpressive.

Sub-Saharan Africa receives world attention for reports about coups, wars and famine but very little is said about the entire continent when it comes to marketing communication strategies especially for top international brands including those that are popularly used in many African countries.

Many marketers and by extension advertising agencies are flooding to the African continent to tap into the potential huge consumer base. According to Martin Sorrell, Chief Executive Officer of WPP, the world's largest advertising company by revenue, "All our major clients, as they are looking for geographical expansion opportunities, have Africa and the Middle East high up on their priority list, if not at the top." WPP Currently generates $500 million in Africa, and a 10% growth is expected in 2011, increasing "profit from under $150 million from four years ago" (Bender and Vranica, 2010).

The business and marketing climate in Africa changed soon after the 2010 Football World Cup, hosted by South Africa. Nigeria, Angola and Ghana became beneficiaries, experiencing large growth potential and a big push from the new focus on Africa. Nigeria experienced a healthy 20 percent growth in advertising. Patrick Ehringer, president of the

Middle East and Africa for DDB Worldwide, a unit of Omnicom Group, says his agency is hoping to "bulk up in Nigeria because of the volume of business that is going on there" (Bender and Vranica, 2010). Africa and the Middle East together represent 2.9 percent or $14 billion of the total $482 billion global advertising market.

Following the global recession, the gloomy world economic landscape took its toll on the advertising market. Visible signs of improvement have been identified. In 2009, overall expenditures dipped by -6.8 percent in the first half of the year. North America's plunge was -15.9 percent while Europe's was -9.1 percent (blog.nielsen.com). There was a rebound in 2010 with a jump in the first half of the year to a total adspend of $238 billion (a 13 percent increase over the 2009 figures). This was attributable to booming emerging markets whose shock absorbent economies were able to withstand the "tsunamis" witnessed in the world market. Latin America was the fastest growing that year, up by 45 percent, while the Middle East and Africa rose by nearly 24 percent (*Adweek*, October 11, 2010).

The Journey of Advertising in Nigeria

Information and data on the history of the marketing communications industry in Nigeria are sparse, and the little that exists is vague and disjointed. What could be considered a crude form of advertising existed in the traditional societies in Africa and Nigeria even before the advent of European incursion into the continent. Africa's oral history tells us of village gong men who disseminated newsworthy events at the market place, and that kings and clan heads had men who served as the liaison between the people and the palace, and that they employed the services of such palace hands to transmit messages from one village or town to the other.

These gong men had the duty of spreading news of meetings, rituals, celebrations and of impending war or danger to the people. Copious messages from the king were meticulously transmitted to the general populations without errors or risk of misinterpretation. Such men chosen for this task possessed, aside from their ability to memorize important facts and paraphrase faultlessly, a sonorous and ringing voice. The gong was bell-shaped cast iron struck by another metal object to produce a ringing tone. In some parts, flute men performed similar tasks to announce the arrival of the king at public functions, to wake up the king every morning and to serve as praise worshippers during important palace functions.

Other crude forms of advertising were sometimes performed on market days by yet another set of professionals who used their creative art form to attract clientele for the advertisers. Traders employed magicians or snake charmers at the market place to direct traffic to their wares, products or services that were on display. Some of these creative professionals also served as celebrities that provided endorsement for the products. Sometimes they even served as guinea pigs for new cure-all traditional potions or showed audiences how to use the product. Many artisans made brisk money through the many bystanders and onlookers who were charmed by the antics of these advertising gurus-cum-magicians.

A practice that could be likened to modern day propaganda featured footmen whose task was to howl the product qualities and attributes to passersby who had earlier been lured to the area by the antics of the magicians. Such moments were interspersed with more direct commercial activities when the products were introduced to bystanders and the actual exchange of goods and services took place. These were the only forms of marketing communications that regularly took place other than the potent word-of-mouth that thrived in oral societies such as Nigeria where news about products and services moved faster than modern-day breaking news.

Prior to modern-day commercial activities and economic processes and structure, most of Africa thrived on subsistence economies and goods were produced for the immediate and extended family members' sufficiency. The only form of commercial exchange occurred through trade by barter when villagers and townspeople exchanged commodities they produced for things they lacked. Soon after the incursion of Europeans into Africa, newer economic patterns ushered in processes of adaptation to the modern methods and improvements in production and distribution strategies.

Printing technology made its way into Nigeria around the nineteenth century, long after the rest of the world was already reaping its fruits. In 1859, Nigeria's first newspaper was established by the Christian Missionary Society (CMS), as part of the evangelization process sweeping through Africa. The vernacular newspaper titled *Iwe Irohin* (*The News*) was first edited by a reverend gentleman, Henry Townsend.

The paper covered mostly religious news such as baptisms, births, marriages and other ecclesiastic stories that were considered appealing to the newly converted Christians in Southern Nigeria. The only advertising section in the newspaper contained snippets that covered the arrival or departure of ships and sometimes what they conveyed. Merchants found information of this type helpful in preparing for the goods that such vessels transported. Trade between Africa and Europe then was mostly one-way—the vessels came to cart away agricultural raw materials that serviced the newly industrialized states of Europe.

It was not until around 1928 that a quasi advertising shop/agency was established. The West African Publicity Limited Company, a subsidiary to the multinational United African Company (UAC), was incorporated in London in August 1928. "It was to provide marketing support for the parent company, the UAC, in response to the marketing demands of the expanding multinational" (*Advertising Annual*, 2000, p. 12).

The advertising industry relied on the print industry for its initial growth, and when in 1959 the first full outdoor advertising service, Afromedia, along with the first television broadcasting service was set up, the industry was ready to take off. The West African Publicity Company assumed a new name, Lintas West Africa, in 1965 as part of the Unilever Group (Lever International Advertising Agency).

In the early years cinema and film were prominently utilized for advertising message delivery while radio and billboards were effective in terms of their reach and utility values in a highly illiterate society. Growth was witnessed in the period between 1970 and early 1990 when Nigeria was reported to be awash with crude oil dollars. Agencies, both fully indigenous and owned jointly with foreign partners, began new business. Media outlets, both print and electronic, grew widely to provide communication channels for the advertising industry.

The global adspend data reviewed reveals that the relationship between the country's share of global adspend was not only indicative of the growth of advertising in the region, but also of the level of growth attained by the country's manufacturing and marketing industries. Advertising revenue figures were also a key "testament to the importance of this element of the marketing communications mix from a public policy perspective" (Harker and Harker, 2002, p. 24).

Advertising Agencies Today

The Association of Advertising Practitioners of Nigeria (AAPN) was set up in 1973 while a statutory regulating body known as the Advertising Practitioners Council of Nigeria (APCON) followed in 1988 through different federal government laws. Under the broad umbrella of APCON are other media-allied associations responsible for coordinating advertising-related issues within their professional sectors. These include the Advertisers Association of Nigeria, the Newspapers Proprietors Association of Nigeria (NPAN), the Broadcasting Organizations of Nigeria (BON) and the Outdoor Advertising Association of Nigeria (OAAN). APCON's organizational structure includes departments dealing with vetting and monitoring, education and training, research/public relations, accounts, administration, inspectorate and publications, among others.

About 84 registered advertising agencies have been identified by APCON, as the registering body for the industry, while about 100 outdoor agencies operate under the aegis of the Outdoor Advertising Association of Nigeria (OAAN). These are serviced by allied industries like the Broadcasting Organization of Nigeria member companies made up of all network and cable channels. In 2000, the total billing for the industry was recorded at N7 billion, approximately $50 million, considered healthy despite dipping fortunes in worldwide global ad revenues.

The challenges are daunting in the face of a growing market; dwindling returns on advertising investments and the stiff competition posed by international agencies who consider agency shops in Nigeria less than equal in their ability to handle international accounts. According to Steve Omojafor, CEO of STB McCann and Universal McCann Nigeria Limited, "the advertising industry, being service-oriented will only survive and successfully play its role, if practitioners are trained to possess creative and innovative minds and are technically equipped to meet the challenges of the ever-changing business environment" (August 18, 2003, personal communication).

Beyond the challenges posed by creativity is the issue of the financial management of the agencies as profitable entities. Account audits, billings and other related information are shrouded in mystery and riddled with guesswork. Most agencies are mere self-serving sole ownership contrivances that fail to conform to globally accepted business criteria. The agencies remain grossly undercapitalized, undermining the prospect for business growth and continuity that would ensure that the attrition rate, currently sky-high, is kept under control (Akinwunmi, 2003).

> *Advertisers run campaigns without budgetary provisions. They either use controversial monitoring reports as excuse or simply sit on invoices until the end of the financial year. Thereafter, they plead that the books have been closed, documentation cannot be accounted for, and so agencies should cancel or drastically renegotiate the debts. (Steve Omojafor, August 2003)*

Ownership structures are rooted in one-person shops and sectional heads and top management officers are left out of the ownership loop. Commitment is tenuous, to say the least, and most accounts remain unstable as agencies witness rapid shifts in human resource from time to time. The Association of Advertising Practitioners of Nigeria (AAPN) was set up with the mandate to register and license agencies and also to ensure that businesses are run according to requisite provisions. However, most agencies remain largely unsupervised and are likely to perform at below par and under the radar of the ineffective AAPN.

Media data and selection have been two areas of concern typically making work in the advertising industry tedious and lacking in authenticity. For many years, media planning and buying of air time and advertising space in Nigeria had been based solely on guesswork, devoid of any scientific, verifiable or evaluative methods. "One area that needs improvement is data generation. We advertise blindly. This is the truth. I don't know which paper that knows its actual circulation and readership" (Emmanul Ekunno, ADVAN President, 2003).

The advertising industry, some say, has seen better days in Nigeria. The need for a regulating body like the Advertising Practitioners Council of Nigeria (APCON) is more relevant now for the purpose of putting the advertising house in some order. APCON's provisions, among many other guidelines stipulate the requirements for qualifying as a practitioner, and require the registration and certification of those qualified to practice, training services for professionals and rules for ethical practices.

A key area of controversy in the industry is the overlapping roles assigned by law to advertising self-regulating agencies that has resulted in friction between such groups and make progressive work impossible.

One major obstacle that has continued to stare Advertising Practitioners Council of Nigeria (APCON) in the face and which sometimes inhibits the full performance of its functions, is the multiplicity of bodies purporting to have regulatory responsibilities. (O. Falomo, AAPN, 2004)

When the APCON was set up in 1988, it was with the charge to "regulate and control the practice of advertising in all its aspects and ramifications" (APCON Decree 55, 1988). A year later, concerned with the rash of fake production of pharmaceutical products harmful to the people, the government set up the National Agency for Foods and Drug Administration and Control (NAFDAC). The task of NAFDAC, however, went beyond controlling fake drugs to other areas such as "advertising of food, cosmetics, medical devices, bottled water and chemicals", an area that APCON felt it was more equipped to regulate. The importance of having structured advertising self-regulating agencies in place is crucial not just for the industry and its image in the country but also because it is reflective of how the industry is perceived and respected in the global environment.

In assessing the role of the mass media in Nigeria, especially the role of advertising, one has to look at the entire mass media industry of which advertising is an integral part. In general, the mass media have been acknowledged to have played crucial roles in shaping and defining the establishment of democracy in Africa (Ojo, 2003). "Around the world, the marketing communications industry is at the forefront in the vanguard of economic development. The reason we hadn't been recognized here may not be unconnected with the sort of government we've had over the years" (Nwaobi, M., CEO Advertising Techniques Limited—J. Walter Thompson affiliate, 2004).

Economic Role

The role of advertising in building strong brands in Nigeria dates back to the early days of advertising when international products like Unilever's OMO washing detergent, Close-Up toothpaste, Smithkline Beecham's Florish, Crest and Pepsodent toothpaste, Star lager beer and Guinness stout became household names.

Agencies like Rosabel, PAL, Sunrise, Grant Advertising and Insight Communications, among many others, grew in billings during the 1970s and the 1980s. The economic impact of advertising was felt more in the area of alcohol marketing where one of the frontline brewers, Nigeria Brewing Limited (NBL), accounted for 6.2 percent of the total market capitalization of the stock exchange.

The current favorable democratic setting has now encouraged the flow of capital into new areas of the economy in Nigeria while the government's trade liberalization policies have opened up the country to foreign investments. All of these help nurture the economy and strengthen the weak advertising industry. Furthermore, the impact of marketing communications in giving a fillip to the ailing Nigeria economy has been acknowledged by industry experts. The industry is estimated to have contributed about N75 billion of the Gross Domestic Product (GDP) out of the total contribution of N30 billion from the blue chip and multinational companies. Overall the AAPN accounted for about N14 billion in billing for the year 2003 (*Vanguard Newspapers*, January 12, 2004).

In no other sector of the Nigerian economy is the role of marketing communications in public information packaging felt more than in the telecommunications industry. Advertising has played a crucial sensitizing role for the on-going privatization policy of the Nigerian government. Before deregulation of the telecom industry, International Telecommunications Union (ITU) figures indicate that only 0.34 telephones lines per 100 people were available. Now deregulated, the government-controlled Nigerian Telecommunications (NITEL) faces stiff competition from foreign companies to break its monopoly.

Consequently, 800,000 new mobile phone lines have been made available to subscribers under the deregulation policy which has galvanized the country into the new telecom mobile age. This created a big boost for the marketing advertising industry, along with new challenges and opportunities. Marketing communication has thus opened a new competitive frontier in the busy telecom industry whereby creative advertising messages try to outdo each other in a bid to win new clientele.

The beer industry continues to do well while banking, oil and allied industries provide a key revenue base for advertising in Nigeria. In the alcoholic drink category, Legend Extra Stout and Star beer pioneered in sales. The huge sales in alcoholic drinks have been of concern to advocacy groups who fear the backlash of drunkenness as a social consequence. New sales marketing strategies like event sponsorships, sales promotions and music shows were used to stir the market's demand for the products. Sona breweries introduced a N75 million sales promotion while a N20 million campaign was launched by Guinness. Sales promotions have been found to be effective in many developing countries where people look to the possible reward of getting rich quickly while enjoying the benefits of their favorite products.

Social Marketing

It is important to review the role of advertising and marketing communication and the mass media in general in the process of what could be termed democratic consolidation. Democratic consolidation is the "challenge of making new democracies secure, of extending their life expectancy beyond the short term, of making them immune to the threat of authoritarian regression" (Ojo, 2003, p. 822).

Such roles played by advertising include educating the people on state affairs and disseminating information on government activities that enable the people to make enlightened decisions on policy issues. Another key area is in disseminating messages to educate people on the scourge of HIV/AIDS in Nigeria through what has been referred to as contraceptive social marketing (CSM). The acronym CSM is limited in its definition as it does not suggest other areas such as the metrification campaign, and the supply of subsidized beneficial products such as contraceptives (including condoms), oral re-hydration salts or nutritionally fortified foods (Harvey, 2002).

Most noticeable in this democratic consolidation is the impact and the role of advertising in the areas of contraceptive social marketing (CSM), political advertising and political mobilization. Highly creative advertising campaigns have proved effective in mobilizing the populace toward the increased need for family planning in Nigeria, especially in the populous cities of southwest Nigeria like Ilorin and Ibadan.

The correlation between exposure to family planning messages and contraceptive use throughout the African continent has been widely acknowledged (Westoff and Rodriguez, 1995). This social marketing role is more relevant now when the scourge of AIDS and other sexually transmitted diseases are ravaging the continent. Zaire, South Africa and Nigeria have invested in social mobilization efforts to stem the tide of the AIDS epidemic through many jingles and slogans.

For effective message penetration in terms of reach and frequency, radio, posters and billboards are still considered the most reliable, for the obvious reason of low literacy levels. Furthermore, newspapers and television are relatively expensive while irregular energy sources make reliance on television less attractive. Radio programs such as Future Dreams, created by the Society for Family Health (SFH), an affiliate of PSI, have been adjudged to be successful. The skit, which was developed using major local languages spoken in Nigeria, was broadcast on 42 radio channels before political controversy over its vulgar content led to its suspension. "The thrust of the campaign should have been the eradication of AIDS and not to encourage promiscuity as its content suggested. People were not cautioned on the consequences of AIDS. The ad gave an erroneous impression" (Akhabue, 2004, p. 34).

Notable public service announcements and social campaign efforts on health issues where advertising and social mobilization messages play a crucial role for effecting behavioral changes include programs dealing with issues such as oral re-hydration therapy (ORT), childhood immunization, female circumcision and safe-sex. The Education and Communication unit of the Society for Family Health in Nigeria estimate that the success of these messages geared toward sexually active men and women will help in promoting behavioral changes in the indiscriminate sexual activities of youngsters. To this end, the division developed and produced a broad range of mass media materials including radio, television, film and folk media programs, and newspaper and magazine articles for, in all, the 31 daily newspapers, 81 radio transmitters, and 71 television stations. Over one million posters, billboards, crown posters, danglers, bumper stickers, indoor stickers and novelty items were produced between 1991 and 1993.

Political Advertising

Whereas the use of political advertising has become a staple of communication in democracies around the world (Kaid, 2004), political advertising as a tool in party politics still remain under utilized in Nigeria. The history and partisan nature of politics make the effective use of political marketing tools, especially political ads, less effective than they should be. Party politics is still enmeshed in ethnic alliances such that no brilliant creative political ad can perform wonders for a candidate if he or she does not belong to a favored specific region, religion or party. Party politics is not robust enough for the electorate to rely on the media presentation and marketing of candidates. This is not to say, though, that politicians are not employing the services of advertising agencies in message dissemination and image packaging.

In 1963 one of the frontline politicians of the era, Obafemi Awolowo, was said to have employed skywriting during rallies for campaign purposes (Nzeribe, 1992). And in 1979 a thematic advertising campaign approach was executed when the two popular parties then, the Unity Party of Nigeria (UPN) and the National Party of Nigeria (NPN), were engaged in the battle over which party would take charge after the military had exited. The use of posters is perhaps the most common print ad medium, while radio has been most effective in reaching the far-flung, highly illiterate populations in the hinterland.

The first nationally televised political debate between two presidential candidates took place in 1992 when the flag bearer for the Social Democratic Party (SDP), M.K.O. Abiola engaged Bashir Tofa of the National Republican Convention (NRC) in a debate on their manifestos and plans for Nigeria. Abiola's performance during the debate has been credited, among other qualities, for his election victory although the elections were unfortunately annulled by the corrupt and rogue military government of Ibrahim Babangida. Abiola, who later died in detention while being incarcerated for claiming his mandate, also employed television jingles that incorporated songs from well known lyrics. The songs soon became the rallying tune to mobilize national support for his candidacy.

Unlike in the United States, where candidates enjoy equal access and equal time provision in air time and news coverage, or in the United Kingdom where party broadcasts are free, political communication laws in Nigeria are silent on the use of print media for party political campaigns. A rich candidate and his party can buy all the air time they need while leaving others with little choice in accessing the electorate. The question of balance and fair coverage are left unanswered. Moreover, the brazen use of negative advertising in political ads is one key outcome of the ineffective regulations in Nigeria's political communication environment.

The nature and content of political ads since the time that Abiola and his peers pioneered political advertising and debates has deteriorated to a level of unprecedented negativity. Although Kaid (2000) observes that, "there is no universally accepted definition of negative advertisements, but most would agree that they basically are opponent-focused rather than candidate-focused" (p. 157), political ads in Nigeria have been caustic and negative in content, to say the least. Devoid of issue discussion or a solid platform for robust debate, the ads compete to determine which would be most debasing. Unlike the party-focused approach commonly used in Britain, the structure of political ads is somewhat candidate-centered, more like that seen in the United States, except that the tone is all negative.

In 2003, Olusegun Obasanjo, the incumbent, and Muhammadu Buhari, the challenger, both retired military dictators, contested the presidential elections as frontrunners. The two were engaged in the most vitriolic of advertising campaigns yet seen in the short history of political advertising in Nigeria. Name calling, outright falsehoods, labeling, personal attacks and other known political advertising vices were put to reckless use. Buhari was likened to Hitler, perhaps more for his trademark moustache that looks like Hitler's, less for his strict and high-handed rule as a military leader.

Olusegun Obasanjo was accused of misdirecting the nation for four years, considered weak and incompetent to lead the country. One of his challenger's ads read: "Let's talk issues—corruption: The only sector of Obasanjo's government that has excelled with distinction is corruption. Corruption has enjoyed unprecedented prosperity since May 29, 1999." Nonetheless, any comparison with Hitler was too callous to use in reference to an opposing candidate in any decent political communication environment. Some of Buhari's opponents accused him of convicting innocent citizens without trial during his tenure as military dictator with the rider: "the leopard's spots are forever."

Financial provisions for campaign ads rest solely with the candidates and the parties, although government provides some financial support in this task. Nevertheless, politicians still employed scaremongering tactics, name calling and outright negativity in the way they packaged their political campaigns during both the 1999 and the 2003 elections. It is clear that the rules of the game as provided in the Transition to Civil Rule (Political Parties Registration and Activities Decree of 1989) have not been followed.

Although the provision of the Transition to Civil Rule (Political Parties Registration and Activities Decree 27 of 1989) prohibits "abusive, intemperate, slanderous or base language designed to provoke violent emotion or reactions in political campaigns," the candidates and their ad agencies ignored such pleas. The decree put in place by the then military junta also requires that, "no political campaigns shall be made on the basis of sectional, ethnic, or religious ground or considerations" (Transition to Civil Rule (Political Parties Registration and Activities Decree 27 of 1989), p. 23). Although the law states that: "Radio and television shall observe balance in political programs, and in the equal presentation of alternative or opposing points of views or interests," the gap left within the law has been abused for partisan language and domination of the air waves by the rich parties.

What then is the effect of these negative ads on voter perception? Perhaps in Nigeria's case it could be political apathy or a brazen resort to candidate evaluation using divisive indicators like religion, ethnicity and financial patronage. However, the overall consequence of negative advertising may result in unhealthy effects for democracy, especially as they relate to voter alienation and cynicism (Kaid, 2004). This is because the role played by negative ads in reinforcing ethnic biases and by crass appeal to religious and geopolitical nepotism may further harm the budding democracy that political communication should help nurture.

Political communication, despite its use by most politicians, is not yet as potent in voter decision formulation as it could be. The winner-takes-all attitude of politicians, the influential role of ethnic politics and the plague of religious dogma make political marketing a tricky terrain. This explains why political ads are still largely negative and say very little about party platforms, issues or electoral promises. There is hope that public enlightenment on democratic principles will help shape the future of political communication in Nigeria and indeed all of Africa.

Conclusions: The Future of Advertising in Nigeria and Africa

The problem of low capital investment and a high rate of attrition is being reversed through affiliations with foreign ad agencies seeking to tap into the nearly 150 million audience base in Nigeria. Agencies like Prima Garnet, STB McCann and The Shops have working relationships with agencies outside of Nigeria. Prima Garnet is affiliated with Ogilvy & Mather Worldwide while STB McCann is affiliated with McCann Erickson, The Shops has a working relationship with the Pittsburg, PA-based Graphic Arts Technical Foundation (GATF) and SO&U Nigeria has affiliations with Saatchi & Saatchi. STB-McCann's Chairman, Steve Omojafor, says: "When agencies merge, corporate growth and survival is assured as the company becomes stronger … The synergy arising from such an exercise enables the company to acquire more technology, retain best staff" (Personal communication, August, 2003).

Considering the vibrant nature of the market and the dynamism and growth witnessed in the industry, the advertising industry in Nigeria remains hopeful. Ad agencies like STB McCann, with its McCann Erickson affiliation, is set to blaze new trails in the ad industry. A subsidiary company, Universal McCann, has been set up with sole responsibility for building a media research database such as the Media in Mind (MIM) tool that other agencies rely on for buying decisions.

With the complex audience composition found in Nigeria, it is helpful to establish a data-driven media measurement system that allows agencies and their clients to determine their return on investments (ROI), as well as evaluate the effectiveness of advertising messages. In 1999, diaries for radio and television audience measurements were introduced in response to arbitrary media pricing that was not based on empirical data. Hence, recently launched scientific media measuring products such as the Media and Product Survey (MPS), the Radio Audience Measurement Survey (RAMS) and the Television Audience Measurement Survey (TAMS) will likely change the operations of the ad agency in Nigeria.

The survey methods used for compiling audience data incorporate personal in-home interviews, diaries and questionnaires, all similar to the universally acceptable and verifiable methods used by Simmons or Mediamark in the United States. Listening and viewing habits will be correlated against product and media usage. The heretofore fairly unknown figures of reach and frequency, which signal the level of dispersion and repetition of advertising messages needed in an ad campaign, and serve as the foundation for media planning in the developed world, are now making their appearance in the advertising market in Nigeria.

All of these should impact the process of Integrated Marketing Communications (IMC) as a tool for marketing in Nigeria. IMC is customer-centric with the requisite knowledge of the customer being the key element of a successful IMC campaign. It provides the ability to go beyond the superficial delineation of data into the consumer's thought process, current and future needs and wants. Beyond this, IMC is data driven. The cohesive and close-knit relationship with marketing cannot materialize when there is only a fleeting knowledge of the consumer.

There is thus a new vista of opportunity in Nigeria for investments in every area of the economy, including the marketing communication industry. New foreign investments in partnerships are taking off in media ownership with total advertising spend for radio having increased from $100 million in 1999 to about $15 million in 2000, an increase of about 24 percent. The quality of newspaper production has also improved drastically with more newspapers produced in color.

About a hundred advertising agencies operate in Nigeria and engage in print, broadcast and outdoor advertising, with a few big international agencies like J. Walter Thomson and Saatchi & Saatchi operating collaborative arrangements with indigenous partners. In 2007 the total ad spend was put at $271 million with television accounting for a share of 51.4 percent while radio accounted for 18.8 percent and outdoor and print taking 17 percent and 12 percent respectively. Besides the full service agencies, outdoor agencies total up to 125.

According to Akanmu (2004), "the combined forces of the 3 D's, Democracy, Deregulation, and Digitization, are fundamentally changing the structure of many industries and with potential seismic effects in some cases. The practice of marketing in Nigeria is entering an era of challenges that has no precedent in the history of the current generation." This is hoping that the industry will avail itself of the immense opportunities that the new environment has made possible. The years of democracy and relative political stability following years of military rule have increased foreign investment confidence in Nigerian markets with a resulting increase in consumer bargaining power due to deregulation and a competitive open market.

References

Adeniyi-Williams, K. (1997). Marketing and advertising in the Nigerian economy. In J. Molokwu and D. Obiaku (eds), *Advertising in Nigeria: Some Fundamental Issues*. Lagos: APCON Publications.

Advertising in Nigeria: some fundamental issues (2000). *Advertising Annual*. Lagos: APCON Publications.

Advertising in the 21st century (2000, March). *Advertising Annual*, vol. 3. Lagos: APCON Publications.

Advertising Overview (2003, December). *APCON Newsletter*, 2(3). Lagos: APCON Publications.

Adweek Global Adspend (2010, October 11). Global adspend rebounds. [Online.] www.adage.com/article (retrieved April 10, 2011).

Akanmu, O. (2004). Democracy, deregulation, digitization and the new challenges of marketing in Nigeria. Paper presented at the *Brand Wagon* Seminar on Democracy and the Nigerian Markets, Lagos, Nigeria, July 20, 2004.

Akhabue, B. (2004, May 28). Aids/STD campaign: who is NBC fighting for? *This Day Newspaper* (Lagos), 34.

Akinwunmi, L. (2003, January 9). The future of advertising in Nigeria. *This Day Newspaper*, 9(2969).

Amuzuo, C. (2004, January 12). Marketing communications: rising investment profile in 2003. *Vanguard Newspapers* (Lagos).

Bender, R. and Vranica, S. (2010, October 22). Global advertising agencies flocking to Africa, *Wall Street Journal*. [Online.] http://online.wsj.com/article/SB10001424052702304741404575564193783950352 (retrieved April 7, 2011).

Doghuje, C. (1992). Political advertising: thoughts and non thoughts. In C. Okigbo (ed.). *Marketing Politics: Advertising Strategies and Tactics*. Lagos: APCON Publications.

Ekunno, E. (2003). Challenges of advertising industry in Nigeria. Presidential Speech delivered at the Annual General Meeting of the Advertisers' Association Nigeria (ADVAN), Lagos, Nigeria, May 2, 2003.

Ethics and professionalism in advertising as tools for national integration (2002, June). *Advertising Practitioners of Nigeria (APCON) Report*, vol. 2.

Falomo, O. (2004, August 6). We will prevent drift in advertising in Nigeria. *This Day Newspaper* (Lagos), 17.

Harker, D. and M. Harker (2002). Dealing with complaints about advertising in Australia: the importance of regulatory self-discipline. *International Journal of Advertising*, 21: 23–45.

Harvey, P.D. (2002). Advertising affordable contraceptives: the social marketing experience. *DKT International*, Washington, DC. [Online.] www.dktinternational.org (retrieved May 23, 2005).

How We Made It in Africa (2011, January 22). Nigerian banks one of the best prospective investment areas in the world. [online]. http://www.howwemadeitinafrica.com/page/2/?s=Nigeria+stock+market (retrieved January 23, 2011).

Kaid, L.L. (2000). Advertising ethics. In R.E. Danton, *Political Communication Ethics: An Oxymoron?* (pp. 147–67). Westport, CT: Praegar.

Kaid, L.L. (2004). Political advertising. In L.L. Kaid (ed.), *Handbook of Political Communication Research* (pp. 155–202). Mahwah, NJ: Lawrence Erlbaum.

Nigerian advertising laws, rules and regulations (2002). *Advertising Annual*, vol. 5. Lagos: APCON Publications.

Nwaobi, M. (2004, May 24). Creativity thrives better in competitive environment. *This Day Newspaper* (Lagos), 28.

Nzeribe, M. (1992). Marketing Nigerian politics. In C. Okigbo (ed.). *Marketing Politics: Advertising Strategies and Tactics*. Lagos: APCON Publications.

Obot, E., A. Akan and N. Ibanga (2002). Beer ads take the lion's share. In *Center for Research and Information on Substance Abuse Report* (p. 36). Baltimore, MD: CRISA Publication.

Ojo, E.O. (2003). The mass media and the challenges of democratic values in Nigeria: possibilities and limitations. *Media, Culture and Society*, 25: 821–40.

Omojafor, Steve (personal communication, August 18, 2003).

Transition to Civil Rule (Political Parties Registration and Activities Decree 27 of 1989). Lagos: Federal Government of Nigeria Printing Press.

Westoff, C. and G. Rodriguez (1995). The mass media and family planning in Kenya. *International Family Planning Perspectives*, 21(1): 26–31.

World Advertising Research Center (2002). Global adspend trends 2002. *International Journal of Advertising*, 21: 551–3.

3 *Patterns of Arabic Taste and Popular Culture: A Social Reading of Arabic Commercials*

ALIAA DAKROURY

Advertising is a buffet of symbolic imagery that advertisers hope will prove tempting and lead to the more difficult exchange of money for goods. Consumers pass down the table of displayed appeals, glancing here and there, but stop only infrequently to oblige a felt inner need for a symbol and a product—and to buy.

(Fowles, 1996, p. 165)

When a group of school children ended their tour of the White House, guided personally by former American President George Bush Sr., journalists and reporters asked one of the children about his opinion on his extraordinary tour guide. The child simply said: "he kept going and going and going," then he added: "like an Energizer bunny" (Fowles, 1996, p. 1).

This anecdote reflects the extent to which advertising influences our lives, informs our discourses, affects our daily language, and creates meaning for us. At the outset, the role of advertising could be viewed as merely one element of a marketing plan, but it is also instructive to regard this important communication medium as a key factor in "shaping," as well as portraying, social culture, art and taste: "advertising not only replicates the social movement ... but also in large measure assisted at its 'creation'" (Cross, 1996, p. 2).

Adopting French sociologist Pierre Bourdieu's conceptualization of "taste," and through the use of a sample of Arabic magazines and pre-recorded video commercials, patterns of Arabic taste and popular culture will be analyzed in this chapter, arguing that advertising does not merely promote the goods and services advertised but rather must represent the audience's taste, values and popular culture in order to achieve its target goal.

Historically, the reason behind the emergence of advertising in the seventeenth century was the consumers' need for information about prices and shipping. This led to merchants creating the "announcements" display, which became known as advertising.

However, with the advent of the twentieth-century's mass market economy, new types of consumers emerged, with more disposable income and needs they didn't even know they had. Hence, advertisers started doing their best to create this type of eager consumers, and encourage them to consume more and more: "in a mass consumption society, this would eventually lead individuals to a continuous quest for new products and new identities in order to keep ahead of the crow" (Patten, 1989, p. 133). In other words, advertising became a tool of social consumption rather than a medium of information.

The Scope

The main purpose of this study is to explore the influence of advertising in constructing, enforcing, and/or changing consumers' behavioral patterns of consumption based on the taste disseminated through advertising and popular culture in Arab society. I am proposing here that the taste pattern suggested in the Arab advertisements incites the audience to imitate and follow. In other words, the taste community that a person lives in may determine his or her preferred model or pattern of taste; I am arguing that advertising plays a key role in reinforcing this role and cultivating Arab society to consume advertised cultural goods and services.

This assumption has been well articulated by many theorists; perhaps best known is French sociologist Pierre Bourdieu (1984) who argues that "there is an economy of cultural goods" (p. 1) in which large organizations and corporations' make an effort to disseminate not merely the goods and services advertised, but also the cultural symbols, life styles and consumption types associated with images, symbols and ideas. Bourdieu explains that

This economy ... finds ardent spokesmen in the new bourgeoisie of the vendors of symbolic goods and services, the directors and executives of firms in tourism and journalism, publishing and the cinema, fashion and advertising, decoration and property development. Through their slyly imperative advice and the example of their consciously "model" life-style, the new taste-makers propose a morality which boils down to an art of consuming, spending and enjoying. (p. 311)

Therefore, by focusing on advertising in this study as only one of these communication media, we can see that the way the language of advertising is expressed is to a great extent influenced by the cultural context. For instance, the structure of language, cultural attributes and incitement of attraction used in Arabic advertising are different from other languages, since the meaning of these advertising messages is defined and perceived within the boundaries of the Arabic cultural framework. The attributes used in the language are particular to a society and its tastes. Dyer (1982) supports this idea since advertisements do not simply manipulate us as audiences, but rather create a structure of "meaning which sell commodities not for themselves as useful objects but in terms of ourselves as social beings in our different social relationships" (p. 116).

Methodology

The analysis for this study was conducted using content analysis; the purpose of this method, according to Krippendorff (1980), is "like all research techniques" to "provide knowledge, new insights, [and] a representation of 'facts'" (p. 21). Here, the text under analysis is the advertising text. This includes pre-recorded video commercials and printed advertising since "text" can refer to any form of expression that can be interpreted, such as verbal, non-verbal, printed, speech, dance and music. The significance of content analysis as a form of qualitative analysis of media texts is worthy of mention. Qualitative research, simply put, is research that is not aimed towards quantifying information or data. It is not primarily concerned with statistics, counting and numbering information. Instead, it is more concerned with how the words and language are established to "mean" something. Alasuutari (1995) explains that content analysis is equivalent to reasoning and argumentation which is based on the construction of meaning and not merely on the quantification of statistical relations between odds, and evens and variables (p. 7). Further, Silverman (1993) adds that "content analysis is an accepted method of textual investigation, particularly in the field of mass communications" (p. 59).

Sampling for this study consisted of a random selection of a variety of advertisements from the November 2004 editions of four Arabic social magazines. Two were from Egypt—*Nos El Donia* (Half of the World) and *Horeyeti* (My Liberty)—and two were from Saudi Arabia—*Zahret El Khalig* (The Flower of the Gulf) and *Saiydati* (My Lady). The main reasons for selecting these magazines are that they are widely distributed and read not only within the two countries but also by Arabs living internationally; they contain a high volume and variety of advertisements, and they are available in local Arabic stores in the city of Ottawa. Moreover, the selected month illustrates the importance of Ramadan, the Muslim Holy month, in the Arabic culture. Due to its social and cultural significance, during this month several advertising campaigns are launched and the number of television viewers watching the shows, soap operas and religious prayers produced specifically for this period increases. Thus, a two-hour videotape of pre-recorded television commercials from Egypt and Saudi Arabia that was recorded in November, was also examined. The commercials advertise a variety of products. The analysis looks only at manufactured products such as electronics, cosmetics, cars, detergents and so on and will not include food products. The former may be more representative of tastes in a particular culture as they tend to be more expensive and have an extended presence in an individual's life, unlike food which is quickly consumed.

Analyzing both print and picture advertising is useful for providing a broader perspective as it allows for different advertising techniques to be studied and related to the theme of the chapter. While the television ads use music, sound and motion, print advertising uses gestures, colors and position. Root (1987) argues that print advertising allows an "indirect" method of analysis of its messages, while television advertising embodies the "direct" form of analysis with its "dynamic dimension." He says, "television commercials … add a dynamic dimension to their message by virtue of their technology. The indirect address may be embodied in changes of state or condition in the course of the commercial or the juxtaposition of several actions with one another" (p. 50). He adds that one key advantage of these features in advertising is that when viewed in the television (as a medium), they embody two dimensions: "the rhetoric of advocacy and the rhetoric of entertainment in the service of the rhetoric of advertising" (p. 60). The same idea is also presented by Dyer (1982), who maintains that visual advertising is more accessible, and perhaps easier to study, since for him, pictures are ways to understand and have a more pervasive impact than words. Moreover, they have the ability to communicate the excitement, mood and imagination (p. 86).

Arab Society and Taste

The selection of Arab society as the case for analyzing taste as produced and portrayed in advertisements and commercials was deliberate and important. This part of the world represents a unique chance to relate the concepts of taste and culture, as many argue that Arab society is not unified by a set of common standards of taste. Instead, the concept of "taste" is differently understood and practiced depending on one's country of origin, economic and social status, and whether one's education was received within the Arab world or in a Western country.

Geographically, the Arab society is divided into two major parts: *Al-Mashreq*, or the East, referring to the Arab Gulf area, and *Al-Maghreb*, or the West, referring to the North African part. These two parts of the Arab World have several commonalities and, naturally, several differences as well, which are relevant to the examination of the concept of taste. Colonization is the key characteristic that both Arab areas share. The *Al-Maghreb* area is closely related to Europe, and depends economically on importing European tourism and exporting a variety of commodities and labor. *Al-Mashreq* is characterized by a "precapitalist economy under the Ottomans" (Patai, 1970, p. 11), followed by the European colonization that deeply affected its conception and evaluation of culture and taste. This latter region is the focus of this chapter.

This area could be plainly called "the oil-rich region," especially after World War II and the increasing capitalist consumption of its people. Family businesses, self-employed persons, international contacts, high exposure to the world through the Western media, culture and fashion are some of the common examples of the lifestyle there; this study uses the example of Saudi Arabia to demonstrate an important pattern of economic and cultural consumption in the Arab world. Altorki and Cole (1997) confirm this assumption noting that the country is not only following Western cultural taste, but is in fact seen as a part of European culture as a result of economic and consumption patterns:

> Saudi Arabia is stereotyped as composed of Bedouin and tribes, as being a super-rich oil producer ... They and other super-rich urban business people, one might conclude, were irrelevant to the local community or perhaps were so involved in the global culture of international business and of foreign capitals and luxurious resorts that they have little in common with the "ordinary" people ... even if it has once been describes as "Paris of Najd." (pp. 48–9)

Egypt was also selected for this study because it represents a certain degree of "openness" to the cultural and social trends around the world, has a non-conservative social and religious atmosphere and, importantly, has a large number of media that are available not only in the Arab region, but also internationally.

Socially, it might be thought to be extremely difficult to characterize the class structure is this region given the diversity at the economic level; on the other hand, it might also be argued that a definition of class structure might depend on both cultural and religious parameters. In other words, there are certain similarities between the two countries, in particular those related to the classification of the social groups "influenced by Islam": "administrators, army, men of religion, merchants, and the proletariat" (Hazen and Mughisuddin, 1975, p. 33). This point can be highlighted with the example of how art is consumed within Arab society. Both tradition and money are important determinants of an accepted art:

> *The beauty of objects everywhere intrudes upon, or complements, their particularity. Art is called in to embellish everything. The richer a man, the more time he can spend at the practice and enjoyment of art, but the poor as well, the great masses of the simple people, live a life in which esthetics play a considerable role. (Patai, 1970, p. 200)*

Deriving from this socio-economic background, we can see that this geographic region is an extremely important example of how emerging economies are affecting cultural consumption especially when it comes to selective exposure to advertising. Therefore, it is key to study the process of how the advertising message is constructed to attract the audience to watch, comprehend and select the goods and services advertised by analyzing the different taste attributes advertised in the selected magazines in this study. What is even more interesting is that social class is a key determinant of the action of consumption; however, the taste disseminated even within lower classes are developed from the same advertising attributes related to taste and social esthetics' value.

Arab Taste as a "Western" Pattern

Herbert Gans (1974), in his *Popular Culture and High Culture: An Analysis and Evaluation of Taste*, argues that there are two sociological assumptions that underlie our social treatment of taste: "[1] popular culture reflects and expresses the aesthetic and other wants of many people (thus making it culture and not just commercial menace); and (2) that all people have a right to the culture they prefer, regardless of whether it is high or popular" (p. vii). It is clear from these assumptions that Gans supports the notion that there is a relationship between taste and advertising in a society. Furthermore, Gans adds that culture is a "social process."

We could also argue that advertising may be one of the tools to identify and map the tastes that are communicated within a society. Indeed, popular culture, like high culture, is a representation of taste in society. Claims have been made against popular culture's content, claiming it has a negative impact on society's values and norms. In contrast to this idea, Gans (1974) suggests that, "if people seek aesthetic gratification and that their cultural choices express their own values and taste standards, they are equally valid and desirable whether the culture is high or low" (p. 127). In other words, Gans sets normative standards to define the popular culture of a particular society based on its individuals' aesthetic preferences. Gans defines three main characteristics for these "social" standards of taste and popular culture:

> *First, it [taste] must respond to and express the demands of its users, offering cultural content that provides the aesthetic satisfaction, information, and entertainment … which they want or think is good. Second, a desirable taste culture must offer material and other rewards to creators*

... Third, a good taste culture must not be socially or psychologically harmful, it should not hurt its users, creators, or the rest of society. (p. 122)

Culture is an important concept in the discussion of the relationship between taste and advertising. Plainly, the meaning of "culture" is intertwined with a set of social, behavioral and historical dimensions, therefore it is not easy to advance one single definition covering all of these aspects. Even scholars admit that this term is one of the two or three most complex words in the English language. We could propose, however, drawing upon the foregoing discussion of taste, that a relevant way to understand culture is to regard it as different patterns of meaning that are transmitted and communicated through symbols and language within a social system. Nevertheless, culture is also seen as the representation of both the ways of life (such as language and attitudes), and the "structure" and practice of those ways, such as its texts, arts, and tastes (Lindlof, 1995, pp. 51–3).

Yet, as discussed, Arabic taste might be influenced by the Western pattern of taste given two basic facts. The first is the long period of colonization and its legacy in the Arab region, and the second is the number of Arab elites who have been educated in Western societies and the Soviet Union. "To a great extent ... the image of the future has been dominated in the past by the use of only two models of development—the Western model and the Soviet model" (Said and Mughisuddin, 1975, p. 73). These two issues are far too complex if analyzed in relation to taste. Colonization has generated acceptance, familiarity and imitation of Western values and aesthetic standards. Additionally, Arab elites who have been educated in the West have not only been confronted with Western values but have chosen to adopt them and believe them to be the ultimate in aesthetics and beauty. This is reflected predominantly in their patterns of consumption. In fact, the Arab elites are considered by some scholars to be a very important subculture. Hazen and Mughisuddin (1975) note:

Arab society remains Western-oriented because of several factors. These are a legacy from the colonial era in which Western culture was anything and everything; Western-educated and bureaucratic subcultures who retain sufficient influence to project their cultural inheritance onto society in general; the vast admiration for Western technology and those technological inventions that the regimes in power feel must be acquired for the greatness of the Arab people ... the positive outlook toward the West has been maintained in spite of Western economic "neocolonialism," [and] Western "infamy" in establishing a Zionist state in the Arab homeland. (p. 175)

Main Findings

In this section, the main results of the content analysis are identified with relation to the foregoing research hypothesis and the theoretical literature of the study that suggest a relationship between culture and taste in the Arab world. In order to illustrate the findings in relation to the purpose of the study, three taste attributes were identified accordingly: 1) Western, 2) luxury and 3) international.

DIFFERENCE BETWEEN PRINT AND MOTION ADS

Here, the first finding was the difference of taste themes illustrated in the television and print ads. For example, while watches, jewelry, clothes, make-up, furniture, cosmetics and electronics ads in the magazines selected used the "Western" taste attribute as a superior and elite taste attribute, the television ads used the opposite, paying more attention to national, traditional and local cultural taste. This result is not so remarkable when one considers that the ads were recorded from local channels and were therefore addressed mainly to the national consumers, not the international audience.

As an example, a Carolina Herrera perfume ad in *Nos Eldonia* magazine used only the brand name New York, associated with a bold font. More interestingly, even with locally made perfumes, ads might use both a Western name and/or a Western symbol or model. For example, the Cazanova Egypt perfume ad in *Horeyeti* magazine used different Western names for its product line such as Professor, Anis, Kenzoom and Cazanova Egypt. Moreover, this ad featured the cowboy hat as a male symbol in one shot. Looking at perfumes in particular, one could argue that, generally, the ads very rarely mention or describe the actual product—its scent components or its scent in this case—rather, they tend to illustrate the "sign" that this perfume implies to the audience. Yet, the main argument of this chapter is that the key determinant of the usage of a specific attribute in an advertisement is the audience's taste. In other words, the sign of the "cowboy" or the word "New York" in the previous two examples imply that unless the perfume is depicted as Western (through its signs, language or models), it is "taste-less." Goldman (1992) confirms this result by arguing that,

> The act of consumption establishes a relationship between the product (the signifier) and what the product means in terms of social relations (the signified). A perfume (the signifier) has been connected to sensual beauty and confidence (the signified), and, just that quickly, the roles of signifier and signified reverse. (p. 24)

THE LUXURY ATTRIBUTE: AN ESSENTIAL THEME

Another important result is the close relation of Arabic taste with the theme of "luxury." This relates to a great extent to Veblen's (1899/1979) *Theory of the Leisure Class* where he questions the desirability of consumption. Recalling his opinion about what represents superior taste, he notes that "if these articles of consumption are costly, they are felt to be noble and honorific" (p. 70).

This particular point worries Patten (1989), who represents a contemporary Veblenian position, in which he suggests that, based on this distinction between cultural identities, a new type of consumption will emerge: a creation of a "higher" and "lower" consumption in society. He adds that it is important in this regard to consider the act of consumption: is it based on *necessity* or as *luxury?*—what he calls "a matter of a 'work and spend' style of consumption"[1] (p. 134). The key point remaining is to question how advertising is related to promoting a certain type of consumption and taste in the Arab region, and setting the criterion to the aesthetic social standards and preferences.

---

1   Patten (1989) explains that "consumers would have to change, to embrace the new consumer economy, and that this change was not only positive but also ethically desirable" (p. 132).

Judith Lichtenberg (1998) in her *Consuming Because Others Consume* explains that socially and psychologically, people tend to consume because they are surrounded by others who also consume; among several reasons for consumption, she points out, is consumption in order to gain status and superiority (p. 156). She rightly adds that with the advances of media technologies, promotion techniques are pushing consumers to consume more and more, and moreover, in this study, to consume certain types of goods and services. This result, according to Lichtenberg is morally alarming as it implies that human characters become more "conformist, greedy, and pre-occupied with material things" (p. 157).

The previous discussion is closely related to the following finding of the research in which it was clear from some of the ads' words and signs, especially those from Saudi Arabia, that the costly, luxurious and expensive products were superior in taste. For example, an ad from the famous Saudi jewelry store Mouawad, illustrates only that "we offer the finest," "the most wonderful" selection of jewelry. Similarly, in the "Rolex" watch ad, only the watch appears and it is simply stated that "it is made of pure gold, and with unique diamonds." Moreover, this ad also uses the close-up, full-page, maximized position to show how "tasteful" the gold-and-diamond watch is.

It is necessary at this point to question critically whether ads represent the current tastes in societies, or form them by encouraging conspicuous consumption and ostentatious behavior with their display of the most luxurious and outstanding forms of goods and products. Veblen (1899/1979) clarifies this point by saying that "the means of communication and mobility of the population now expose the individual to the observation of many persons who have no other means of judging his reputability than the display of goods" (p. 86).

MUSIC USAGE

Music is another important characteristic used by every one of the television ads, which seems to indicate the possibility of a unified cultural taste in the Arab world. On the importance of music in general, James Lull (1992) says that "music has the ability to stimulate extraordinary emotional feelings" (cited in Fowles, 1996, p. 120). For the Arab world in particular, Patai (1970) argues that "music ... is perhaps the most individualistic of arts in the Middle East" (p. 200). With a more complex analysis of the different music genres in the ads, one could see that Oriental and traditional music is not the only kind used. Instead, modified versions of Ricky Martin's and Britney Spears' popular songs accompanied by Arabic words are used in some advertising, such as for Pepsi and Coca-Cola. This is to some extent comparable with the first finding showing the domination of Western taste in the Arabic ads.

Amin (1974) in his *The Modernization of Poverty*, says that "traditional Arab forms whether in music, dress, furniture, and architecture are indiscriminately replaced by western forms" (p. 112). This result is also important in relation to the idea of popular culture. In this age of globalization, music—and popular singers around the world—holds an important significance for the receivers of ads, especially those of a younger age. Western music genres and symbols represent a "high-culture" taste for youths of the Arab world at least.

SIGNS AND CELEBRITIES

Another interesting result is the usage of "sign" language in both the television and magazine ads, especially in association with make-up, cosmetic and beauty products, to relate the meaning of these particular products and their possession with psychological position and high standards of taste. For example, the words: "golden," "outstanding," "unique," "best," "elegant" and "finest" imply a certain hierarchy in social status and position. Here, it is worth quoting at length Bourdieu's (1984) understanding of how the usage of language could be one of the "social markers" especially within a cultural and economic context:

> All the deliberate modifications of appearance, especially by use of the set of marks—cosmetic (hairstyle, make-up, beard, moustache, whiskers, etc.) ... which, because they depend on the economic and cultural means that can be invested in them, function as social markers deriving their meaning and value from their position in the system of distinctive signs ... which is itself homologous with the system of social positions (p. 192).

An example for this kind of language is the Longines watches ad which simply asserts that "Elegance is an attitude." In addition, the L'azurde jewelry ad writes "The stamp of pureness ... A light for your beauty" and "For golden occasions." Focusing on taste characteristics, the findings showed that there are two different realms, or practices, of taste in the Arabic ads that are used consistently in both television and magazines: models and celebrities. First, the constant use of foreign models in ads was very prevalent in the research findings. Women, men and even children have to have [in all the ads] blond hair and light eye color. This pattern was used in ads for men's, women's and children's clothes, electronics and other kinds of products. Second, celebrities are an important feature in ads, depicting the choice of the product as tasteful. Both Western figures such as Cindy Crawford in a Moulinex ad, and national or local Arabic celebrities such as an actor, singer or soccer player in a soap or car ad are used. In examining the role of celebrities in ads, and its relation to popular culture, Fowles (1996) argues that popular culture is "correctly understood as the domain that provides individuals with the symbolic material they can use to help normalize their lives" (p. 117).

A final finding that is quite interesting is the representation of foreigners in the television ads. One ad particularly represents how a concept of taste exists within the social and cultural domain. In a laundry detergent ad, the housewife is speaking about her dedication to her family and her involvement in every detail even in doing the laundry. On that note, she asks her maid, who seemed to come from the Far East, to hand the detergent to her. Moreover, at the end of the ad, she asked the maid again to show how this detergent made the laundry so clean. In fact, this ad represents more than just a detergent, it may be implying that a "tasteful" housewife living in this region has to have a maid, which is again related to some extent to Veblen's theory of conspicuous consumption.

Conclusion

Overall, this chapter has highlighted and illustrated some aspects of taste that are communicated in one of the important forms of communication media, advertising. In analyzing a collection of Arabic magazine and television ads, we can conclude that although officially we are living in the post-colonial era, there are different manifestations of Western cultural, social and aesthetic domination in previously colonized countries. No wonder we read about Yves Saint Laurent or Pierre Cardin producing a special line of women's clothes for the *Al-Mashreq* region. We can start questioning that if Arab women living in this region do not wear a designer model, will they be tasteless? Alternatively, will one show a high-taste pattern if they do wear such a model? A number of preliminary findings came out of this pilot study, but the practices of taste in the Arab world would definitely be worth further exploration, perhaps by interviewing a selection of people to discover more about their patterns of consumption, and relate it psychologically to Veblen's or Bourdieu's concepts of taste.

A possible path to take might be to follow Immanuel Wallerstein's[2] modern world systems approach, where the global picture proposes a global capitalist market economy point of view, in which a hierarchy of power relations is built between the "core" countries, the capitalist, Western and developed countries, as well as the "periphery" countries, i.e., those that follow the core countries economically, politically and also culturally, and finally, the "semi-periphery" countries, which combine both situations.

This view assumes a sort of dependency theory, which suggests that the less-developed former colonial regions, although officially independent from their colonizers, arguably are still dependent on the developed world's move toward "modern global capitalism" (Tomlinson, 1991, pp. 36–7). Multinational media corporations are good examples of this perspective, in which those corporations that operate on a transnational scale are producing and distributing the media products which emphasize those values and consumeristic ideals that the capitalist imperial powers promote, thereby leading the world's tastes and culture in that direction.

Cees Hamelink (1983), in his *Cultural Autonomy in Global Communications: Planning National Information Policy*, argues that many international practices reflect this discourse in daily life. For example, he says, "in a Mexican village the traditional ritual dance precedes a soccer match, but the performance features a gigantic Coca-Cola bottle" (p. 2). In other words, he believes that the various capitalist transnational corporations are the primary agents responsible for hegemony, particularly in the Third World, impacting even those cultural practices[3] related to future generations; for instance,

> *replacing breast-feeding by bottle feeding [which is promoted by companies like Nestlé for instance] has had disastrous effects in many Third World countries. An effective, adequate,*

---

2   See Immanuel Wallerstein in his "The rise and future demise of the world capitalist system: concepts for comparative analysis" (1974), and his "Semi-peripheral countries and the contemporary world crisis" (1976), in which he argues that the world economy became a fixed model as early as the 1640s because this is where unequal exchange between the core–peripheries countries first becomes evident, not only in terms of economic factors but also in power relations.

3   A relatively recent example of the application of this cultural homogenization of global capitalist powers is the work of neo-Marxist, Armand Mattelart, in particular, his criticism of Disney comics and cartoons, which are widely distributed in the developing countries. He believes that these cultural products are "carriers" of American capitalist cultural values (Tomlinson, 1991, p. 42).

and cheap method has been exchanged for an expensive, inadequate and dangerous product. (Hamelink, 1983, p. 15)

This view may be observed not only with commodities, such as cigarettes, but also in depicting the position and image of a nation, an idea suggested by Baudrillard, as cited in Goldman (1992), who argues that the best way to treat a commodity is to regard it as a sign. In this study, it was shown that with the advent of global advertising channels streaming to Middle Eastern and Arab countries, "Oriental" taste has been changed to follow the "Western" type. Blond models are replacing dark-haired models and Western words and attributes are attracting the audience and encouraging consumption of Western goods and services. This is an alarming but existing reality that needs more investigation and research.

References and Consulted Sources

Alasuutari, Pertti (1995). *Researching Culture: Qualitative Method and Cultural Studies*. London: Sage.

Altorki, Soraya and Donald Cole (1997). Change in Saudi Arabia: a view from "Paris of Najd." In Nicholas Hopkins and Saad Elddin Ibrahim (eds), *Arab Society: Class, Gender, Power, and Development* (pp. 29–52). Cairo: The American University in Cairo Press.

Amin, Galal (1974). *The Modernization of Poverty: A Study of the Political Economy of Growth in Nine Arab Countries (1945–1970)*. Leiden: Brill.

Barker, Chris (1999). *Television, Globalization and Cultural Identities*. Philadelphia, PA: Open University Press.

Bourdieu, Pierre (1984). *Distinction: A Social Critique of the Judgment of Taste*. Cambridge, MA: Harvard University Press.

Brawley, Edward A. (1983). *Mass Media and Human Services: Getting the Message Across*. Beverly Hills, CA: Sage.

Chester, Mills and Rebecca Chaisson (1996). The betrayal of media. In Mary Cross (ed.), *Advertising and Culture: Theoretical Perspectives* (pp. 113–25). London: Praeger.

Cross, Mary (1996). Reading television texts: the postmodern language of advertising. In Mary Cross (ed.), *Advertising and Culture: Theoretical Perspectives* (pp. 1–11). London: Praeger.

Deacon, David, Michael Pickering, Peter Golding and Graham Murdock (1999). *Researching Communications: A Practical Guide to Methods in Media and Cultural Analysis*. London: Arnold.

Dyer, Gillian (1982). *Advertising as Communication*. London: Methuen.

Farsoun, Samih (1997). Class structure and social change in the Arab world. In Nicholas Hopkins and Saad Elddin Ibrahim (eds), *Arab Society: Class, Gender, Power, and Development* (pp. 11–28). Cairo: The American University in Cairo Press.

Fowles, Jib (1996). *Advertising and Popular Culture*. Thousand Oaks, CA: Sage.

Gans, Herbert (1974). *Popular Culture and High Culture: An Analysis and Evaluation of Taste*. New York: Basic Books.

Goldman, Robert (1992). *Reading Ads Socially*. London: Routledge.

Green, Martin (1996). Some versions of the pastoral: myth in advertising; advertising as myth. In Mary Cross (ed.), *Advertising and Culture: Theoretical Perspectives* (pp. 29–49). London: Praeger.

Hamelink, Cees (1983). *Cultural Autonomy in Global Communications: Planning National Information Policy*. New York: Longman.

Harindranath, Ramaswami (2000). Ethnicity, national culture(s) and the interpretation of television. In Simon Cottle (ed.), *Ethnic Minorities and the Media Changing Cultural Boundaries* (pp. 149–63). Philadelphia, PA: Open University Press.

Hazen, William and Mohammed Mughisuddin (1975). *Middle Eastern Subcultures: A Regional Approach*. Toronto: Lexington Books.

Jugenheimer, Donald (1996). Advertising as educator. In Mary Cross (ed.), *Advertising and Culture: Theoretical Perspective* (pp. 105–12). London: Praeger.

Krippendorff, Klaus (1980). *Content Analysis: An Introduction to Its Methodology*. Beverly Hills, CA: Sage.

Lichtenberg, Judith (1998). Consuming because others consume. In David A. Crocker (ed.), *Ethics of Consumption: The Good Life, Justice, and Global Stewardship: Philosophy and the Global Context* (pp. 155–75). Lanham, MD: Rowman and Littlefield.

Lindlof, Thomas, R. (1995). *Qualitative Communication Research Methods*. Thousand Oaks, CA: Sage.

McLuhan, Marshall (1967). *The Mechanical Bride: Folklore of Industrial Man*. Boston, MA: Beacon.

McLuhan, Marshall (1998). *Understanding Media: The Extensions of Man*. Cambridge, MA: The MIT Press.

Patai, R. (1970). Middle East as a culture area. In Lutfiyya Abdulla and Churchill Charles (eds), *Readings in Arab Middle Eastern Societies and Cultures* (pp. 187–204). Paris: Mouton.

Patten, Simon N. (1989). *The Consumption of Wealth*. Philadelphia, PA: University of Pennsylvania Press.

Root, Robert (1987). *The Rhetorics of Popular Culture: Advertising, Advocacy, and Entertainment*. New York: Greenwood Press.

Said, Abdul A. and Mohammed Mughisuddin (1975). Subcultures in the Arab world. In William Hazen and Mohammed Mughisuddin (eds), *Middle Eastern Subcultures: A Regional Approach* (pp. 73–90). Toronto: Lexington Books.

Schor, B. Juliet (1998). A new economic critique of consumer society. In David A. Crocker (ed.), *Ethics of Consumption: The Good Life, Justice, and Global Stewardship: Philosophy and the Global Context* (pp. 131–8). Lanham, MD: Rowman and Littlefield.

Silverman, David (1993). *Interpreting Qualitative Data: Methods for Analyzing Talk, Text and Interaction*. London: Sage.

Tomlinson, John (1991). *Cultural Imperialism: A Critical Introduction*. London: Printer Publishers.

Veblen, Thorstein (1899/1979). *Theory of the Leisure Class*. Boston, MA: Houghton Mifflin.

Wallerstein, Immanuel (1974). The rise and future demise of the world capitalist system: concepts for comparative analysis. *Comparative Studies in Society and History*, 16(4): 387–415.

Wallerstein, Immanuel (1976). Semi-peripheral countries and the contemporary world crisis. *Theory and Society*, 3(4): 461–83.

4 *Advertising in Israel: From Traditional Dilettantism to Professional Westernism*

AMIR HETSRONI

The history of Israeli advertising, which stretches for nearly one hundred years, had started decades before the state of Israel was established. Over the years, the fate of the industry has been strongly shaped by Israel's unique political conditions—a Jewish country built by European immigrants with a sizeable Arab minority and lingering ethno-political conflict.

In this chapter we review how Israeli advertising matured from a few agencies that put all of the eggs in the printed press basket and produced dilettante advertisements that rarely made up any thoughtful campaign to a modern industry that often takes after American models for inspiration and contains a large number of agencies that generate carefully constructed campaigns.

We will examine this development in four facets: the structure of the industry, the size and allocation of budgets, the content of advertisements and market regulation.

Industry Structure

Historical changes in the advertising industry in Israel have been closely related to technological innovations and were also affected by historical events such as tides of immigration and wars. We notice five eras in the history of Israeli advertising:

DAYS OF THE WILDERNESS (1930–1960)

This period is characterized by reoccurring attempts to establish advertising as a profession. Many of the attempts were ill fated, since they failed to build an economic backbone that could sustain the industry during recession.

The first agencies were established in the 1930s as single-man workshops (Gornichovsky, 1998). The meager local market (fewer than 500,000 inhabitants at the time) could not provide enough work to the industry that relied, to a great extent, on public funding. The main products were, therefore, advertisements that glorified Zionist organizations and enticed people to make altruist deeds for public causes. This situation did not change radically after Israel had gained independence in 1948, as the country remained poor by Western standards and the lion's share of its economy was directly or indirectly owned by the government (Bar-Magen-Rosenberg, 2000). While in the Western world Carnegie's separation principle that splits the creative team from the budget personnel had already become common in advertising agencies, in Israel the minute size of billings did not let the agencies keep more than a person or two (usually the owners) on the payroll (Friedman, 2003). The production was limited to print advertisements and a few posters.

THE INNOCENT GENERATION (1960–1967)

This era is marked by great expectations of the industry to break out and specialize. Radio and cinema joined the printed press as advertising channels, and commercial corporations joined the government as suppliers of work. However, the much looked-for creative and economic break did not happen in those years, because the advertising professionals themselves still lacked the skills of modern advertising (Friedman, 2005). One sign of maturity that, nonetheless, emerged was the formation of the Israeli Union of Advertising Agencies (IUAA) in 1961. Although this organization never gained legal standing in Israel, it has been representing the industry for decades in its negotiations with the government.

THE BEGINNING OF MODERN ADVERTISING (1967–1980)

The massive change in the business occurred after the country's victory in the Six-Day War of June 1967 that brought with it an unprecedented economic prosperity (Almog, 2004). Population growth and standard of living increased, creating larger markets for non-viable goods. International brands such as Coca-Cola and Sony swept the country. Not only did these imports give work to advertising firms, but they also brought demand for American-style campaigns and a general increase in local corporations' interest in marketing communication (Hornik, 1980). This interest found expression in the issuing of a trade journal Otot ("Signals," in Hebrew) that since 1975 has been published on a monthly basis. The advertising industry itself went through a generational change of guards, as young people who studied the profession overseas returned to Israel determined to modernize the industry, which was lagging by at least 30 years behind Europe and America (Friedman, 2003). These "young Turks" established the first modern agencies that distributed the work between different departments.

THE PROFESSIONAL AGE (1980–1993)

By these years, the market was filled with half a dozen modern agencies. Rapid technological developments (such as offset printing and digital color separation) opened new opportunities and pushed advertising professionals to be more innovatively creative. However, the fact that television (which had only one governmentally funded non-commercial station) was not allowed to broadcast any advertisements except for public service announcements still put considerable limitations on the capability of campaigns to be multifarious.

THE BELATED TV AGE (1993 AND ONWARD)

The embarking of commercial advertising on television in 1993 brought about a dramatic transformation in the make-up of advertising budgets. Other technological developments, particularly the coming of age of the Internet, caused further changes. Besides the shifting in media planning strategy, the basic structure of the industry changed, as new professions (e.g., TV directors) and firms that specialize in TV and Internet campaigns flooded the market. The last of the few pioneering agencies that had stood at the industry's cradle and were still active in the 1980s could not survive the last changes, and closed their offices. Partnerships of local agencies with foreign conglomerates (e.g., McCann Erickson, BBDO) have become common. These global conglomerates brought with them some of their global customers. While the hope of these customers to use the Israeli market as an entry ticket to Middle Eastern markets has so far been denied in light of the upheavals in the Israeli–Palestinian peace process, global corporations have learned to consider the Israeli market worthy enough on its own (Friedman, 2003). The increased interest among young people in joining the prosperous trade encouraged colleges and universities to include advertising courses in the curriculum and, in 2002, led to the establishment of a school devoted solely to advertising professions under the auspices of the Israeli Union of Advertising Agencies (IUAA, 2006). The rapid growth of the population, as an influx of Jews immigrated to Israel from the former Eastern Bloc, and the improvement in the standard of living have placed the Israeli economy on a par with southern European countries such as Spain and Greece and have contributed to the attractiveness of the local market to global (and local) advertisers (Friedman, 2003). The local advertising industry discovered the power inherent in the different subpopulations that comprise the body of consumers, and opened departments that target the Arab minority and Russian-speaking Jews who are more responsive to ads in their mother tongue.

By the new millennium, the advertising industry in Israel had become large and decentralized. It is composed of more than 100 full service agencies (IUAA, 2006). Ten percent of these agencies are large and bill more than $10 million annually; 40 percent are medium size and run budgets in the range of two to ten million dollars per year; 50 percent of the full service agencies are small or regional and manage budgets that are less than two million dollars per year. There are also several firms with a specialty emphasis, such as media planning, new media advertising and graphic design.

Budgets Size and Allocation

Advertising's share of the country's gross national product (GNP), which was barely half a percent in 1985, reached 1.1 percent 20 years later. Considering the annual spending on advertising per capita as an indicator of industry growth, the following benchmarks are notable: in the early 1960s, the annual spending on advertising per capita was only five dollars. It crossed the $50 threshold in the late 1970s and reached $110 by the mid 2000s.

Until the mid 1990s, the printed press' share of advertising budgets was at least 80 percent. This resulted from a ban on commercial advertising on television. When the ban was lifted, the share taken by television of all advertising budgets grew quickly from 6 percent in 1993 to 33 percent a decade later. The share of the printed press, on the other hand, has been dropping throughout the last decade and is expected to fall below

50 percent in the next few years. While by Western standards the current share of the printed press is still somewhat high and the current share of television is still slightly low, if the existing trends persist, then the allocation of advertising budgets in Israel will become similar to budgets in North America and Europe in a few years.

The change in allocation of budgets led to a reduction in the number of newspapers—from six major dailies in 1995 to three a decade later. Commercial television, on the other hand, flourishes as it receives an increasing share of the advertising budgets. The number of advertising-based TV networks has grown from one in 1995 to four in 2005. Yet, one network ("Channel 2") continues to attract more than 80 percent of all budgets allotted to television (Keinan-Dinar, 2004).

While newspapers and magazines, together with television, receive six sevenths of all the budgets, there are four additional advertising channels—radio, billboards, cinema and the Internet—that have (or at least used to have) notable presence. One can learn about the changes in share of different channels over the years from considering Table 4.1.

Radio has been keeping a steady share (around 7 percent of the budgets) since the 1970s, amid technological developments and changes in regulation policy that opened up new opportunities for advertisers. One global reason why radio kept its share is that it continues to be the most ample medium for people under specific circumstances, such as commuting to work. Another explanation, more particularly related to Israel, is that along with the decline in people's exposure to public radio, dozens of regional commercial stations, which received their operation licenses during the second half of the 1990s, have been attracting young audiences who are highly sought by advertisers (Keinan-Dinar, 2004).

Finally, the Internet is the newest player in the field. It offers a relatively inexpensive alternative to traditional mass media channels and, therefore, has a particular appeal to smaller firms that cannot pay the prices demanded by television networks and large circulation newspapers. Recently, the Internet has also been discovered by larger corporations that seek to target segmented audiences (Hanson, 2000). The high penetration of the Internet in Israel (about 70 percent of the adult population have Internet access—see Peri, Tsfati and Tukachinsky, 2005) and the dramatic increase in the number of Hebrew news sites and portals that since the late 1990s have been offering advertising space in Hebrew contribute to the growing attractiveness of the medium from the advertiser's perspective.

Changes in the size of advertising budgets in Israel (like changes in the economy in general) have been closely related to the political circumstances. While the rapid economic growth of the mid 1990s after the signing of the Oslo interim accord with the Palestinians went along with an unprecedented prosperity within the advertising industry, the *intifada* riots of the early 2000s brought about stagnation and some signs of recession. Improvements in macro-political conditions that occurred toward the mid 2000s, following a possibility of renewal of the peace process between Israel and the Palestinians, is correlated with a general increment in the spending on advertising in Israel (Keinan-Dinar, 2004).

Table 4.1   Allocation of advertising budgets between different media over four decades

	1961	1963	1968	1973	1979	1983	1988	1993	2002	2003	2004
Overall spending on advertising (in million dollars)	11.3	8.6	16.0	41.0	94.3	205.0	432.0	788.0	791.0	746.0	766.0
Newspapers and Magazines	79.3%	69.8%	69.0%	83.0%	82.7%	81.5%	81.0%	80.4%	56.4%	53.1%	51.00%
Television	–	–	–	–	0.3%	0.5%	3.5%	6.0%	30.4%	33.3%	34.00%
Radio	2.7%	7.0%	12.5%	7.3%	6.5%	6.3%	6.7%	4.5%	7.0%	7.0%	7.00%
Billboards	9.0%	11.6%	12.5%	7.3%	8.5%	9.7%	7.2%	8.5%	5.1%	4.1%	4.00%
Cinema	9.0%	11.6%	6.0%	2.4%	2.0%	2.0%	1.6%	0.6%	0.1%	0.1%	0.05%
Internet	–	–	–	–	–	–	–	–	1%	2.4%	3.95%

Advertising Content

Content analyses of advertisements often use values as an indicator of cultural change and stability (see, for example, Cheng and Schweitzer, 1996). This indicator is used to discover, again, the gradual shift from featuring traditional Israeli distinctions to presenting global Western values. For many years, Israeli advertisements were predominated by national myths. In the pre-independence years (up to 1948) and during the 1950s and 1960s, Israeli advertising celebrated national symbols to such an extent that it was sometimes hard to see where the sponsorship of Zionist ideals ends and the promotion of goods and services begins. In those years, it was typical to see politicians appearing in commercial advertisements, e.g., David Ben-Gurion in a real estate ad from 1968 (Dankner and Tartakover, 1996). These historical figures were not celebrities for hire (as Bob Dole, for example, was a spokesman for Viagra in the 1990s). They were unpaid actors willingly participating in campaigns that had, in addition to their commercial value, a justified national cause like the building of new settlements in the country's peripheral regions (Bar-Magen-Rosenberg, 2000).

Over the last few decades, the appearance of state leaders, national myths and traditional Israeli values typified by altruism (e.g., collectivism, patriotism) in advertisements has become less and less the norm, as Western values, typified by hedonism and pragmatism, have increased their prominence (Lemish, 2000). A comparison of the value systems presented in print advertisements from the 1950s and 1990s shows that the frequency of Western values substantially increased throughout the years, whereas the frequency of collectivism, militarism and Zionism sharply declined (Bar-Magen-Rosenberg, 2000). Amply demonstrating this trend is the use of national flags. While in advertisements from the 1950s the only flag in sight had been the Israeli national flag, in the 1990s the appearance of this flag was already outweighed by the presence of the Star-Spangled Banner (Avraham and First, 2003).

To obtain an impression of the content of Israeli advertising in the last decade, consider two content analyses of the values presented in TV advertisements that were conducted by the author. Some figures from the first analysis, which consists of 861 ads from the years 1994–1997, were previously published (Hetsroni, 2000). The results of the second analysis, which is composed of 2,353 ads from the years 2000–2004, are published here for the first time. Both analyses used the same coding book, and were based on a random stratified sampling of commercials that were aired on the most popular network ("Channel 2") during the prime-time hours (for a complete description of the sampling, the coding procedure and the operational definitions, see Hetsroni, 2000). Table 4.2 presents the results of the analyses.

The figures point out a remarkable stability over time. In both analyses, Western values—either hedonistic such as joy or pragmatic like saving, efficiency and excellence— predominate. Traditional Israeli values, e.g., patriotism and collectivism, have only a minor presence. The stability across time found in this study, which covers the era of TV advertising in Israel, stands in contrast with what Bar-Magen-Rosenberg (2000) found in her analysis of print advertisements from the 1950s and 1990s, perhaps because the major part of the Westernization process that Israeli culture went through had been completed by the 1980s, before television advertising in Israel even started (Almog, 2004). Currently, in terms of basic content elements, the major bulk of Israeli advertising is a mixture of pragmatic and hedonistic values. The share of pragmatic values is considerably larger than the share of hedonistic values. This picture has a notable resemblance to what is seen in American advertising (Cheng and Schweitzer, 1996).

Table 4.2   The appearance of Western and Israeli values on TV advertisements in 1990s and the 2000s

	1994–1997 N=861	2000–2005 N=2353
Western Values—Pragmatic		
Saving	23.3%	29.4%
Efficiency	22.9%	30.7%
Competitiveness	12.2%	12.1%
Excellence	28.6%	38.0%
Comfort	20.0%	19.3%
Modernization	11.6%	16.5%
Quality	22.6%	23.7%
Western Values—Hedonistic		
Individualism	9.2%	8.7%
Beauty	11.7%	10.0%
Joy	38.2%	31.9%
Leisure	15.0%	11.6%
Sexuality	12.5%	10.4%
Popularity	7.9%	9.6%
Israeli Traditional Values—Altruistic		
Collectivism	8.7%	9.2%
Charity	2.1%	2.5%
Patriotism	3.5%	2.3%
Tradition	5.2%	2.5%

Note: Since there was no limitation on the number of values coded per ad, the columns do not add up to 100 percent.

Market Regulation

While there is no law in Israel that refers specifically to advertising, advertised material is subject to laws and ordinances that regulate the mass media. This section refers to the regulation of the two major advertising channels—the printed press and television and starts with the former. Draconian ordinances, inherited from the British colonial regime, allow the home office minister to censor any part of any newspaper and even completely halt the printing and selling of a publication, when the minister perceives that there is "public danger" embedded in the content (Caspi and Limor, 1999). This bylaw was never used to censor print advertisements, which are practically left with little public regulation except for laws that generally regulate press activities (e.g., prohibition of defamation).

Television advertising, on the other hand, is, at least apparently, strongly regulated, since in the eyes of Israeli law the airwaves are, unlike newspapers, a dear national asset. However, the Second Authority for Radio and Television, a governmental body in charge of regulating TV advertising, which has the right to disqualify advertisements, has preferred to push a voluntary code of conduct and not use this right too frequently. In recent years, the average number of TV ads that are censored each year has been no more than five (Second Authority for Radio and Television, 2006). The code of conduct aims to prevent potential disagreement over what is allowed to be seen in advertisements by stating in advance what is forbidden to be shown. The largest section of the code refers to sexuality and nudity. For example, frontal nudity is prohibited, but revealing clothing is allowed in cases where the advertised product has a clear relationship to the clothing (Second Authority for Radio and Television, 2006). Indeed, while most of the cases that are dealt with by the FTC, the body in charge of advertising regulation and consumers' complaints in the USA, pertain to deceptive advertisements (Keenan, 1994), in Israel the most often voiced public concern is over female nudity and the appearance of sexual stereotypes.

In practice, the most potent censorship does not come from state appointed officers but from consumers, whose activities have a significant effect on advertisers. Just like conservative groups in America (e.g., "The Moral Majority") enforce effective pressure by boycotting advertisers that cross the line, so do ultra-orthodox Jews in Israel. In addition to their economic boycotting power, these consumers have demonstrated symbolic violent resistance to (what they consider to be) promiscuous advertising by defacing street billboards (Friedman, 2005). Although few advertisers have publicly condemned this vandalistic behavior, calling it a threat to free speech, in practice, many of them have given this protest high consideration in their marketing decisions. For example, when billboards showing a cosmetics advertisement that featured Sarah Jessica Parker (a very popular starlet in Israel in the early 2000s due to her part in "Sex and the City") were physically ruined by angry ultra-orthodox consumers, the advertiser ordered the agency to use computerized touch-up techniques to cover some parts of the actress' body (Yefet, 2004). Perhaps, the reason that only a small number of advertisements are officially censored is that the market applies a strict self censorship policy that has much in common with the clearance policy enacted by American TV networks, when it comes to provocative advertisements (Keenan, 1994).

Summary

This chapter has shown how Israeli advertising has developed from a small number of self-contained miniature agencies that rarely connect separate ads into a unified campaign to a multitude of organizations with distinct inter-specification that generate carefully constructed campaigns. While the weight of advertising budgets gradually shifted from newspapers to television, so did the content replace traditional national symbols with Western values. US advertising sets the example to Israeli advertising professionals in many areas, from the structure of agencies to self regulation of advertisements. While in a few aspects, such as the share of the budget taken by television, Israeli advertising has not yet reached North American and European standards, it is expected to be on a par with these countries in just a few years, if current trends persist.

References

Almog, O. (2004). *Farewell to Srulik: Changing Values among the Israeli Elite*. [In Hebrew] Haifa: University of Haifa Press.

Avraham, E. and A. First (2003). I buy American: the American image as reflected in Israeli advertising, *Journal of Communication*, 53(2): 282–99.

Bar-Magen-Rosenberg, M. (2000). The reflection of the value change in print advertisements in Israel since the country's establishment. [In Hebrew] Master's thesis, Bar-Ilan University, Ramat Gan, Israel.

Caspi, D. and Y. Limor (1999). *The In/Outsiders: The Mass Media in Israel*. Cresskill, NJ: Hampton Press.

Cheng, H. and J.C. Schweitzer (1996). Cultural values reflected in Chinese and US television commercials. *Journal of Advertising Research*, 36(3): 27–45.

Dankner, A. and D. Tartakover (1996). *Where We Were and What We Did: An Israeli Lexicon of the Fifties and Sixties*. [In Hebrew] Tel-Aviv: Keter.

Friedman, G. (2003). On the way to the wilderness days. [In Hebrew] *Otot*, 274: 7–9.

Friedman, G. (2005, December 5). Advertisers should understand culture. *Ynet*. [Online.] http://www.ynet.co.il/articles/0,7340,L-3179143,00.html (retrieved March 27, 2006).

Gornichovsky, D. (1998). Issues in the history of advertising in Israel. [In Hebrew] *Otot*, 100: 58–60.

Hanson, W.A. (2000). *Principals of Internet Marketing*. Cincinnati, OH: South-Western College Publishing.

Hetsroni, A. (2000). The relationship between values and appeals in Israeli advertising: a smallest space analysis. *Journal of Advertising*, 29(3): 55–68.

Hornik, J. (1980). Comparative evaluation of international vs. national advertising strategies. *The Columbia Journal of World Business*, 151(1): 36–45.

Israeli Union of Advertising Agencies (IUAA) (2006). [Online.] http://www.pirsum.org.il (retrieved March 27, 2006).

Keenan, K.L. (1994). Advertising. In E.K. Thomas and B.H. Carpenter (eds), *Handbook on Mass Media in the United States* (pp. 3–18). Westport, CT: Greenwood Press.

Keinan-Dinar, R. (2004). Decline in print advertising, increase in television. [In Hebrew] *Haaretz*, C5.

Lemish, D. (2000). If you are not there, you do not exist: the reflection of the Israeli society in advertising. In C. Hertzog (ed.), *Fifty Years: A Society in the Mirror*. [In Hebrew] (pp. 539–59). Tel Aviv: Ramot Press.

Peri, Y., Y. Tsfati and R.H. Tukachinsky (2005). *News Consumption on Internet Sites. Media Trust Index: Report Number 4*. [In Hebrew] Tel Aviv University: Hertzog Institute for Media, Society and Politics.

Second Authority for Radio and Television (2006). [Online.] http://www.rashut2.org.il (retrieved March 27, 2006).

Yefet, O. (2004, November 22). LUX "dressed" Sara Jessica Parker. [In Hebrew] *Ynet*. [Online.] http://www.ynet.co.il/articles/0,7340,L-3007963,00.html (retrieved March 27, 2006).

Asia

5 Cambodia: From Conflict to Consumerism, through Chaos to Progress

JAN QUARLES

Cambodia's history is written in the language of a great fallen kingdom and the legacy of a more recent genocidal bloodbath in the twentieth century. As the small country struggles to join the world economy, it faces hurdles high and wide. In the last 30 years, Cambodia has had one of the most horrendous human rights records in history, and its transition, aided by the United Nations, has been marked by continuing repression, political instability, and slow economic development.

Cambodian authors have written that most Westerners have only a basic knowledge of the country, and Van Roeun (2002) has written that "most don't understand the complexity of its political, social, and economic situation ... Westerners have little knowledge of the challenges confronting Cambodia in its efforts to become a less-impoverished country" (p. 27), but he also writes that many are beginning to shed stereotypes about the Southeast Asian region as a whole and its strategic importance.

To understand why Cambodia has been ranked as one of the poorest countries in the world, and to ascertain the obstacles it must overcome to play on the world stage, one must look at its history. Today, the country struggles to overcome these obstacles to create an attractive business and investment environment. Cambodia's advertising industry, evolving alongside its business and legal structures, must still be considered very young. A look at the country's past, and its current economic status, will help explain why the country faces substantial infrastructure and development challenges and why its conditions vary so widely from those of the more dominant nations in the region.

From its ancient roots in a realm that in the tenth century stretched from Laos to Burma and the Gulf of Thailand, after many conquests and kings, a weakened Khmer kingdom turned for help to Siam and Vietnam, and lost a great amount of territory. In the late 1800s, the French, who had colonized Southern Vietnam, forced Cambodia to become first a protectorate and then a colony. The country was occupied by Japan during World War II, but gained its independence in 1953 from France with a "royal crusade for independence" by King Norodom Sihanouk. In 1955, the King abdicated in favor of his son to form a political movement and won all seats in parliament. His rule became authoritarian and an opposition movement grew. In the 1960s, Sihanouk withdrew from diplomatic relations with the United States, but during the Vietnam War eventually renewed the relationship that allowed the United States to begin the secret bombing of Vietnam's "sanctuaries" and to incur a brief invasion into the country to eradicate Communist bases. Afterward, for complex reasons, the former king aligned himself with the Vietnamese and Laotian communists against his former prime minister, Lon Nol, and through an extended series of events, Lon Nol's government, given the name of the Khmer Republic, grew autocratic. When his military forces were defeated, Lon Nol fled to the United States, and the Khmer Rouge gained power (Kamm, 1998).

In April 1975, the Khmer Rouge captured and evacuated Phnom Penh and other towns and declared the country to be the People's Republic of Kampuchea. More than 1.5 million Cambodians were forced into the countryside, families were divided and people died (estimates have ranged from hundreds of thousands to two million) from execution, forced labor or starvation during the rule of the leader, Pol Pot, and his Khmer Rouge regime. During this time, the non-communist world imposed economic sanctions. The Vietnamese drove the Khmer Rouge from the cities in late 1978, and a 10-year Vietnamese occupation began.

An internal civil war raged between the Vietnamese-allied government troops and the Khmer Rouge for 13 years, but the 1991 Paris Peace Accords mandated democratic elections and a ceasefire. The accord was a major turning point for the country, and many attribute the growth of Cambodia today to that agreement that, for a country that had no communication infrastructure, was effectively allowed to "start from scratch" (Barisoth, 2000). The United Nations Transitional Authorities in Cambodia (UNTAC) worked to restore a country that had been stripped "to nothing." UNTAC worked to develop a free press system in a country with almost no infrastructure of any sort, with few human resources, and with few basic necessities. Little trace of the vigorous press freedom that had existed in the period from 1945 to 1955 or 1970 to 1972 (a brief window between the overthrow of Prince Sihanouk and the emergence of Pol Pot) still existed (Barisoth, 2000).

The UN-sponsored elections of 1993 helped restore some aspects of Cambodian life, but since that time the country has been referred to as a semi-democracy (Eng, 2000) because the dominant political party, the Cambodian People's Party (CPP) ruled by Hun Sen, has remained in power. Cambodia also retains a royal family, with Norodom Sihamoini recently named King after his father, Norodom Sihanouk, retired; it is, therefore, a constitutional monarchy.

In 1993, after Norodom Sihanouk was chosen as king, he named his son, Norodom Ranarriddh, first prime minister and Hun Sen second prime minister and a coalition ruled. Ranarriddh had chosen to forgo any royal position to lead the pro-Sihanouk royalist party, but Hun Sen had been involved in the pro-Vietnamese regime of the late 1980s and had a hold over much of Cambodia (Kamm, 1998). In 1997, the coalition fell apart, and Hun Sen eventually staged a coup against all opponents at the time, postponing elections until 1998. For international investors watching the new Cambodia emerge, it was a time to "wait and see," until a government formed in 1999 (Ang, 2006).

Many have alleged that Hun Sen is a former Khmer Rouge official, a charge he repeatedly denies. He is one of the world's longest-serving prime ministers, as he has been in power in various coalitions since 1985. His party's failure to win an outright majority in elections means he has turned to several other parties to form coalitions. But the spirit of authoritarian rule and suppression of freedom of expression remain in spite of constitutional declarations; the coalition governments formed over the decade have been fragile and Khmer media have been suppressed in various ways. Press freedom is not guaranteed, and the Prime Minister and his allies control several broadcasters ~

(BBC, 2006). An *Economist* (You can't say that here: Cambodia, 2005) report notes that when Cambodian elections are being held and the country is under international scrutiny, Hun Sen allows his opponents to speak their minds, but at other times he "undermines civil liberties, prevents his opponents from organizing and makes an example of a few of the most outspoken." A recent example was the arrest of the leader of the primary opposition party, Sam Rainsey, for corruption and the arrest of the owner of the independent radio station Beehive (You can't say that here: Cambodia, 2005). Rainsey and Hun Sen since had a tentative reconciliation in 2006, but the relationship remains as it has always been—troubled.

Hun Sen has his concerns about his international image. In 1999, his CPP party hired a Washington-based public relations firm, the David Morey Group, and two law firms to lobby on Hun Sen's behalf and against a resolution condemning him for war crimes in Cambodia after 1978 (Crispin, 1999).

The last Khmer Rouge surrendered in early 1999 and some of the leaders will be tried by a UN-sponsored tribunal for crimes against humanity. Funds are being raised to hold the tribunal, and a site, Kandal province, has been chosen (Berthiaume, 2005). The elections in 2003 were only marked by sporadic violence, but a coalition government did not form for more than a year (CIA Factbook, 2006). Since the Peace Accord, the media landscape in Cambodia has been populated and decentralized, as this chapter will note, and the country has set its sights on growing its economy.

In early 2003, a Thai actress, Suwanan Kongying, allegedly commented in a cable television interview that she would perform in Cambodia only after the country returned Angkor Wat's temples to Thailand. The comment, which remained unproven, evoked long-standing cultural tensions. The Prime Minister made a remark at a televised ceremony regarding Kongying, saying she was "not even worth the blades of grass at Angkor Wat." Riots broke out in Phnom Penh and demonstrators burned the Thai embassy, and attacked other Thai businesses and several hotels. The Cambodian government reacted slowly but eventually undertook a campaign to clarify the relationship to Thailand. Full diplomatic relations resumed in April of 2003, but some long-term effects, including changes in television programming on some networks to be discussed later, can still be felt (Report to the Congress, 2003).

Cambodia Today as an Emerging Economy

Cambodia is one of the world's 49 least-developed countries (LDCs), although Prime Minister Hun Sen in March 2006 announced his forecast that the country would no longer be an LDC as of 2020, basing his optimism on "the maintenance of peace, the reduction of poverty, and the reduction in the prevalence of AIDS" (Chinaview.cn, 2006). It is a member of the association of Southeast Asian nations (ASEAN) and the Asian Free Trade Area (AFTA). At present, Cambodia struggles deep in the shadows of the top competitors in the Asian region, countries such as Singapore, Japan, China and South Korea. In terms of subregions of Asia when exports of services and merchandise are considered, Cambodia is seen as peripheral to the countries of Southeast Asia (with Singapore being seen as the center) (Gunaratne, 1999).

A predominantly Buddhist country (95 percent), Cambodia is homogenous, as 90 percent of its 14.8 million residents are Khmer (5 percent are Vietnamese, Chinese 1 percent and other ethnic groups 4 percent). The official language is Khmer, but many younger Cambodians are also learning English. The literacy rate is 84 percent for males and 64.1 percent for females (CIA Factbook, 2006). Nearly two thirds of the population are under 30 years old, a statement on the heavy toll the older generation paid during the time of the Khmer Rouge (Kazmin, 2003).

The Khmer have an average annual per capita income of about $320 USD (World Bank 2005 estimate). The gap between the rich minority in the urban areas and the poor majority in the countryside remains wide. The World Bank designates Cambodia as a low-income country (along with Vietnam, Laos and Myanmar) and as a low HDI (human development index) country. The country has only one viable export industry, garments, but construction is now booming and contributes to growth. The garment industry, threatened in early 2005 with the end of US garment quotas, also thrives with the imposition of further quotas (now called safeguards) on China until 2008 (Bethiaume, 2005).

A promising tourism industry is developing, given that the temples of Angkor Wat, considered by some as one of the "new" seven wonders of the world, are open to tourists once again. The temples, built between the ninth and the thirteenth centuries by Khmer kings, are designated World Heritage sites. The tourism industry is growing rapidly, with foreign visitors surpassing one million annually in 2005.

While the two major industries are growing in fits and starts, 75 percent of the population remains engaged in subsistence farming, and the rural countryside has almost no basic infrastructure. An estimated 40 percent of the population lives below the poverty line. Many of the population remain uneducated, and more than 50 percent are 20 years old or younger.

Cambodia's economy relies heavily on imported goods and services, as the local manufacturing that does exist cannot meet consumer demands. Most imports come from neighboring countries, and smuggling and piracy remain significant issues. Imports exceeded US$3.5 billion in 2005 (CIA Factbook, 2006).

The genocide during the Khmer Rouge effectively wiped out a generation of educators, lawyers and doctors and the impact is seen in many ways, including in the country's need to develop the sophisticated judicial and legal system that qualifies it for membership in the World Trade Organization. Cambodia received the first invitation given to a least-developed country to join the WTO at Cancun in 2003, and ratification of the invitation is underway with the early 2006 seating of the Cambodian National Assembly to vote. But legal and judicial reform is slow, and the long-term development of the country remains daunting, as an investment guide to Cambodia notes:

> The problems endemic to countries at an early age of economic development are exacerbated in Cambodia by the conflict and instability of the 1970s and 1980s. The brief and bloody rule of the Khmer Rouge, in particular, did much long-term damage. Professional qualifications are a scarce commodity; road infrastructure is limited ... and administrative capacity is limited. (UNCTAD, 2003)

The World Economic Forum ranked Cambodia for the first time in 2005, but placed it 112th out of 117 countries in terms of competitiveness, citing corruption, inefficient bureaucracy, inadequate education of workers, poor infrastructure and access to loans, tax rates, crime and "burdensome labor laws," while noting in a positive light the country's mobile phone network, low inflation, a stable exchange rate and a lack of discrimination against foreigners. Vietnam was ranked at 81 and Thailand at 36 (Wasson and Kimsong, 2005).

But Sok Siphana, Secretary of State in the Ministry of Commerce and the chief architect of Cambodia's accession to the WTO, is optimistic. He says, "We have completely reintegrated into the world trading system ... we are moving Cambodia away from the old Killing Fields image with an economic embargo to acceptance in the world economic community" (Asia Inc., 2004).

Many non-governmental organizations (NGOs) remain in Cambodia today and play vital roles in day-to-day life, and the government works with donors, including the World Bank and the International Monetary Fund (IMF). Estimates place Cambodia's GDP at the official exchange rate at $4.92 billion for 2005 with a real growth rate, estimated to be 4 percent. Cambodia is still heavily dependent on foreign assistance to fund public investment, with aid totals around 14 percent of GDP. The United States has been one of Cambodia's largest trading partners and donors (official assistance in 2004 was $70 million). The economy is heavily dollarized, and the US dollar accounted for 70 percent of the nation's total liquidity in 2003 (US Embassy Phnom Penh, 2004). Cambodia has a foreign debt of $2.4 billion owed largely to Russia and its second largest creditor is the United States. Major donors also include Japan and the European Union. China pledged 20 million Yuan (US$2.4 million) for military training and hospitals.

The Cambodian government adopted a free market, pro-investment policy and offers incentives to foreign businesses, but the lack of transparency, weakness of key financial institutions, young legal system and continued presence of corruption continue to dampen such investments.

Corruption still affects the country's development, as it occurs in activities from citizens paying unofficial fees for public services to granting of improper tax exemptions. A World Bank survey in 2000 found that citizens and businesses ranked corruption as the first or second problem blocking development in Cambodia (Christoff, 2002). A 2003 Human Rights Watch report noted that Cambodia was ranked in the lowest category for its failure to comply with minimum international standards to combat human trafficking (Human Rights Watch, 2003).

A report on the emerging economies of Southeast Asia notes that markets such as Cambodia do not have the same quality of data as do more developed countries, and information networks have developed differently, with trust limited to networks of family and friends because businesses have been developed intuitively. Management decisions are often made holistically and intuitively. This culturally different approach has made it difficult for new entrants into business, and a lack of transparency exists in information available for the examination of many business practices (Haley and Tan, 1996). Market information, therefore, is not always available.

The Media in Cambodia

For many people, daily life in Cambodia is still very basic. Almost 80 percent of the population lives in rural areas of the country. The information and communication structures are still very fragile in those areas, but many homes do have access to radios. Cell phones account for much of the telephone use as lines are limited to major residential towns and cell phone businesses have sprung up in Phnom Penh. An entrepreneur will buy a cell phone and service, and then sell calls for a few riels (Cambodian currency where 4,034 riels equal $1 USD) (Quarles, 2003b). Four foreign firms offer cell technology, and the services are heavily advertised. In 1993, Cambodia was the first country in the world where the number of mobile telephone subscribers passed the number with fixed lines (International Institute of Cambodia, 2005).

During the Vietnamese occupation, the country's media were monopolized by the Vietnamese-backed government. The media scene changed very quickly with the arrival of UNTAC in 1991. UNTAC opened its own radio station, distributed radios and aired spots on state television (Chanadra, 2000). Today, Cambodia has more media organizations than its neighbors Vietnam, Laos and Myanmar (Burma) combined. (See Clarke (2000) for a succinct media history before 1991.)

Newspapers can be found in Khmer, English, French and Chinese, and all are published in Phnom Penh. People often do not have the money to buy copies, so the practice of renting a copy for a short period of time evolved (kiosks rent them for about 400 riels per viewing), and the young boys selling copies at hotels and in the city often "resell" discarded papers two or three times a day or negotiate repurchase from one reader to sell to another (Borton, 2002). The two daily Khmer-language papers are *Rasmei Kampuchea* and *Koh Santepheap*. The daily English paper is *The Cambodia Daily*, and it is set up as an NGO and independent voice. The *Phnom Penh Post*, established in 1992, also publishes in English on a bi-weekly basis. Both English-language newspapers are available online by subscription. The English newspapers are considered important, as they are the most professional and protected because they are foreign-owned and staffed, and they cover issues self-censored in Khmer language publications (Eng, 2000).

The Ministry of Information lists around 300 print publications, but not all publish regularly. Only 20 to 30 publish regularly. (Most local papers are small, depend on government sources for news, and focus on advertising and entertainment.) They have been called more opinion papers than newspapers (Hodson and Kimsong, 1998). Many of the small papers, says Sek Barisoth (2000), can actually be described as political leaflets because "they publish mostly political advertisements in favor of one party and attacking the other." They are usually a single folded broadsheet with poor photographs and political cartoons.

As Cambodia's economy developed slowly throughout the 1990s, many newspapers accepted subsidies from political parties because the economy provided a meager advertising base. Owning a newspaper was sometimes seen as an investment in political pull to be traded for influence in other areas (Foster, 2005). Stories were published lambasting their supporter's political opinions, and retaliation was sometimes violent. Today, however, newspapers do have some information and often investigative coverage even if the papers themselves are tabloids. Foster (2005) says that today's economy and the more open economic environment demanded by the WTO may benefit Cambodian media organizations, bringing investors and new businesses as advertisers.

Barisoth (2000) notes that the Cambodian press have been described as "chaotically free … and also criticized as very unprofessional and sensational, using swear words, sexy women, and gory crime stories to attract readers." Other have called the press "free but foul-mouthed" for their vicious verbal assaults on political leaders, but have noted that civility is improving, but on a "slow road" (Hodson and Kimsong, 1998).

Cambodia has no restrictions on foreign publications, and international broadcasting is available through three cable stations, but only to those who can afford to subscribe to cable services. Cambodians who can afford satellite service watch Star-TV and other regional stations (Clarke, 2000).

Television in Cambodia includes:

* TV3, a joint venture of KCS Cambodia and the municipality of Phnom Penh. It broadcasts government information and official live concerts as well as entertainment. It also broadcasts in the provinces;
* TV Channel 5, owned by the Royal Cambodian Armed Forces;
* TVK, National Television of Cambodia, owned by the government of Cambodia;
* Cambodian TV Station 9;
* Apsara TV, owned by the Apsara Media Group, with close ties to the Cambodian People's Party (the CPP, Hun Sen's political party);
* CTN, launched in 2003 and available by subscription in the US;
* Bayon TV, also with connections to the CPP.

Radio stations include 13 Khmer-language stations in Phnom Penh, with as many in the regional centers (Ang, 2006). Many are affiliated with the CPP. FM105 is the most-listened to station in Cambodia. FM102 is run by the Women's Media Center (a groundbreaking group for women in Cambodia as journalism is still largely a male-dominated profession in the country) and is considered independent (Sarayeth, 2002), as is Radio Beehive, an independent station covering corruption and unrest left untouched by other media outlets (Chandara, 2000). The station has been closed, and reopened, and its owner recently arrested for defaming Hun Sen by airing an interview in which he was accused of selling land in Vietnam (Bethiaume, 2005). Beehive Radio was praised during the 2003 elections for being "virtually the only station in Cambodia to offer airtime to all political parties." The main opposing party, headed by Sam Rainsey, would have no broadcast platform without Beehive, and thus the small radio station's presence is crucial (Neumann, 2003). Radio remains the most accessible medium in Cambodia as access is cheap, radios can run on batteries where electricity is unavailable, and radios can be used outdoors in rural environments.

A 2000 survey cited by Sarayeth (2002) found that only 57 percent of the population owns or has access to a television set (for group viewing), while 62 percent of the population listens to radio daily. Radio stations broadcast for 18 hours a day (television programming is much more sporadic in the provinces), and listenership increases in rural areas.

The ruling CPP controls nearly all of the broadcasting industry in Cambodia. As recently as November 2005, the Cambodian Ministry of Information was ordering all television and radio stations to cease reading newspaper content on air in light of an August ban on inserting commentary into the reading (Malamed and Van Roeun, 2005). Also, a government regulation allows all political parties to buy airtime from private media companies, mainly owned by the CPP. This brings the risk that economic sanctions could be directed at individuals with media companies who sell airtime to parties that are in competition with their owners (Weiss, 2003). A United Nations Center for Human Rights report (2003) noted that the government procedures for licensing and allocating radio and television frequencies were not impartial (Clarke, 2000).

The first Internet portal in the Khmer language with access points in all 20 provinces of the country was launched in 2003 (Klein, 2005). The Internet was only introduced into Cambodia in 1997 with the assistance of Canada. There are seven ISPs in the country, but Internet penetration is relatively low and the price of access high (International Institute of Cambodia, 2005). Former King Norodom Sihanouk, in his retirement undergoing treatment in China, has written for three years on a personal blog, and papers have commented on his musings about current events and his personal life. He has recently stopped commenting (Cambodian ex-monarch joins blogger community, 2005).

A 2003 report found that Cambodia still lacks a "culture of literacy," with few newspaper readers among the country's largely rural population. Writers and booksellers often struggle to make a living, and no culture of reading exists. The report does say a market is developing for glossy magazines for young urban Cambodians and those magazines recover their printing costs through advertising and sales (Reed, 2003).

Few hard statistics are available on films and cinema, book production or daily newspaper circulation. UNESCO has no available current data on these aspects of Cambodian life. Cambodian cinema is in rapid decline, due to a lack of resources, insufficient copyright protection, and censorship. Cambodian movies struggle to make money when local productions can cost 20 times more than the $50 it takes to show the pirated movies that floods the Cambodian market (Sisovann, 2002). Movies cannot be broadcast on television without permits, but obtaining a permit is chancy. All movies and even advertisements seen on the state-owned TVK must be approved. "Advertisements for medicines must go to the Ministry of Health, and traditional dramas can't be sponsored by modern products," says Mao Ayuth, 2002 head of the association of television stations (Sisovann, 2002).

Education

The Cambodian Communication Institute (CCI), the educational program providing training for Khmer students wishing to work as journalists, merged in 2003 with the Department of Communication at the Royal University of Phnom Penh. The RUPP program is a four-year course leading to a Bachelor of Arts in Media Management and accepts a small class each year. As the university states, the course is "designed to train students across a broad range of media-related academic disciplines ... to create and maintain the highest-quality independent journalism and media management that will serve the needs of the Cambodian people" (RUPP, 2006). The program also offers several shorter degrees (one year) and intensive workshops. The BA program began in 2001 with help from the Konrad Adenauer Foundation, as well as Ateneo de Manila University (Philippines) and Ohio University, and today the faculty includes Khmer professionals and experts from sponsoring universities and from expert international sources. Students take courses in journalism, media law and ethics, online journalism, graphic design, and media production. In their third and fourth years, they also take allied subjects in principles of advertising, public relations and marketing. Some advertising agencies in Phnom Penh also provide on-the-job training to their Khmer staff (Quarles, 2003b).

Advertising in Cambodia

Emerging markets are defined by "low rates of mobilizing savings which in turn impact the ability to acquire the infrastructure to receive communication messages" (Fletcher and Melewar, 2001). For example, a Bates Indochina managing director said that his agency in 2002 worked with advertisers to fund and develop programming for clients who wanted to advertise on television but became frustrated by the immaturity of the market for making standard commercial media buys (Osborne, 2002). Therefore, in working in an emerging economy, communicators must ask what infrastructure is available to receive the message they create, and what cultural norms must be considered (such as the use of information provision versus persuasion) (Fletcher and Melewar, 2001).

Cambodia's market is small, its infrastructure is young, and demand for local consumption is limited compared to such markets as Thailand and Vietnam, but Cambodia, as described in an UNCTAD report (2003), possesses such strengths for industry as a young population, openness to free trade, a dollarized economy and an adaptable workforce. The small size of the market may make brand recognition and loyalty easier to achieve, and it has a desirable location within the Mekong region.

The report also cited weaknesses for those looking to do business in Cambodia, including price sensitivity and a narrow market for high-end goods, low education, limited marketing mechanisms (the country is segmented into minimarkets in the provinces), counterfeit products, smuggling, a low incidence of mass media outreach, lack of quality retail outlets and a small domestic market. Investors, the report recommends, should take the long view and learn to understand and work with the local culture. But many of those working in the business culture in Phnom Penh are optimistic if the government remains stable.

You Ang, director of Bassac Orchid (an agency affiliated with JWT internationally), observes that advertising has grown steadily at a rate of 12 percent since 1999. Prior to 1999, very few multinationals (Unilever, Procter & Gamble, Nestlé, Coca-Cola, etc.) spent money in Cambodia, and the coup in 1997 kept investor confidence low (Ang, 2006). Media spending jumped dramatically in 1999, by 144 percent, and by 85 percent in 2000. Since then, it has maintained growth. However, an agency director (of Bates Cambodia) worried in 1993 that Cambodia's economy may not be able to keep up with the growth in its advertising sector (Woodsome, 2003a), but as of 2006, the advertising industry continues its steady, but not dramatic, growth. This growth will continue only if the political climate is stable. With elections to be held in 2008, some turmoil had already erupted.

Cambodia, as an emerging economy, does not currently offer international advertisers a high level of profitability, but some companies such as Unilever see the potential in the country, reshaping their products to fit the purchasing abilities of rural consumers and shaping advertising to fit the very basic market. Companies looking to advertise in Cambodia must also consider the cultural environment. The predominant language, Khmer, is difficult to learn and to write, making localized production essential and visual appeals a must. Literacy issues must be considered, as should cultural issues and values in the primarily Buddhist country. Having multinational companies in Cambodia is important. Their presence "helps lower costs for creative ... and raises the quality bar higher. Decreasing costs in the local market means more and more local clients are able to afford to develop better quality advertisements" (Ang, 2006).

A Cambodian Ministry of Commerce report notes an abundance of marketing services, including Khmer and English newspapers, periodicals, television, event sponsoring, advertising agencies and government ministries (Cambodian Ministry of Commerce, 2005). Furthermore, local vendors use promotional campaigns such as gifts or lucky draws to introduce new products. Billboards, leaflets and loudspeakers on trucks are also used to promote products and political parties. Personal apparel campaigns for awareness, similar to the AIDS ribbons campaigns worldwide, have reached Cambodia, as the Alliance for Freedom, a group of 20 NGOs seeking more awareness for freedom of speech, distributed yellow ribbons in Phnom Penh and the provinces (Plaut and Chandara, 2005).

Advertising in 2006 is centered around services and leisure. Mobile phone service providers and Internet providers are sub-categories, with mobile phone providers driving the division with 80 percent of spending. (Other drivers are travel agents and hotels.) Home personal care is second, followed by pharmaceuticals, alcoholic beverages, non-alcoholic beverages and tobacco (Ang, 2006). Clothing is now near the bottom of the list in terms of media spending.

In some instances, certain companies adapt their products and advertising approaches to fit Cambodia. Unilever Thai Trading Ltd. made smaller shampoo sizes available for a few riels and approached hair salons and barbers to push the product in addition to using broadcast advertising and billboards (Asawanipont, 2005).

Agencies moved into Cambodia as part of their regional strategies for Asia. Although billings are smaller than those of neighboring countries like Thailand, networking in Cambodia makes strategic sense (Frith, 1997). In 1992, Bates Cambodia was the first international advertising agency in Cambodia. A full service agency, it is French in origin, owned by the Cordiant Group, and headquartered in Singapore. Its subsidiaries include 141 Cambodia and Zenith Media. Its major clients included British American Tobacco, CamGSM (mobile phone network), Tele 2 (an international gateway), Caltex (petrol stations and convenience stores), Dumex (infant formula) and International SOS (medical emergency services) (http://www.bates141.com/).

Other larger agencies in Phnom Penh include the giant Publicis through Prakit/ FCB, Tonle Orchid (now RiverOrchid) and Red Dot (the first Khmer agency). Red Dot's clients have included Sony, Ericsson, Visa, Caltex, InterContinental Hotel, Cambodian Ministry of Tourism, World Vision, Mobitel and Nikon (Red Dot, 2006). The *Cambodian Yellow Pages* lists 79 companies as advertising agencies, but most are small enterprises or businesses handling only a few aspects of advertising.

Bassac Orchid, part of the River Orchid group operating throughout the Mekong Basin, has a commitment to diversity in its mission and an agency team of "14 nationalities from four continents: Khmer, Lao, Thai, British, Singaporean, American, Vietnamese, Japanese, Filipino, Malaysian, Zambian, Canadian, Ukrainian and Burmese." The agency spend more than $1,000 USD per week in consumer research across Laos and Cambodia through their research component, Orchid Insight. They work with clients including Nestlé, Coca-Cola, Unilever, ANZ Royal, Equal, Western Union, Johnson & Johnson, Pfizer, USAID and Motorola (Ang, 2006).

One agency head who wished to remain anonymous (Quarles, 2003a) outlines the difficulties of doing advertising in a culture where awareness of the importance of advertising still evolves. Corruption, in terms of kickbacks from contracts, and political influence used in awarding contracts remain problems. Ethical copyright understandings are evolving. No professional association has formed, but the agency head hopes to see professional standards and practices in the near future. Most Cambodian businesses have yet to think of the economics of the long term, and many CEOs need a basic education in the benefits of advertising. He notes that many of the first advertising agencies to form had roots in other cultures (Thailand, France) and that native-owned agencies are relatively new.

Pascal Buriez directs the office of Bates Cambodia, the first international agency in Phnom Penh. He says Cambodians today understand more about advertising than they did in the 1990s and attributes this change in exposure to international publications. The baby boom generation born after the fall of the Khmer Rouge are young adults now, and in the urban areas, at least, they purchase mobile phones, clothing, Internet services and "motos (motorcycles)."

Although agency billings are not readily available in a culture where information is shared with only family or trusted friends (one observer says "it is not in the Khmer psyche to share information" (Eng, 2000)), an indicator of how much a company might spend to reach urban consumers is Mobitel marketing director Sitha Porm's estimate that his company spends $15,000 to $20,000 for print campaigns and $30,000 for television campaigns about six times a year to convince consumers to use its SMS services. Porm said the campaigns resulted in a rise in message use.

Other companies may want to launch similar campaigns but do not have the resources to do so. Members of Phnom Penh's growing advertising community say that Cambodian companies have yet to identify or tap the potential buying power of the Cambodian consumer (Woodsome, 2003a). But the growing multinational presence, as noted previously, is changing the climate. Advertising in the urban area is subtle and sophisticated, as seen in the creative approach taken by Bassac Orchid for Equal. Agency Director You Ang calls the copy and visual, "very simple and very Cambodia ... an international quality ad with a local aesthetic." The headline reads: "Have you ever wondered why Khmer women have such nice figures?" The tagline reads: "Equal. Great taste minus the calories."

Advertising in the rural areas is basic, as life is very different, rural Cambodians have less income and the rate of illiteracy is high, precluding heavy print campaigns. Advertising agencies must use "simple techniques," and they often create traveling road shows and point of promotion offerings.

Alcohol advertising is not restricted, but health warnings are placed on advertisements (WHO, 2004). A Cambodian form of point-of-purchase is the phenomenon of the "beer girl." The girls wear gowns in the colors of the biggest brands and compete for customers, hoping to be picked to pour the brand. Reports say some of the "beer girl" relationships extend past closing time and encourage the spread of AIDS. Beer companies believe the girls are an essential part of marketing efforts and far more effective than billboard, print or broadcast advertising. But Ministry of Health officials worry about the 4,000 to 5,000 beer girls plying their trade (Schiffrin, 1999) and an NGO has formed to lobby for a makeover of the beer girls.

Tobacco advertising is banned only in government media in Cambodia, with no other restrictions in a society where more than 60 percent of people smoke. Cambodia is a signatory to (but has yet to ratify) the Framework Convention on Tobacco Control (FCTC), a treaty sponsored by the World Health Organization. Those countries that ratify will "outlaw tobacco advertising and sponsorship, demand that tobacco firms cover at least 30% of every cigarette pack with health warnings, and ... ban the use of euphemistic adjectives like 'light' or 'mild' to describe cigarettes" (Fitzpatrick, 2005).

Since 1991, Cambodia has had an influx of cigarette advertising in many forms, from billboards to mass media advertising to promotions at point of sale. In 2001, advertising expenditures on all Cambodia media were more than $5 million USD, with most of that money going to television (MacKenzie, Collin, Sopharo and Sopheap, 2004). Outdoor advertising is not monitored, but it is believed to have increased by 20 percent in 2005 because of the partial return of spending on cigarettes (Ang, 2006). Cigarette advertising is currently banned on state-owned television, but private stations still sell airtime.

But change does occur. The monks of the Samrong Andet Pagoda have been smoke-free since 2002 and seven other pagodas have followed, an impressive number in a country where many monks smoke and receive up to seven packs of cigarettes as alms each month (Wilson, 2002). Roth Saroeun, the Venerable Head Monk of the Samrong Andet Pagoda, and other monks now head a "Khmer Quit Now" campaign. Saroeun has been featured in an anti-smoking documentary, "Holy Smoke" (Kong, 2004).

In terms of advertising-related law, Cambodia has drafted a new trademark law to comply with the Trade-Related Aspects of Intellectual Property Rights (TRIPS) rules for WTO membership. The law defines a trademark as any "visible sign" of distinguishing the goods and services of an applicant and provides for a 90-day opposition period (Esler, 2002). Copyright enforcement is split between the Ministry of Culture (phonograms, CDs and other recordings) and the Ministry of Information (printed materials), and a new law on copyright enacted on March 8, 2003 has yet to be enacted. A draft law on patents also remains before the National Assembly. While not a center for production of pirated materials, Cambodia's markets sell a plethora of pirated goods, including imported pirated products (US Embassy Phnom Penh, 2005).

A law adopted in 2003 guaranteed political parties equal access to private newspapers, and television and radio stations. The levels of illiteracy make broadcast media very important during elections. In the May 1998 elections, studies found that Hun Sen's party, the CPP, was featured 448 times in the electronic media while coalition party FUNIPEC and the opposition party SRP received 14 reports between them. The law was created to address such imbalances (Carmichael and Sokheng, 2003). The law was designed to give equitable coverage to parties and their issues during news, to allow all parties to buy time on private radio and TV and in print media, and to clarify the role of NGOs in broadcasting political debates (Carmichael and Sokheng, 2003). However, many of the private media companies refused election advertisements other than those of the party they backed (Samean, 2003).

The biggest Khmer-language newspaper financed primarily through advertising is *Rasmei Kampuchea*, owned by Teng Boon Ma, one of the country's richest men and a friend of Hun Sen. The paper has gained a reputation for accuracy, although it is generally pro-CPP in its political coverage (Eng, 2000). It dominates the market, with a circulation of about 35,000 a day (Tenove, 2001), and commands from 25 to 45 percent of the total advertising revenues available to Cambodian publications. It is a 12-page broadsheet daily, with a full-color front page offering color advertising. It has its own printing press with four-color capability (Clarke, 2000). However, the founder and publisher of the *Phnom Penh Post*, Michael Hayes, says that few people understand the advertising culture in Cambodia. "A lot of people think my paper is subsidized by the US government. They can't understand that I do this by selling ads and selling copies and subscriptions and doing layout jobs on the side" (Tenove, 2001).

Radio stations most often have commercial clients, and sometimes programs are sponsored. FM102, run by the Women's Media Center, has clients such as jewelry stores, grocery stores, battery stores and schools. FM90 has two sponsored programs—one by a driving school and one by a pharmaceutical company. Radio Apsara has advertisements for cigarettes, private schools, universities and drinking water on one of its live music or singing programs (White and Reagan, 2003). Radio's reach is a little more than 50 percent of the 92 percent reach of television nationally. Print has a 45 percent reach and the Internet reach is still niche, around 3 percent (Ang, 2006).

Radio Beehive is different. Mam Sonando is an important broadcaster in Phnom Penh, as his station is the most independent voice. He told a media sales trainer from Western Kentucky University's NPR station that he has "two classes of advertisers": independent businesses and what he called "non-independent" companies:

The independent businesses are the small merchants that sell things like medicines, clothing, and eyeglasses. Many potential advertisers in this category are afraid to advertise with him due to his political leanings, which do not favor the government. The "non-independent" businesses are big companies that are not fearful of advertising with him, but he has few of these due to his 1kw signal ... Sonando loves analogies, so he explained his challenges in the marketplace this way. "In America, you play football on a level field with non-biased referees. In Cambodia, our field has many holes and a biased referee." (White and Reagan, 2003, p. 13)

Sonando does not accept "vice" advertising such as cigarettes. Many businesses are afraid to advertise with him, so his station's "revenue picture" comprises donations received from listeners.

Cambodia's television ad spend is $5 million dollars a year. In the cluttered landscape of advertising in the country, television dominates. TV5 traditionally brought in much of the revenue, but recent monitoring by Orchid Insight shows that CTN viewership is rising, as is that of TV3, and TV5's viewership is declining. After the anti-Thai riots of 2003, TV5 and others pulled Thai programming from their lineups and replaced it with Chinese and Indian serials. TV5's general manager says the station with the new lineup now has 60 percent of the audience share. The top three programs are "Super Joke" on TV3, "Top Teen" on TV5 and the Khmer Soap "Broken Heart" on CTN (Corben, 2004). Zenith Media, a part of Bates Cambodia, offers television ratings, and Nielsen ratings are available as well.

The Cambodian government itself launched a "shoestring advertising campaign" on CNN in late 2004 with a "Visit Cambodia" spot created for under $1,000 USD by the Tourism Ministry itself and carried by CNN over a week-long period at an 85 percent discount rate (Cambodia ecstatic, 2004).

Not all communication messages in Cambodia are commercial. With the prevalence of NGOs in the country, many public service campaigns are developed for awareness of social issues, using the same paths shared by commercial messages. These organizations include United Nations programs as well as independent charities. Numerous job advertisements in *The Cambodia Daily* directed at the NGO community in Cambodia called for public relations and advertising skills (Personal observation, 2003).

The UN development program and the national AIDS authority have launched several campaigns to break the silence regarding sex, sexuality and AIDS, using spots on television, radio and in cinemas to raise awareness of the disease as a development concern (Woodsome, 2003b). The BBC World Service Trust sponsors a soap opera directed to rural Cambodians. *Rous Cheat Chivit* (Taste of Life) is a hospital drama with plot lines on HIV and AIDS designed to educate viewers in the country with the worst HIV rate in Southeast Asia. Many cases result from a husband's transmission of the infection after he has visited one of the country's many sex workers (Marks, 2004).

The US embassy in 2005 sponsored a Cambodian version of "Sesame Street" called "Sabai Sabai Sesame" in Khmer. The program is aired on Apsara Television (Sesame opens, 2005) and produced by Educational Television Cambodia, a project of World Education.

A typical public safety spot shows a rural woman inside a simple home. "She lifts a chicken to check for eggs, then goes over to lift her newborn. The baby's lips move, saying "No!" and a disembodied hand appears holding a bar of soap. The woman will remember to wash first next time" (Cambodian TV commercials, 2006).

Cambodia's Future

Cambodia continues to make progress in its journey toward status as a developed country, but much remains to be done. In the 15 years since the Peace Accords in 1991, the country has continued its slow but steady economic development in spite of political instability, corruption and weak judicial and legal systems in a situation where most citizens still live in a rural environment and depend on agriculture. *Voices of the Least Developed Countries in Asia and the Pacific* (UNDP, 2005) states that Cambodia is likely to meet few of its development goals by 2015 because the rest of the world has lost focus on the country's needs for "reform, increased government revenue for education, teachers and health … and an economically broad base of employment" (Wasson and Prak, 2005).

But for many in the advertising industry, future growth will depend on other factors as well. The presence of multinationals, as noted, encourages the growth of the local industry in addition to channeling dollars into a sometimes shaky economy. For those investors seeking to enter the Cambodian landscape, factors such as political stability also play an important role, as seen in the growth of the industry from 1999 to 2006. With elections to be held in 2008, You Ang (2006) of Bassac Orchid believes that advertising spending will increase at least for the next two years. What will happen beyond that date? Only time will tell, in a country where both the economy and the political structure remain somewhat shaky.

References

Ang, You (2006). Personal interview, Phnom Penh, March 4, 2006.
Asawanipont, Nitida (2005, January 28). Unilever puts focus on Cambodia, Laos, *The Nation*.
Asia, Inc. (2004, November). *Who's Hot in Asia/Cambodia*. [Online.] http://www.asia-inc.com/November04/Hcambodia_sok_nov.htm (retrieved November 13, 2006).
Barisoth, Seth (2000). Cambodia: country report. In Asian Media information Centre, *Media and Democracy in Asia* (pp. 16–30). Singapore: Asian Media Information Centre.
BBC (2006). Country profile: Cambodia. [Online.] www.BBC.org (retrieved October 10, 2006).
Berthiaume, Lee (2005, December 29). For Cambodia, a year of hope and controversy. *The Cambodia Daily*.

Borton, James (2002, September 14). Sex, scandal and the Cambodian press, *Asia Times*.

Cambodia ecstatic with shoestring CNN exposure (2004, November 22). Deutsche Press-Agentur.

Cambodian ex-monarch joins blogger community (2005, May 26). *Taipei Times*.

Cambodian Ministry of Commerce (2005). [Online.] http://www.moc.gov.kh/ (retrieved October 31, 2006).

Cambodian TV commercials (2006). [Online.] www.brash.com/brash_dot_com/2006/01/cambodian_comme.html (retrieved November 13, 2006).

Carmichael, Robert and Vong Sokheng (2003, May 9). Telling it like it is. *Phnom Penh Post*, 22.

Chandara, Lor (2000). Media in Cambodia's emerging democracy. In Asian Media Information Centre, *Media and Democracy in Asia* (pp. 31–45). Singapore: Asian Media Information Centre.

Chinaview.cn (2006, March 14). UN optimistic about Cambodia's economic future. [Online.] www.chinaview.cn (retrieved November 15, 2006).

Christoff, Joseph (2002, June 13). Cambodia: government reform progressing, but key efforts are lagging. *GAO Report to the Subcommittee on Foreign Operations*. Washington, DC: Government Accountability Office.

CIA Factbook, 2006, Cambodia (2006). [Online.] http://www.cia.gov/cia/publications/factbook/geos/cb.html (retrieved October 30, 2006).

Clarke, Judith (2000, September 4). Cambodia. *Handbook of the Media in Asia. Communications Law in Transition* newsletter, published by Oxford and Yeshiva Universities. [Online.] http://pcmlp.socleg.ox.ac.uk/transition/issue07/cambodia.htm (retrieved June 14, 2005).

Corben, Ron (2004, May). Little goes a long way: Indochina is still a flickering blip on Asia's television radar. *Television Asia*, 22: 2.

Crispin, Shawn (1999, January 7). Cosmetic surgery: Hun Sen tries to remake his image in Washington. *Far Eastern Economic Review*.

Eng, Peter (2000, December 25). Cambodian journalists moving towards professionalism. *The Korea Herald*.

Esler, Lindsay (2002, May 17). Cambodia's new trademarks and unfair competition law. *Mondaq Business Briefing*.

Fitzpatrick, Liam (2005, March 2). Can Asia kick the habit? *Time Asia*.

Fletcher, Richard and T.C. Melewar (2001). The complexities of communicating to customers in emerging markets. *Journal of Communication Management*, 6(1): 9–23.

Foster, Michelle (2005). Lost profits. *Knightline*, Winter.

Frith, Katherine Toland (1997). Asian advertising: charting the trends. *Media Asia*, 24(2): 94–8.

Gunaratne, Shelton (1999). The media in Asia: an overview. *Gazette*, 61(3–4): 197–223.

Haley, George and Chin-Tong Tan (1996). The black hole of Southeast Asia: strategic decision making in an informational void. *Management Decision*, 34(9): 37–48.

Hodson, Jeff and Kay Kimsong (1998). Cambodian newspapers take slow road to respectability. *The Cambodia Daily*. [Online.] www.kamnet.com/kh/cambodia.daily/Fifth_Anniversary/page_8.htm (retrieved June 14, 2005).

http://www.bates141.com/ (retrieved March 29, 2011).

http://www.stat-usa.gov (retrieved January 6, 2005).

Human Rights Watch (2003). *World Report 2003: Cambodia*. [Online.] www.hrw.org/wr2k3/asia3.html (retrieved November 3, 2006).

International Institute of Cambodia (2005). *Country Progress Report*. [Online.] http://www.afact.org/include/getfile.php?fid=1099 (retrieved November 15, 2006).

Kamm, Henry (1998). *Cambodia*. New York: Arcade Publishing.

Kazmin, Amy (2003, July 22). Cambodia's disenchanted younger grow restless for a brighter future. *Financial Times*, 9.

Klein, Norbert (2005). KH: Cambodia. *Digital Review of Asia Pacific.* [Online.] http://www.digital-review.org/05_Cambodia.htm (retrieved November 3, 2006).

Kong, Mom (2004, January). The situation in Cambodia. *The Globe.*

Mackenzie, Ross, J. Collin, C. Sopharo and Y. Sopheap (2004). Almost a role model of what we would like to do everywhere: British Tobacco in Cambodia. *Tobacco Control*, 13: 112–17.

Malamed, Samantha and Van Roeun (2005, November 24). TV, radio ordered not to read newspapers. *The Cambodia Daily.*

Marks, Naomi (2004, September). Far EastEnders: how a Cambodian soap opera brings hope. *BMJ.* [Online.] www.bmj.com (retrieved November 4, 2006).

Neumann, A. Lin (2003). An independent voice. In Committee to Protect Journalists, *Dangerous Assignments* (Fall-Winter).

Osborne, Magz (2002, January 14). Making programs adds up for advertisers. *Variety*, 385(8): 47.

Plaut, Ethan and Chandara, Lor (2005, December 2). Alliance forms for freedom of expression, begins campaign. *The Cambodia Daily.*

Quarles, Jan (2003a, October). Interview with agency head, identity confidential.

Quarles, Jan (2003b). Personal observations during October, during residency at Royal University of Phnom Penh.

Red Dot (2006). [Online.] www.reddot.com.kh (retrieved November 13, 2006).

Reed, Matt (2003, January 17). Survey: Cambodia lacks a culture of literacy. *The Cambodia Daily*, 13.

Report to the Congress on the Anti-Thai Riots in Cambodia on January 29, 2003. [Online.] www.state.gov (retrieved November 15, 2006).

Roeun, Van (2002). Beyond a sideshow: better understanding between Cambodia and the West. In Anura Goonasekera and Jin Chua Chong, *Under Asian Eyes* (pp. 13–30). Singapore: SPF, AMIC and Nanyang Technological University.

RUPP (2006). [Online.] rupp.edu.kh/rupp_wsite/stud-info/dmc/dmc.htm (retrieved 2006).

Samean, Yun (2003, June 3). Some private media shun election ads. *The Cambodia Daily.*

Sarayeth, Tive (2002). Media reform experiences in Cambodia. Paper presented at Beyond Media Education, Manila, September. [Online.] http.wacc.org/asia (retrieved October 10, 2006).

Schiffrin, Anya (1999, July 19). Doctors say foreign brewers risk promoting spread of AIDS in Cambodia. Associated Press Business News.

Sesame opens: Apsara TV-11 to broadcast Sesame Street (2005, December 9). *Hollywood Reporter.*

Sisovann, Pin (2002, June 29–30). Behind the screen: a closer look at the troubled world of Cambodian cinema. *The Cambodia Daily*, weekend edition.

Tenove, Chris (2001, April). Cambodian media: a "mad dog" not a watchdog. *Thunderbird Online Magazine.* [Online.] http://www.journalism.ubc.ca/thunderbird/archives/2001.04/cambodia.html (retrieved October 10, 2006).

UNCTAD (2003). *An Investment Guide to Cambodia.* New York and Geneva: United Nations. [Online.] http://www.unctad.org/TEMPLATES/WebFlyer.asp?intItemID=2703&lang=1 (retrieved November 15, 2006).

UNDP (2005, July). *Voices of the Least Developed Countries in Asia and the Pacific.* New Delhi: UNDP and Elsevier.

US Embassy Phnom Penh (2004). *Cambodia Commercial Guide, 2004.* [Online.] http://phnompenh.usembassy.gov/uploads/iages/_NsauSuPw3T52EFXwBg/country_cguide04.pdf (retrieved November 15, 2006).

US Embassy Phnom Penh (2005). *Country Commercial Guide*. [Online.] http://phnompenh. usembassy.gov/economic_affairs.html (retrieved November 15, 2006).

Wasson, Erik and Kay Kimsong (2005, September 30). Businesses put Cambodia near bottom of list. *The Cambodia Daily*.

Wasson, Erik and Chan Thul Prak (2005, July 5). Development in Cambodia falling short. *The Cambodia Daily*.

Weiss, Raimund (2003, May 23–June 5). NEC and the media: TV3 and TV5. *Phnom Penh Post*.

White, Bart and Terry Reagan (2003). *Cambodian Manager Residency Field Report, December 26, 2002– January 10, 2003*. Prepared for Internews and Western Kentucky's NPR. [Online.] http://www.wku. edu/ijmmt/sessions/cambodia/02_cam_fo/docs/cam_m_res.pdf (retrieved October 10, 2006).

Wilson, Sophie (2002, January 18–31). Tobacco advertising in Cambodia. *Phnom Penh Post*.

Woodsome, Kate (2003a, January 6). Advertising evolves with country's awareness. *The Cambodia Daily*.

Woodsome, Kate (2003b, May 20). UNDP, AIDS authority launch media spots. *The Cambodia Daily*.

World Health Organization (WHO) (2004). *Global Status Report: Alcohol Policy*. [Online.] www.who. int/entity/substance_abuse/publications/policy_Cambodia.pdf (retrieved October 10, 2006).

You can't say that here: Cambodia (2005, November 5). *The Economist*, 77.

6 *The Role of Indirect Advertising in Establishing Social Legitimacy: An Analysis of Tobacco Sponsorship in China*

AMY O'CONNOR AND MARY FRANCES CASPER

Introduction

Around the world, 11,000 people die every day from illnesses associated with tobacco use. Of those who die, over 2,000 live in China. It is estimated that by the year 2050 this number will expand to over 8,000 Chinese deaths each day (The Framework Convention Alliance for Tobacco Control, 2004; *An International Treaty for Tobacco Control*, 2003). Recently, China surpassed the United States in the number of tobacco related deaths. "Chinese adults severely underestimate smoking risks. A 1996 nationwide survey revealed that two-thirds believe smoking does little or no harm. Professor Richard Peto of Oxford University states that 'Sixty percent of Chinese adults don't know that smoking can cause lung cancer, and 96% don't know it can cause heart disease'" (Wilson, 1998).

China represents a growth market for multinational tobacco companies in what has become an increasingly hostile world climate. In China tobacco companies find reduced advertising and promotional restrictions, a population underinformed about the hazards of tobacco use, and an increasing public interest in Western products. This chapter explores the role of indirect advertising in establishing social legitimacy for tobacco companies in China. To do so, first the use of tobacco in China is summarized. Next, the chapter examines the concept of social legitimacy as a means to create favorable public opinion and weave corporations into the fabric of society. Third, the indirect advertising efforts of tobacco companies in China are examined through the lens of legitimacy. Finally, the chapter assesses the practical applications of using indirect advertising to create social legitimacy and circumvent efforts to curb tobacco use.

Background

Tobacco consumers in high income countries such as Britain, Canada and the United States have become increasingly aware of and responsive to the adverse health effects of tobacco, largely due to increased government controls on the tobacco industry and its advertising practices. However, much of the developing world remains underinformed about the hazards of cigarette consumption (Cornwell, 1997). Among countries with emerging economies, China represents the global hotspot for tobacco companies due to its large number of smokers and the increasing openness to Western products. China has seen tobacco use rates increase dramatically in the last four decades. Between 1952 and 1996, the Chinese male smoking rate has risen from one to 15 cigarettes per day (WHO targets Asian tobacco ads, 2002). Teens make up a large number of new smokers. "Up to 50,000 Asian teenagers start smoking each day" (WHO targets Asian tobacco ads, 2002, p. 569). In total, China's smoking population is expected to rise to 400 million by 2050 (Roberts, 2002).

Currently, China accounts for 33 percent of all cigarettes smoked worldwide (Fitzpatrick, 2005) and it is estimated that tobacco consumption rates in China will rise by 4.07 million tons and China's share of the total world tobacco demand will reach 43 percent in 2010 (*Projections of Tobacco Production, Consumption and Trade to the Year 2010*, 2003). The rate of increase indicates that currently China is in the second stage of smoking proliferation (Brown, 2001). During stage two, smoking starts to catch on; the rates for men are over 50 percent and rates for women may extend as high as 40 percent (Brown, 2001). While over 66 percent of the male population smokes, only 1 percent of Chinese women currently smoke cigarettes (Wilson, 1998). While male smoking rates may have reached saturation, these statistics indicate that tobacco companies may experience growth by convincing women to start smoking cigarettes (Roberts, 2002). This strategy was successful in Western countries decades ago and included the introduction of cigarettes packaged specifically for women (Roberts, 2002).

In addition to being one of the largest consumers of tobacco, China is also one of the world's largest tobacco producers (Northoff, 2004). As of 1997, China accounted for one third of the world's output of tobacco (Richmond, 1997). In 2003, China produced 1.75 trillion cigarettes of which only one percent were exported (Fitzpatrick, 2005). One reason for the demand may be that tobacco is relatively inexpensive in China when compared to more developed countries. In the United States a pack of cigarettes sells for approximately $3.50 with the majority of the cost being federal and state taxes (Chan and Capehart, 2004). In contrast, a pack of cigarettes in China sells for around 50 cents (Fitzpatrick, 2005).

Tobacco production provides much needed jobs in China, yet decimates the environment and the health of the population. The China National Tobacco Corp (CNTC) is one of the country's biggest employers ... [providing] work for 500,000 people [and] 10 million peasant families who grow tobacco (Richmond, 1997, p. 1139). However, as farmers cultivate tobacco as a cash crop, less land is available for growing nutritious foods, leading to malnutrition (Richmond, 1997). There is an additional affect on health caused by the cost of tobacco consumption. Money used to purchase tobacco results in less food in many Chinese households. "The tobacco habit consumes 9.5% of the household income in urban areas and 14% among rural Chinese" (Richmond, 1997, p. 1139).

China's large population represents a lucrative market for tobacco companies facing severe image and legal hurdles in Western countries. One indication of the potential of emerging economies to help tobacco companies realize their long-term growth strategies is summed up as follows: "You buy Philip Morris in the long term for their international business," says Bonnie Herzog, an analyst at Credit Suisse First Boston in New York City. "That's their growth engine" (Brown, 2001). This statement highlights the opportunities available for tobacco companies in emerging economies and signals the need for advertising to help encourage consumption while communicating the social legitimacy of Western tobacco companies in Chinese society.

The Legitimacy Construct

The concept of legitimacy has a long history in corporate communication activities beginning in the nineteenth century. Early entrants seeking to gain legitimacy through advertising in the United States included AT&T, General Motors and General Electric (Marchand, 1998). These corporations demonstrated their fit in society through the rhetorical construction of image(s) that met with societal expectations and desires of corporate behavior. As such, legitimacy is a theoretical construct with its roots in rhetoric (Bostdorff and Vibbert, 1994; Crable and Vibbert, 1983; Hearit, 1995) and strategic management (Aldrich and Fiol, 1994; Dowling and Pfeffer, 1975; Esrock and Leitchy, 1998; Suchman, 1995). Consistent with each perspective is the following definition:

> legitimacy is the congruence between the social values associated with or implied by (organizational) activities and the norms of acceptable behavior in the larger social system of which they are a part. (Dowling and Pfeffer, 1975, p. 122)

The emphasis on congruence with organizational behavior and social values highlights the importance of corporations engaging in activities that demonstrate to publics the corporation's commitment to upholding social and cultural norms and mores. Researchers contend that for an organization to survive it must maintain legitimacy with its publics (Dowling and Pfeffer, 1975; Hearit, 1995; Perrow, 1970). While corporations control the construction of the messages and images associated with legitimacy, it is the public that determines whether an organization has legitimacy based on their perceptions and interpretations of organizational behavior (Perrow, 1970). Seeger (1997) summarizes, "Judgments of legitimacy are matters of interpretation and are in part a function of the public statements made about organizations and their activities" (p. 108).

One way a corporation can attempt to establish legitimacy is to create linkages between itself and society (Seeger, 1997). Corporations create links through activities such as sponsorships and financial contributions to events or issues that have social significance. Seeger contends that "this linkage of the organization to universally positive symbols is a common and effective legitimizing strategy" (p. 107).

For tobacco companies, China represents both an emerging economy and an opportunity to establish social legitimacy anew. Economically, legitimacy is a valuable resource for Western tobacco companies entering the Chinese market because it enhances an emerging corporation's odds of survival (Aldrich and Fiol, 1994; Rao, 1994; Singh, Tucker and Meinhard, 1991; Suchman, 1995). Legitimacy helps the corporation attract resources (Parsons, 1960), and increase the level of resource transactions flowing into an organization (Terreberry, 1968). For Western tobacco companies that expand into China and face competition from the Chinese cigarette monopoly, social legitimacy may provide a foothold in a country steeped in culture and tradition.

The search for legitimacy has been described as a "battle between frames" (Hargreaves, 2004, p. 61). In this sense entrance into new markets provides a tobacco company with opportunities to decouple its Western markets from its efforts in China. In other words, corporations can separate illegitimate behaviors (e.g., US marketing efforts) from those perceived as acceptable (e.g., promotional activities in China) (Elsbach and Sutton, 1992). The framing of issues by country allows corporations to focus on gaining legitimacy through the issues or actions that are of central concern to important publics rather than seeking legitimacy for the entire organization (Boyd, 2000).

Corporations seeking to gain legitimacy have three primary strategies to consider: 1) connect themselves to elements in the social scene that already possess legitimacy, such as charities or cooperative partnerships with respected organizations; 2) use communication (e.g., advertising) activities to alter the environment to be more congruent with corporate interests; and 3) alter its behaviors, products, services to fit with social norms and expectations. While distinct, each of the three strategies is grounded in the basic premise that there must be congruence between the organization and its operating environment for legitimacy to be conferred. Each strategy, however, has a different central focus.

When organizations seek to develop linkages with other organizations that possess the type of legitimacy desired, the corporation is seeking to associate itself with social norms without actually changing its core business operations. Typically legitimacy is achieved this way through corporate funding of philanthropic entities or sponsorship of socially and culturally important events or causes. For example, in the United States Philip Morris has made large donations including employee support to Meals on Wheels and various charities associated with stopping homelessness and domestic violence (Bryne, 1999).

Second, corporations can rely on traditional forms of advertising to present the corporate image desired. Over time research suggests that these campaigns can alter the environment in support of the corporation (Marchand, 1998). This strategy, however, takes considerable time, effort and money to be successful. The most notable example of this type of campaign working is the US tobacco industry's "no harm from cigarettes" campaign that lasted nearly 40 years during which time no legislation or litigation occurred that the tobacco companies did not support (Bryne, 1999; Hilts, 1996; Orey, 1999; Kluger, 1996).

Third, corporations can choose to alter their product, service or means of production in an attempt to meet the social and cultural expectations of key publics. When corporations choose this strategy it is often as a last resort. In the case of tobacco, the decision to alter marketing and advertising practices was not voluntary. Rather, political and legal sanctions worldwide have forced all tobacco companies to change their fundamental marketing practices in an attempt to salvage enough legitimacy to continue operating.

This chapter is primarily concerned with the use of indirect advertising by tobacco companies in an attempt to attach themselves to elements in the social scene that can provide legitimacy. Therefore, its focus will be on the first two strategies and how tobacco companies are woven into the social and cultural fabric of society.

Tobacco Advertising in China

The increase in recent years of advertising and promotion in China have opened the door for Western companies. The rise in advertising and promotion are due to a plethora of factors including China's entrance into the World Trade Organization, an increasingly global marketplace, the expansion of the Internet, the need among Chinese media for funding and the appeal of the Western lifestyle among the Chinese. For Western tobacco companies the interest in Western products has provided the impetus needed for them to gain access to the largest consumer market in the world. Tobacco companies have seized upon the opportunity to advertise their products in China as a means to increase market share, distance themselves from legal difficulties in the United States and continue to meet the expectations of shareholders (Brown, 2001).

The Internet continues to introduce new products and lifestyles into China. The opportunity for corporations to use the Internet as a means to promote their products is great. China currently has approximately 80 million Internet subscribers and it is estimated by 2006 that number will reach 153 million (Green, 2004). Internet access coupled with relatively inexpensive traditional forms of advertising (Strasser, 1994) and the need by Chinese media outlets for Western revenue have increased the opportunities for tobacco companies to promote their products and corresponding lifestyles.

Emerging economies face unique challenges when dealing with tobacco promotion. Often there is a lack of local resources to fund media programming. The challenge facing media companies is summarized as follows: "Because developing countries depend more on international sources for programming, they are more likely to exempt international media from their tobacco advertising bans" (Cornwell, 1997, p. 249). The need for financial support on the part of the media is coupled with the need for access in a concentrated market that forces tobacco corporations to rely on advertising rather than pricing strategies (Saffer, 2000). The result is the creation of an alliance between Chinese media, Western tobacco companies and consumer desires for Western products.

As Western advertisers moved into the Chinese market in the early 1990s, the Chinese public responded favorably to Western advertising strategies (Strasser, 1994). Advertisers commonly play on Chinese desires for the new and the Western (Strasser, 1994). Western products, including tobacco, are considered to be "fashionable, and quite often, progressive" (Watson, 1997, p. 41). Tobacco companies have tapped into the desire for things Western and communicate tobacco use in the frame of a lifestyle, rather than a product.

Cigarette advertising is not designed to convey information about the physical characteristics of the product or to convey important product information, but rather to create a fantasy of sophistication, pleasure, and social success ... In developing countries this imagery can be designed to associate the product with a glamorous fantasy of American or European life-styles. The relatively small expenditure on tobacco provides a link to this fantasy lifestyle. (Saffer, 2000, p. 217)

Advertisers exploit the Chinese desire for Westernism by rhetorically constructing an image for their product that is simultaneously Western yet Chinese in its application (Strasser, 1994). The advertisements use Chinese actors enjoying Western tobacco thus allowing for a break from tradition without becoming a Westerner. This imagery fits well with the role of tobacco as a symbolic declaration of independence. "Smoking a cigarette for the beginner is a symbolic act. I am no longer my mother's child, I'm tough, I am an adventurer, I'm not square ... As the force from the psychological symbolism subsides, the pharmacological effect takes over to sustain the habit" (Jarvis, 2004, p. 277).

While initially unfettered in their advertising strategies, tobacco companies have recently come under increased scrutiny for their advertising and marketing practices. In 2002 the World Health Organization Western Pacific called for a ban on tobacco advertising and sponsorships (WHO targets Asian tobacco ads, 2002). As of 2002, China required health warnings on cigarette packs, banned tobacco advertising on television, print and electronic ads, and banned advertising at indoor sporting events (Roberts, 2002). However, loopholes in the law still exist that allow indirect marketing in the form of sponsorships, apparel and promotional activities (Roberts, 2002).

Indirect Advertising

Indirect advertising applies the strategies and outcomes of traditional advertising (e.g., generate awareness, recognition, recall and increase sales) using alternative methods such as sponsorship of events and programming, product tie-ins and product placement in films or other media venues (Cornwell, 1997; Harper and Martin, 2002; Saffer, 2000). Tobacco companies have used indirect advertising as a means to reach consumers for decades. Most cigarette brands depict a strong image in their advertising, such as the Marlboro Man as an iconic image of the West or Joe Camel as an adventurer and playboy. The aim of indirect tobacco advertising is to promote, to reinforce or to maintain the impact of the brand name and its theme. This is accomplished without specifically mentioning the tobacco product (Joossens, 2001). Rather, indirect advertising uses brand names, trade names, trademarks, emblems or other distinctive features of tobacco products with the aim or the indirect effect of promoting a tobacco product (Joossens, 2001).

In more recent years, tobacco companies have increased their use of indirect advertising due to heightened restrictions on tobacco promotion in traditional advertising channels. Studies indicated that when tobacco advertising is banned, expenditures on indirect advertising increase (Heloma, Nurminen, Reijula and Rantanen, 2004). As early as 1979, British American Tobacco realized the importance indirect advertising would have in the future.

> *Opportunities should be explored by all companies so as to find non-tobacco products and other services which can be used to communicate the brand or house name, together with their essential visual identities. This is likely to be a long-term and costly operation, but the principle is nevertheless to ensure that cigarette lines can be effectively publicised [sic] when all direct forms of communication are denied. (Joossens, 2001)*

Even when direct forms of communication are denied, brands continue to have salience due to strong brand imagery and social connection to the brand and individual use patterns. Multiple studies have found a strong positive relationship between sponsorship and recognition, recall, and awareness both in the United States and internationally (Cornwell, 1997; Joossens, 2001). In all likelihood, this is due to the ability of indirect advertising to provide an increased temporal exposure to brand imagery (McQuistan and Squier, 2001) and to attach the brand to an activity or idea that the audience feels positively about (O'Connor, 2004). As Western tobacco companies have entered China, they have relied heavily on indirect advertising, particularly sponsorship, to increase sales while simultaneously establishing social legitimacy.

Sponsorship and Legitimacy

Sponsorship has been found to be as effective as traditional advertising in developing brand loyalty and recognition (Cornwell, 1997; Harper and Martin, 2002). Sponsorship involves an exchange between the sponsor and the activity or event. Specifically, the sponsor (e.g., Philip Morris) provides financial support to the event (e.g., auto racing) in exchange for the right to associate itself with the event and communicate that association to select target audiences (Cornwell, 1997). Due to the reciprocal nature of the agreement, bans on sponsorship are often unpopular. "Events become so dependent on the sponsorship fees coming from tobacco companies that they themselves become advocates for the tobacco companies" (Cornwell, 1997, p. 246). Stotlar (1992) contends that "television, sponsors, and event owners have become a triumvirate in sport. The event owner depends on the sponsor for an operating budget, yet the sponsor is willing to provide the needed assets only if television coverage can be guaranteed" (p. 16).

The use of sponsorship offers tobacco companies a presence that traditional advertising does not. In China, Philip Morris sponsors a popular television series. The show has a large audience in China and through the sponsorship, Philip Morris becomes a welcomed guest in the Chinese home. Similarly, tobacco companies have sponsored the world's largest tobacco museum. Located in Shanghai, the museum opened in July 2003, at a cost of over $22 million which was donated primarily from the local branches of the tobacco companies, and promotes the joys of smoking (Fitzpatrick, 2005). "There are a lot of limitations on advertising," says Wang Chuanqing, the museum's vice curator. "So we use the museum format to showcase tobacco" (Fitzpatrick, 2005, p. 5). The museum features historical and contemporary displays on tobacco use, production and social connection in China and other parts of the world. Typical of any museum which houses cultural artifacts, the Shanghai museum presents tobacco in connection to society and how Chinese use and enjoy the product (Fitzpatrick, 2005).

By sponsoring socially and culturally popular programming and activities, the sponsoring tobacco company is first identifying itself with something the audience enjoys, second demonstrating its fit within society, and third providing a form of entertainment or leisure that might not be available without sponsorship. Legitimacy is conferred to the sponsoring company through its attachment to a desirable cultural icon. Because it is a sponsorship rather than a traditional advertisement, audience members may view the corporation as supporting a cultural expression rather than selling a product. Over time, audience members may consider the corporation not as a sponsor but as a participant in the social and cultural expressions it funds thereby increasing its legitimacy and possibly increasing the number of linkages it can acquire.

In addition to the sponsorship of cultural events, tobacco companies frequently sponsor sports teams and corresponding events. For example, Marlboro sponsored the Chinese National Football League for five years; The British Tobacco Company sponsors the Chinese basketball team; and Philip Morris and R.J. Reynolds brands sponsor the

Marlboro Open and the Salem Open tennis tournaments in Hong Kong (McQuistan and Squier, 2001). Sporting event sponsorships connect tobacco products to a healthy, vibrant and successful lifestyle (McQuistan and Squier, 2001). Philip Morris (1990) explained, "While sports are by far the best avenue to attract, sample, and influence our core target smokers, it's not the only way. International movies and videos also have tremendous appeal to our young adult consumers in Asia."

The sponsorship of sports and musical events, particularly those aimed at a younger demographic, provide tobacco companies with a channel to establish legitimacy through the support of events that are young, sexy and have strong Western associations. These events link an event's excitement to smoking thereby creating positive associations between the product and social role models (Maurice, 2002). For example, R.J. Reynolds promoted a popular rock concert series in Hong Kong using five empty Winston cigarette packages as the cost of admission (Cornwell, 1997). The link between product usage and engaging in desired social and cultural events is inextricable and becomes inescapable when other promotional material is added.

As part of the brand personality and imagery, event sponsorship it often paired with another form of indirect advertising known in the trade as merchandising. Point-of-sale materials such as lighters, displays and promotional items display cigarette brand names packaged in attractive and novel ways. Brand name recognition has been linked to the increased likelihood of smoking (Jamner et al., 2003) and advertisers have found that merchandising enhances brand recognition particularly in restrictive advertising environments. Tobacco names and logos on "carrying bags, shops and kiosks, clothing, cafes, snack bars and restaurants" increase brand name recognition (Braverman and Aaro, 2004, p. 1232). The pairing of event sponsorship and product merchandising is exemplified in Marlboro's sponsorship of motor racing. During the event young Chinese women dressed as Marlboro cowgirls and offered free samples of Marlboro products. Events and car racing sponsorships that appeal to the thrill seeker extend the brand's appeal to include "I am a Westerner" (The Framework Convention Alliance for tobacco control, 2004). Coupled with Western television programs, music and fashion, smoking a Marlboro completes the picture.

In greater Asia, other forms of indirect advertising are being introduced. In Malaysia, for example, tobacco advertisers use trademark diversification to establish small companies that are projected as independent of tobacco. These brands then select activities or events to sponsor, which ties the name of the parent tobacco company to the event or activity without that company acting as a direct sponsor (Assunta and Chapman, 2004). An alternative method with a similar result is for the tobacco company to offer a non-tobacco product or retail operation which can be used to promote cigarette brand names (Cornwell, 1997). For example, R.J. Reynolds established "Salem Holidays," a travel agency in Malaysia. Ads for the firm use the slogan "a world of refreshment," yet can be said to be promoting vacations, rather than Salem cigarettes (Cornwell, 1997).

Sponsorship provides Western tobacco companies with the opportunity to connect to important events in China while increasing the time target audience members spend interacting with the brand and its visual imagery. In addition, sponsorships allow tobacco companies to create legitimacy linkages with media outlets, rock bands and other socially sanctioned events, thereby increasing the likelihood that the corporation will be viewed as a good corporate citizen and worthy of support.

Conclusion and Practical Applications

Tobacco is the second major cause of death in the world. It is estimated that if current smoking patterns continued, tobacco will cause more than 10 million deaths by the year 2020. Tobacco also has economic costs that include high public health costs of treating tobacco-related illness, decreased worker productivity due to illness, and premature death leaving families with reduced economic security. The annual global net loss due to tobacco related issues is US$200 thousand million, with a third of the loss being in developing countries (WHO, 2005). The statistics are clear that tobacco use has significant economic and social consequences. Yet, in emerging economies tobacco companies are finding ways to gain legitimacy in the face of increasing Western resistance.

China represents the global hotspot in the tobacco wars of the developing market economies due to its population, large number of smokers and only partial adoption of restrictive advertising and promotional practices. The importance of advertising in emerging economies is understood by the tobacco companies. A 1996 study found that when US cigarette companies entered Asian markets tobacco advertising increased and total tobacco use surged by 10 percent (Chaloupka and Laixuthai, 1996). Indirect advertising provides companies in highly concentrated or regulated industries with an important method of competition. It allows corporations to break through the clutter of traditional forms of advertising while simultaneously gaining legitimacy through the support of socially and culturally important events. In addition, indirect advertising allows tobacco companies to continue brand imagery and promotion when direct forms of advertising are prohibited.

Tobacco companies are adept at finding new markets and developing strategies to sustain their product even when direct avenues of advertising are blocked. Indirect advertising as a means of promoting products when other direct channels of advertising are banned highlights the centrality of communication to tobacco companies in creating and maintaining presence in society. "Tobacco is a communicated disease. It is communicated through advertising and sponsorship. The most pernicious and pervasive form of that marketing is found in sports stadiums and arenas worldwide," said WHO Director-General Dr Gro Harlem Brundtland (Maurice, 2002, p. 80).

Legitimacy, too, is a communicative act. As tobacco companies engage in activities that demonstrate their social worth, they are in effect asking publics to accept the corporation as a part of the community and by proxy its products. For emerging economies this creates both an ethical and economic conundrum. The influx of Western corporations and the economic development that is associated with their presence is needed and at times courted by emerging economies. In the case of tobacco companies, however, a public health risk comes along with the economic development. When publics in emerging economies confer legitimacy upon corporations based on support of certain cultural values (e.g., Western ideals, youth, freedom) there may be other, less immediately obvious, values that are not being supported (e.g., health and wellness). In this vein, indirect advertising, as a form of legitimacy creation, offers publics an association with supported social and cultural ideals without forcing the company to disclose the potentially damaging effects of their product. In the case of emerging economies the challenge will be to see if the lessons learned in the West about tobacco must be re-learned in the East.

References

Aldrich, H.E. and C.M. Fiol (1994). Fools rush in? The institutional context of industry creation. *Academy of Management Review*, 19(4): 645–70.

An International Treaty for Tobacco Control (2003). [Online.] http://www.who.intfeatures/2003/08/en/print.html (retrieved April 25, 2005).

Assunta, M. and S. Chapman (2004). The tobacco industry's accounts of refining indirect tobacco advertising in Malaysia. *Tobacco Control*, 13(Supplement 2): ii63–ii70.

Bostdorff, D. and S.L. Vibbert (1994). Values advocacy: enhancing organizational images, deflecting public criticism, and grounding future arguments. *Public Relations Review*, 20: 141–58.

Boyd, J. (2000). Actional legitimation: no crisis necessary. *Journal of Public Relations Research*, 12(4): 341–53.

Braverman, M.T. and E. Aaro (2004). Adolescent smoking and exposure to tobacco marketing under a tobacco advertising ban: findings from 2 Norwegian national samples. *American Journal of Public Health*, 94(7): 1230–38.

Brown, E. (2001, September 5). The World Health Organization takes on big tobacco (but don't hold your breath). *Fortune*.

Bryne, J.A. (1999, November 19). Philip Morris: inside America's most reviled company. *Business Week*, 176–92.

Chaloupka, F.J. and A. Laixuthai (1996). *US Trade Policy and Cigarette Smoking in Asia*. National Bureau of Economic Research Working Paper 5543. National Bureau of Economic Research.

Chan, K.K. and T. Capehart (2004). Health concerns or price: which takes credit for declining cigarette consumption in the US? *Choices* (1st quarter), 43–6.

Cornwell, B.T. (1997). The use of sponsorship-linked marketing by tobacco firms: international public policy issues. *Journal of Consumer Affairs*, 31(2): 238–53.

Crable, R.E. and S.L. Vibbert (1983). Mobil's epideictic advocacy: "observations" of Prometheus bound. *Communication Monographs*, 50: 380–94.

Dowling, J. and J. Pfeffer (1975). Orgnaizational legitimacy: social values and organizational behavior. *Pacific Sociological Review*, 18, 122–36.

Elsbach, K.D. and R.I. Sutton (1992). Acquiring organizational legitimacy through illegitimate actions: a marriage of institutional and impression management theories. *Academy of Management Journal*, 35: 699–738.

Esrock, S.L. and G.B. Leichty (1998). Social responsibility and corporate web pages: self presentation or agenda setting? *Public Relations Review*, 24(3): 305–19.

Fitzpatrick, L. (2005). Can Asia kick the habit? *Time Asia*.

The Framework Convention Alliance for Tobacco Control (2004). [Online.] http://www.fctc.org/ (retrieved April 4, 2005).

Green, H. (2004). The quest to click in China. *Business Week*. [Online.] http://www.businessweek.com/technology/content/jun2004/tc20040622_0004.htm (retrieved September 12, 2005).

Hargreaves, S. (2004). Conceptualising legitimacy for new venture research. *Journal of New Business Ideas and Trends*, 2(2): 54–65.

Harper, T.A. and J.E. Martin (2002). Under the radar: how the tobacco industry targets youth in Australia. *Drug and Alcohol Review*, 21: 387–92.

Hearit, K.M. (1995). Mistakes were made: organizations, apologia, and crises of social legitimacy. *Communication Studies*, 46: 1–17.

Heloma, A., M. Nurminen, K. Reijula and J. Rantanen (2004). Smoking prevalence, smoking related lung diseases, and national tobacco control legislation. *Chest*, 126(6): 1825–31.

Hilts, P.J. (1996). *Smoke Screen*. New York: Addison-Wesley.

Jamner, L.D., C.K. Whalen, S.E. Loughlin, R. Mermelstein, J. Audrain-McGovern and S. Krishnan-Sarin (2003). Tobacco use across the formative years: a road map to developmental vulnerabilities. *Nicotine and Tobacco Research*, 5(Supplement 1): s71–s78.

Jarvis, M.J. (2004). ABC of smoking cessation: why people smoke. *BMJ*, 328: 277–9.

Joossens, L. (2001). *How to Circumvent Tobacco Advertising Restrictions: The Irrelevance of the Distinction between Direct and Indirect Advertising*. [Online.] http://www.globalink.org/tobacco/docs/eu-docs/0102joossens.shtml (retrieved September 14, 2005).

Kluger, R. (1996). *Ashes to Ashes: America's Hundred-year Cigarette War, the Public Health and the Unabashed Triumph of Philip Morris*. New York: Alfred A. Knopf.

Marchand, R. (1998). *Creating the Corporate Soul: The Rise of Public Relations and Corporate Imagery in American Big Business*. Berkeley, CA: University of California Press.

Maurice, J. (2002). WHO attacks tobacco sponsorship of sports. *Bulletin of the World Health Organization 2002*, 80(1): 80–81.

McQuistan, M. and C. Squier (2001). Tobacco, health and the sports metaphor. *Culture, Sport, Society*, 4(2), 101–21.

Northoff, E. (2004, January 8). Higher world tobacco use expected by 2010: growth rate slowing down. FAO News. Rome: Food and Agriculture Organization of the United Nations.

O'Connor, A. (2004). In the boardroom of good and evil: an assessment of the persuasive premises and social implications of corporate values advocacy messages. Unpublished dissertation, Purdue University.

Orey, M. (1999). *Assuming the Risk: The Mavericks, the Lawyers, and the Whistle-blowers Who Beat Big Tobacco*. New York: Little, Brown and Company.

Parsons, T. (1960). *Structure and Process in Modern Societies*. Glencoe, IL: Free Press.

Perrow, C. (1970). *Organizational Analysis: A Sociological View*. Belmont, Ca: Wadsworth.

Philip Morris, *Marlboro 1990*, Bates #2504034844.

Projections of Tobacco Production, Consumption and Trade to the Year 2010 (2003). Rome: Food and Agriculture Organization of the United Nations.

Rao, M.V.H. (1994). The social construction of reputation: certification, contests, legitimization, and the survival of organizations in the American Automobile Industry: 1895–1912. *Strategic Management Journal*, 15: 29–44.

Richmond, R. (1997). Ethical dilemmas in providing tobacco to developing countries: the case of China. *Addiction*, 92(9): 1137–41.

Roberts, D. (2002, September 23). China's healthy ban on foreign butts. *Business Week*. [Online.] http://businessweek.com/bwdaily/dnflahs/sep2002/nf20020923_8326.htm (retrieved September 12, 2005).

Saffer, H. (2000). Tobacco advertising and promotion. In P. Jha and F. Chaloupka (eds), *Tobacco Control in Developing Countries* (pp. 215–36). New York: Oxford University Press.

Seeger, M.W. (1997). *Ethics and Organizational Communication*. Gresskill, NJ: Hampton Press.

Singh, J.V., D.J. Tucker and A.G. Meinhard (1991). Institutional change and ecological dynamics. In Walter W. Powell and Paul J. DiMaggio (eds), *The New Institutionalism in Organizational Analysis* (pp. 390–422). Chicago, IL: University of Chicago Press.

Stotlar, D. (1992). Sport sponsorship and tobacco: implications and impact of Federal Trade Commission vs. Pinkerton Tobacco Company. *Sport Marketing Quarterly*, 1(1): 13–17.

Strasser, S. (1994, March 14). Where the admen are. *Newsweek*, 123: 39.

Suchman, M.C. (1995). Managing legitimacy: strategic and institutional approaches. *Academy of Management Review*, 20(3): 571–611.

Terreberry, S. (1968). The evolution of organizational environments. *Administrative Science Quarterly*, 12: 590–613.

Watson, J.L. (1997). *Golden Arches East: McDonald's in East Asia*. Stanford, CA: Stanford University Press.

WHO (2005). Why is tobacco a public health priority? [Online.] www.who.int/tobacco/health_priority/en/print.html (retrieved April 8, 2005).

WHO targets Asian tobacco ads (2002, October). *Environmental Health Perspectives*, 110: 569.

Wilson, M. (1998). Three million tobacco deaths a year in China by middle of next century. [Online.] http://www.ctsu.ox.ac.uk/tobacco/inat.htm (retrieved April 25, 2005).

CHAPTER **7**

Advertising in Indonesia: Balancing an "Asian" Socio-Culture with Economic Growth, Multimedia Convergence and Expanded Consumerism

ANURADHA VENKATESWARAN

Introduction

Technological innovations in the 1990s, particularly in the area of information and communications, have helped transform the world into a giant global marketplace. In the mid-to-late 1990s, multinational corporations (MNCs) in developed countries, such as the United States, faced market saturation, increased competition and declining profit margins within their own geographic boundaries. Consequently, they increasingly looked toward penetrating the rapidly expanding economies in many developing countries. The Asian region, in particular, presents some of the fastest growing economies in the world. In the mid 1990s, the World Bank had projected that Asia would account for more than half of global GNP growth and half of the global trade growth by the end of the decade (Frith, 1996a). Thus, billions of US dollars are being spent on advertising in Asia, targeting a burgeoning middle class and aiming to increase consumerism and build loyalty to multinational brands.

Advertising is a "form of commercial mass communication designed to promote the sale of a product or service, or a message on behalf of an institution, organization, or candidate for political office" (MSN Encarta, 2004). It is worth noting that advertisements serve not just to build and promote brands but also to increase market share by inducing purchase. A major industry since the twentieth century, advertising influences the buying habits of billions of consumers worldwide. Global ad expenditure exceeded $400 billion/annum in 2006 (*Advertising Age*, 2006), dropped significantly in the worldwide recession of 2007–2009, and is projected to recover to over $448 billion in 2010 (Associated Press, 2010). Media studies reveal that the average person in the United States encounters 500–1,000 advertisements in a single day. While proponents of advertising point out important economic and social benefits stemming from stimulated consumer demand (Frith, 1996a), its critics argue that it is often deceptive, encourages an excessively materialistic culture, promotes the consumption of nonessential goods and services, and concentrates power in the hands of large multi- or trans-national corporations (MNCs or TNCs) that possess large economies of scale. Multinational advertisers are held to perpetuate monopolies by driving out smaller, local firms with insufficient capital to accommodate the high cost of advertising. Furthermore, advertising has been accused of furthering the gap between the "haves" and the "have nots" (Frith, 1996a), effectively perpetrating a "consumer divide." Finally, advertising by MNCs is said to have contributed to the creation of a heavily Western influenced popular culture, particularly among easily influenced and status-conscious youth in developing countries in Asia (Frith, 1996a) and elsewhere. In the process, indigenous cultural values are seen as likely to erode.

To what extent the above criticisms of advertising are valid, would depend on the cultural perspective of the country in question. Culture, a complex blend of language, social norms and traditions, values and ethics, and religious and ethnic belief systems, serves to drive the creation of policies and laws, which in turn serve to limit the content and therefore the potential influence of advertisements. Whereas individualistic cultures, such as that found in the United States, stress values that benefit individual/personal goals, collectivistic cultures, as are prevalent in several Asian countries, emphasize values that subordinate personal goals for the sake of preserving group structure and the common good. Thus, in several Asian nation-building states, government, while conscious of the need to promote economic growth and encourage upward social mobility, nevertheless pursues an active strategy of restricting/curbing advertising content to maintain an appropriate balance within a traditional Asian value system.

This chapter assesses the political, social, economic and cultural (including religion, language and ethnicity-based value systems) influence on advertising in the Southeast Asian country of Indonesia. Although unique in its own way, Indonesia shares some similarities *vis-à-vis* advertising with some other Asian countries, due to its being part of the same Asian "regional bloc," harboring a similar state of economic development and economic affiliation (as a member of the Association of Southeast Asian Nations— ASEAN), and, particularly in regards to neighboring Malaysia, exhibiting congruencies on the level of modernization/democratization, as well as cultural similarities associated with natural affinities of religion, ethnicity and language. Indonesia's government is trying to maintain a tenuous equilibrium between maintaining/preserving indigenous cultural values and an Asian democratic system on the one hand, and encouraging economic growth, multi-media convergence and consumerism on the other. This poses some interesting challenges while also providing opportunities for advertisers striving to promote goods/services in response to increasing consumer demand from a growing middle class.

Background

HISTORICAL, GEOGRAPHIC AND ETHNIC BRIEF

Indonesia, the world's largest archipelagic nation state, was colonized by the Dutch in the early seventeenth century, and experienced Japanese occupation from 1942 to 1945. Although Indonesia declared independence following Japan's surrender on August 17, 1945, it took years of negotiations, on-off hostilities and UN mediation before the Netherlands relinquished their hold on Indonesia, formally recognizing Indonesian independence on December 27, 1949. With an area of about 1,904,567 sq. km., Indonesia's border countries are East Timor, Malaysia and Papua New Guinea (World Factbook, CIA—Indonesia, 2010).

Indonesia, the third largest Asian country in population (after China and India), consists of the three major islands of Java, Sumatra and Kalimantan and over 13,500 small and medium-sized islands, and is home to over 200 different ethnic groups (Indonesia Capsule, 2002). Although not an Islamic state, 86 percent of the population is Muslim, 9 percent Christian, and 2 percent each are Buddhist and Hindu. Indonesia's original inhabitants were Malays, which together with the geographical proximity and religious affiliation, accounts for many cultural similarities between the country and neighboring Malaysia. Ethnicity is a huge component in Indonesian diversity and cultural affiliation, with Javanese constituting 41 percent of the population, Sundanese 15 percent, Madurese 3.3 percent and coastal Malays 11 percent. The remainder is comprised of over 200 ethnic tribes. Thus maintaining unity is a prime concern for Indonesia's government—Bahasa Indonesia, for instance, is a manufactured language expressly designed to bring various ethnic groups together.

GOVERNMENT AND POLITICAL BRIEF

Indonesia (capital Jakarta), is a Republic with 30 provinces, two special regions, and one special capital city district. With the implementation of decentralization on January 1, 2001, the 440 districts or regencies became the key administrative units responsible for providing most government services (World Factbook, CIA—Indonesia, 2007). Indonesia's legal system, rooted in Roman-Dutch law, has been modified by indigenous concepts and new criminal procedures and election codes. Since October 20, 2004, the elected chief of state and head of government is President Susilo Bambang Yudhoyono, the first Indonesian president to be directly elected by the people (Arnold, 2005). He took over from Megawati Sukarnoputri, who is credited with bringing stability to Indonesia following the 30-plus years of Sukarno's authoritarian military rule (USAID, 2003). The legislative branch is the unicameral House of Representatives or Dewan Perwakilan Rakyat (DPR) with 550 seats, whose members serve five-year terms. Various political parties include the Functional Groups Party (GOLKAR), the Democrat Party (PD), the Indonesia Democratic Party-Struggle (PDI-P), the Great Indonesia Movement Party (GERINDRA), the National Awakening Party (PKB), the Peoples Conscience Party (HANURA), the Prosperous Justice Party (PKS) and the PPP or United Development Party (World Factbook, CIA—Indonesia 2010).

CHANGING ECONOMIC CLIMATE IN INDONESIA

Historically, natural reserves of timber, tin, gas and precious minerals, and particularly oil, have been the major economic drivers of the country. Indonesia is the only Asian member of OPEC, and in 2004 was ranked seventeenth among world oil producers, sixth in gas production, and the world's largest exporter of liquefied natural gas (US Department of State, 2004). However, declining oil production and a lack of new exploration investment in recent years, has turned Indonesia into a net oil importer (World Factbook CIA—Indonesia, 2007).

Indonesia's market-based economy, like Malaysia's, has government playing a strong role. Some 160-plus state-owned enterprises exist, and government exerts price control on several staple goods such as fuel, rice and electricity (World Factbook CIA—Indonesia, 2007). In the mid 1980s government took steps to eliminate regulatory obstacles to economic activity, particularly in the external and financial sectors, with a view to stimulate growth and employment. Private investment, both foreign and domestic, accelerated. Real progress was made, with annual real GDP growth averaging nearly 7 percent over 1987–97; and Indonesia gained respect as a newly industrializing economy and as an emerging major market. Foreign investment reached a record high of $33.8 billion in 1997. However, the Asian financial crisis of 1997 hit Indonesia hard, derailing its economic progress and altering its political and economic landscape, unlike in neighboring Malaysia, which weathered the Asian financial crisis remarkably well thanks to immediate government controls. Consequently, even in 2002, Indonesia's economy had barely recovered to pre-1997 levels (World Factbook CIA—Indonesia, 2007). The official debt burden meanwhile had increased from 27 percent of GDP prior to the Asian financial crisis, to 100 percent of GDP by year-end 2000. Foreign investment approvals fell from pre-1997 levels by 73 percent, to roughly $9.8 billion in 2002, rising only to $13.6 billion in 2003 (World Factbook CIA—Indonesia, 2007). Imports from the United States, in 2003, totaled $2.5 billion, a figure still well below the $4.5 billion in 1997, prior to the Asian crisis (World Factbook CIA—Indonesia, 2007). Additionally, terrorist activities in 2002, particularly the Bali bombings on October 12, adversely affected tourism and related sectors such as transportation and restaurants, leading to a loss of 350,000 jobs in 2003 (Embassy of the United States of America, Jakarta, 2003). On the political front, Indonesia has seen four different presidents since 1997, adding to the instability. In recent years the country has also weathered the loss of East Timor, independence demands from provinces, bloody inter-ethnic and religious conflict, the devastating tsunami of December 2004, and a May 2006 earthquake in central Java that caused over US$3 billion in damages.

Indonesia's economic prowess will depend critically on moving faster to implement legal and judicial reforms. Additionally, re-privatizing the bulk of the country's banks and reforming the banking sector is thought to be crucial for increased commercial lending. Following the trickling down of foreign financing post-1997, there was very little real investment in infrastructure in the early 2000s, which has created bottlenecks, particularly in the area of electric power generation (Country Commercial Guide: Indonesia, 2003). Unlike in neighboring Malaysia, the protection of intellectual property rights in Indonesia is hampered by the inadequate enforcement of laws and regulations (Country Commercial Guide: Indonesia, 2004). Violations range from the piracy of software, audio and video discs, to trademark counterfeiting and patent infringements on drugs. Although President Megawati Sukarnoputri's tenure during 2001–2003 is credited with reducing political instability and strengthening Indonesia's relationship with the International Monetary Fund, even as of 2004 the Indonesian estimated GDP growth of 4.1 percent was judged to be far below the 7 percent level needed to accommodate new job seekers. The unemployment rate had increased from an already high 9 percent in 2004 (Country Commercial Guide: Indonesia, 2004), to an estimated 12.5 percent in 2006 (Table 7.1). Thus, President Susilo Yudhoyono, elected in September 2004, was faced with the need to grow the economy much faster and to produce more jobs. In this he has American support and assistance. America has a vested interest in Indonesia—long regarded as a key country due to its strategic location in the region. USAID has provided developmental assistance to Indonesia since 1950 (USAID, 2003). Following (then) President Bush's initiative of October 12, 2003, such assistance is geared toward advancing the country's effective democratization, de-centralized governance, community-driven development, sector reform and economic stabilization (USAID, 2003).

In recent years, Indonesia's economic outlook has improved noticeably. The Asian Development Bank (ADB) had forecast the Indonesian economy to grow moderately, at about 6–6.5 percent over 2006–2008 (Asian Development Bank, 2005). Per capita income (Table 7.1) had finally reached its pre-1996 peak, and sales of publicly-owned assets, combined with reduced fiscal deficits and relaxed government control over the economy, had finally pushed the ratio of public sector debt to GDP down from a high of 94 percent in 2000 to an estimated 39 percent in 2006 (Lingle, 2007). Under Presidential Decree No. 150/2000, government has established 14 distributed regional "growth zones," in which special tax incentives are available for economic growth fueled by private enterprise. There are also four "growth triangles" involving Indonesia and neighboring ASEAN countries such as Singapore, Thailand, Malaysia and Brunei, and an Australia–Indonesia development area (AIDA). US firms with a strategic alliance with either Indonesian or Australian companies can participate in AIDA projects. All of the above growth nodes offer intra-regional incentives for regional distribution and assembly/manufacturing, which should help alleviate the infrastructure problem (Country Commercial Guide: Indonesia, 2004).

Overall, Indonesia still classifies as one of the lower-middle income countries of the world (World Economic Profiles, 2005, World Bank 2010). However, in terms of purchasing power parity, Indonesia's per capita GDP has risen to US$4,000 in 2009 (Table 7.1). Much of the "higher" purchasing power in recent years is concentrated in the densely populated island of Java, where the country's largest cities, including the capital Jakarta, are situated. This has led to a dichotomy where modern retail structures— shopping malls, hypermarkets, supermarkets and discount stores—are rapidly increasing in the urban areas, however 75 percent of the retail market still comprises traditional street markets and kiosks dispersed in parts of urban areas and in rural Indonesia (Indonesia's rapid retail development, 2006). In 2007, government, trying to ensure that rural areas were not left behind in the country's effort to transform to an informational society, collected Universal Service Obligation (USO) funds from telephone operators, to develop telephone access for 40,000 villages that had no telephone connectivity (Goswami, 2007). This is important since only 52 percent of the population lives in urban areas and 16.7 percent overall still live in poverty (World Bank, 2010; World Economic Profiles— Indonesia, 2005; World Factbook CIA—Indonesia, 2007).

Table 7.1   Select demographic and economic data for Indonesia

Population, July 2009 est.	229,964,723
Population growth rate (2009 est.)	1.1%
Population 0–14 years (2010 est.)	28.1% (male 34.3 million, female 33.2 million)
Population 15–64 years (2010 est.)	66% (male 79.5 million, female 78.9 million)
Population 65 years and over (2010 est.)	6% (male 6.3 million, female 7.9 million)
Literacy (age 15 and over who can read and write)	90.4%
Ethnic groups (2000 Census)	Javanese 41% Sundanese 15% Madurese 3.3% coastal Malays 11% other or unspecified 29.9% (approx.)
Main religions (2000 Census)	Muslim 86% Protestant 6% Roman Catholic 3% Hindu 2% Buddhist 2%
Languages	Bahasa Indonesia (official, modified form of Malay) English Dutch Various dialects—popular Javanese
GDP (PPP), 2009 est.	$960 billion (US 2009 dollars)
GDP (official exchange rate) (2009 est.)	$539.4 billion (US)
GDP—real growth rate (2009 est.)	4.5%
GDP per capita (PPP)	$4,000 (2009 est.)
GDP composition by sector (2009 est.)	agriculture 15.3% industry 47.6% services 37.1%
Investment (gross fixed)	31.1% of GDP (2009 est.)
Distribution of family income (Gini Index)	34.8 (2006)
Inflation rate (consumer prices)	13.2% (2006 est.); 4.8% (2009 est.)
Labor force	113.7 million (2009 est.)
Unemployment rate	8.1% (2009 est.)
Public sector debt	39.0% of GDP (2006 est.)*

Source: World Factbook CIA—Indonesia (2007 and 2010); and *Lingle (2007).

DEMOGRAPHICS AND GROWTH OF CONSUMERISM IN INDONESIA

Indonesia's population ranks fourth in the world, and the country is home to a growing middle class. The Indonesian middle class, estimated at about 21 million people in 2000 (World Bank Development Indicators, 2002) is projected to grow by more than 60 million in the coming decade (Deutsch, 2010). This creates very attractive global growth prospects for American MNCs. A crucial assumption about Indonesia's (and other Asian countries') spending potential is that along with anticipated good economic growth prospects, the distribution of income will also expand, thus expanding the middle class (World Bank, 2005). A growing middle class is associated with an increased level of disposable and discretionary income, typically resulting in increased expenditures on consumable goods and household durable goods such as food, water, petrol, electricity, TVs, telephones, cell phones, computers, refrigerators and automobiles.

Segmentation studies carried out in 2002 by Taylor Nelson Sofres revealed that the Indonesian market can be meaningfully segmented (Lindgren, 2002) into five consuming groups, ranging from the "A" households with monthly expenditures over Rp. 1,500,000, to "E" households characterized by monthly expenditures of less than Rp. 300,000. Marketers are particularly interested in the top three, or "ABC" categories. The relative percentages of these segments, along with their penetration by select major consumer product categories, for the capital Jakarta, is shown in Tables 7.2a and 7.2b. The largest proportion (43 percent) of households in Jakarta is classified as "C," with monthly household expenditures in the range Rp. 500,000 to 1,000,000. There are also significant numbers (14 percent each) of A and B households with sizeable consumption of products ranging from cars to washing machines to mobile phones and computers (Lindgren, 2002). A subsequent study by ACNielsen in 2004 revealed that the number of "A" consumers had increased to 15 percent of the population, or about 12 million people—four times the entire population of Singapore! Similarly, the percentage of "B" spenders had increased from 14 to 15 percent, and their monthly expenditures had increased from Rp. 1–1.5 million, to Rp. 1.25–1.75 million (Hakim, 2004). Such an expanding middle class is a boon to marketers and to advertising professionals aiming to promote/encourage the consumption of goods and services.

The mobile cellular phones market, in particular, has seen spectacular growth, and in 2009 such phones were owned by 159.25 million Indonesians (World Factbook CIA—Indonesia, 2010), up from 58 million in 2006 (Indonesia's recent regulatory and policy development, 2006) and reflecting a huge increase from the 2003 estimate of 20 million cell phones, or about 8 percent of the total population (Indonesia: mobile communications market, 2004–2007). In 2009 Indonesia had 33.96 million fixed telephone lines in service (World Factbook CIA—Indonesia 2010). By contrast, in 2006 Indonesia only had 6.3 fixed telephone line subscribers per 100 people, or about 15 million lines in total (Indonesia's recent regulatory and policy development, 2006). However, that is considerably higher than 3.9 phones for every 100 people in 2003, which, in turn, is a substantial improvement over the 1990 number of 0.7 telephones per 100 people (MSN Encarta, 2004). Internet penetration has increased from 8 million in 2003 (Indonesia's regulatory update, 2004) to 16 million users in 2006 (World Internet Statistics, 2007), to a projected 30 million users in 2008 (World Internet Statistics, 2007). Overall, therefore, given the optimistic economic outlook, the sheer size of the market, and the large and increasing numbers of purchasing middle class, consumerism is big business in Indonesia. In the

Table 7.2a **Segmentation of Indonesian consumer market by household monthly expenditures, in Jakarta, in 2001–2002**

Segment class	Monthly household expenditure (Rp)	Percentage of households
A	> 1,500,000	14
B	1,000,000–1,500,000	14
C	500,000–1,000,000	43
D	300,000–500,000	20
E	< 300,000	9

Table 7.2b **Penetration (in %) of ABC market segments in Jakarta, in 2002, by select product categories***

Product category	A	B	C
Television	99	99	97
Refrigerator	91	73	47
Telephone	78	55	27
Mobile phone	59	30	11
Washing machine	56	26	9
CD player	35	24	19
Car	35	14	3
Credit card	32	12	4
Personal computer	24	9	4
Air conditioning	19	3	1

Note: *Based on a sample size, n = 1,004.

Sources: Lindgren (2002) and Hakim (2004).

first semester of 2006, sales of consumer goods grew to Rp. 60.1 trillion (around US$6.5 billion), an increase of 10 percent, and were expected to grow by at least 15 percent over 2006 (Haswidi, 2006). In 2005, Indonesia's growth in consumer goods revenues was 18 percent, the second highest among 15 Asian nations. Use of credit cards had increased by 20 percent in the first semester of 2006 (Haswidi, 2006). Citibank, the largest credit card issuer in Indonesia, enjoyed a 40 percent market share in 2006 (Indonesia: Citibank named "Best Credit Card" in inaugural banking loyalty awards, 2006). By 2006, some 15 million Indonesians were qualified for premium cards (Gold or Platinum status).

Growth in advertising correlates positively with growth in consumerism. Indonesia is currently the largest Southeast Asian economy and is projected to be the fastest growing consumer market after India and China (Deutsch, 2010). Thus total advertising (ad) spending increased 26 percent in the first quarter of 2010 (Ad spending rises 26 percent, 2010) as mobile phone operators spent more on promotion amid increasing competition within the telecommunications industry. This growth trend carries over from previous years—in 2002, for instance, Indonesia recorded the second highest growth rate (39 percent) in advertising expenditures in Asia, behind Japan, with total ad spending in TV and print media alone reaching $531 million (ACNielsen, 2002; Moestafa, 2003). This was despite the fact that (as discussed previously) the economy was still struggling in many respects. As will be discussed subsequently, Internet advertising in Indonesia is still nascent, though growing reasonably fast. The aforementioned growth in Internet subscribers, and in the number of cell/mobile phone users over the past decade, has positive implications for the future of Internet advertising and mobile advertising in Indonesia.

Advertising in Indonesia

THE CULTURAL CONTEXT OF ADVERTISING

Discussions of differences among cultures at a national level are usually grounded in the four/five dimensions postulated by Hofstede—femininity vs. masculinity, power distance, collectivism vs. individualism, uncertainty avoidance, and long-term versus short-term orientation or Confucian dynamism (Hofstede, 1991; 1997). Hofstede's rankings on these dimensions for select Asian countries is tabulated in Table 7.3, with the rankings for the United States included as a point of reference. In this section, the meaning and significance of these cultural dimensions will be reviewed briefly. In a subsequent section, the implications of these scores for marketing and advertising will be discussed.

Masculine countries are those where there is a clear demarcation in social gender roles—men are perceived as being assertive, tough and focused on material success whereas women are modest, tender, nurturing and supportive (Hofstede, 1997). The "masculine" pole thus reflects a job culture featuring opportunity for high earnings and job advancement, recognition for performance and an adequate level of challenge to foster a sense of personal accomplishment. In contrast, countries and organizations at the feminine end of the spectrum value a good working relationship with direct superior(s), working in cooperation with other people and having job security (Hofstede, 1997). Hofstede's original work on 53 countries/regions located Japan at a masculinity index of 95 (rank 1), with the USA at an index of 62 (rank 15). Indonesia (at 46, rank 30) and Malaysia (at 50, rank 25) are very closely positioned, and reflect more of the "feminine" traits cited.

Power distance is "the extent to which the less powerful members of institutions and organizations within a country expect and accept that power is distributed unequally" (Hofstede, 1997, p. 28). In large power distance countries, due to considerable dependence of subordinates on bosses, organizational power is centered in as few hands as possible. Also, due to a large emotional distance, subordinates are unlikely to approach and contradict their bosses directly. According to Hofstede's study, both Malaysia and Indonesia are characterized by large power distances—Malaysia ranked number 1 out of 53 countries/regions, with Indonesia weighing in at number. 8. By comparison, the United States, ranked 40 out of the 53 regions, has much less of a distance separating superiors

Table 7.3   Hofstede's cultural-dimensions scores for select countries

Country	PDI		IDV		MAS		UAI		LTO	
	index	% Deviation*	index	% Deviation*	index	% Deviation*	index	% Deviation*	index	% Deviation*
China	80	1.27	20	-9.6	66	30.37	30	-16.96	118	69.7
Hong Kong	68	-13.92	25	12.99	57	12.59	29	-19.72	96	38.1
Indonesia	78	-1.27	14	-36.72	46	-9.14	48	32.87	–	–
Malaysia	104	31.65	26	17.51	50	-1.23	36	-0.35	–	–
Philippines	94	18.99	32	44.63	64	26.42	44	21.80	19	-72.7
Singapore	74	-6.33	20	-9.60	48	-5.19	8	-77.85	48	-30.9
Thailand	64	-18.99	20	-9.60	34	-32.84	64	77.16	56	-19.4
Vietnam	70	-11.39	20	-9.60	40	-20.99	30	-16.96	80	15.1
Mean	79		22		51		36		70	
United States	40		91		62		46		29	

Note: **PDI** (power-distance index); **IDV** (individualism index); **MAS** (masculinity index); **UAI** (uncertainty avoidance index); **LTO** (long-term orientation).

Source: Hofstede and Hofstede (2005) and *Willer (2006).

and subordinates. Studies document that Malaysia and Indonesia are still characterized by minimal power of the media, and minimal consumer activism, compared to a country such as the United States, and that mediated communication between government and organizations or consumers reflects a highly unequal status, and a one-way asymmetric flow (Taylor and Kent, 1999; Venkateswaran, 2004; Thomas, 2004).

In individualistic societies such as the United States, individuals are expected to look out for self and immediate family. In collectivistic societies, on the other hand, people belong to, and are expected to be loyal to strong cohesive "ingroups." Furthermore, the degree to which one can differentiate between vertical and horizontal individualism and collectivism in turn affects the nature of communication (one-way or two-way, symmetric or asymmetric), and thus impacts advertising. Hofstede's work (1991; 1997) reveals a large difference along this dimension, between a nation such as the United States with an individualism index value of 91, compared to Malaysia at 26 or Indonesia at 14. These numbers again underscore that in cultures such as Malaysia or Indonesia, collective responsibility, interdependency and accountability are stressed.

A country's culture will also influence the high or low context (Hall, 1976; Hall and Hall, 1990) of communication (advertisement). High-context cultures such as Indonesia, Malaysia or other Asian countries tend to have more restricted code systems, relying more on contextual elements such as the physical, socio-relational or perceptual, than on actual language/words. Within such high-context transactions, participants are acutely aware of their social relationships, particularly status and role, and therefore words are not necessary to convey the meaning of the context. In contrast, in a culture such as the United States (individualistic, low context), the verbal content of the communication is a primary source of information. Thus, for a US multinational corporation engaged in marketing/advertising in a country such as Indonesia, it is important to bear the following (LeBaron, 2003) in mind:

- nonverbal messages and gestures may be as important as what is said;
- status and identity may be communicated nonverbally and require appropriate acknowledgement;
- face-saving and tact may be important, and needs to be balanced with the desire to communicate fully and frankly;
- building a good relationship can contribute to effectiveness over time; and
- indirect routes and creative thinking are important alternatives to problem-solving when blocks are encountered.

Freedom of mass communication via advertisement is also influenced by the level of tolerance for uncertainty and ambiguity within the culture. Uncertainty avoidance— Hofstede's fourth dimension, has been described as the degree to which members of a particular culture feel threatened by uncertain or unknown situations. This manifests as a need for predictability—a need for control through written and unwritten rules. At first sight, it is surprising that both Malaysia and Indonesia feature in Hofstede's uncertainty index as medium to low, at no. 36 and 48, with the United States at no. 46. Hofstede's findings, however, suggest that this dimension of culture has its basis in a desire to uncover the "truth." The search for an absolute "Truth," while very relevant to people of Western nations, may not be a valid indicator to characterize the behavior of "Eastern" nations. Eastern nations, are more inclined to value virtue than truth, and favor a long-term orientation for economic development that emphasizes thrift, perseverance and respect for social obligations (Hofstede and Bond, 1988; Hofstede, 1997). Such cultural leanings, as will be discussed in subsequent sections, are manifested in a strongly negative attitude toward any advertising that promotes heavily Western values, and which conceivably could erode strongly held Asian values and cultural beliefs.

SOCIO-POLITICAL CONTEXT: INDONESIA'S PANCASILA

When the constitution of Indonesia was drafted in 1945, the nation's fundamental beliefs were set forth as five ideological guiding principles, or *Pancasila*: belief in one Supreme God, humanitarianism, nationalism expressed in the unity of Indonesia, consultative democracy and social justice for all Indonesians (US Library of Congress—Indonesia, n.d.). The *Pancasila* thus "promulgates a culturally neutral identity, overarching the vast cultural differences of a heterogeneous, multi-ethnic and multi-religious society" (US Library of Congress—Indonesia, n.d., p. 86), and, as is the case with Malaysia's *Rukunegara*, has been used as an instrument to effect social and political control by the government. Such policies are deemed essential to unify and to hold together Indonesia's multi-racial and multi-religious society. In keeping with the above, media in Indonesia and in neighboring Malaysia (except the Internet) have a long history of government control, and have the responsibility of helping support governmental efforts toward nation building, maintaining racial harmony and national integration, and fostering social stability in tandem with economic growth. Indeed, even the private sector in these countries is expected to cooperate with the government to further the above ideals (Venkateswaran, 2004).

Advertising aims not just to sell products, but also to acquire "cultural capital" by communicating values to the consuming populace (Holden, 2001). Thus, countries like Indonesia and Malaysia, while striving to partake of the economic benefits of globalization, nevertheless view advertising as an "intentional, constructive, social reproductive tool to promote a ... multiethnic, unified, harmonious, consumptive lifestyle" (Holden, 2001, p. 275).

In order to be successful, therefore, advertisers need to understand the country's political infrastructure including government attitudes and media content limitations and restrictions, in the context of the country's culture. Nationwide advertising with a single message is further complicated by the existence of a diverse population featuring various regional groups, each not only with its own language or dialect but also with unique deep-rooted cultural and religious biases and attitudes. Companies particularly need to respect the cultural influence of Islam, women and ethnic identifications in advertisements.

LEGAL AND CULTURAL ADVERTISING RESTRICTIONS AND LIMITATIONS IN MALAYSIA AND INDONESIA

The early history of advertising in Indonesia, is detailed by Anderson (1984). Frith (1996b, p. 263), in a subsequent review of advertising in Indonesia through the mid 1990s, has pointed out that the industry has always "been fraught with tensions." Despite this, advertising expenditures had grown from about $1 million a year prior to President Suharto's New Order (1966), to about $70 million by 1977 (Anderson, 1984; Frith

1996b). As multinationals and (therefore) ad agencies began to proliferate in the early 1970s, the government helped organize the Persatuan Perusahaan Periklanan Indonesia (PPPI)—the Indonesian Association of Advertising Agencies, charged with restoring order to the industry. However, animosity grew between the PPPI, and foreign multinationals as well as Chinese owned agencies. Such anti-foreign sentiments escalated further with the "Malari" demonstrations in 1974, after which the Suharto government clamped down on luxury living as exemplified by the use of foreign products. Advertising began to be viewed as "promoting conspicuous consumption," and all TV commercials for luxury products were banned (Frith, 1996b). Nevertheless, public anti-sentiment towards advertising continued into the 1980s, resulting in a total ban of all TV commercials from the airwaves in 1981. After a decade the ban was finally lifted in 1991, multinationals were welcomed again, and the ad industry began to revive (Frith, 1996b).

Indonesia's Code of Ethics and Practices of Advertising, formulated in 1981, stresses the social responsibilities of advertising and notes that it should be in line with the guiding principles of *Pancasila* and the 1945 constitution (Frith, 1996b). Thus, just as in Malaysia, advertising is required to be in accordance with the policies for national development. Consequently, it comes as no surprise that all advertisements are required to be "truthful, responsible, and not in conflict with current legal regulations; not be offensive or degrade religious faiths, moral ethics, traditions, culture and any race or interest group; and keep with the spirit of healthy competitiveness" (Frith, 1996b, p. 271). Furthermore, encouraging violence, preying on people's superstitions, portraying children in dangerous situations, using doctors/pharmacists/health professionals to promote medicines, use of cigarettes and/or alcohol advertisements to promote consumption of the same, are all restricted per the Code (Frith, 1996b). TV commercials, in particular, must be previewed by the Censor Board of the government, and must earn a Certificate of Approval. Overseas commercials must be approved before telecast. As in Malaysia, foreign models or locations are frowned upon, except for international non-consumer products.

Recognizing the expanded importance of broadcasting as a strategic means of channeling information and forming public opinion in an "information society," Indonesia enacted Broadcast Law No. 32 on December 28, 2002. This law was revolutionary in that it removed government's authority to issue and revoke broadcasting licenses, instead according that power to a new independent body—the Indonesian Broadcasting Commission (KPI). Commenting on the importance of the law (Supplement to statute book of the Republic of Indonesia—number 4252, 2002), PPPI stressed that it was necessary to:

- guarantee that broadcasting protected the freedom of thought and expression while adhering to the principles of justice, democracy and supremacy of law;
- observe all aspects of life in nation and state "without ignoring the important and strategic role of broadcasting as an economic agency, both on national and international scales";
- accord the community at large more social control to participate in the development of national broadcasting—with this in mind an Indonesian Broadcasting Commission (KPI) was simultaneously established and given powers to work with the government to formulate rules and regulations specific to broadcasting issues;

- anticipate the growth of information and communication technologies (ICT) as they relate to broadcasting, in areas such as digital technology, compression, computerization, cable TV, satellite, the Internet and others;
- ensure that broadcasting embodied "quality" and that it reflected "various aspirations of the community to increase their ability to thwart the bad impact of foreign cultural values."

Despite these signs of relaxing government control and modernization, there are disturbing reports that much of this apparent shift toward democratization of the media might be a smoke screen (Freedom up in the air!, 2005; Yamin, 2006). Subsequent regulations, particularly No. 50/2005 effectively demoted the role of the KPI to that of an administrative body, while the actual power to censure and shut down broadcasting in effect reverted back to the government (Alamudi, 2005). Government intrusion reportedly dictated that even changes in internal rules or appointments to the executive board of broadcasters must first be reported to the Ministry of Communications and Information. Yamin (2006) reports that government still controls Indonesian media, citing that weeks before making a politically unpopular decision to raise domestic fuel prices, President Yudhoyono had all TV stations air multiple ads promoting the need to lift oil subsidies for "the good of the country." Additionally, regulations were issued in late 2005, and signed by President Yudhoyono (Regulations nos 49–52/2005) that significantly curtailed foreign broadcasts. For instance, Article 17 (5a) of regulation no. 50/2005 on Private Broadcast Institutions, signed into law on November 16, 2005, stipulates: "Private broadcasting institutions are forbidden to relay regular broadcast programs originating from foreign broadcasting institutions, which include program types: (a) news (b) music programs with improper performances and (c) sports broadcasts which show sadistic acts" (Alamudi, 2005). Media outcry was so intense, however, that government postponed the implementation of these new regulations for two months, until February 6, 2006 (Public service broadcasting regulations, 2006). An appeal of the foreign news ban and a push for unambiguous regulation by the KPI was subsequently drafted and submitted to the Indonesian Supreme Court on May 11.

On April 20, 2000, the Indonesian Consumer Protection Law (Law No. 8 of 1999 on Consumer Protection) became effective. This law specifically lays out the rights and obligations for both consumers and businesses. Of special concern to advertisers is the following:

> ... the right of the consumer to "obtain accurate, clear and honest information on goods and/ or services. This means that advertisements must give true and correct information on the products" ...

The law specifies how business players can advertise or promote their products to the consumers, vis-à-vis misleading information, including a provision that an advertising agency can also be held accountable if an advertisement is deemed to be misleading (E-commerce Legal Guide: Indonesia, 2001). Additionally, gambling and soliciting gambling is strictly illegal in Indonesia, and is treated as a criminal offense. Thus, for instance, the use of gambling advertisements (banner or pop-up ads) on the Internet that target Indonesians is criminally punishable even if the gambling is carried out overseas (E-commerce Legal Guide: Indonesia, 2001).

From the above discussion, it appears as though the basic dilemma confronting Indonesia (identical to that faced by neighboring Malaysia) is how to participate in the expanding economic benefits and consumerism stemming from globalization, while simultaneously disassociating from the influx of perceived negative "Western" cultural influences (Venkateswaran, 2004).

MEDIA AND THE ADVERTISING INDUSTRY IN INDONESIA

Media in Indonesia, as in other countries, includes newspapers, magazines, a variety of other smaller-scale regular and casual publications, television, satellite, radio, cinema, posters and billboards, video vehicles including VCs and DVDs and the World Wide Web, and related technologies (Venkateswaran, 2004).

The period 2000–2006

Considered one of the most promising media markets in terms of growth potential, advertising expenditures in Indonesia at the turn of the century were growing at a rate 2.5 percent faster than the rate of growth of the country's GDP (Zenith Optimedia, 2002). The Adex/GDP ratio for Indonesia, in the early 2000s, was about 0.7 percent (Francis, 2002). According to Nielsen Media Research (January 2007, 2006), corporate expenditures on advertising in 2006 were around Rp. 28 trillion, representing a 17 percent increase over the Rp. 23 trillion (US$2.4 billion) figure in 2005. The 2005 figure, in turn represented a 5 percent increase over that in 2004 (Abe, 2006). The top ten advertisers in 2005, courtesy Nielsen Media Research, are tabulated in Table 7.4, along with their spending in US dollars.

Table 7.4 Top ten advertisers in Indonesia in 2005 and 2004 by Nielsen Media Research

Advertiser	2005 ($)	2004 ($)	% CHG
Unilever	157.9	155.4	1.7
Metro TV	47.3	45.6	3.7
Rajawali Citra Televisi	43.8	33.0	32.6
Televisi Pendidikan Indonesia	37.5	35.2	6.7
Global TV	36.5	4.1	782.8
Surya Citra Televisi	34.5	39.9	-13.3
Wings Corp.	33.6	38.1	-11.7
Indosiar Visual Mandiri	33.6	34.9	-3.7
Cakrawala Andalas Televisi	30.7	32.2	-4.8
Duta Visual Nusantara TV7	28.6	25.5	11.8

Note: Figures are US dollars in millions, discounted by *Advertising Age*.

Source: *Advertising Age* (2006).

Zenith Optimedia's figures for 2001, for the breakdown of advertising expenditures by media, featured TV at 59.8 percent, newspapers at 28.5 percent, magazines at 6.1 percent, radio at 3.5 percent and others (cinema, outdoor etc.) at 2.0 percent. Unlike in Malaysia where newspapers command almost 60 percent of the advertising revenues, it is the television sub-sector that boasts the largest share of advertising and the best future prospects for growth in Indonesia (Zenith Optimedia, 2002). In 2006, TV held strong at 68 percent of total adspend, with newspapers accounting for 27 percent, and magazines 5 percent of the total (Krismantari, 2006). Daily reach for TV weighed in at almost 70 percent (Djalal and Reen, 2003), compared to about 28 percent for newspapers (Zenith Optimedia, 2002). Indonesia's main government-owned station, TVRI (Yayasan Televisi Republik Indonesia), was founded in 1962, and the first private commercial TV station, RCTI (Rajawali Citra Televisi Indonesia), aired in 1989 (MSN Encarta, 2004). The number of TV households in 2001 was 30 million, and the penetration rate was 61 percent. However, cable and pay TV penetration were still extremely low at the time (ACNielsen, 2002). The top five commercial TV channels in 2001 were TPI, ANTEVE, Indosiar, SCTV and RCTI, with viewership shares of 14 percent, 4 percent, 28 percent, 24 percent and 26 percent, respectively (ACNielsen, 2002). As of 2006, the Indonesian TV sector had grown to include one public TV station, 10 national private TV stations, 70 local private TV stations, and two major cable providers. Potential viewership is now upward of 160 million people. At year end 2006, Indonesia was getting set to switch from analog technology to digital broadcasting (CNET Asia, 2006). Digital cable pay TV service via fiber optic cable is also available in certain regions, and digital satellite pay TV transmission (DVB-S) is available throughout Indonesia (Media of Indonesia, 2006).

Not surprisingly, given the stringent constraints on what the media could cover in previous years, the main focus for all private TV and radio has been entertainment (Muted voices, 1996). However, each of the top private channels is aimed at a specific target market segment. Rajawali Citra Televisi (RCTV) and Surya Citra Televisis (SCTV) target the middle and upper middle classes with a mix of foreign films, American programs, sports and Indonesian *sinetrons* (dramas). Televisi Pendidikan Indonesia (TPI), which had initially focused on education, acquired the nickname *Televisi Pembantu Indonesia* (Indonesia Maids' Television), owing to the rising popularity of its Latin American soap operas with domestic workers. ANTEVE targeted youth and the sports-minded public, and Indosiar aimed its programming at the affluent Chinese market (Muted voices, 1996). In 2001, total TV ad spending was about Rp. 10,000 billion, and the top five categories advertised were toiletries and cosmetics, beverages, food, pharmaceuticals and household products/supplies (Muted voices, 1996). *Survei Pemilih Indonesia*, a survey on the 2004 election, conducted by The Asia Foundation in collaboration with Charney Research, NY and ACNielsen, Indonesia in June–August 2003, revealed that TV was the medium of choice for educating/informing Indonesians about the 2004 election (Nielsen news: Indonesia, 2004). In 2003, the five most watched channels were: Indosiar (45 percent), RCTI (19 percent), SCTV (12 percent), Trans TV (5 percent) and TVRI (4 percent). The best time to air advertisements was found to be the evening slot from 5 to 9 pm.

Print media in Indonesia relish the country's newly found press freedom after the repressive 32-year regime of Suharto, which ended in 1998. Under Suharto, journalists were censored, publications were banned, and reporters and writers were frequently jailed along with political prisoners (Goodman, 2000). Suharto's successor, B.J. Habibe is credited with lifting repressive restrictions on the press, and introducing the September

1999 (Free) Press Law which replaced the 1966 and 1982 Press Laws, and also created the independent Press Council to help develop press freedom and increase the standards of the national media. This new law resulted in an explosion of publications—Southeast Asian Press Alliance (SEAPA) reckons that by year-end 1999 there were 299 newspapers, 886 tabloids, 491 magazines and 11 bulletins as well as several media-related websites (Goodman, 2000). Problems arose, however, with regards to sustainability, stemming from a lack of quality, professionalism and experience on the part of many journalists. Thus the number of publications had dropped to a more reasonable 700, by mid 2002 (Goodman, 2000; Moestafa, 2003). The World Association of Newspapers (www.wan-press. org) reports that there are about 172 dailies and 425 non-daily newspapers published in Indonesia. Most of Indonesia's large daily newspapers are published in Jakarta, in Bahasa Indonesian. Major newspapers include *Kompas*, *Pos Kota*, *Berita Buana*, *Berita Harian* (pro-government), *Media Indonesia*, *Indonesia Times*, *Tempo*, *Java Post*, *Harian Ekonomi Neraca*, *Bernes*, *Bola*, *Sinar Indonesian Baru*, *Republika* and *Suara Pembaruan* (MSN Encarta, 2004; Country Commercial Guide: Indonesia, 2004, 2005; worldpress.org/newspapers). The leading English daily is *The Jakarta Post* (Frith, 1996b; MSN Encarta, 2004). *Kompas* is the market leader with an average daily readership, measured across nine major cities, of 2.22 million (ACNielsen, 2004). *Tempo* is the leading weekly news magazine. Additionally, the *Asian Wall Street Journal* (English) and the *International Herald Tribune* (English) are popular with the elite. Advertising in local media as well as in newspapers is recommended for introducing new products, particularly in areas of high purchasing power such as Jakarta and West Java (Country Commercial Guide: Indonesia, 2005). In 2001, the proportion of display ads to classified ads was 67 percent to 33 percent (World Association of Newspapers, 2006). Although total ad spend in newspapers trails was well below TV, it is reportedly growing at a faster rate (Krismantari, 2006). The rationale is believed to be the ability of newspaper advertisements to provide more in-depth product information—particularly relevant in inducing purchase of high-tech and/or expensive products. Thus, in 2006, the largest chunk of newspaper advertising was from companies in the communication services and devices area, followed by motorcycle producers. Government restricts advertising space in newspapers to 35 percent of the paper's content (Encyclopedia of the Nations, 2006).

Magazines in Indonesia are a growing medium for advertisers, accounting for 5–6 percent of total advertising expenditures. Magazine advertising was at Rp. 919,000 million in 2003, having grown 27.3 percent over 2002. The 2004 estimate was Rp. 1,081,000 million (Magazine advertising forecasts, 2004/2005). The top ten most visited online magazines are *Nova*, *Femina*, *Hanyawanita*, *Popular*, *Gatra*, *Gadis*, *Tempo*, *Bisnis Indonesia*, *Ayahbunda* and *Inside Indonesia*. Popular business magazines include *JIEF Economic Monthly*, *Warta Economi*, *Bisnis Indonesi*, *SWA* and *Warta Economi*. Popular women's magazines are *Femina*, *Kartini* and *Sarinah*. Islamic news magazines also exist such as *Sabili* (weekly) and *Media dakwah* (weekly) (worldpress.org/newspapers).

Since the fall of Suharto, the biggest change has been in the number of radio stations scattered throughout the huge archipelago, from about 798 in 1998 to 1,500 by 2003 (Djalal and Reen, 2003), to around 1,800 as of 2006 (CNET Asia, 2006). Radio reaches 85 percent of the archipelago, and contributes about 4 percent to the total adspend. In addition to hundreds of local broadcasting stations, most of which are private (www.tvradioworld.com/region2/ins), radio stations include the government operated Radio Republik Indonesia (RRI) which operates six national networks, and shortwave broadcasters including BBC—Indonesian service, Radio Australia—Indonesian service, VOA—Indonesian service and Voice of Indonesia (www.tvradioworld.com/region2/ins). Radio stations are also available as free streaming audio services on the web, the first of which was Indoradio (www.indoradio.net). Since 2006, several radio stations in Jakarta have gone digital, using digital audio broadcasting (DAB) or hybrid HD-radio (Media of Indonesia, 2006). Commercial time on radio has been restricted to a maximum of 25 percent of total airtime (Frith, 1996b). Although sometimes disparaged as a poor man's TV, a 2006 survey by Nielsen Media Research of 1,105 people from the upper income brackets in greater Jakarta and Surabaya revealed that 68 percent listened to the radio. These consumers were found to be avid media consumers, with 53 percent reading tabloids, 43 percent browsing the Internet, and 78 percent reading the newspapers every day (Indonesia: new generation of media consumers emerges, 2006).

The period 2006–2010

Total adex in 2009 reached IDR 48.6 trillion, a 16.5 percent increase from IDR 41.7 trillion in 2008. The three largest sectors in the media industry continue to be TV, newspapers and magazines (including tabloids). TV media still represents the largest adex, relatively stable at 62 percent of the total in 2008 and 2009. However, the adex percentage for newspaper media has increased from 26.9 percent in 2005, to 34.8 percent in 2009. Table 7.5a shows the gross adex for the three largest media segments in Indonesia, for 2006–2010 (projected). Table 7.5b shows the corresponding share of adex over the same period.

In the first half of 2010, the top five advertisement sectors (PEFINDO, 2010) were telecommunications (IDR 2.6 trillion), government and political spending (IDR 1.4 trillion), corporate (IDR 1.1 trillion), cigarette/tobacco (IDR 0.9 trillion), and hair care products (IDR 0.8 trillion). While traditional media have done quite well in recent years, advertising spending in Indonesia is anticipated to move past the confines of traditional and into new arenas such as the Internet, event marketing, trade shows, store promotions, viral marketing and loyalty marketing, in coming years (Amojelar, 2006). A complex market, media fragmentation and increasing numbers of advertisements are forcing advertising professionals to think more strategically, not just about ad content but also about ad placement and alternative media vehicles. Thus a new "twist" has been the emergence of "media specialists." Until recently, ad agencies handled both the creation of ads as well as their placement—thus they charged a commission/fee for the creative job, and another for the media placement service. Nowadays, media specialists (Kasdiono, 2006) can take orders from any advertisers, independent of who actually designed the ads, and receive significant profit margins from the act of "strategic placement." This has given them significant bargaining power compared to the advertising agencies *vis-à-vis* the media (Kasdiono, 2006). Competition among advertising agencies is thus becoming increasingly tougher, and advertising price wars in which advertisers are offered the lowest possible agency fees, are reportedly forcing small advertising companies out of competition. Although capable local advertising agencies like Matari, DM Pratama, Dwi Sapta, Hotline and others retain a significant share of the advertising pie, a large part of the business is shifting toward companies with foreign affiliations (Abe, 2006).

Indonesia's large and widely scattered population represents a viable market for Internet marketing and advertising, and e-commerce. As consumerism and the demand for high-

Table 7.5a   Gross adex for the three largest media segments in Indonesia, 2006–2010, in IDR trillion

Gross adex	2010 (p*)	1st half 2010	2009	2008	2007	2006
TV	37.1	17.0	29.9	26.2	23.1	20.6
Newspaper	20.8	10.0	16.9	13.8	12.0	9.0
Magazine, tabloid and other	2.1	1.5	1.8	1.7	2.6	2.7
Total	60.0	28.5	48.6	41.7	37.7	32.3

Table 7.5b   Share percentage of total adex by segment, 2006–2010

Media share of adex	2010 (p)*	1st half 2010	2009	2008	2007	2006
TV	61.8%	59.6%	61.5%	62.9%	61.2%	63.9%
Newspaper	34.7%	35.1%	34.8%	33.1%	31.9%	27.9%
Magazine, tabloid and other	3.6%	5.3%	3.7%	4.0%	6.9%	8.2%

Note: * = projected value.

Source: AGB Nielsen Media Research; and Media Scene data processed by PEFINDO (2010).

tech and premium products grows, a need for "mass customization" of advertisements is anticipated. In this context, the Internet offers a unique advantage over traditional media—not only is dissemination instantaneous and technologically easy, but the reach is immense, and the message can be customized. In various countries across the world, the Internet is growing faster than any other medium, powered by rapid innovation in types of Internet advertising, as well as advances in measurement and tracking of consumer's responses to advertisements. Worldwide spending on Internet advertising is expected to continue to recover next year, led by expanded Internet marketing and outlays in emerging economies. Zenith Optimedia reports estimated worldwide ad spending of $449.7 billion in 2010, and predicts that web spending will rise from 14 percent of the market in 2010 to 18 percent in 2013, driven by video and social media (Schweizer and Rabil, 2010). The fastest growing Internet markets are the BRIC countries (Brazil, Russia, India and China), with relatively low penetration rates, yet characterized by strong, rapidly growing economies. The Boston Consulting Group added Indonesia to BRIC; i.e., BRIIC because of its population of 243 million coupled with its proportion of mobile phone users which, at 66 percent, is higher even than China and India (Harrison and Lee, 2010).

In regards to the extent of Internet advertising in Indonesia, it is important to keep in mind that this is limited by Internet connectivity (PC ownership/shared Internet access), as well as download speeds (dial-up using telephone lines vs. broadband/high speed). At the start of 2001, Internet penetration (Boerhanoeddin, 2000) in Indonesia was estimated as 0.4 percent, compared to Malaysia's 4.8 percent, and Singapore's 19.6 percent. Stated reasons for the low penetration were the reported lack of fiber optic infrastructure, a lack of phone lines and PC connectivity, and culture, habits and privacy concerns (Boerhanoeddin, 2000). However, since then the Internet has rapidly become a vital need in big cities, and Internet cafés are filled to capacity (Boerhanoeddin, 2000). In 2005, Indonesia was ranked 14th worldwide (World Internet Statistics, 2007) on the basis of total number of Internet users—16 million (compared to Malaysia's 11.0 million and Singapore's 2.4 million). This number has since increased to around 30 million in 2008 (World Factbook CIA—Indonesia, 2010) While this appears very impressive, one must keep in mind that the population of Indonesia is much higher than that of these countries—thus a higher number of users does not translate to a higher Internet penetration. Nevertheless, a higher number of users implies that a higher number are exposed to advertisements. Regardless, the Admax Network, a digital advertising network for sites in Southeast Asia, reports Indonesian online ad spending to be rather low, accounting for only 0.14 percent of the total adex, in 2009. By contrast, in Europe the online ad spending represented 12 percent of the total in 2009 (Indonesia Internet advertising, 2009).

APPLYING THE CULTURAL CONTEXT TO ADVERTISING CONTENT IN INDONESIA

Historically, in a collectivistic society such as Indonesia, the extended family format has been a way of life. In such an environment involving continuous social contact, harmonious co-existence is a key virtue that then extends to spheres beyond the family. Thus the word "no" is seldom used as it is seen as confrontational. Furthermore, the pronoun "I" is seen as too individualistic, and is frequently dropped from sentences in collectivistic societies. For instance, when using the Bahasa Indonesian language, the word "Saya" ("I" in English) is often dropped (Willer, 2006, p. 52). Tag lines in advertising campaigns in individualistic countries often refer to the individualistic self, for instance, "Designed for the individual" (Mitsubishi, UK) or "Go your own way" (Ford Probe), or "Mein Magnum und Ich"—which translates to "My Magnum and I" (Germany), referring to the Magnum brand of ice cream. In contrast, examples of good taglines in collectivistic countries are "Prospering together" (Chiyoda Bank) or Phillips Electronic's "Together we make your life better"—rendered in the country's local language (Willer, 2006, p. 54).

Unlike in an individualistic society such as the United States, the need to communicate verbally in order to confirm one's relationship to another is not necessary. Thus many advertisements are high-context ones in which the physical environment and the nature of the participants conveys the necessary message—a written, coded, explicit part is redundant. For instance, in advertisements (as in Indonesian society in general), the manner of speaking perceptibly shifts in register according to the age, gender and relative social position of the participants in the conversation, conveying the necessary social context (Willer, 2006, p. 45). When language is used in Indonesian commercials, it needs to be controlled. The higher the status of the product advertised, the lower and flatter is the preferred tone. A cool and self-possessed demeanor is admired in contrast to loud, over the top behavior, or the use of extravagant gestures. Thus, advertising statements are often read out in a monotonic fashion, particularly when promoting high-status or prestige products, since shouting is associated with loss of "face" (Willer,

2006, pp. 72, 73). Particularly when dealing with technical products, Indonesians need more rational reasons (neutral orientation) to purchase compared with Malaysians, but fewer rational reasons than the Chinese; and advertisements for such products should emphasize specific features and qualities, product benefits and guarantees, while being read in a relatively neutral, low emotive language. In contrast, during emotionally charged times such as Ramadan (Muslim holy period), companies come up with special advertisements that are much more emotionally charged and affective, with moving cultural and religious gestures and symbols (Willer, 2006, p. 74).

It has been observed in collectivistic societies, that corporate brands are favored over product brands (de Mooij 2005, p. 64; cited in Willer, 2006, p. 50). Since trust and relationships are very important in Indonesia, it is postulated to be easier to build a relationship between a company and its consumers, than to build a relationship between a company's "brand" and consumers. Trust and quality are reflected in the company or its logo, rather than in the individual product/brand name. For example, Unilever's campaign for Sunsilk shampoo in Indonesia clearly exhibits the Unilever name, unlike in other European countries where the Unilever logo in Sunsilk campaigns is not shown (Willer, 2006, p. 50). This is also reflected in the case of advertorials, or newspaper articles about the company, where the "client" is often not named.

Another cultural aspect reflected in advertisements in collectivistic societies is sharing of meals in a group setting, as opposed to the depiction of people eating alone in individualistic societies where privacy is cherished and respected. Thus visuals in advertisements for McDonald's, Indonesia never show people eating alone but rather in the company of family and friends (Willer, 2006, p. 53). A Leo Burnett McDonald's commercial in the mid 1990s, aired in Malaysia—also a collectivistic society with similar Asian values—was cited by several agencies as a culturally sensitive, value-promoting example. The ad, which showed children enjoying a birthday party at McDonalds, emphasized respect to elders, harmony between different races and the importance of family values (Kilburn, 1995). Advertisements in Indonesia showing the Marlboro man as implicitly part of a group, were judged by a group of Indonesian interviewees to be more successful than an advertisement by rival cigarette Camel, that featured a lonely (though ruggedly masculine) Camel man (Willer, 2006, p. 53).

Another interesting facet in many Indonesian advertisements is the necessity to demonstrate clearly the intended use of the product using visual product depictions. Interviews with Indonesians, conducted by Willer (2006, pp. 62, 63), revealed that Indonesians tend to be very creative in using products for a wide range of activities beyond the specific intended use for which the product was designed. Two examples cited were the use of toothpaste to clean teapots, and the use of soap bars to wash hair. Thus advertisers need to be very careful to forestall any misuse of products that could lead to injuries. On the other hand, if an advertiser can creatively come up with multiple uses for a product (or if a product can be designed with multiple uses in mind), this aspect of Indonesian behavior would be a big advantage. This orientation has been dubbed a "diffuse orientation" by Trompenaars and Woolliams (2004, p. 72), as opposed to a "specific orientation." An interesting characteristic associated with such "diffuse" societies is the very effective use of celebrities in advertisements to sell products. Just as a product's use can be "diffuse," a celebrity, even if famous in only one specific field, is believed to be automatically capable of success in various other fields. Yet another facet of advertising to a "diffuse-oriented society" is that the company itself is seen to have "diffuse" responsibilities, i.e., is viewed as being responsible for the personal welfare and problems of its customers, as well as the whole society/community. Thus, such an orientation stresses that the corporation, along with government, is accountable for the economic, social and political development of the country. The latter concept holds equally true in the case of Indonesia's neighbor, Malaysia (Venkateswaran, 2004).

Indonesia is known to be a very status-oriented society (Willer, 2006, pp. 79, 84–7). The status orientation correlates positively with Hofstede's power distance index. Status and prestige in Indonesia stem from seniority in rank, or age (associated with experience), nobility, job titles, gender (male), family names, and ethnic and religious background. These are considered attributes of "being," thus contributing to an "ascribed" status; rather than attributes from "doing," that impart an "achieved" status. Although the aforementioned attributes have been, and continue to be very important to status, in an increasingly materialistic Indonesia, objects such as TVs, cars, mobile phones etc. can impart status to their possessor. Furthermore, Palmer (2004, p. 48, cited in Willer, 2006, p. 84) observes that status is increasingly being associated with Westernization in housing, dress, manners, education, interests and speech. In recent years globalization has resulted in the "mallification" of Jakarta. Malls have become the place where status conscious Jakartans, especially Jakartan youth, visit for the cultural purpose of "*mejeng*"— behaviors that reflect a certain level of consumption such as wearing trendy clothes and meeting with people of the same upwardly mobile social status, in a public space. Thus, in Jakarta, "malling" has also become a symbol of consumption and lifestyle (Ansori, 2009). However, as Willer is quick to point out, this does not mean that the ascribed status of Indonesian society is shifting toward an achievement-based one. He emphasizes that it is "not activity (doing) through which affluence is accomplished, but the symbols and their display which primarily creates status" (Willer, 2006, p. 85). Thus marketing and advertising strategies are being tailored to capitalize on this orientation. To illustrate, in Indonesia, a BMW print advertisement exhibited the tag line "Just in case you refuse using words to tell your success stories," shown alongside a BMW picture. This text seems to imply that mere possession of a BMW confers status/success. In contrast, in Singapore, which is considered to be a much more "achievement-oriented" society, a similar BMW advertisement touted the tagline: "For all the late nights, for all the missed occasions, for all the hard work …"

Lastly (E-commerce Legal Guide: Indonesia, 2001), advertisers should be very careful not to air/print material (including on the Internet, which is classified as a kind of broadcast media) that could be construed as being:

- immoral/offensive to morality;
- offensive to certain ethnic or religious groups in Indonesia; or
- interpretable as containing political messages, particularly left-wing politics.

Summary and Conclusions

Countries such as Indonesia and Malaysia, both regarded as "moderately Islamized polities" (Jones, 1994) and as "restricted and stable semi-democracies" (Leventoglu, 2003), illustrate the dilemma confronting Asian governments aiming for economic modernization. According to economic modernization theory, economic modernization comes hand in hand with political liberalization. Initially, authoritarian rule serves to provide the stability to implement economic growth. However, the by-product of such modernization is typically a materialistic, upwardly-mobile, highly urbanized consuming middle class (Jones, 1994). As discussed in this chapter, Indonesia's middle class is expanding, and consumerism is very much on the rise. As a result, advertising is also rapidly expanding—Nielsen Media Indonesia reported that total advertising spending by just print and TV media alone rose 26 percent, to Rp. 13.02 trillion, in the first quarter of 2010, the highest in first-quarter spending since 2005 (Ad spending rises 26 percent, 2010).

Such an urbanized middle class, subject to forces of globalization and to increased exposure to Western lifestyles and philosophies via advertising and the marketing of Western (multinational) brands, is usually seen as likely to shift the political balance toward liberalization, i.e., to increasing political participation, an end to corruption, increased consumer activism and a freer press (Jones, 1994). Such a lifestyle change also exposes children to a very different atmosphere, one characterized by significant exposure to world pop culture, technological innovation and materialism. Thus along with economic optimism, there is great concern that Indonesian (and other Asian countries') youth are moving away from traditional morals and virtues and increasingly embracing individualism (Willer, 2006, p. 58). It is worth noting that about 28 percent of the population, or about 67.5 million people are in the 0–14 years age group (World Factbook CIA—Indonesia, 2010), with an estimated (by linear extrapolation) additional 16–20 million in the 15–20 age group.

It should come as no surprise then, that government in these Asian countries, while aspiring to the economic opportunities stemming from globalization, has nevertheless been very careful to maintain and re-enforce ideological "Asian values" that emphasize community and conformity rather than tolerance of individualistic interests. Such values are propagated not only via state education programs, and mass media and public relations campaigns, but also through procedures, policies and acts that serve to control and restrict the content of advertising in the country.

As demonstrated by Hofstede, countries such as Indonesia or Malaysia favor a long-term orientation for economic development that emphasizes thrift, perseverance and respect for social obligations (Hofstede and Bond, 1988; Hofstede, 1997). Such cultural leanings, stemming from strongly held socio-political guiding principles—Malaysia's *Rukunegara* and Indonesia's *Pancasila*—are manifested in a strongly negative attitude toward any advertising that promotes heavily Western values, which conceivably could erode strongly held Asian values and cultural beliefs. Thus, in such Asian countries, there is a constant tug-of-war between the inflow of images and information associated with globalization and the resulting economic and technological modernization, and the stated necessity of maintaining socio-cultural integrity.

Whether the rapid onslaught of globalization and technological modernization will transition the country's youth into exhibiting more individualistic behavior, remains to be seen. Whether Internet advertising, which presently is not subject to the same stringent levels of regulation as other media forms, will gradually acclimatize increasing numbers of consumers to more Westernized advertising also remains to be seen. Currently, however, Internet advertising is still in a relatively nascent stage in Indonesia (although growing rapidly), and therefore lacks the power to sway consumer opinion significantly. Furthermore, as has been pointed out with reference to Indonesia (Djalal and Reen, 2003), another interesting trend is beginning to emerge, namely that as the Indonesian media expands in accessibility, content and quality, the need for, and consequently the use of, foreign media appears to be declining somewhat.

At least in the near future, therefore, multinational advertisers in Indonesia will still have to be careful to balance the desire for economic growth and increasing consumerism on the one hand, with the necessity of upholding traditionally held "Asian" socio-cultural principles/beliefs on the other.

References

Abe, B. (2006, March 14). Between competition and creativity in ads industry. *The Jakarta Post.com.* [Online.] (accessed February 1, 2007).

ACNielsen Reports (2002–2005).

Ad spending rises 26% as telecoms ring up even more (2010, April 21). *The Jakarta Post: Business.*

Advertising Age (2006, November 20). 20th Annual Global Marketers.

Alamudi, A. (2005, December 5). Repression of information again. *The Jakarta Post.com: Opinion.* [Online.] (accessed February 16, 2007).

Amojelar, D.G. (2006, July 1). Ad spending to spread beyond trimedia—ACNielsen. *The Manila Times: Business.*

Anderson, M. (1984). *Madison Avenue in Asia: Politics and Transnational Advertising.* Cranbury, NJ: Associated University Press.

Ansori, M.H. (2009). Consumerism and the emergence of a new middle class in globalizing Indonesia. *Explorations*, 9(Spring): 87–97.

Arnold, W. (2005, February 17). Indonesia's president vows to make changes to bring in foreign investment. *The New York Times.*

Asian Development Bank (2005, April 6). Indonesian economy forecast to pick up speed over next three years, despite tsunami.

Associated Press (2010, July 20). Global ad spending 2010 forecast at a glance: a look at global advertising spending by region.

Boerhanoeddin, Z. (2000). E-commerce in Indonesia. *I-net 2000 Proceedings.* Indonesian Satellite Corp.

CNET Asia (2006, November 15). From Bali to a digital world. [Online.] (accessed February 8, 2007).

Country Commercial Guide: Indonesia (2003, 2004, 2005). Chapters 2, 4 and 6. [Online.] http://www.usembassyjakarta.org/ccg (accessed April 5, 2005).

Deutsch, A. (2010, November 18). Indonesia's middle class comes of age. *FinancialTimes.com.* [Online.] http://www.ft.com/cms/s/0/3a7c963a-f335-11df-a4fa-00144feab49a.html (accessed DATE).

Djalal, D. and K. Reen (2003, July 2). Media trends in Indonesia. *USINDO Open Forum.* Washington, DC.

E-commerce Legal Guide: Indonesia (2001). APEC. [Online.] http://www.bakerinfo.com/apec/indoapec_mail.htm (accessed February 8, 2007).

Embassy of the United States of America, Jakarta (2003). *Executive Summary to the Country Commercial Guide.*

Encyclopedia of the Nations (2006). *Indonesia.* Thomson Corporation.

Francis, S. (2002, May 8). Is the Indian advertising industry lagging behind? *agencyfaqs.* [Online.] (accessed December 5, 2005).

Freedom, up in the air! (2005, December 5). Editorial. *The Jakarta Post.com.* [Online.] (accessed February 8, 2007).

Frith, K.T. (1996a). Introduction: Dependence or convergence? In K.T. Frith, *Advertising in Asia: Communication, Culture and Consumption* (pp. 3–10). Ames, IA: Iowa State University Press.

Frith, K.T. (1996b). Advertising in Indonesia: Unity in Diversity. In K.T. Frith, *Advertising in Asia: Communication, Culture and Consumption* (pp. 260–72). Ames, IA: Iowa State University Press.

Goodman, A. (2000, October). Indonesian media suffer growing pains. *UBC Journalism Review,* 3(1).

Goswami, D. (2007, January 26). Evaluating ICT policy in Indonesia: interview with LIRNEasia researcher. [Online.] http://www.lirneasia.net/2007/01 (accessed February 3, 2007).

Hakim, Z.P. (2004, October 14). Number of big spenders increases: ACNielsen. *The Jakarta Post.com.* Business News. [Online.] (accessed February 7, 2007).

Hall, E.T. (1976). *Beyond Culture.* New York: Doubleday.

Hall, E.T. and M.R. Hall (1990). *Understanding Cultural Differences.* Yarmouth, ME: Intercultural Press.

Harrison, C. and M. Lee (2010, September 1). BRICs, Indonesia to double Internet use, report says. *Business Week.*

Haswidi, A. (2006, September 4). Consumer goods sales grew by 10% in first semester: study. www.thejakartapost.com. [Online.] (accessed February 7, 2007).

Hofstede, G.H. (1991, 1997). *Cultures and Organizations: Software of the Mind.* New York: McGraw-Hill.

Hofstede, G.H. and M. Bond (1988). The Confucius connection: from cultural roots to economic growth. *Organizational Dynamics,* 16(4): 4–21.

Hofstede, G. and G.J. Hofstede (2005). *Cultures and Organizations: Software of The Mind.* New York: McGraw Hill.

Holden, T.J.M. (2001). The Malaysian dilemma: advertising's catalytic and cataclysmic role in social development. *Media, Culture and Society,* 23: 275–97.

Indonesia Capsule (2002, June 19). Indonesian Market Capsule Review. www.asiamarketresearch.com. [Online.] (accessed March 9, 2005).

Indonesia: Citibank named "Best Credit Card" in inaugural banking loyalty awards (2006, May 23). [Online]. www.citigroup.com/citigroup/press/2006/data/060523b.htm (accessed February 7, 2007).

Indonesia Internet advertising is predicted to grow by 30% (2009, March 13). Admax Network Press Release.

Indonesia: mobile communications market 2004–2007 (2004, July 22). Asia Pacific Research Group.

Indonesia: new generation of media consumers emerges (2006, April 5). *The Jakarta Post.*

Indonesia's rapid retail development (2006, February). *Elsevier Food International,* 9(1).

Indonesia's recent regulatory and policy developments (2006, October 23–27). APEC Telecommunications and Information Working Group, 34th meeting, Auckland.

Indonesia's regulatory update (2004, March 21–26). Document no. telwg29/PLEN/14. Plenary Agenda Item. APEC Telecommunications and Information Working Group, 29th meeting, Hong Kong, China.

Jones, D.M. (1994). Asia's rising middle class: not a force for change. *National Interest,* 38(Winter): 46–50.

Kasdiono, E.P. (2006, March 14). Trends in ads business. *The Jakarta Post.*

Kilburn, D. (1995, July 17). Malaysia: strict rules relax a little in advertising. *AdWeek: Eastern Edition,* 36(29): 26–8.

Krismantari, I. (2006, December 1). Indonesia: change in strategy boosts newspaper ad sales. *The Jakarta Post.*

LeBaron, Michelle (2003, June). Communication tools for understanding cultural differences. In Guy Burgess and Heidi Burgess (eds), *Beyond Intractability*. Conflict Research Consortium, University of Colorado, Boulder, CO. [Online.] http://www.beyondintractability.org/essay/communication_tools/ (accessed February 13, 2007).

Levontoglu, B. (2003, September 1). *Social Mobility, Middle Class and Political Transitions*. Stony Brook, NY: Stony Brook University.

Lindgren, D. (2002). *Consumer Segmentation Survey: Jakarta and Surabaya, April 2002*. Jakarta: Taylor Nelson Sofres (TNS)—Indonesia.

Lingle, C. (2007, February 4). Restoring Indonesia's economy to a higher growth path: economic outlook. www.thejakartapost.com. [Online.] (accessed February 3, 2007).

Magazine advertising forecasts in Asia Pacific by country (2004/2005). *Media Convergence e-Newsletter*. [Online.] http://www.mediaconv.com/newsletter/issue12/forecast.htm (accessed March 5, 2005).

Media of Indonesia (2006, February 20). *Wikipedia*. [Online.] (accessed December 8, 2006).

Moestafa, B.K. (2003, February 10). Gray days for colourful print media. *The Jakarta Post*.

MSN Encarta (2004). Indonesia.

Muted voices: censorship and the broadcast media in Indonesia (1996, June). *Article 19*. [Online.] www.article19.org/docimages/442.htm (accessed March 9, 2005).

Nielsen Media Research (2000–2006).

Nielsen news: Indonesia (2004, May). Nielsen Media Research. 11th edition.

PEFINDO (2010, July). Media industry: adex breakdown in Indonesia. PT Pemeringkat Efek, Indonesia. [Online.] http://new.pefindo.com/files/201007_id_media.pdf (accessed December 6, 2010).

Public service broadcasting regulations inhibit media freedom in Indonesia (2006, February 2). International Federation of Journalists. [Online.] http://www.ifj.org (accessed February 8, 2007).

Schweizer, K. and S. Rabil (2010, December 6). Internet, emerging markets to lead worldwide advertising growth next year. www.bloomberg.com. [Online.] (accessed December 7, 2010).

Supplement to statute book of the Republic of Indonesia—number 4252 (2002). *Elucidation of Law No. 32/2002 on Broadcasting*. Jakarta: Perusahaan Persatuan Periklanan, Indonesia.

Taylor, M. and M. Kent (1999). Challenging assumptions of international public relations: when government is the most important public. *Public Relations Review*, 25(2): 131–44.

Thomas, A.O. (2004). The media and reforms in Indonesia. In Donn J. Tilson and Emmanuel Alozie (eds), *Toward the Common Good: Perspectives in International Public Relations* (pp. 387–404). Boston, MA: Allyn and Bacon.

Trompenaars, F. and P. Woolliams (2004). *Business Across Cultures* (Culture for Business Series). Chichester: Capstone.

US Department of State (2004, October). *Background Note: Indonesia*. Bureau of East Asian and Pacific Affairs. [Online.] http://www.state.gov/r/pa/ei/bgn/2748.htm (accessed February 22, 2005).

US Library of Congress—Indonesia (n.d.). [Online.] http://countrystudies.us/indonesia/86.htm (accessed January 8, 2006).

USAID (2003). Indonesia: program briefing [Online.] http://www.usaid.gov/locations/asia_near_east/countries/indonesia/indonesia_brief.html (accessed April 24, 2005).

Venkateswaran, A. (2004). The evolving face of public relations in Malaysia. In Donn J. Tilson and Emmanuel Alozie (eds). *Toward the Common Good: Perspectives in International Public Relations* (pp. 405–23). Boston, MA: Allyn and Bacon.

Willer, R.K. (2006, July 19). Dispelling the myth of a global consumer: Indonesian consumer behavior researched by means of an analytical diagram for intercultural marketing with a case study of Sunsilk shampoo for the veiled woman. Dissertation, University of Berlin.

World Association of Newspapers—Indonesia (2006).

World Bank (2002–2005, 2010). Data by country [Online.] http://www.worldbank.org/country/indonesia (accessed December 5, 2005 and December 4, 2010).

World Bank World Development Indicators (2002–2005).

World Economic Profiles (2005).

World Factbook (2004, 2007, 2010). CIA—Indonesia. [Online.] https://www.cia.gov/library/publications/the-world-factbook/geos/id.html (accessed December 13, 2004, February 2, 2007 and December 4, 2010).

World Internet Statistics (2007, January 2). ASEM TFAP. *e-Commerce Statistics*. [Online.] (accessed February 8, 2007).

www.indoradio.net (accessed July 21, 2006).

www.tvradioworld.com/region2/ins (accessed March 9, 2005).

www.universalmccann.org. *Insider's Reports* (June 1, 2006). (accessed February 8, 2007).

www.wan-press.org (accessed February 8, 2007).

www.worldpress.org/newspapers (accessed February 8, 2007).

Yamin, K. (2006, October 31). Half a century of turmoil for Indonesia's media. *Asia Media Forum*. [Online.] http://www.asiamediaforum.org/node/572 (accessed February 5, 2007).

Zenith Optimedia (2001, 2002, 2006, 2008). Global Advertising Expenditure Forecasts. www.zenithoptimedia.com.

Zenith Optimedia (2006, December 12). Global Internet ad spend to grow seven times faster to hit $ 31.3 b in 2007. [Online.] www.metrics2.com/blog/2006/12/05_global_Internet_ad_spend (accessed February 1, 2007).

8 The Dynamics and Entrepreneurship of Advertising in India

TEJ K. BHATIA AND MUKESH BHARGAVA

Introduction

Unchanged for centuries, rural populations constitute the heart of India. Most of India (about 72 percent of the total population) lives in more than half a million (total 627,000) villages and speaks in numerous tongues.

The dispersion phenomenon poses a two-fold challenge for advertisers and mass communicators wishing to reach rural audiences:

- *Geographic dispersion*: rural audiences are scattered over many small villages, many of which are still beyond the reach of conventional media, and rural corporate giants and champions of rural marketing, such as Hindustan Lever (see McDonald 1993/94, p. 47), are struggling to reach them.
- *Linguistic dispersion*: India is a multilingual country with dozens of major languages and hundreds of dialects/varieties.

The question of language and dialect choices together with spatial dispersal makes the task of reaching the rural audience of India an even more daunting one. There are other variables too, such as religion, gender income disparity and social stratification scatter, that can complicate their already nightmarish problem. However, they are not as fundamental and immediate as the issues of geographical and linguistic dispersion. Therefore, the following three focal issues involving Indian media are the most urgent concerns of mass communicators, advertisers and marketers.

1. How do media planners, advertisers and marketers reach the unreachable with the most suitable media to ensure maximal spatial reach?
2. How can they be reached linguistically and effectively?
3. How is global vs. local paradox resolved?

Furthermore, due to the economic forces of globalization and the emergent trend for seeking out new hot markets (called B2-4B—business to 4-billion) among others, rural marketing is gaining new heights in India and the other BRIC (Brazil, Russia, India and

China) nations. While answering the above questions, this chapter examines particularly the marketing, linguistic and advertising aspects of new emerging markets of rural India in the age of globalization.

A central theme of globalization for international companies is how to resolve the paradox of globalization *and* localization (national and regional interests, appeals, affiliations etc.; question 3). In this chapter we focus on these issues in the communication and advertising fields, identified as a critical concern in the past research (Mueller, 1992). The concern has manifested itself in terms of a "standardization" vs. "adaptation" debate in international advertising, media and marketing (see Agrawal, 1995; Onkvisit and Shaw, 1999).

The choice of advertising positioning globally faces a new and unusual challenge. The choice internationally is no longer just communication globally in markets with somewhat similar demographic groups (e.g., urban, teenagers from affluent economic classes). These segments are saturated with the presence of global brands and do not offer opportunities for growth. The challenge in the future is the large and different consumer segments that are just beginning to join the organized markets. This challenge is summarized in phrases such as B2-4B (business to 4-billion), selling to the pre-markets and marketing to the "bottom of the pyramid" (Chomsky and McChesney, 1998; Razin and Sadka, 1999; James, 2001; Kilpatrick, 2001; Prahlad, 2004; Friedman, 2005).

Catering to these segments requires a very different strategy in terms of the marketing structures and programs. The case in point is the innovative programs by Hindustan Lever that involve packaging design changes combined with distribution and advertising communication (Balu, 2001; for other programs such as Pepsi, see Saran, 2004).

The overlap between tapping these segments and improving the quality of lives of the poor generates an interesting group of companies combining business acumen and cause-related efforts. For example, the World Resources Institute lists projects with numerous companies such as Microsoft, Hewlett Packard, Cargill, Bristol Myers Squibb. Other high-profile cases are the Media Lab at M.I.T. (Young, 2001). These investments are not a fad. For the pioneers, the current investment is paying off. Lever's contribution from the less developed markets is already the largest segment in a variety of product lines.

For these programs to succeed, marketers will need to catalog various innovations used to learn and reach these consumers worldwide. These include details about the segments as well as the existing infrastructure. From the perspective of the communication task, an understanding of the unorganized/unregulated media and messages would provide the foundation for developing appropriate strategies in these markets. These would compliment what is known about the organized mass media, some of which are beginning to reach the rural and poor segments around the world.

The aim of this chapter is to examine the three facets—marketing, language and advertising—of new emerging markets of rural India in the age of globalization. The main focus is on "unconventional" media in general and wall advertising in particular. In the process, an attempt has been made to provide a detailed analysis of the communication messages in rural settings painted on walls and other structures. Our logic is that reaching hot rural markets in India particularly poses a formidable challenge to marketers and media experts in view of the linguistically diverse and geographically scattered market. To reach such markets requires innovative solutions. Specifically we attempt to show how globalization and localization (both themes and appeals) get coded in terms of the choice of languages, scripts and linguistic structures in the body of rural advertisements.

Economic, Market and Communicative Environment

The Indian economy is expected to grow at the annual rate of more than 8 percent through 2015 (*The New York Times*, November 7, 2010, p. 8). No wonder that on President Obama's Indian trip in November 2010, the first stop was not the capital city, Delhi, but Mumbai, the economic capital of India. While the population of India is over 1.2 billion people, the income, urbanization and other demographic details are often not used to understand the similarities and differences between these and the Western markets. According to the Census of India 2001, India is the land of villages, with over 627,000 villages and over 72 percent of the population living in rural areas (*India 2004*, p. 15). This is a land of contrasts with many major religions such as Hinduism (dominant), Islam, Christianity, Buddhism, Sikhism and Jainism. There are 24 major languages and many vernaculars.

The linguistic situation and communication networking in India can be represented diagrammatically by a pyramid-type structure, shown in Figure 8.1. Hindi and English are the two national and link languages of India. While Hindi is the language of the masses in the north-western and north-central part of India, English is the pan-Indian language of the educated elite. Thus, English and Hindi represent the peak of the pyramid. Hindi is written in the Devanagari script. "Scheduled" languages (i.e., state languages) are spoken predominantly in their respective states. Hindi, along with English, is the only state

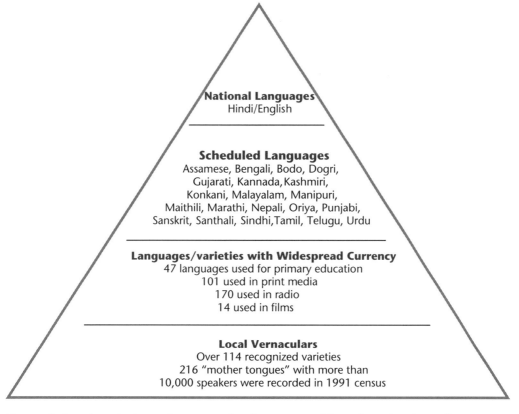

Figure 8.1   Linguistic and communication networking situation in India

language that is spoken in more than one state. Urdu is the official language of the state of Jammu and Kashmir. However, not all "scheduled" languages are spoken in a particular state. Sindhi is not the official language of any Indian state. Kashmiri is spoken in the state of Jammu and Kashmir but the official language of the state is Urdu. Finally, rural dialects (mother tongues or vernaculars) are shown at the base of the pyramid.

A common misperception is to treat the urban–rural divide as the boundary of the market and non-market activities. Thanks to the significant improvement of infrastructure, rural digital connectivity and the distribution of income, the contribution of the rural markets has become a significant part of the overall market. Moreover, the gap between the urban middle class and the rural middle class is narrowing. Table 8.1 further exhibits the growing power of the rural households. This lends further support to the claim that middle-class rural Indians have "higher disposable incomes than urban Indians" (Rao and Natarajan, 1996).

The data shows that the absolute size of the rural market is becoming bigger than that of the urban market. During the period 1989–94, the purchase of color TVs, videocassette recorders (VCRs), and washing machines by rural households increased by 200 percent. In 1993–94, shampoos and nail polishes registered 25 percent and 24 percent of total sales, respectively, in rural areas, a 1 percent jump from 1992–93. The rural markets now constitute more than 70 percent share of durables such as bicycles, radios (portable), and mechanical wristwatches and nondurable/consumable, such as washing cakes (soaps). Rural India is not just any other emerging market. This is a market where marketers can make profits almost instantly. Along with economic gains, the consumption pattern even among the poorest strata is steadily growing. A villager who used to save for special events, such as the marriage of a daughter where pieces of gold or jewelry were bought for the eagerly awaited event, is today looking for a refrigerator, VCR or car.

A travelogue by Mishra (1995) elegantly documents the wealth and changing face of rural and small town India. The transformation is resulting in the homogenization

Table 8.1   Distribution of households between rural and urban areas by income groups

Income class	Rural (in thousands)		Urban (in thousands)		Rural share (%)		Rural share
	1987–88	1993–94	1987–88	1993–94	1987–88	1993–94	% increase
L	67,162	74,736	14,769	15,804	74.18	82.54	+.64
LM	25,173	26,457	13,021	14,228	65.87	65.03	-.87
M	4,207	8,618	3,820	7,345	52.41	53.99	+1.58
UM	718	2,864	1,818	3,378	28.31	45.88	+17.57
H	352	1,622	1,119	2,272	23.93	41.65	+17.72

Note: L = lower income class; below Rs. 20,000 annual per household; LM = lower-middle income class; Rs. 20,001–40, 000 annual per household; M = middle income class; Rs. 40,001–62,000 annual per household; UM = upper-middle income class; Rs. 62,001–86,000 annual per household; H = upper income class; over Rs. 86,000 annual per household; Rs = Rupees (approximately 45 Rupees = $1 US).

Source: Rao and Natarajan (1996, p. 163).

of urban and rural consumption patterns. The prime-time TV programs, which used to give tips about agriculture, are being occupied with urban messages, which are in turn transforming the nature and pattern of consumption in villages. Mishra observed that small towns and villages, which were at one time "inconsequential little dots on the map," are now transformed beyond recognition. The signs of prosperity and growing consumerism and globalization now "threaten to upstage metropolitan India." (See also, Bhatia, 2007 and Ninan, 2007 for expansion of the rural market in India and transformation of advertising in Hindi and other local language magazines.)

The global market has come full circle. With recent economic liberalization, local companies which once feared competition with multinationals for shares of the rural Indian market are now competing for markets in Western countries. A case in point is Indian farm products and equipments companies. Indian companies such as Mahindra and Mahindra are now not only targeting the rural Indian population but have also begun to forge their paths into Western markets. With new-found success from the emerging Indian rural market, they have begun to venture out of India to sell and advertise their tractors and other products in the United States.

It is in this setting that the transformation of the pre-markets to large potential and vibrant markets is taking place. As noted earlier, these markets require a transformation of the elements of the mix as well as the institution and players involved. For example, Hindustan Lever's plan involved a change in the packaging, distribution as well as advertising but capitalized on the well established brand image in the detergent and soap markets. Other examples include the entry of well-known international brands such as Sony, Honda, Gillette among others. These compete actively against some of the national brands for their future.

With 600–700 million potential consumers and the second largest growing economy in Asia, rural India is no longer perceived by global business as an economic basket case. On the contrary, the rural market in India is hot. However, the formidable challenge for marketers and advertisers is how to tap this market which exhibits a remarkably high degree of geographical and linguistic dispersion. The simplest and common solution is to reach rural consumers by means of organized "conventional" media (e.g., TV, radio and print). However, such a solution is too simplistic and is subject to serious limitations for the following five primary reasons: 1) some rural areas are still beyond the reach of the conventional media, particularly television; 2) energy crunch and rampant power failures even in the urban areas; 3) it is rather expensive; 4) a very limited exposure time; and 5) channel surfing. Therefore, in order for advertisers to reach the unreachable, it is imperative for them to find a balance between conventional and non-conventional media modalities. The two main forms of non-conventional advertising are: video van advertising and wall advertising. Pioneered in the late 1980s, video van advertising is called a "miracle medium" by some media experts, and "magic media" by others. Renowned for linguistic innovations, successful reach and impact on rural marketing and advertising, the video van modality has been the subject of national and international media attention (e.g., BBC, CNN and Japan's NHK). (For a detailed treatment of video van advertising, see Bhatia, 2000, pp. 70–80; Bhatia, 2007, pp. 67–74.)

Wall Advertising/Paintings

If one travels from an urban area in India, the urban landscape gives way in favor of green and open farms. Along the railroad track or highways, one will find every standing structure is covered with bright yellow, red, green, pink or white colors, with something written on it. To an uninitiated foreign eye it might appear to be graffiti, but it is in fact a message displayed by some advertiser. What is more remarkable is that even private structures are not spared. The outer wall of a private house or shop might be painted with or without the permission of its owner.

The same scene is repeated over and over again with even more intensity as one goes deeper into the rural heartland of India. In short, wall paintings are a mark of a vibrant economic and social life. Their location is very central in the sense that they are located next to a village shop, highway stop/railway station, or an area where villagers gather or pass daily. While villagers can view these ads at their leisure, this is not true of other outdoor forms of advertising. Furthermore, it is very traditional and economic (costing a couple of dollars) in nature. Wall paintings are a combination of various forms of outdoor media (such as the poster and kiosks) that are common in developed countries. These take on a variety of forms and shapes.

Wall paintings combine the size of posters and kiosks with point-of-purchase displays. The major advantage is the location of the advertisement. Additionally, since a wall advertisement is only replaced if another advertisement covers it, the message has a longer life than a print and broadcast commercial. The disadvantages are that since these are unregulated, the quality of the location and the message cannot be controlled. For our purpose, this is an advantage as it allows us to observe the actual execution of the advertisements as they are displayed in the markets and not what the advertisers would design sitting in their offices. Moreover, given how these are produced and viewed, they will necessarily be used to carry short messages (like other outdoor media).

The only study on the effectiveness of the medium compared this to other outdoor media (Jethwaney and Dyal, 1992). Wall paintings are ranked third in terms of recall, lower than hoarding and kiosk advertising. The study compared the relative impact of advertising campaigns in seven media forms: hoarding, kiosk, wall painting, film, song/dance/drama, print and bus-panel advertising. There is some recent research on the effectiveness of outdoor media (Bhargava, Donthu and Caron, 1994) but the differences in the media, messages and context make the comparison difficult.

Study Sample and Selection

Data for the first phase of this research were part of a larger project on rural advertising (Bhatia 2000 and 2001). The overall study involved detailed visits over five months covering various states in India in 1997. The study collected audio and video data on a variety of commercials. This chapter is based on a sample of over 2,000 wall advertisements collected from villages in three zones in India. From the eastern zone, the villages were located in Bengal; from the Western Zone, in Rajasthan and Maharashtra; and from the Northern Zone, in Uttar Pradesh and Punjab. The advertisements were in six languages: English, Hindi, Urdu, Punjabi, Marathi and Bengali. Some were viewed in photographs, others on videotape. The advertisements covered a variety of products and services as well as social/developmental messages (ideas).

During the second phase (2005–2007), the scope of this wall sample size was further extended by 300 samples drawn from the following two cities from the Western zone: Jaipur, Rajasthan and Ahmedabad, Gujarat. The Ahmedabad sample included the seventh language, Gujarati.

Although this is a large sample, it still remains a convenience sample. With the "population" of the universe an unknown—how many wall advertisements exist in the market place?—it is impossible to claim that a representative sample has been selected. However, this sample size, covering three out of four regions and seven major languages, comprises a fairly representative sample on typological grounds. Therefore, the generalizations drawn may not hold for all the regions and languages in an absolute sense but are representative in a number of ways.

As mentioned earlier, the structure of wall advertising is different from the print advertising in the sense that usually it avoids the body-copy or main-text component of the print ads. This is a natural consequence of wall advertising, which prefers conciseness over elaborate explanation about the properties of the product. This gap is filled by means of providing an evaluative statement about the product. In short, wall advertising comes close to the banner type of advertising witnessed in sports arenas in the West, rather than the elaborate print advertising found in magazines.

Color schemes and the physical properties of a wall are usually exploited (un) consciously and systematically to impose a structure on an ad and distinguish at the same time its different structural properties. Consider, for example, a Dabar ad for hair oil. The ad is in the Hindi language written in the Devanagari script. The attention-getter phrase carries the company's name, Dabar, in a calligraphic style of the Devanagari script. The second structural property, product name, is displayed on the bottle in the left corner. The attention-getter is separated from the display of the product name and the sub-attention getter (second line). The sub attention-getter conveys product attributes (*aanvalaa kesh tail*, amla hair oil) in Hindi. The fourth structural property, slogan, is in Hindi too: *asli poshan baalon ko de nayaa jiivan* (the real nourishment which gives a new life to hair). The repetitive use of two sounds, *l* and *n*, adds a rhythmic character to the slogan which facilitates easy recall. The product in question is local; therefore, the local appeal is created entirely by means of the Hindi language and the Devanagari script. The color scheme is not only utilized to impose a structure on the ad but is also in agreement with the sensory and inter-religious perception of the Indian culture. Interestingly, the artist leaves his/her signature mark on the ad in English immediately following the slogan in the right-most corner.

Analysis and Observations

INFORMATION CONTENT

Wall advertising is overwhelmingly an information-only ad form. Thus, it is neutral and has wider appeal. Only 12.8 percent of the ads analyzed contained additional information. All the advertisements provided the product name. Some ads carried generic product identification, e.g., *davaiiyāā* (medicines), jewelry. All of the ads had product names, 40 percent of the ads were in Hindi, 36 percent were mixed languages, and 24 percent were in English. Only 4.2 percent of the commercial ads provided contact information. Service and social ads were exceptions though, since they displayed contact information very prominently. 2.8 percent of the ads provided details about the information cue, taste, while 1.4 percent made mention of price and assurance. The rank ordering of information cues present in wall advertising of commercial products is given below in descending order of importance (i.e., product name=most important; slogan=least important).

- product name
- company's name
- contact information
- taste or other properties
- price and/or assurance
- invitation to use the product
- slogan

Global Products, Advertising and Ecology

Although the recent samples (2005–2007) did not show any significant shift in terms of structural properties, qualitative and quantitative distribution of information cues, a change was evident in the advertising of product types. The incidence of global products advertised on walls increased dramatically. This led to a remarkable expansion and reinvention of public space for advertising, particularly by beverage industry global giants such as Coca-Cola and Pepsi. For example, in a fierce competition for advertising, Coca-Cola and Pepsi began to invade the ecologically-sensitive Himalayan region with their ads painted on rocks. This resulted in a law suit in which both companies agreed to the punitive damage and promised to clean the rocks.

Globalization: Two Views and Underlying Strategies

It is intriguing to observe that advertisers, either unconsciously or by design, have developed two distinct models of globalization and its relation to localization, which govern their linguistic representational strategies and linguistic choices. These views can be characterized "competitive" and "cooperative." The two divergent views naturally lead to two distinct underlying linguistic representational strategies: the competitive view leads to language segregation, whereas the cooperative view yields language integration. The language segregation is the natural outcome of the perception of globalization and localization as opposites, while the language integration is the consequence of the perceived accommodation between the two.

Past research found that English is found more appropriate to voice the theme of globalization, whereas Hindi (and other regional languages) are found more suitable for national and local themes. (For further details about how different languages—Hindi, Sanskrit, Persian and English—carry different functional loads in Indian advertising, see Bhatia, 1987, p. 31; Bhatia, 1992, p. 201.)

Now let us turn to the question of the pattern of language choice and use to mark globalization and localization in rural advertising. The following two patterns are rendered by the "competition" model of globalization: 1) think global and act global; 2) think local and act local. The following discussion will further illustrate and detail these two patterns found in commercial, social/developmental and service industry ads.

THINK GLOBAL AND ACT GLOBAL

This pattern is carried out by means of English only. Here are some examples:

Domino's Pizza

Castrol

Coca-Cola

Pepsi

Gulf Lubricants (worldwide since 1901)

Kellogg's Frosties: the energy to win

The linguistic composition of such messages is restricted either to product name or the logo in English. The text size rarely goes beyond one word. The script chosen for the product is Roman. The content transmission beyond product name and logo is not deemed necessary. The main perception of advertisers is that villagers will process an English word as a visual image and will retain it as such. In other words, the language use is primarily symbolically and the appeal is exclusively visual in character. Only the commercial products with international product positioning in mind follow this pattern.

THINK LOCAL AND ACT LOCAL

This pattern represents the reversal of the "think global, act global" pattern, as is evident in the following examples:

fenaa saabun
(foam soap)

sonaa biij
(*sona* seeds [pun: golden seeds])

Dabar haajmola—chat pat swaad jhat pat aaraam
(Dabar's Hazmola—spicy taste and quick relief)

The text size in these ads is relatively large. It is three or four times larger than the size of the ads employing the "think global and act global" approach.

Social/Developmental and Service Campaigns

Social developmental and service ads prefer the "think local and act local" approach. They depend upon Hindi or the regional dialects for the transmission of the message. Consider the following three ads.

graamiiN vikaas aur rozgaar kaa vaaydaa
(rural development and the promise of employment)

javaahar rozgaar yojnaa kaa dohraa faaydaa
(the double benefit of the Jawahar Employment Plan)

pancaayatii raaj … jantaa kaa apnaa raaj
(*panchayati* rule … people's self rule)

All three ads are in Hindi. Themes are highly local in character; therefore the natural choice is Hindi and the Devanagari script over English. The rural employment plan is named after the beloved first prime minister of India (Jawahar Lal Nehru). Consider some service industry ads below:

gais chuulhaa, preshar kukkar ripeyar
(gas stove [and] pressure cooker repairs)

minii tiffan sarvis
(mini tiffin service)

The first slogan advertises a repair service. Although all the words except for *chuulhaa* (stove) are from English, they are assimilated into Indian languages and thus are written in local scripts (Devanagari in this case). The second advertises "the hot lunch delivery" service. Taking its cues from the renowned hot lunch delivery service in Bombay, the service announces the lunch delivery service aimed at rural workers in urban areas within the vicinity.

Most of the service ads (including commercial ads) are gender neutral. The only exception is alternative medical ads. These ads are placed by doctors (called "*vaidya*" or "*hakim*"), who practice indigenous medicine.

vaidya ruup kishor raa Thii … strii purush rog, mardaanaa kamzori,
svapan-dosh virya kii kamii viirya-shkraaNu—[sperm]—kii kamii
joRoõ kaa dard [gaThiyaa], safed daag keliye mailē

(meet Vaidaya [Dr] Rup Kishor Rathi for [the treatment of] female, male diseases,
masculine weakness, nocturnal emission, shortage of virility, sperm [count]
shortage, arthritis, [and] white spots)

These ads are overwhelmingly aimed at males, and the topic is male impotence. Such ads are heavily indigenous in content, appeal and approach. Within the monolingual framework of the ad, they sometimes strive for bilingual strategies. Notice the paraphrasing in the concept of low sperm count is paraphrased as *virya kii kamii* (shortage of virility) in colloquial Hindi, then by using more Sanskritized Hindi (*viirya-shkraaNu*—[sperm]—*kii kamii*). This time the Sanskrit word is followed by its English translational equivalent in square brackets. Similarly, arthritis is first mentioned in colloquial Hindi as, *joRõ kaa dard* (pain of the joints) and then in a rural dialectal form as [*gaThiyaa*]. We summarize these themes and the pattern of language use Table 8.2.

Table 8.2 Codification pattern: Globalization and localization

Approach	Ad-type	Language	Script	Structure	Text size
Think global —act global	Commercial	English	Roman	Attention-getter (i.e., product name)	1–4 words
Think local —act local	Product	Hindi/ regional languages	Devanagari/ regional scripts	Attention-getter; slogans; invitation	6–8 words
	Services	Hindi/ regional languages	Devanagari/ regional scripts	Attention-getter; slogans; invitation	8–12 words
	Social/Idea	Hindi/ regional languages	Devanagari/ regional scripts	Attention-getter; slogans; invitation	8–12 words

Globalization and Localization: Bridging the Gap

With the cooperative integrative model in mind, advertisers break the barriers posed by linguistic segregation and attempt to integrate the globalization and localization themes by integrating the participating linguistic systems. This is an optimization strategy which subscribes to the "think and act both global and local at the same time" approach. The following ads are illustrative of glocalization by language and script mixing.

> Whirlpool ... Home Appliance—refrigiators ... washing machines
> (Whirlpool ... Home Appliance—refrigerators ... washing machines)

> Philips ... In service to the service TV ... *saalõ saloõ aap ke saath* ... Radio
> (Philips ... in service to the service ... for years and years with you ... TV [and] Radio)

The Whirlpool ad achieves integration by displaying the first clause—Whirlpool—home appliance in English and elaboration of home appliance in the second clause in Hindi—refrigerator and washing machine. On structural grounds, it imposes a topic–comment type of structure on the ad in which the topic is in English and the comment is in Hindi. A Phillip's Radio and TV ad, on the other hand, displays the company's name with prominent fonts followed by the slogan ("in service to the service") in English with the font size smaller than the font displaying the company's name. In the third line is the picture of a TV on the left and a Radio on the right, with "TV" and "Radio" written in English. Sandwiched between these two images is the Hindi text *saalõ saloõ aap ke saath* (years and years with you).

In short, the glocalization is achieved by mixing two languages and scripts within a single ad. The language and script allocation process is not random. It appears that the onset and termination points prefer English connected by a long, content-sensitive string of Hindi text (Bhatia, 2002). The mixing of different languages and scripts sets the stage for bilingualism, which enables the masses to overcome the problem of content transmission caused by the use of English. Furthermore, the interface of verbal and visual cues further maximizes the degree of bilingualism and, thus, yields the relatively easier grasp of the content of an ad in question. By linking the visual message with the verbal message, the social campaigns overcome the limitations of understanding caused by the low literacy in Hindi in rural India.

Integrating the findings of our analysis, we develop a typology which is indicative of the dynamics of Indian advertising. First, while we use Hindi for this analysis, this can be substituted by the proper language in the context of the research. Second, the typologies of the ads studied were product, services and social/ideas, which can again be modified depending on the research issues. What we observed in the language use was in two dimensions. The first was the integration of the local and English language in a variety of settings for the marketing. This use ranges from the selection of the brand name, the packaging and logo design, to the attention-getter lines and slogans. Some of the hypotheses of the "appropriate" use of the English, the local language (in this case Hindi) and language mixing is summarized in Table 8.3.

Table 8.3   Parameters of content and language choice

Ad type \ Language	English product	Hindi product	Mixed product	Hindi service	Hindi social/ideas
Product Information					
Name	+	+	+	+	+
Wrapper/picture	+	+	+	+	+
Logo	+	+	+	+	+
Company name	+	+	+	+	+
Content	-	+	-	+	+
Contact info.	+	+	+	+	+
Special offer	-	+	-	+	+
Properties					
Packing	+	+	+	-	-
Utility	+	+	+	+	+
Price/value	+	+	+	+	-
Taste	+	+	+	+	-
Quality					
Research	-	+	+	+	+
Assurance	-	+	+	+	+
Safety	-	+	+	+	+
Guarantees	-	+	+	+	-
Evaluation					
Ranking/new	+	+	+	-	-
Endorsement	-	+	+	+	+

In our context, both services and ideas are better communicated in terms of the local language. These categories may provide interesting test cases where the discourse patterns may be different from those observed for the products (and brands). Clearly, in addition to this typology, what are also required are valid measures of effectiveness of the advertisements. With the growing importance of advertising to the rural areas, this would form the next stage for future work.

English and the Marketization of Discourse

English is the single most important linguistic tool for the promotion of globalization of the global discourse. Globalization is penetrating rural India by means of both overt and covert means:

- overtly by product naming, logo, and colors
- covertly by marketization of the rural discourse

With English and the rapid spread of globalization, the scope and intensity of branding of local brands and availability of global brands in India advertising has gained new strength. Consider, for example, the expressions "No 1", "new" or "super." Before the onset of globalization, the concept of being best was expressed by means of a native expression, *avval darzaa* (excellent/first class), but today it is completely replaced either by "No. 1" or the expression, *nambar* (number) *ek* (one) (or by the numeral substitution) even in rural advertising in India. Information about size and models is usually presented in English, although words such *size* and *model* are written in Devanagari characters and demonstrate that a long string of juxtapositioning of nouns is another example of overt global advertising discourse through English. Consider, for example, the following wall ad:

kolgate rakshaa dant manjan
(Colgate teeth protector Manjan)

The emerging trend of "I-generation" themes is rapidly becoming part of Asian societies that are renowned for their preference for a "societal" value system over "individualistic" values. Rural advertising is no exception in this regard. The Hindi collective discourse is being replaced by the individualistic discourse. Observe the following ad in this regard:

meraa parivaar, meraa raashtra, meraa laks anDarwiay evam baniyaan
(my family, my country, my Lux underwear and undershirts)

Notice the order in the first two noun phrases: country comes after family.

Conclusions

In order to overcome the formidable challenge of reaching more than half a million villages through conventional media in rural India, advertisers rely on a complex mix and manipulation of conventional and unconventional media. Non-conventional advertising (particularly wall advertising) represents an integral part of rural as well as urban India in the age of globalization. While conventional advertising methods in the West are losing their punch, marketers are turning to non-traditional methods and media to carry advertising messages (Eisenberg, 2002). The case of wall (outdoor) advertising in India is particularly instructive and is worthy of serious attention.

The analysis of wall advertising reveals that globalization even at the margins favors an integrative view, which we term "glocalization." The best kind of practice of globalization, either at the center/middle or at the margin, should take its cues from glocalization. Advertisers can optimize the strength and appeal of their messages by mixing languages and scripts, rather than by taking a puritan "either–or" approach. Although advertisers are remarkably homogeneous in their choice of English as the language of globalization and in their choice of discourse rendered through English (Bhatia and Ritchie, 2004), rather than creating a black or white piece of work, they prefer to create a mosaic with different languages and scripts (Bhatia 1987 and 1992). This integration is achieved through insightful accommodations of the different linguistic systems in the structure of an advertisement which underscores the entrepreneurship of Indian advertising. The deeper need of glocalization is so compelling that even fierce proponents of the "either–or" approach to globalization sometimes end up using the bridging techniques to undercut its intrinsic limitations.

The safest path to standardization is to standardize logo and product name. The logo does not need to be adapted and the same is true with the product name (unless the product name has negative connotations in the target market). However, the challenge is to stretch the association of the logo with the product name beyond iconic association to the level of linguistic comprehension. Multinational companies that follow the "think global and act global" approach can achieve their goal with more efficiency in this regard if they follow the "bridging" strategies such as those used by Whirlpool in rural India. Thus, they can bypass the localization of brand names (e.g., the translation of brand names in local languages). In rural advertising, even the transliteration of an Indian product name is challenging, let alone the translation of a global product name from English to Indian or other languages. (See Chan, 1990 for Chinese translation of English product names.)

The greatest challenge to standardization comes from those ads that rely more on content, which in turn require the use of a language. Universal themes such as peace, motherhood, etc., with the proper visual mix, reduce language dependency, thus creating more room for standardization. If the standardization has to be carried out within the limits of a content-based ad, integration strategy can yield better results.

References

Agrawal, Madhu (1995). Review of a 40 year debate in international advertising. *International Marketing Review*, 12(1): 26–49.

Balu, Rekha (2001). Strategic innovation: Hindustan Lever. *Fast Company*, 47: 120–36.

Bhargava, Mukesh, N. Donthu and R. Caron (1994). Improving the effectiveness of outdoor advertising: lessons from an analysis of 288 campaigns. *Journal of Advertising Research*, 34 (March/April): 46–55.

Bhatia, Tej K. (1987). English in advertising: multiple mixing and media. *World Englishes*, 6(1): 33–48.

Bhatia, Tej K. (1992). Discourse functions and pragmatics of mixing: advertising across cultures. *World Englishes*, 11(2–3): 195–215.

Bhatia, Tej K. (2000). *Advertising in Rural India: Language, Marketing Communication, and Consumerism*. Tokyo: Tokyo Press.

Bhatia, Tej K. (2001). Language mixing in global advertising. In Edwin Thumboo (ed.), *The Three Circles of English* (pp. 195–215). Singapore: Singapore University Press.

Bhatia, Tej K. (2002). Globalization, localization or glocalization? In Richard Grant and John Short (eds), *Globalization and the Margins* (pp. 53–71). London: Palgrave Macmillan.

Bhatia, Tej K. (2007). *Advertising and Marketing in Rural India*. Delhi: Macmillan.

Bhatia, Tej K. and William C. Ritchie (2004). Bilingualism in global media and advertising. In Tej K. Bhatia and William C. Ritchie (eds), *Handbook of Bilingualism* (pp. 513–46). Oxford: Blackwell.

Chan, Allan K. (1990). Localization in international branding: a preliminary investigation of Chinese names of foreign brands in Hong Kong. *International Journal of Advertising*, 9: 81–91.

Chomsky, Noam and R. McChesney (1998). *Profits over People*. New York: Seven Stories Press.

Eisenberg, Daniel (2002). It's an ad, ad, ad, ad world. *Newsweek*, 38: 41.

Friedman, Thomas L. (2005). *The World is Flat: A Brief History of the Twenty-First Century*. New York: Farrar Straus and Giroux.

India 2004. Complied by the Research, Reference and Training Division. New Delhi: Ministry of Information and Broadcasting, Government of India.

James, Dana (2001, November 5). B2-4B spells profits: billions of Third World buyers are rich opportunity. *Marketing News*, 1: 11–12.

Jethwaney, J. and R. Dyal (1992). *Impact of the Multi-Media Publicity Campaign at Ardh Kumbh Mela 1992: An Analysis*. New Delhi: Indian Institute of Mass Communication.

Kilpatrick, David (2001, February 5). Looking for profits in poverty. *Fortune*, 143(3): 174–6.

McDonald, Hashim (1993/94). Review 200-India. *Far Eastern Economic Review*, December 30, 1993–January 6, 1994, 46–7.

Mishra, Pankaj (1995). *Butter Chicken in Ludhiana: Travels in Small Town India*. New Delhi: Penguin.

Mueller, Barbara (1992). Standardization vs. specialization: an examination of Westernization in Japanese advertising. *Journal of Advertising Research*, 32(1): 15–24.

Ninan, Sevanti (2007). *Headlines from the Heartland*. New Delhi: Sage.

Onkvisit, Sak and John J. Shaw (1999). Standardized international advertising: some research issues and implications. *Journal of Advertising Research*, 39(6): 19–24.

Prahlad, C.K. (2004). *The Fortune at the Bottom of the Pyramid*. Upper Saddle River, NJ: Prentice Hall.

Rao, S.L. and I. Natarajan (1996). *Indian Market Demographics: Consumer Classes*. Delhi: Global Business Press, National Council of Applied Economic Research (NCAER).

Razin, A. and E. Sadka (eds) (1999). *The Economics of Globalization: Policy Perspectives from Public Economics*. Cambridge and New York: Cambridge University Press.

Saran, Rohit (2004, December 13). Call of the countryside. *India Today*, 46–7.

Young, Jeffrey R. (2001, October 12). MIT's media lab, a media darling seeks global role and new missions. *The Chronicle of Higher Education*, A41–3.

9 *Advertising Communication Styles in Eastern Asia*

FEI XUE

Introduction

Eastern Asia (especially China, Japan and South Korea) is one of the most robust advertising markets in the world. Currently, Japan is the largest advertising market in Asia and the second largest advertising market in the world in terms of advertising expenditure ($37.48 million in 2005). China, with a staggering 37 percent growth in 2004 ($18.96 million), has risen from nowhere to rank second in advertising expenditures in Asia and third in the world (Interpublic Group, 2005). Other places in this area, such as South Korea (35 percent growth in 2000) and Hong Kong (20 percent growth in 2000), also show great promise (ACNielsen, 2000). In fact, some predict that by 2006 Asia may overtake Western Europe as the world's second largest advertising region (Interpublic Group, 2005). Therefore, it has become a pressing issue for both marketers and researchers to understand the effective advertising strategies that can be used in this part of the world.

Although many global marketers would prefer to have a consistent advertising campaign across countries, advertising plans are frequently modified to fit in a specific market, sometimes because of legal restrictions but more often because of cultural differences. As Pollay and Gallagher (1990) put it, cultural values are the core of advertising messages, and typical advertisements endorse, glamorize and reinforce cultural values. Many studies have confirmed that advertising works best when it is culturally based (e.g., Mueller, 1994; Taylor, Miracle and Wilson, 1997). Therefore, it is important for advertisers to understand the cultural values in Eastern Asia and their impact on advertising.

Influenced by the values of Confucianism, the countries in Eastern Asia share similar communication styles that are very different from those in Western societies. Through content analysis, many researchers have revealed differences in cultural values conveyed in advertising between the United States and Eastern Asia, representing two hugely different cultures—Western culture and Ancient Eastern culture. For example, Taylor and colleagues (1997) noted that Koreans prefer high-context and less information-oriented ads than Americans do. Cheng and Schweitzer (1996) analyzed 1,105 Chinese and US television commercials and found that Chinese commercials resorted more often to symbolic cultural values, whereas US commercials tended to use both symbolic and utilitarian values.

What is causing the differences? How are the differences influencing the practice of advertising in Eastern Asia? What should global marketers know about the impact of culture on advertising? To help answer these questions, this chapter will summarize the general characteristics of communication styles in Eastern Asia and how they influence advertising messages. First, two major constructs—high/low-context cultures and the individualism/collectivism dimension—that have been frequently used to explain the cultural differences between Western and Eastern societies are briefly discussed. Then, the chapter will look at the differences between Eastern Asia and Western countries (mainly the United States) that have been found in both advertising themes and advertising executions (Cho et al., 1999).

Theoretical Framework

Before we start examining the general characteristics of advertising communications in Eastern Asia, we need to look at the determinant factors underlying cross-cultural differences. A wide variety of constructs have been proposed and used in advertising content analysis to explain the differences in advertising messages across cultures, drawn mostly from the models of Geert Hofstede (1980) and Edward T. Hall (1976), such as power distance, individualism/collectivism, masculinity/femininity, uncertainty avoidance, long-term/short-term orientation, high-context/low-context, etc. Among the most utilized dimensions were high-context/low-context cultures (e.g., Biswas, Olsen and Carlet, 1992; Taylor, Wilson and Miracle, 1994) and the individualism/collectivism dimension (e.g., Han and Shavitt, 1994; Albers-Miller and Gelb, 1996).

HIGH-CONTEXT VS. LOW-CONTEXT CULTURES

"Context" refers to the amount of implicit versus explicit information used in the creation of meaning (Callow and Schiffman, 2002). A continuum scale of cultures with high and low context at either extreme is typically used to represent the extent to which "contexting" occurs in the culture (see Table 9.1; Mueller, 2004). Toward the high end of the continuum are cultures typically found in countries like China, Korea and Japan, and at the low end are cultures typically found in the United States and most Western European countries. Toward the middle are France, Spain, Africa and the Middle Eastern Arab countries (Onkvisit and Shaw, 1993; Zandpour et al., 1992).

The construct of context summarizes how people in a culture relate to one another, especially in their social bonds, responsibility, commitment, social harmony and communication (Kim, Pan and Park, 1998). In high-context cultures intimate human relationships and well-structured social hierarchy and norms serve as a broad context in which human communication takes place. These cultures are intuitive and contemplative. They tend to use indirect and ambiguous messages (Miracle, Chang and Taylor, 1992). The communicators assume a great amount of shared knowledge and views, so that less information is offered explicitly and much more is implicit or communicated in indirect fashions. Therefore, the audience needs to put the messages in appropriate context in order to understand their right meanings. On the other hand, a low-context culture is one in which messages are spelled out as concisely and thoroughly as possible. The mass of the information is vested in the explicit code, that is, in the words, sentences and

Table 9.1   High-context versus low-context cultures

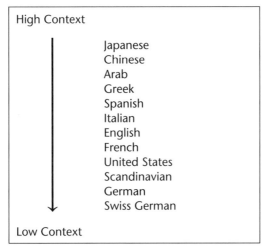

High Context

Japanese
Chinese
Arab
Greek
Spanish
Italian
English
French
United States
Scandinavian
German
Swiss German

Low Context

Source: Mueller (2004).

grammar, so the audience relies less on symbolic interpretations than on explicit cues (Callow and Schiffman, 2002; Hall, 1976; Zandpour et al., 1992).

A group of researchers has confirmed that context could be a predictor of advertising content (e.g., Cho et al., 1999; Lin, 2001). Generally, the advertising in high-context cultures frequently employs indirect information, uses less informational and more visual cues, and stresses depth rather than breadth (Lin, 1993; Roth, 1992; Tai and Pae, 2002). Advertising in low-context cultures is prone to be more informative and stresses breadth rather than depth to meet the need for explicit communication (Lin, 1993; Roth, 1992). In addition, in high-context cultures, people try to avoid direct confrontation to maintain social harmony and intimate bonds among people. Therefore, advertising in high-context cultures uses more of a soft-sell approach and indirect and harmony-seeking appeals, whereas advertising in low-context culture uses more of a hard-sell approach and more direct and confrontational appeals such as price information and comparative advertising (Cutler and Javalgi, 1992; Miracle et al., 1992; Mueller, 1987 and 1994).

INDIVIDUALISM VS. COLLECTIVISM

Sociologists also use the concepts of individualism and collectivism to differentiate cultures. In individualistic cultures, individual uniqueness and self-determination are valued. Collectivistic societies, however, expect individuals to identify with and work well in groups that protect them in exchange for loyalty and compliance (Hofstede, 1980). In other words, individualism represents a social pattern in which loosely linked individuals see themselves as independent of collectives and look after themselves. Collectivism, on the other hand, symbolizes closely linked individuals who see themselves as belonging to one of more collectives and who are inclined to give priority to the goals of the groups before one's own (Earley and Gibson, 1998; Triandis, 1995). Researchers believe that the difference in the individualism/collectivism dimension represents one of the major distinctions between Eastern Asian culture and American culture (e.g., Ho, 1979). Eastern Asian countries, such as China, Japan and South Korea, are typically considered as collectivistic cultures, which consist of historically emphasized family, social interests, and collective actions, and deemphasized personal goals and accomplishments (e.g., Li, 1978; Oh, 1976). The United States, on the other hand, is known for "rugged individualism," the belief that each person is an entity separate from others and the group and, as such, is endowed with natural rights (Spence, 1985). Hsu (1981) described the US way of life as "individual-centeredness," characterized by a greater emphasis on "self-reliance," equality, resentment of class-based distinctions, and rejection of the past. The Chinese way of life, however, is centered on a set of relationships defined by Confucian doctrine, including women's chastity, benevolent fathers and filial sons, submission to authority and ancestor worship.

In relation to advertising strategies, a high value on collectivistic behaviors may lead to a need for companies to develop some type of personal relationship with the audience. For example, Miracle (1987) reported that the goal of advertising in Japan and South Korea is often to make friends with consumers and to encourage them to depend on the seller. Japanese advertisements often follow the sequence described as follows:

1. make friends with the audience;
2. prove that you understand their feelings;
3. show that you are nice;
4. consumers will then want to buy from you because they feel familiar with you and trust you.

The logic behind Western advertising is hugely different. For instance, the audience is often given clear-cut information to show why one brand is preferable to others. Then, if consumers are satisfied with the purchase, they will begin to develop trust in the company and in its products (Taylor et al., 1997).

Previous research has demonstrated that this individualism and collectivism framework has important implications for the content of advertisements. For example, Lin (1993) suggested that, in a collectivist society, it is considered impolite to be direct or "boastful." Within that context, specific comparative or logically-based appeals are often desired in an individualistic culture, but not in a collectivistic culture, to more effectively convey product images. Content analyses of magazine ads suggested that Korean ads tend to use more collectivistic appeals, whereas US ads tend to use more individualistic appeals (Han and Shavitt, 1994). Similar results were found when comparing Japanese ads and US ads (Javalgi, Cutler and Malhotra, 1995).

Advertising Communication in Eastern Asia

With these two theoretical frameworks in mind, now let us look at how advertising communication style in Eastern Asia is different from its Western counterparts. The differences in advertising messages between Eastern Asia and Western countries have been found both in terms of advertising themes and execution. Advertising theme is the content of the message, that is, the "what is communicated." Advertising execution is the creative presentation of the message, or "how the message is communicated" (Cho et al., 1999).

ADVERTISING THEMES

Themes of advertising messages are typically discussed in term of advertising appeals. An advertising appeal is defined as any message designed to motivate the consumer to purchase (Mueller, 1987). Cultural values, norms and characteristics are embedded in advertising appeals, which are used to different degrees in various cultures. It is important to choose appropriate advertising appeals that match consumers' interests, needs and cultural beliefs in order to persuade them. There are several traditional advertising appeals that are commonly used in Eastern Asia and are different from those used in Western cultures.

Group consensus appeal

The emphasis of this advertising appeal is on the individual in relation to others, typically the reference group. The individual is depicted as an integral part of the whole (Mueller, 1987). Just as individualism and modernity are found to represent typical Western cultural values (Frith, 1990; Lin, 1993), collectivism and tradition are typical of Eastern culture (Maynard and Taylor, 1999; Wheeler, Reis and Bond, 1997). Pan and colleagues (1994) noted US culture values the individual personality, whereas traditional Chinese culture weights heavily a person's duties to family, clan and state. Therefore, it is expected to see group values emphasized in Eastern Asian advertising. For example, in a comparative content analysis between US and Korean television commercials, Cho and colleagues (1999) found that US commercials used more individualistic appeals, such as enjoying being unique or being adventurous; while Korean commercials used more collectivistic appeals such as having a conversation with others. Ji and McNeal (2001) reported that Chinese children's commercials were less likely to portray the fun/happiness appeal and adventure appeal, which were related to individualism, than were those in the United States. Almost 45 percent of the US children's ads promoted fun and happiness children can have in their lives, while only 14 percent of the Chinese children's ads conveyed the same message. Similarly, about 17 percent of the US children's ads promoted adventurous behaviors, while in China only a mere 3 percent of the children's ads contained the same message.

Veneration of the elderly and traditional appeal

In this advertising appeal, wisdom of the elderly, as well as the veneration of tradition, is stressed (Mueller, 1987). Older group members are depicted being asked for advice, opinions and recommendations, and historic images are frequently used in the advertisements. Pan and colleagues (1994) noted that US culture places primary faith in rationalism and is oriented toward the future, whereas traditional Chinese culture rests on kinship ties and tradition with a historical orientation. In advertising research, Cheng (1994) indicated that, even though Chinese society is changing, veneration of elderly people remains a typical feature of Chinese culture and a common theme in Chinese advertisements. In a comparative content analysis (Cheng and Schweitzer, 1996), it was found that the dominant values reflected in Chinese commercials were "family," "technology" and "tradition"; whereas the dominant values reflected in the US commercials were "enjoyment," "individualism" and "economy." Zhou and colleagues (2005) also found that there were more visuals regarding veneration of the elderly and tradition in Chinese television commercials than in US commercials. There were more elderly people used as models in Chinese television commercials than in the US commercials for a broad array of products from soap and drink to medicines. A lot of historic images were used in Chinese commercials such as a picture of a famous ancient Chinese character or a historical event or an old Chinese saying.

Status appeal

This advertising appeal emphasizes how the use of a particular product will improve some inherent quality of the user in the eyes of others. Position and rank within the context of the group are stressed (Mueller, 1987). The value of social status is often reflected by a person's material possessions, which are reflective of economic achievements, and economic upward mobility is an important goal for which people are expected to strive in a Confucian society (Wong and Ahubia, 1998). This contrasts with the expression of economic achievement in Western culture, where the display of material wealth is an individual tendency rather than a social expectation. It was found that Japanese ads have a greater tendency to illustrate the importance of social status than do US ads (Mueller, 1987). Cheng and Schweitzer's (1996) study also provided similar results suggesting that advertisements in China were more likely than Western advertisements to use status appeals. This includes words like "success," "power," "boss," or pictures of people with successful careers or abundant material possessions. Such status appeals can also include use of foreign words, phrases, models and foreign celebrity endorsements. In Asian countries, foreign goods have always been related to higher social status. It was found that Chinese consumers generally prefer foreign-sourced, standardized commercials to their localized counterparts (Tai and Pae, 2002). Another survey (Nishina, 1990) showed that about 70 percent of Japanese thought foreign goods were better in design than domestic ones. Table 9.2 summarizes the advertising themes and appeals used in Eastern Asia.

ADVERTISING EXECUTIONS

To convey successfully the messages to the audience, one also has to consider the appropriate techniques to be used in advertising, which calls attention to the importance of specialized advertising executions in a global market. Advertising execution is the creative presentation of the message, or the "how the message is communicated." The use of words, visuals and audios in advertisements varies across cultures. In general, soft-sell advertising is more popular than hard-sell advertising in Eastern Asia. In this approach, mood and atmosphere are conveyed through a beautiful scene or the development of an emotional story or verse. Human emotional sentiments are emphasized over clear-cut, product-related appeals, which is the focus of a hard-sell approach (Mueller, 1987). There are several advertising executions that have been proven effective in Eastern Asia.

Table 9.2   Advertising themes in Eastern Asia

Advertising appeals	Examples
Group consensus appeal	For example, Cho and colleagues (1999) found that US commercials used more individualistic appeals, such as enjoy being unique; where Korean commercials used more collectivistic appeals such as having a conversation with others.
Veneration of the elderly and tradition appeal	For example, Cheng (1994) indicated that veneration of elderly people remains a typical feature of Chinese culture and a common theme in Chinese advertisements. Cheng and Schweitzer (1996) reported that the dominant values reflected in the Chinese commercials are "family," "technology" and "tradition."
Status appeal	For example, Mueller (1987) found that Japanese ads have a greater tendency to illustrate the importance of the social status than do US ads. Cheng and Schweitzer's (1996) study also provided similar results that advertisements in China are more likely than Western advertisements to use status appeals.

Indirect speech style

Eastern Asian countries often display traditional values that reflect a less direct style of speech in the advertisements (Lin, 1993; Mueller, 1994). For example, compared to US commercials, which are prone to pursue "the completeness and perfection of either a rational or an emotional appeal in their product information strategy," Japanese commercials tend to seek "the sophistication of either a physical or emotional embodiment" (Lin and Salwen, 1995, p. 63). Cho and colleagues (1999) found a similar distinction between US and Korean television commercials. In a similar vein, Cheng (1994) suggested that, in China, stressing company reputation and image is a more effective way to persuade consumers than directly demonstrating specific product attributes and quality. This is because the latter approach can be perceived as an "insult" to the consumer's intelligence concerning their abilities to make a sound judgment (DiBenedetto, Tamate and Chandran, 1992). Other indirect speech techniques used in Eastern Asian countries include using shorter messages, using more celebrities to build interpersonal relationships with the consumers and using still graphics (instead of animation) to assure a slower pace, etc. (Lin, 1993).

Information level in advertising

Another variable that has been of particular interest to international advertising researchers is the level of information included in the typical advertisement, such as price, quality, supply, packaging, availability and warranty. Based on the high-context/low-context cultures framework, consumers in high-context cultures are likely to rely more on the contextual elements (e.g., mood and tone) of an ad and less on the explicit claims made. Therefore, they seem likely to react more positively to an ad with low levels of information than to ones with high levels. For example, *the results of a four-country, four-media study* (Keown et al., 1992) *indicated that degrees of information cues in advertising were different between the United States and Eastern Asian countries, including Japan, Korea and China.* Taylor and colleagues (1997) also found that Koreans prefer high-context and less information-oriented ads more than Americans do. Ramaprasad and Hasegawa (1992) noted that the emotional approach was more common than the informational strategy in Japanese television commercials. Advertising in Eastern Asia is more about brand images, not product features.

Comparative advertising

Comparative advertising involves either directly or indirectly naming competitors in an ad and comparing one or more attributes in an advertising medium (Shao, Bao and Gray, 2004). Comparative advertising is commonplace in the United States, but it is not widely used in Eastern Asian countries, where confrontation is avoided and harmony is sought (de Mooij, 1998; Ramaprasad and Hasegawa, 1992). "Boasting" of product quality and "bribing" consumers into submission conflict with the customs of respectful treatment of consumers and a projection of a respectable company image (Lin, 1993). In Zhou, Zhou and Xue's (2005) study, only four out of 200 Chinese TV commercials used indirect comparison between brands. Comparative advertising is not as effective in Eastern Asia as in the United States. It was found that when evaluating direct comparative ads, consumers in low-context communication cultures were more likely to be persuaded than those in high-context cultures (Shao et al., 2004). In a comparison between US and Korean samples, Korean participants reported fewer positive attitudes toward the comparative advertisements and the advertised brands (Choi and Miracle, 2004).

Brand acknowledgement

High-context cultures are intuitive and contemplative and tend to use indirect and ambiguous messages. Low-context cultures are analytical and action-oriented and tend to use clearly articulated and spoken messages. Therefore, one could expect that advertising in high-context cultures will be devoted more to establishing the context before mentioning the brand, company name or product. For instance, it was found that brand names were mentioned later in Chinese television commercials than in US television commercials (Zhou, Zhou and Xue, 2005). Similar results were found in Miracle and colleagues' (1992) study that the company names were mentioned later in Korean television commercials than in US television commercials.

Other techniques

There are some other advertising executions that have been mentioned by researchers but have not yet been widely investigated. For example, DiBenedetto and colleagues (1992) discovered that, when it comes to humor appeals, Japanese are unlikely to use demeaning or slapstick portrayals, relying instead upon earthy, family-based or black-humor appeals. Zhou and colleagues (2005) discussed visual differences between Chinese and US television commercials and reported that Chinese commercials contained less

Table 9.3   Advertising execution in Eastern Asia

Advertising execution	Examples
Indirect speech style	For example, Cheng (1994) suggested that, in China, stressing company reputation and image is a more effective way to transfer the intended "feelings" to consumers than directly demonstrating specific product attributes and quality. Lin (1993) summarized some soft-sell techniques used in Japan such as using shorter messages, using songs to set moods, using female voice, etc.
Information level	For example, Taylor and colleagues (1997) found that Koreans prefer high context and less information-oriented ads more than Americans do. Ramaprasad and Hasegawa (1992) noted that the emotional approach was more common than the informational strategy in Japanese television commercials.
Comparative advertising	For example, Shao and colleagues (2004) suggested that when evaluating direct comparative ads, consumers in low-context communication cultures indicated higher persuasion effect than those in high-context cultures. Choi and Miracle (2004) found Korean participants reported less positive attitude toward the comparative advertisements and the advertised brands than US participants.
Brand acknowledgement	For example, Zhou and colleagues (2005) found that the brand names were mentioned later in Chinese television commercials than in US television commercials. Miracle and colleagues (1992) also reported the similar findings betwen Korean and US television commercials.
Others	For example, DiBenedetto and colleagues (1992) discovered that Japanese are more likely to use earthy, family-based or black-humor appeals. Lin (2001) reported that, compared to Chinese ads, the US ads were more likely to depict products as time-saver.

clear visual story lines and more historical images than US commercials. Lin (2001) reported that the US ads were more likely to depict products as time-savers, while Chinese ads were less likely to use this type of time-oriented advertisements. Table 9.3 summarizes types of advertising execution in Eastern Asia.

Discussion

Eastern Asia has its own unique advertising communication style. It represents a collectivistic and high-context culture. Generally speaking, advertising in Eastern Asian countries emphasizes family values, group consensus, history and traditions. Compared to Western cultures, advertisements in these countries contain less information, use more of a soft-sell approach, and utilize indirect and harmony-seeking appeals. This is something global marketers need to understand. However, with the development of a global economy, there have been many changes regarding the values and lifestyles reflected in advertising.

Globalization enables people to understand and accept different cultures. Today, you can find Western cultures and values in advertising messages in Eastern Asia. They emphasize appeals of individualism and independence, youth and modernity, and product merit, especially when the advertising is targeting young people and using a niche medium such as magazines (e.g., Zhang and Shavitt, 2003). For example, in a comparative content analysis (Cheng and Schweitzer, 1996), it was found that "modernity" and "youth" are common values reflected in advertising in both Chinese and US commercials. Cho and colleagues (1999) also reported in their study that both Korean and US television commercials demonstrated strong present-time orientation.

The impact of new technology on advertising communication in Eastern Asia needs our attention, too. Internet users in Eastern Asia represent 87 percent of Asia's online population, and over 18 percent of the world's total (Ciolek, 2002). There is space to grow considering that only 7.2 percent of the Chinese population is online (Dobson, 2005). The short messaging service (SMS) is also gaining popularity in Eastern Asia. In China, SMS more than tripled from 19 billion messages in 2001 to 60 billion in 2002 and is expected to grow as the number of mobile subscribers in the country climbs to 500 million by 2007 (Normandy and Ali, 2002). Does culture still play a role in this hi-tech advertising communication? How can we understand consumers' responses toward these advertising messages? These are questions that need to be addressed in future studies.

Finally, although we have discussed how most countries and districts in Eastern Asia share similar communication styles, there are differences among them in terms of the degree of economic development, legal systems and political environments. This chapter describes the big picture of the advertising communication in Eastern Asia, but individual research is certainly necessary for questions regarding advertising in specific countries.

References

ACNielsen Research (2000). *Asia Pacific News* [Online.] http://www.acnielsen.com/news/asiapacific/hk/2000/20001016.htm (retrieved March 28, 2006).

Albers-Miller, N.D. and B.D. Gelb (1996). Business advertising appeals as a mirror of cultural dimensions: a study of eleven countries. *Journal of Advertising*, 25(4): 57–70.

Biswas, A., J.E. Olsen and V. Carlet (1992). A comparison of print advertisements from the United States and France. *Journal of Advertising*, 21(4): 73–81.

Callow, M. and L. Schiffman (2002). Implicit meaning in visual print advertisements: a cross-cultural examination of the contextual communication effect. *International Journal of Advertising*, 21: 259–77.

Cheng, H. (1994). Reflection of cultural values: a content analysis of Chinese magazine advertisements from 1982 and 1992. *International Journal of Advertising*, 13: 167–83.

Cheng, H. and J.C. Schweitzer (1996). Cultural values reflected in Chinese and US television commercials. *Journal of Advertising Research*, 36: 27–45.

Cho, B., U. Kwon, J.W. Gentry, S. Jun and F. Kropp (1999). Cultural values reflected in theme and execution: a comparative study of US and Korean television commercials. *Journal of Advertising*, 28(4): 59–73.

Choi, Y.K. and G.E. Miracle (2004). The effectiveness of comparative advertising in Korea and the United States: a cross-cultural and individual-level analysis. *Journal of Advertising*, 33(4): 75–87.

Ciolek, T.M. (2002). Electronic environments of Eastern Asia: a background survey. *Asian Studies Review*, 26: 233–60.

Cutler, B.D. and R.G. Javalgi (1992). A cross-cultural analysis of the visual component of print advertising: the United States and the European community. *Journal of Advertising Research*, 32(1): 71–80.

De Mooij, M. (1998). *Global Marketing and Advertising*. Thousand Oaks, CA: Sage.

DiBenedetto, C.A., M. Tamate and R. Chandran (1992). Developing creative advertising strategy for the Japanese marketplace. *Journal of Advertising Research*, 32(1): 39–48.

Dobson, C. (2005, November 18). China's online world ready for great leap in ad opportunities. *Media Asia*, 17.

Earley, P.C. and C.B. Gibson (1998). Taking stock in our progress on individualism-collectivism: 100 years of solidarity and community. *Journal of Management*, 24: 265–304.

Frith, K.T. (1990). Western advertising and Eastern culture: the confrontation in Southeast Asia. In James H. Leigh and Claude R. Martin, Jr. (eds), *Current Issues and Research in Advertising* (pp. 63–73). Ann Arbor, MI: University of Michigan, Graduate School of Business Division of Research.

Hall, E.T. (1976). *Beyond Culture*. Garden City, NY: Doubleday.

Han, S. and S. Shavitt (1994). Persuasion and culture: advertising appeals in individualistic and collectivistic societies. *Journal of Experimental Social Psychology*, 30: 326–50.

Ho, D. (1979). Psychological implications of collectivism: with special reference to the Chinese case and Maoist dialectics. In L. Eckensberger, W. Lonner and Y. Poortinga (eds), *Crosscultural Contributions to Psychology*. Amsterdam: Swets and Zeitlinger.

Hofstede, G. (1980). *Culture's Consequences*. Beverly Hills, CA: Sage.

Hsu, F.L.K. (1981). *American and Chinese: Passage to Differences*. Honolulu, HI: University of Hawai'i Press.

Interpublic Group (2005). *Spheres of Influences: Global Advertising Expenditure 2005* [Online.] http://www.interpublic.com/read_file.php?did=282 (retrieved March 25, 2006).

Javalgi, R., B.D. Cutler and N.K. Malhotra (1995). Print advertising at the component level: a cross-cultural comparison of United States and Japan, *Journal of Business Research*, 34: 117–24.

Ji, M.F. and J.U. McNeal (2001). How Chinese children's commercials differ from those of the United States: a content analysis. *Journal of Advertising*, 30(3): 79–92.

Keown, C., L.W. Jacobs, R.W. Schmidt and K. Ghymn (1992). Information content of advertising in the United States, Japan, South Korea and the People's Republic of China. *International Journal of Advertising*, 11: 257–67.

Kim, D., A.Y. Pan and H.S. Park (1998). High- versus low-context culture: a comparison of Chinese, Korean and American cultures. *Psychology and Marketing*, 15: 507–21.

Li, D.J. (1978). *The Ageless Chinese*. New York: Scribners.

Lin, C.A. (1993). Cultural differences in message strategies: a comparison between American and Japanese TV commercials. *Journal of Advertising Research*, 33(4): 40–48.

Lin, C.A. (2001). Cultural values reflected in Chinese and American television advertising. *Journal of Advertising*, 30(4): 83–94.

Lin, C.A. and M.B. Salwen (1995). Product information strategies of American and Japanese television advertisements. *International Journal of Advertising*, 14(1): 55–64.

Maynard, M. and C. Taylor (1999). Girlish images across cultures: analyzing Japanese versus US Seventeen magazine ads. *Journal of Advertising*, 28(1): 39–48.

Miracle, G.E. (1987). Feel-do-learn: an alternative sequence underlying Japanese consumer response to television commercials. In F. Feasley (ed.), *Proceedings of the 1987 Conference of the American Academy of Advertising* (pp. 73–8). Columbia, SC: University of South Carolina.

Miracle, G.E., K.Y. Chang and C.R. Taylor (1992). Culture and advertising executions: a comparison of selected characteristics of Korean and US television commercials. *International Marketing Review*, 9(4): 5–17.

Miracle, G.E., C.R. Taylor and K.Y. Chang (1992). Culture and advertising executions: a comparison of selected characteristics of Japanese and US television commercials. *Journal of International Consumer Marketing*, 4: 89–113.

Mueller, B. (1987). Reflections of culture: an analysis of Japanese and American advertising appeals. *Journal of Advertising Research*, June/July, 51–9.

Mueller, B. (1994). Degrees of globalization: an analysis of the standardization of message elements in multinational advertising. In James H. Leigh and Claude R. Martin (eds), *Current Issues in Advertising*, 12 (pp. 119–33). University of Michigan, Division of Research.

Mueller, B. (2004). *Dynamics of International Advertising: Theoretical and Practical Perspectives*. New York: Peter Lang.

Nishina, S. (1990). Japanese consumers: introducing foreign products/brands into the Japanese market. *Journal of Advertising Research*, 30(2): 35–45.

Normandy, M. and Q. Ali (2002). Text messaging ads on fast track in Asia. *Advertising Age*, 73(48): 12.

Oh, T.K. (1976). Theory Y in the People's Republic of China. *California Management Review*, 19: 77–84.

Onkvisit, S. and J.J. Shaw (1993). *International Marketing: Analysis and Strategy*. 2nd ed. New York: Macmillan.

Pan, Z., H.C. Steven, G.C. Chu and Y. Ju (1994). *To See Ourselves: Comparing Traditional Chinese and American Cultural Values*. Boulder, CO: Westview Press.

Pollay, R.W. and K. Gallagher (1990). Advertising and culture values: reflections in the distorted mirror. *International Journal of Advertising*, 9(4): 359–72.

Ramaprasad, J. and K. Hasegawa (1992). Information content of American and Japanese television commercials. *Journalism Quarterly*, 69: 612–22.

Roth, M. (1992). Depth versus breadth strategies for global brand management. *Journal of Advertising*, 21: 25–36.

Shao, A.T., Y. Bao and E. Gray (2004). Comparative advertising effectiveness: a cross-cultural study. *Journal of Current Issues and Research in Advertising*, 26(2): 67–80.

Spence, J.T. (1985). Achievement American style: the rewards and costs of individualism. *American Psychologist*, 40: 1285–95.

Tai, S.H.C. and J.H. Pae (2002). Effects of TV advertising on Chinese consumers: local versus foreign-sourced commercials. *Journal of Marketing Management*, 18(1/2): 49–72.

Taylor, C.R., G.E. Miracle and R.D. Wilson (1997). The impact of information level on the effectiveness of US and Korean television commercials. *Journal of Advertising*, 26(1): 1–18.

Taylor, C.R., R.D. Wilson and G.E. Miracle (1994). The impact of brand differentiating messages on the effectiveness of Korean advertising. *Journal of International Marketing*, 2: 31–52.

Triandis, H.C. (1995). *Individualism and Collectivism*. Boulder, CO: Westview Publications.

Wheeler, L., H.T. Reis and M.H. Bond (1997). Collectivism-individualism in everyday social life: the middle kingdom and the melting pot. In L.A. Peplau and S.E. Taylor (eds), *Sociocultural Perspectives in Social Psychology: Current Readings* (pp. 297–313). Upper Saddle River, NJ: Prentice Hall.

Wong, N.Y. and A.C. Ahubia (1998). Personal taste and family face: luxury consumption in Confucian and Eastern societies. *Psychology and Marketing*, 15(5): 423–41.

Zandpour, F., C. Chang and J. Catalano (1992). Stories, symbols, and straight talk: a comparative analysis of French, Taiwanese, and US TV commercials. *Journal of Advertising Research*, 32: 25–38.

Zhang, J. and S. Shavitt (2003). Cultural values in advertisements to the Chinese X-Generation: promoting modernity and individualism. *Journal of Advertising*, 32(1): 23–33.

Zhou, S., P. Zhou and F. Xue (2005). Visual differences in US and Chinese television commercials. *Journal of Advertising*, 34(1): 111–19.

10 Advertising Practice in Post-Communist Kazakhstan: Improvising on Capitalist Communications

AMOS OWEN THOMAS

Introduction

Advertising is a relatively new industry in Central Asia, dating from the demise of the Soviet Union in the early 1990s. But more than that it symbolizes the radical change of ideology and political economy involved in the transition from communism to capitalism. As the closest country to Russia, both geographically and culturally, Kazakhstan has been a trendsetter within the region and hence the development of its media and advertising industries are worthy of analysis. While the countries in Central Asia might now be politically independent, there is still considerable economic and cultural dependence on Russia and other former Soviet states and dependencies. The advertising industry in Kazakhstan is no exception, taking its cue from Russia- and Ukraine-based counterparts, often affiliates of transnational advertising agencies and multinational marketers themselves. Within Kazakhstan, despite rapid growth of commercial media, advertising agencies face a virtual cartel of media ownership by the political elite. These are some of the challenges facing the practice of advertising in this emergent free-market economy, the improvisations on which need to be analyzed for their pertinence to other transitional, developing and emergent economies.

Concise Chronology

PAST GEOPOLITICS

Geographically the region of Central Asia is roughly demarcated by the Caspian Sea in the west, Iran and Afghanistan in the south, Russia in the north and China in the east. From the early eighteenth century the Russian Empire had extended its control over the

Asia steppes, then used by the largely nomadic Turkic tribes, through diplomatic and trade means. Whenever there were periodic uprisings, successive Tsars resorted to military conquest and colonization of the region, though with due respect afforded to cultural and religious traditions. The Islamic faith was a unifying factor among all the Central Asian peoples and the launch-pad for various movements for autonomy and independence in the eighteenth and nineteenth centuries. However, most intellectuals leading those political movements were in favor of pan-Turkism as an alternative to Westernization and pan-Islamism, some of them even flirting with socialism (Hiro, 1995, pp. 1–7).

The abdication of the Tsar in 1917 raised hopes of independence in Central Asia. The Bolsheviks subsequently took power and initially pledged equal sovereignty and self-determination for all nations of the former empire. Lenin had argued that nationalism as a reaction to capitalism would be replaced by internationalism as socialism gained ascendency. But Stalin, who came to power in 1924, advocated the establishment of nations with a shared official language and territory. Consequently, under his direction the region that had once held such historic names as Turkestan, Bukhara and Khorezm underwent radical territorial reorganization. This was to result in Kazakh, Uzbek, Kyrgyz, Tajik and Turkmen Soviet republics that were the predecessors of the current nation-states. Soon after, the redistribution of lands previously owned by Russian colonizers to the landless was superseded by collectivization and settling of nomadic peoples (Hiro, 1995, pp. 8–23). Khrushchev, who succeeded Stalin, was determined to make the Soviet Union self-sufficient in grain and meat, and so Kazakhstan was selected to have millions of hectares of nomadic grazing land converted to this task. Settlers of Russian, Ukrainian and German ethnicity sent to create this agricultural "miracle," were resented by the native Kazakhs and this fuelled further calls for cultural autonomy (Hiro, 1995, pp. 24–35).

RECENT POLITY AND ECONOMY

The agitation for autonomy came to a head during Gorbachev's *perestroika* era when a Russian apparatchik was appointed as party head in Kazakhstan. Subsequent riots and their violent suppression by the government led eventually to the appointment of a Kazak national as party leader. The appointee, Nazabayev, was later to push for the formation of the Commonwealth of Independent States to replace the Soviet Union, and become president of the sovereign nation (Derbyshire, 1993, pp. 329–30). Despite claiming to advocate democratic reforms, Nazabayev extended his tenure, first via a referendum in 1995, then by legislative amendments to the constitution and finally through an election in 1999. In that election the key opposition candidate was banned and, upon his self-imposed exile, sentenced to 10 years imprisonment. Subsequent attempts to mount serious political opposition have also been subject to similar harassment. Still, supporters of Nazabayev claim that he has been instrumental in preserving inter-ethnic peace and political stability through the difficult years of economic reform (BBC News, 2004).

Economically and socially, the country continued to cope in the early 2000s with high unemployment, poverty, inflation, prostitution, drug addiction and AIDS. Infrastructure was declining while environmental degradation remained a tragic consequence of the Soviet Union's nuclear testing, space exploration, draining of the Aral Sea for irrigation and toxic dumping on its soil. Nonetheless the country is rich in mineral resources, particularly oil in its west bordering the inland Caspian Sea, though until recent years the lack of international pipelines from this largely land-locked country have been an impediment to oil export. Culturally, the country comprises largely Kazaks who make up 53 percent of the population, and Russians totaling about 30 percent and declining through migration due to discrimination since the collapse of the Soviet Union. Independence has witnessed the renaissance of Kazak language and culture through government policy, although Islamization has been resisted in favor of secularism and freedom of religion. In recent years the Kazakhstan government has had a successful track record at negotiating long-standing disputed borders with neighboring Russia, China, Uzbekistan and Kyrgyzstan (Daniel, 2003).

Broadcast Policy

SOVIET ERA

During the Soviet era all television broadcasts were state-run and subject to communist party influence. In the initial years of television, the lack of technology to broadcast nationally enabled some regionalism in programming, thus Russian and Kazak language television developed together. But this was soon replaced by centralization of control over television from Moscow in keeping with the typically Stalinist ethos, and consequently the Russian language and culture was privileged throughout the Soviet Union. This Russian hegemony remained the status quo until the era of *glasnost* under Gorbachev in the 1980s which unleashed demands for ethnic and localized television in the non-Russian states (Mickiewicz, 1988, pp. 207–8). While not-for-profit broadcasting was the dominant paradigm, advertising on television came into being minimally (Interview Kzs04). Such advertising tended to be by local tourism bodies promoting holiday destinations within the Soviet Union such as Black Sea resorts. Advertising was used also in conjunction with social policy such as promoting fruit juice over alcohol. Given the planned economy, advertising was also used to fix mismatches between things produced and consumer demand (Mickiewicz, 1988, p. 29). Sponsorship has had a shorter history, beginning even in the lead-up to the demise of the Soviet Union in 1991. For then multinational corporations had sponsored American-origin programming which carried a corporate message, but no product commercials (Interview Kzs05) for reasons that will be elaborated on later in this chapter.

INDEPENDENCE ERA

With the rapid growth of channels that followed political independence, the television industry experienced relative chaos. In 1996 tenders were called for broadcast frequencies when the first Mass Media Law was enacted which was strengthened in 2002. Local interviewees claimed that most television owners conceded the need for regulation to stabilize the situation (Interview Kzs07). However foreign sources argue that it was the growing popularity of the independent television stations that compelled the government to regulate broadcasts via its Decree No. 1523. This decree required payment to obtain a broadcasting license, and depending on transmitter capacity the fee could be up to US$200,000 for three years. The high prices caused about 20 stations to close down, including some that had been critical of the government. Hence by the late 1990s, the television industry was dominated by the state broadcaster and a few stations controlled by members of the president's family or inner circle, although details of ownership remain a tightly held secret. Only four private television stations, ORT-Kazakhstan, Khabar, NTK and KTK received approval to broadcast nationally (Internews, 2003). By the early 2000s, most media were believed to be unofficially part of larger Kazakhstan conglomerates, because the ownership structures were not made transparent and explicit. Ownership of the various media was overlapping via holding companies that in classical fashion owned clusters of print, radio and television. One respondent even thought that there might even be some minority foreign ownership of media through "money laundering" which was nonetheless able to exercise influence through control of technology infrastructure (Interview Kzs07).

Through its various agencies at the national and provincial levels, the government monitored programming on all the licensed television stations (Interview Kzs02). The Department of Information in the commercial capital Almaty regulated those that broadcast nationally (Interview Kzs01). In earlier days, regulation tended to be more of technical aspects rather than programming content. However, by the early 2000s the focus had shifted to the use of the Kazak language and imported materials (Interview Kzs04). According to the 1999 Law on Mass Media, by 2002 transmission of foreign programs was not to exceed 50 percent of total programming hours on television and radio, and by 2003 this figure reduced to 20 percent (US-English Foundation, 2004). Some interviewees believed though that if a Russian program was translated or dubbed, it counted towards the 80 percent Kazak-language requirement. In practice only about 50 percent of programming was in Kazak by 2002 (Interview Kzs04). But dubbing was said to be only an option until the end of 2002 as the legal requirement was for local production thereafter. It was believed that licenses would be lost if stations failed to comply with this requirement. According to one respondent, this stipulation needed to be seen in the context of Uzbekistan and Kyrgystan television, where programming was already 100 percent in their respective national languages (Interview Kzs03).

Media Scene

BROADCAST MEDIA

As of the early 2000s there were 38 television channels of varying professionalism and technological quality (Internews, 2003), of which no more than eight were national in audience reach and the rest provincial or municipal. Together, all the national channels in Kazakhstan raised US$25–30 million from advertising annually, which was sufficient for them to survive financially but to not be very profitable. There were estimated to be 3.88 million television sets in the country or about 231 sets per 1,000 people (NationMaster. com, 2003), which constitutes a fair-sized audience market for competition by broadcasters and advertisers. Yet strictly speaking these national channels were not competitors, even though they had roughly the same reach. For instance, their advertising rate rises were said to be done in quick succession suggesting price-fixing characteristic of a cartel (Interview Kzs09).

Of the national broadcasters, Kazakhstan-1 had a 98 percent audience reach in Kazakhstan, ORT 89 percent and Khabar TV 85 percent in 2002 according to the social research firm Concom Eurasia. Yet this figure was alleged by an interviewee to differ somewhat from that reported privately by the media research firm Gallup (Interview Kzs04). Khabar TV was believed by some interviewees to be part state-owned but it was certainly managed by the daughter of the president of Kazakhstan, Nazabayev. She had inaugurated Khabar TV as something novel and commercial, but government control had been extended over it, albeit informally (Interview Kzs02). The public broadcaster Kazakhstan-1 had technically the highest penetration or potential audience reach in the country but in reality it had low viewership or audience ratings because much of its programming was considered dull by the populace.

ORT-Kazakhstan was the leading Russian-language channel in Kazakhstan by ratings and while of Russian origin was said to be an affiliate of Khabar TV. Its programming was produced in Russia and not broadcast "live" but with a two-hour delay which allowed for the insertion of Kazakhstan advertising, news, weather and so on (Interview Kzs09). Some of its programs are purchased from the Russian broadcaster Perviy for rebroadcast in Kazakhstan (Interview Kzs12). Though ORT was not state-owned in either Russia or Kazakhstan, it came under strong political influence in both (Interview Kzs04). It was argued that only because ORT was careful with its news and other programming was it granted a license to broadcast in Kazakhstan. Many of its innocuous talk-shows, game-shows and interview programs are cloned from Western formats. While copyright laws governing such contraventions existed in Kazakhstan, they were thought to be not very effective (Interview Kzs01). Most other channels from Russia ceased to be available as free-to-air broadcasts with regulation in the late 1990s, though were made accessible via subscription cable. Hence the channel RTR, previously a free-to-air broadcast rival to ORT that was also aggressively pro-ethnic Russian, was consequently relegated to pay-TV (Interview Kzs09).

Due to personal links with the government, NTK was a network permitted to broadcast nationally, without having to undergo the tendering process for a television license (Internews, 2003). Rahat TV was yet another major network and owned by another family member of the Kazakhstan president. KTK, a dominant player in the television market, was once affiliated with the independent Karavan print media group but was believed since to have been transferred to a pro-government conglomerate. Arna television station was formerly known simply as the second channel of Khabar TV and broadcasts exclusively in Kazak. Although with less than half of ethnic Kazaks or about 16 percent of the total national population able to speak the language, its audience was relatively small. Other networks like Tan TV and Channel 13 have paid financially for their independent and often oppositional political stance. Some 30 such small television stations existed around the country, coping with allegedly unfair competition from the major players for advertising revenue. The major business firms that were sources of advertising revenue or investors in channels were either closely associated with the political elite or at least reluctant to antagonize them by supporting these independent stations. Table 10.1 summarizes details of the key television stations in Kazakhatan.

There were also 35 non-state-owned radio stations in Kazakhstan in the early 2000s. A province like East Kazakhstan, visited by the researcher, sustained just one commercial broadcaster in the early 2000s, though there had been others prior. The government-owned Kazakh Radio broadcasts in nine languages which includes minorities within the country which are often majorities in neighboring countries. There were estimated to be 6.47 million radios in the country or about 386 sets per 1,000 people (NationMaster.com, 2003). On short-wave, apart from the government-owned Radio Alma-Ata, the BBC Kazak

Table 10.1   Key television stations in Kazakhstan, early 2000s

Title	Ownership	Language	Reach
Kazakhstan-1	government-owned	Kazak/Russian	national
Khabar	private/government	Kazak/Russian	national
ORT-Kazakhstan	private	Russian	transnational
KTK	private	Russian	national
NTK	private	Russian	national
Rahat TV	private	Kazak/Russian	national
Tan TV	private	Russian	major cities
Elarrna	private/government	Kazak	national
31 Channel	private	Kazak/Russian	national
Caspionet	private	English	transnational
Astana	private/government	Kazak/Russian	major city
Almaty	private	Kazak/Russian	major city

Source: Adapted from Internews (2003), supplemented by research respondents.

service and Radio Free Europe/Radio Liberty were accessible in principle (TvRadioWorld. com, 2004). Unlike its domestic radio and television, the influential BBC World Service is funded by the British government's Foreign Office, while Radio Free Europe/Radio Liberty is a US government-sponsored legacy from the Cold War era (Wikipedia.org, 2005).

PRINT MEDIA

Since advertising revenue was very limited, print media particularly were dependent on government subsidies. With about 80 percent of the 1,260 print media allegedly under government control, there could not be said to be an independent press in Kazakhstan. There were 39 newspapers and 26 magazines based in Almaty while every major city supported at least one weekly of its own. However only 11 newspapers were considered politically independent and they have been subjected to well documented repression (International Policy Fellowship, 2004). Among the forms of harassment alleged were inspections by tax, fire and sanitary authorities, legal actions, physical attacks by unknown persons on employees, editors, journalists and their families, death threats, arson and cancellation of work visas. Hence private ownership of media has not implied autonomy of operation in the Kazakhstan context. Just prior to presidential elections in 1999, 15 independent newspapers were closed down. Furthermore, the leading media holding company, Karavan, was compelled to sell its newspaper and radio of the same name as well as its television station KTK. Their new holding companies, TV-Media and Premier Inter Asia, were believed owned by people loyal to the government (Kuzainov, 2002). Regardless of ownership, most of the major newspapers, both dailies and weeklies, appear to publish in Russian rather than in Kazak (Table 10.2).

Table 10.2   Key newspapers in Kazakhstan, early 2000s

Title	Ownership	Language	Frequency
Kazakhstanskaya Pravda	government-backed	Russian	daily
Yegemen Qazaqstan	government-backed	Kazak	daily
Ekspress-K	private	Russian	daily
Zhas Alash	private	Kazak	daily
Vremya	private	Russian	daily
Nachenem s ponedelnika	private/opposition	Russian	weekly
Soz	private/opposition	Russian	weekly
Assndy Times	private/opposition	Russian	weekly
Karavan	private	Russian	weekly
Megapolis	private	Russian	weekly
Argumenty y Fakty	private	Russian	weekly
Komsomolskaya Pravda	private	Russian	weekly
Panorama	private	Russian	weekly
Novoye pokoleniye	private	Russian	weekly
Delovaya nedelya	private	Russian	weekly
Kapital	private	Russian	weekly

Source: Adapted from BBC (2004), supplemented by research respondents.

OTHER MEDIA

Under the media law, Internet sites were classified as mass media and thus came under strict monitoring of the authorities. This effectively closed off an avenue for independent journalists to recycle foreign-posted articles critical of the government (Pannier, 2001). There were only 1,129 cinemas in the country, or just 0.06 per 1,000 of population (NationMaster.com, 2003), in keeping with a worldwide trend of decline fostered by television and videos. The spurt in publicly-funded movie production in the immediate post-Soviet era, characterized as the "New Wave" celebrating Kazakh cultural identity, peaked soon after as the realities of the market economy set in (Waller, 1996). Nonetheless, 33 percent of the residents of Almaty surveyed claimed to have visited a cinema with the last six months (Brif Agency, 2002). Outdoor advertising such as billboards, pylons, light boxes, roof-tops, sides and fronts of buildings had become increasingly available in the post-Soviet era, contesting the spaces once reserved for nationalistic statues, propaganda murals and communist slogans. While Kazakhstan had a reasonably wide range of advertising media by the early 2000s, this chapter will concentrate on the television industry, due to general constraints of obtaining data in the country and especially within the limited time of a fieldtrip made from overseas.

Agencies and Accounts

ADVERTISING AGENCIES

The advertising industry in Kazakhstan was just over a decade old when fieldwork for this research was done in mid 2003. Multinational corporations had been instrumental in introducing advertising after the fall of the Soviet Union in 1991, with most of the creative work initially produced in Moscow and primarily of a sales promotional nature (Interview Kzs05). Many local agencies in Kazakhstan that represented transnational advertising agencies, were known locally as "chain agencies." They were often referred to within the local media marketplace by their own original names as much as that of their transnational affiliates. However, advertising in Kazakhstan continued to be dominated by multinational marketers as indicated by the fact that six of the top ten advertisers were global corporations (Table 10.3). In fact, the remaining four would best be described as regional rather than domestic corporations. Together these ten firms contribute a third of all advertising expenditure in Kazakhstan.

After political-economic liberalization in the early 1990s, publishers had initially provided some advertising services directly to clients. But because their facilities and structures for creating print advertising were below standard, some of the staff left to start their own fledgling advertising agencies. Styx, the first ad agency, was formed by people with a background in journalism and publication, and they have since come to represent the transnational advertising agency Leo Burnett (Interview Kzs03). Still, their first clients back in 1990 were Russian companies selling commodities such as grain

Table 10.3 Major advertisers on television media in Kazakhstan, 2000

Advertiser	Adspend	Percentage*	Time	Percentage#
Procter & Gamble	US$3,849,409	7.34 %	3,618 min	2.87 %
Sugar Corporatn	US$3,464,163	6.61 %	3,730 min	2.96 %
Unilever	US$2,826,396	5.39 %	2,554 min	2.02 %
LG Electronics	US$1,914,221	3.65 %	2,907 min	2.30 %
Bank Turanalem	US$927,648	1.77 %	1,204 min	0.95 %
Air Kazakhstan	US$850,873	1.62 %	3,938 min	3.12 %
Colgate-Palmolive	US$838,934	1.60 %	844 min	0.67 %
Coca-Cola Almaty	US$730,598	1.39 %	553 min	0.44 %
Urker Cosmetics	US$715,275	1.36 %	594 min	0.47 %
Stimorol	US$672,303	1.28 %	519 min	0.41 %
Total	US$16,789,820	32.02 %	20,460 min	16.21 %

Note: * = percentage of total media expenditure by all advertisers in Kazakhstan; # = percentage of total broadcast airtime on television in Kazakhstan.

Source: Gallup Media Asia, cited in Advertising (2001).

in Kazakhstan, rather than branded manufactured goods (Interview Kzs06). Despite the growth of advertising agencies, television and radio stations had successfully continued to offer their own creative production services in-house (Interview Kzs05), significantly supplementing their funding. Advertising media sales itself was thought to represent only about 45 percent of television station revenue in Kazakhstan with much of the rest coming from production services (Interview Kzs07). Yet the line between ad agency and media owner was not clearly drawn as demonstrated by one agency, Alna Media Marketing, publishing a magazine entitled *Moth* targeting youth 16 and above for its clients.

ACCOUNT HANDLING

Advertising agency remuneration was either via media and production commissions, or negotiated on a contractual basis. Generally, agency income from their multinational clients tended to be on a set media commission basis, while the fee was more negotiable in the case of local clients (Interview Kzs05). Advertising budgets were set by marketers on the conservative percentage-of-sales basis, in which sales during the previous advertising year were monitored to plan the next year's advertising. The advertising budgets of multinational corporations were generally set in Moscow for the region and then allocated to the national markets (Interview Kzs05). Even the method by which the budget was set by the client was sometimes not disclosed to the local agency, which was simply given a fixed budget to work with for advertising in Kazakhstan. Hence the Kazakhstan agencies seemed in the dark regarding whether the method used was percentage of sales, objective-and-task, comparative parity, another or neither. Little or no regional advertising for Central Asia was organized in Almaty even by major agencies based there, because those decisions were also generally made by agency offices in Moscow (Interview Kzs06). Hence the essential role of advertising agencies within Kazakhstan was confined to advising their marketer clients, both foreign and local, on creating, adapting and placing advertising locally.

Media Planning and Monitoring

MARKET/AUDIENCE RESEARCH

Television viewership research in Kazakhstan was carried out using the out-dated diary method rather than the more reliable people-meters used in developed countries. Print readership surveys were done only twice a year. There was only limited monitoring of advertising, while pre-testing/post-testing of advertising was known to be done only on behalf of one client, Procter & Gamble (Interview Kzs06). Two different firms, Gallup Media and Brif, collected data on television audiences and print readership respectively (Interview Kzs05). However, both their research was said to confirm that the growth of advertising spending in Kazakhstan had been quite steady over the previous decade, and demonstrated that television was the leading medium (Interview Kzs03).

Television ratings were the sole basis for advertising media decisions but this fact was allegedly the motivation for some television stations setting a precedence for bribing the media research firms that produce the ratings. Because ratings were not necessarily factual or transparent in Kazakhstan, one station preferred to evaluate audiences via its advertisers' intuitive preferences. In other words, if advertiser clients judged a certain program qualitatively suitable for their products, the station deemed its audience segment valuable and the program worth retaining on its schedules. Hence public relations by the television station were thought to be more important to attracting advertising than ratings (Interview Kzs07). Nonetheless in Kazakhstan generally, news programming received top ratings, movies came second with sports programs receiving the third-highest ratings, followed then by music channels (Interview Kzs10). ORT was thought to have the largest share of prime time audiences estimated at around 50 percent, with Khabar TV and KTK each at about 13 percent, while Kazakhstan-1 had less than one percent (Interview Kzs11). This situation was reflected also in their respective shares of the television advertising expenditure pie based on published data of the top ten advertisers in Kazakhstan (Figure 10.1).

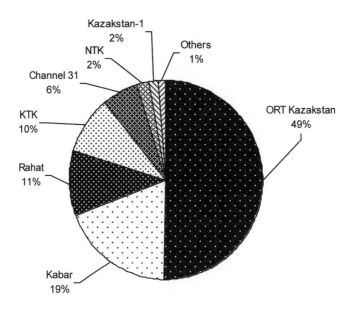

Figure 10.1 Allocation of advertising to Kazakhstan channels by major marketers, 2000

MEDIA BUYING

Previously in the 1990s advertising agencies had bought time first from the television stations and then sold it on to their clients. There were also multiple media brokers then but by the early 2000s, one of them, TV Media Holdings, was said to have a near-monopoly on television media sales and almost all the national newspapers. It was controlled by the Kazakhstan president's daughter who also owned Khabar TV (Interview Kzs05). Its only competitor was Alma Media which sold media on the major newspaper *Karavan*, on a major television station KTK, and on some radio stations (Interview Kzs03). It was also the holding company for both *Karavan* and KTK, and worked on a commission basis for the Russian channel RTR. Yet, its management saw no conflict of interest since it used different teams to market each media entity (Interview Kzs10). Hence an effective duopoly has characterized media broking and constrained media buying within the advertising industry in Kazakhstan since the early 2000s.

As is characteristic of many advertising markets, especially in the developing world, there was said to be considerable discounting of advertising rates, with volume discounts negotiated by the media brokers with clients and kept strictly confidential. Hence advertising expenditure (adspend) figures such as those for television (Table 10.4) were thought to be about 20–30 percent inaccurate since they were based on rate-card costs. A media research firm estimated that press advertising was discounted by 20 percent, while outdoor advertising was said to be not discounted at all, and television advertising discounts were subject to volume of purchase (Interview Kzs08). In summer, television viewing declined in Kazakhstan, as in most other countries, and hence advertisers concentrated their spending on print media then (Interview Kzs03). As with account management, there was very limited media buying on a regional Central Asian or former Soviet Union basis, and most was on a national or provincial or local basis (Interview Kzs06).

Local ads were usually inserted into Russian channels and programming that were rebroadcast in Kazakhstan, but the advertising revenue was not shared with the Russian channels (Interview Kzs04). The Russian-origin channel ORT-Kazakhstan was dominant in the local media scene but it was deemed rather expensive to buy advertising time on. Therefore only major marketers like leading Kazakhstan banks and multinational corporations like the Korean consumer electronics firm LG used it. On the other hand, the locally created KTK channel was considered the most effective national media buy for most other advertiser clients. A few cable channels, such as the Russian ones and Nickleodeon, also accepted local Kazakhstan advertising for insertion in the programming.

Table 10.4 Total advertising spending on television in Kazakhstan, 2000

Channel	US dollars	Percentage	Time	Percentage
ORT Kazakhstan	$15,868,734	30.3%	7091.0 min	5.6%
Channel 31	$8,591,185	16.4%	40,226.0 min	31.9%
Kabar	$8,145,711	15.5%	9,688.3 min	7.7%
Rahat	$7,314,421	13.9%	23,023.9 min	18.2%
KTK	$5,797,278	11.1%	10,182.4 min	8.1%
Shahar	$1,970,011	3.8%	19,461.9 min	15.4%
Tan	$1,763,350	3.4%	7,641.9 min	6.1%
NTK	$1,755,541	3.3%	5,791.6 min	4.6%
Kazakhstan-1	$1,233,329	2.4%	2,869.8 min	2.3%
Kabar 2/El-Arna	–	–	243.3 min	0.2%
Total	$52,439,559	100.0%	126,211.1 min	100.0%

Source: Gallup Media Asia, cited in Advertising (2001).

But on many other channels for which the cable networks did not pay royalties for carrying, foreign advertising came along with the programming which was broadcast in "real-time" (Interview Kzs10).

The situation for provincial television stations was quite different. Generally, they had better quality of broadcast signal in the local area and were more efficient than the national stations (Interview Kzs03). For example, with a population of just 320,000, Oskemen, the capital of East Kazakhstan province, was generally regarded as an "immature" market. Some firms there did not advertise at all, while others preferred print or outdoor advertising. With regard to local television ratings, sometimes the provincial commercial station Kalkent TV was in the lead, and at other times the government-owned provincial broadcaster BKTB was. Of Kalkent TV's programming in the early 2000s, 48 percent was from the Russian channel NTV (or HTB) and 52 percent was local. Kalkent TV sometimes bought its programs from other Kazakhstan stations or bartered advertising for them (Interview Kzs02). Some local ad agencies also produced their own programs on behalf of marketer clients. Kalkent TV had some permanent local advertising clients which it serviced directly and not through an ad agency. Though the owner of Kalkent TV was a major businessman in Oskemen, his other companies were said to not advertise much on the station, for reasons not disclosed (Interview Kzs02). Market and audience research was done *ad hoc* in Oskemen by professors and students from the local university on behalf of stations and being proprietary was not publicly available.

Production Creativity or Adaptation

SPONSORSHIP

The practice of sponsorship in the region has had as long a history as advertising in Kazakhstan, if not longer. For soon after the demise of the Soviet Union in 1991, Johnson & Johnson brought Disney cartoons to Kazakhstan with a corporate sponsorship message, namely a tag-line promising "care for your family with premium health products." There was no product advertising as such because Johnson & Johnson products were not yet available for sale within the country. But the positive attitude developed in audiences paid off two years later when the products were launched successfully in the market (Interview Kzs05).

Across the television channels only about 15–20 percent of promotional expenditure was on sponsorships versus advertising spots in the early 2000s (Interview Kzs06). Still there appeared to be a growing trend towards sponsorship rather than advertising on Khabar TV, for instance (Interview Kzs03). However due to the tax structure in Kazakhstan, only 1 percent of sponsorship was exempt from tax. This was perhaps a means of denying "grey" economic capital or gains from the "black market" being allowed such a legal outlet (Interview Kzs07). The trend towards sponsorship was evident in adaptations of program formats like "Who Wants to be a Millionaire?", which in Kazakhstan was sponsored by Kommerzbank (Interview Kzs11), though sponsorship data was not collected by the research firm Gallup/Brif until mid 2002 (Interview Kzs08), making trend analysis impossible.

COMMERCIAL PRODUCTION

Back in 1994, when Procter & Gamble and Philip Morris came to Kazakhstan, they sent "pool books" of advertisements. These samples of advertising created in international markets were meant for adaptation to the local market by local agencies. But by the early 2000s most of these clients' advertisements were locally created and their agency claimed to be the only marketer that did pre-testing and post-testing of its advertisements (Interview Kzs06). Advertising creativity was still sometimes adapted from overseas materials provided by multinational marketers and their ad agencies. But admittedly most "Western" television commercials did not work in the region for obvious reasons of differences in culture and economic development. Original creative production became a very competitive business because there were many local agencies in Kazakhstan. Furthermore some newspapers and television stations did creative work in-house for their advertiser clients (Interview Kzs05). Advertising agencies began specializing in specific forms of creative production and so were sometimes sub-contracted as creative "hot-houses" by different clients (Interview Kzs03).

As of the early 2000s, there was no advertising law *per se* and the industry was believed subsumed under the media law, though there were some laws governing pharmaceuticals and alcohol that were pertinent to their advertising (Interview Kzs11). While no specific law regarding local content in advertising existed like the Mass Media Law governing television, agencies like Styx/Leo Burnett sought early to demonstrate a capability to create local advertising. About 80 percent of its Kazakhstan advertising reportedly involved new creative work and the remaining 20 percent comprising adaptation of foreign advertising. Styx/Leo Burnett did most of its own creative development but outsourced production. Initially it used television and radio stations for broadcast advertising but more recently used independent studios. Print advertising was being outsourced to the Baltic states for their higher quality production (Interview Kzs06). Yet generally the trend in Kazakhstan has been to develop its own creativity and even to export its creative products to culturally similar countries such as Turkey (Interview Kzs05).

Transitioning or Developing?

The experience of other post-communist countries with media reforms and privatization should prove invaluable for comparing the Kazakhstan experience. In Bulgaria in the first decade of liberalization, the new politically credible print media faced serious competition from more market-oriented "infotainment" periodicals, culminating in the takeovers by a German media corporation. In television, the introduction of private television and unregulated access to satellite and cable television from abroad led to serious competition for market dominance. Together the reluctance of the government to relinquish intervention in the media industry, dependence on developed countries for media hardware and software, and the amateurish adoption of a free-market model meant that media in Bulgaria had not risen to the challenge of playing "Fourth Estate" in society (Raycheva, 1999). In Kazakhstan, it is the distaste of the government towards any other entity including civil society having such a watchdog role that has seen it maintain an iron grip on media ownership.

Similarly in Estonia, a post-Soviet state like Kazakhstan rather than an Eastern bloc one like Bulgaria, the press and television sector expanded dramatically in the 1990s. Privatization of local television and availability of foreign channels eventually resulted in the state-owned media losing market share. According to Lauk (1999) the advertising market grew exponentially with growth rates of up to 46 percent annually. The press media received the largest share of advertising spending at 47 percent with television commanding 27 percent. One publishing group introduced the idea of free newspapers subsidized fully by advertising that became popular with citizens with limited income. In a form of imitative or reverse hegemony the largest advertising agency in Estonia not only owned four agencies within the country but others in other former Soviet states in the Baltic states as well as in Ukraine and Russia. But adopting the market model had not profited the local media themselves which have survived only as parts of large media corporations with substantial foreign ownership, largely Scandinavian. In Kazakhstan, survival of local media seems to have been achieved by their oligopolistic control of advertising revenue, mostly from foreign multinationals, via media brokerages and government patronage.

The former communist countries bordering Western Europe seemed to have embraced the capitalist system with greater enthusiasm than those of Central Asia. This has included less government intervention in the media and advertising industries though that soon saw heavy involvement by foreign multinationals. In the immediate post-Cold War period Hungary's print media mushroomed to over 2,800 publications but Western media conglomerates such as News Corporation and Bertelsmann began taking an interest. The Czech national broadcaster entered into an arrangement with a French firm to sell its advertising spots. Transnational ad agencies such as Saatchi & Saatchi, McCann-Erickson and Young & Rubicam formed joint ventures in Hungary as well as Poland, then Czechoslovakia and the former Yugoslavia. Their multinational clients such as General Electric, Procter & Gamble, Eastman Kodak, McDonalds and Mobil were on the scene soon after the collapse of communism, these US firms somewhat ahead of their European counterparts (Lane and Smith, 1991). Similarly transnational advertising agencies have formed partnerships with fledgling Kazakhstan agencies and been a conduit for advertising from multinational corporations.

In the case of Russia itself, privatization of the media did not necessarily leave the state out of ownership because it came to coexist with corporate interests. In the post-Soviet era, television has grown in importance but, much as in Kazakhstan and unlike other ex-communist European countries, it remains in the hands of domestic politicized capital with the relatively inaccessible Internet left as the only hope for counter-cultural dissent (Rantanen, 2002, pp. 92–104). The hopeful trends of *glasnost* and *perestroika* initiated by Gorbachev in the 1980s for greater autonomy of the media comprehensively portrayed by Gibbs (1999) seem not to have continued. As with globalization worldwide in the post-Cold War capitalist era, a characteristic outcome of television in Russia has been the growth of entertainment content, much of it imported and dubbed, even if the highest rating programs tend to remain domestic serials. The complementary advertising industry took off in the early 1990s by tapping into pent-up consumer demand for all things new and foreign. Yet it peaked in the mid 1990s when goods advertised drifted out of affordability of many Russians in the traumatic shift to a market economy (Rantanen, 2002, pp. 115–24).

Though generalizations concerning vast regions have their limitations and exceptions, the state of development of media and advertising in Kazakhstan appears closer to that of the developing countries of Asia than the developed countries of Europe. Television in sub-Saharan Africa, for instance, grew rapidly over the 1990s as a result of economic liberalization and commercialization, as well as the use of satellite, cable and MMDS technologies. But Paterson (1998) argued that it was still an urban and affluent phenomenon promoting wasteful consumerism. It served primarily to profit private business interests which were often large regional corporations with foreign business partners and local political backers. Claiming dubiously to be aiding an African renaissance, these new broadcasters offered little indigenous cultural production, information, education or news, and made no contribution to national or regional development apart from fostering consumption and materialism. Likewise programming in Kazakhstan has been largely imports from the West and from Russia, the latter being largely clones of Western programming, with little effort at socio-economic development despite some rhetoric.

The recent history of developing countries, previously having authoritarian governments with media reforms and privatization, should also prove instructive for Kazakhstan. The media-owners of Kazakhstan might take a leaf out of the experience of those in the Philippines and Indonesia which had been closely identified with the Marcos and Soeharto regimes respectively, both crony capitalist. For instance, conglomerates in Indonesia owned at least in part by the president's family or his cronies largely controlled the media during the Soeharto regime of the early 1970s through late 1990s. Advertising expenditure then was essentially being channeled from one part of these conglomerates to another as revenue via advertising agencies (Thomas, 2004). When the regional economic recession in the late 1990s triggered political revolt in the country, various media found themselves in dire financial straits. Disassociation with cronies of the former regime was deemed essential to the long-term viability of those media in the post-revolution economic restructuring and industry reforms.

Ideological Cross-Over

In comparing and contrasting three perspectives on the transition in political, economic and media systems, Sparks and Reading (1994) take issue with those who seek to portray the communist and capitalist approaches as diametrical opposites. In both systems the leadership is bureaucratic and the consequence of the ideological change has been that the former communist elite retained control by transforming themselves into capitalists, as indeed was the case in Kazakhstan. They point out though that among the former communist countries in Central and Eastern Europe there has been an outright rejection of the US model of complete privatization of the television industry in favor of the Western European model of mixed private and public broadcasting. Surveying the literature, Hughes and Lawson (2004) found that political liberalization in developing and transitional economies have consistently not resulted in the democratization of the media, as evidenced in Mexico. Instead of playing a civic role as the Fourth Estate, media owners have traded favorable coverage of the government in return for its patronage policies and concessions for their related businesses, including advertising revenue from political campaigns. Owners and managers that they appointed, rather than the journalists, were found to play a critical part in promoting establishment-oriented and tabloid-style news, which could attract more advertising. Consequently the largely privatized media, controlled by crony capitalists, in developing and transitional economies such as Kazakhstan are no less partisan than the state-run media from the communist era that they have superseded.

Quite apart from government regulation of programming content and the domination of media brokering by the larger players, independent media face the reluctance of marketers to advertise on media critical to the government and thus incur its displeasure. While such media might be popular with their audiences, their economic survival is dictated by advertising revenue that can be manipulated by authoritarian regimes. Thus not only were the number of media vehicles limited by the government through licensing and censorship, the number of those considered politically astute to advertise in was smaller yet. Executives in the industry made no mention of these constraints in the interviews, but a search on the Internet revealed the repression of the media to be well-documented by international observers, academics, non-governmental organizations, even some foreign governments as well as opposition Kazakhstan leaders in exile. Advertising agencies and their marketer clients might plead innocence by claiming to be merely placing their advertising in the most efficient of the limited media available. Doubtless they are constrained by the media brokering cartel formed by the associates of the political leadership. In the case of Kazakhstan the hegemony of a political elite over the mass media seems no less total under a capitalist regime than under a communist one. Regardless, agencies and marketers in developing and transitional economies, especially those of multinational origin, cannot exactly claim impartiality, let alone practicing ethical principles and corporate social responsibility when choosing to avoid politically controversial media for largely pragmatic commercial reasons, given the political and economic influence they can wield through their advertising budgets.

References

Advertising (2001). Television. *Advertising*, 4(16): 4.

BBC News (2004). Country profile: Kazakhstan. BBC News World Edition website. [Online.] http://news.bbc.co.uk/2/hi/asia-pacific/country_profiles/1298071.stm (accessed July 2, 2004).

Brif Agency (2002). Untitled factsheet, provided by Brif Agency, Almaty, Kazakhstan.

Daniel, Kate (ed.) (2003). *SBS World Guide* (pp. 396–7). Melbourne: Hardie Grant Books.

Derbyshire, Ian. D. (ed.) (1993). *The Hutchinson Dictionary of World History*. Oxford: Helicon Publishing.

Gibbs, Joseph (1999). *Gorbachev's Glasnost: The Soviet Media in the First Phase of Perestroika*. College Station, TX: Texas A&M University Press.

Hiro, Dilip (1995). *Between Marx and Muhammad: The Changing Face of Central Asia*. London: HarperCollins.

Hughes, Sallie and Chappell Lawson (2004). Propaganda and crony capitalism: partisan bias in Mexican television news. *Latin American Research Review*, 39(3) (October): 81–105.

International Policy Fellowship (2004). Overview of public service broadcasting in Kazakhstan. Public Service Broadcasting in Central Asia. [Online.] www.policy.hu/padhy/kazak_overview.htm (accessed July 2004).

Internews (2003). Television and radio companies operating in the Republic of Kazakhstan. *Internews Kazakhstan*. [Online.] www.internews.kz/eng/stations/ (accessed July 2004).

Interview Kzs01, middle manager, provincial public broadcaster.

Interview Kzs02, senior manager, provincial commercial broadcaster.

Interview Kzs03, middle managers, local advertising agencies.

Interview Kzs04, middle manager, local market research firm.

Interview Kzs05, senior manager, local advertising agency.

Interview Kzs06, senior manager, international advertising agency.

Interview Kzs07, senior manager, national commercial broadcaster.

Interview Kzs08, middle manager, international market research firm.

Interview Kzs09, middle manager, international advertising agency.

Interview Kzs10, middle manager, media brokering firm.

Interview Kzs11, senior manager, media brokering firm.

Interview Kzs12, professional interpreter and university lecturer.

Kuzainov, Aldar (2002). Kazakhstan's critical choice. International Eurasian Institute for Economic and Political Research. [Online.] http://iicas.org/libr_en/kz/03_01_15kz.htm (accessed August 2004).

Lane, W. Ronald and Otto W. Smith (1991). A perspective of advertising/marketing/media research. In Al Hester and L. Earle Reybold (eds), *Revolutions for Freedom: The Mass Media in Eastern and Central Europe* (pp. 211–27). Athens, GA: University of Georgia.

Lauk, Epp (1999). Trends in the development of the Estonian media market in the 1990s. *Media Development*, 3: 27–32.

Mickiewicz, Ellen (1988). *Split Signals: Television and Politics in the Soviet Union*. New York and Oxford: Oxford University Press.

NationMaster.com (2003). Asia: Kazakhstan: Media. *NationMaster.com*. [Online.] www.nationmaster. com/country/kz/media (accessed March 25, 2005).

Pannier, Bruce (2001). Kazakhstan: parliament moves to further restrict media independence. Radio Free Europe/Radio Liberty. [Online.] www.intellnet.org/news/2001/03/24/4036-1.asp (accessed July 2, 2004).

Paterson, Chris A. (1998). Reform or re-colonisation? The overhaul of African television. *Review of African Political Economy*, 78: 571–83.

Rantanen, Tehri (2002). *The Global and the National: Media and Communications in Post-Communist Russia*. Oxford and Lanham, MD: Rowman and Littlefield.

Raycheva, Lilia (1999). Turn-of-the-century challenges facing the mass media in Bulgaria. *Media Development*, 3: 9–12.

Sparks, Colin and Anna Reading (1994). Understanding media change in East Central Europe. *Media, Culture and Society*, 16: 243–70.

Thomas, Amos Owen (2004, July). Emancipating media from authoritarian capitalism: reflections on Indonesia's transition to democracy. *International Journal of Business and Society*, 5(2): 49–58.

TvRadioWorld (2004). Kazakhstan: radio and television. *TvRadioWorld*. [Online.] www.tvradioworld. com/region2/kaz/ (accessed July 7, 2004).

US-English Foundation (2004). Kazakhstan: language research. *US English Foundation Official Language Research*. [Online.] www.us-english.org/foundation/research/olp/viewResearch.asp? CID=49&TID=1 (accessed July 2, 2004).

Waller, Gregory (1996). National cinema and film culture in Kazakhstan. *Asian Cinema*, Spring, 39–49.

Wikipedia.org (2005). Radio Free Europe/Radio Liberty, and BBC World Service. [Online.] http:// en.wikipedia.org/wiki/ (accessed August 2005).

11 *Challenges and Opportunities for Advertising in Moldova: A Nation in Transition*

MICHAEL H. MCBRIDE

An unnamed Moldovan poet was said to have written many years ago: "When Moldovans get together and feast, they cry at one side of the table and laugh at the other. Their soul seems to resemble a globe with two hemispheres—one is day, the other night. Joy and sorrow." If true, it helps to explain dualities inherent in Moldovan culture: a divided nation historically, linguistically, economically and politically. No wonder Moldovans have survived so long, yet it is a wonder that a thriving advertising industry estimated at $14 million USD in 2005 took hold, given complex, dynamic roadblocks to progress (Dodonu, 2000).

This chapter briefly examines Moldova's history and culture, overviews its economy and consumers (including tourism and key agricultural industries), backgrounds Moldovan advertising and reviews agencies and clients (including financial and political spheres), discusses legal activities affecting advertising, analyzes print and broadcast media (plus telecommunications, mail service and the Internet), and describes marketing and media measurement services.

Moldova's unique location, at the perimeter of Eastern and Western cultures, has contributed to long, difficult struggles to maintain sovereignty. During the Middle Ages, and in modern times, Moldova chose political policies that reinforced its independence, defense of its territory and preservation of its frontiers. The most glorious era was during the reign of Stefan cel Mare (Stefan the Great). Between 1457 and 1504, Moldovans won brilliant victories over Turks, Tartars, Hungarians, Poles and other invaders; however, this temporary success did not assure future stability. Under the constant threat of invasion, unification was the region's only means of resisting aggression (Horton, 2003).

The Bessarabian area of Moldova was first annexed to Russia in 1812. Following the Crimean War, in 1856, Russia lost the southern region of Bessarabia to Moldova, only to gain it back from Romania in 1878. With the collapse of the Russian Empire in 1918, the area declared its independence and reunited with Romania. The newly-formed Soviet Union refused to recognize this reunification, however, and in 1924 created the Moldavian Autonomous Soviet Socialist Republic (MASSR). In 1940, the remainder of present-day Bessarabia was annexed by the Soviet Union, and part of it was combined with the MASSR to form the Moldavian Soviet Socialist Republic (MSSR). In the early 1940s, Romania again claimed territory of the MSSR, but after World War II the region was annexed again, for a final time, by the Soviet Union (Horton, 2003).

Subsequent to final annexation, the Soviet Union began Russification in an attempt to create a uniform, patriotic and Soviet-cultured empire. This process included official introduction of the Moldovan language, created by writing the native Romanian language using the Cyrillic alphabet and introduction of the Russian language into everyday life, plus cultural re-education of the population into the Soviet/Communist tradition. Immigrants and government bureaucrats were granted jobs and residences, while the native population was subjected to mass deportation (mainly to Siberia), organized famine and forced denationalization (Horton, 2003).

The tone of Soviet leadership changed in 1986 with the introduction of *glasnost* (openness) by Soviet President Mikhail Gorbachev. This new policy permitted the pursuit of traditional culture by the Moldovan population and leadership, setting the stage for the Republic's independence. Following a failed coup in Moscow resulting in ousting Gorbachev from power, combined with the subsequent Soviet collapse, the Moldovan Parliament and the Republic's General Assembly declared Moldova's independence on August 27, 1991.

Of two different autonomous regions within its territory, each born of separate political visions, the self-declared state of Transniestria, meaning "beyond the Dneister (River)," known as "Pridnestrovskaya Moldavskaya Republika" (PMR), is not recognized by the international community. In the dying days of the Soviet Union, alarm grew in the region over possible reunification with Romania. A 1989 law making Moldovan an official language added to the tension, sparking Transniestria to proclaim its secession. A brief civil war ensued, leaving 700 dead. A ceasefire was signed in 1992, setting up a demilitarized zone enforced by Russian military forces. Their continued presence remained a stumbling block in peace talks, continuing a tense standoff with Moldova. Based on a 2004 census, a near equal mix of ethnic Moldovans, Russians and Ukrainians are among the estimated population of 500,000, yet local experts believe only 325,000 live there, two-thirds of them impoverished elderly. Authorities exercise tight control over the all-Russian-language media. The territory's first private radio station, Inter FM, opened in 2003. Radio Pridnestrovye is state-run. Dniester Moldovan Republic TV is also state-run, and owned by the President's son. Three newspapers run limited advertising: *Pridnestrovye* (state-run), *Dnestrovskaia Pravda* and *Novyy Dnestrovskiy*. Most of Moldova's industrial infrastructure is in Transniestria, including munitions and steel factories, but its best-known factory, Kvint, produces well-known cognac. Its economic potential, however, is limited due to international isolation. Plagued by poverty, corruption, organized crime, smuggling (ethanol, cigarettes and drugs) and trafficking (fuels, arms and people), Transniestria has its own currency, constitution, parliament, flag and anthem.

The second region, Gagauzia, a southern territory of roughly 150,000 population, also has its own flag, police, university and weekly public periodicals, but it is only a self-governed area recognized by Moldova in 1994. The Turkish-speaking minority was allowed to settle in Moldova in exchange for conversion to Christianity.

Chisinau, the capital city, is the economic, political, cultural and geographic center of the country. More than 500 years old, it is home to some 700,000 residents. Despite being burned five times, Chisinau is considered one of the greenest cities in the world and is poetically called "a flower of stone that is washed upon the soft and sunny rain." It emerged as an important regional center for trade and is a model of development for the country. According to a 2004 final report from the Business Consulting Institute, Chisinau's economic district represents about one-third of Moldova's population and accounts for about 80 percent of total imports and 60 percent of exports, excluding Transniestria.

Moldova is known for its hospitality, rich customs and traditions, enriching its culture by adopting and preserving aspects of ethnicities inhabiting its territory over time. Its arts and crafts, including pottery, carpets, weavings and carvings (stone and wood), are special. Age-old traditions also are important, notably family customs like *shezatorile* (social evenings), *clacile* (group work), *plugushorul* (decorated processions) and calendar holidays like *colinda* (Christmas) and *sorcova* (New Year). The most important personal custom is inviting family, neighbors and even strangers into the home's *casa mare*, the living space memorializing the family clan, for obligatory food, drink and conversation. National celebrations include "Woman's Day," "Victory Day," "City Day" and "National Language Day," and "Martisor," a special celebration of spring.

Music and cuisine also are part of the cultural landscape. A moment of national pride occurred in 2005 when a Moldovan musical group called Zdob si Zdub, roughly meaning the sound of a drumbeat, placed sixth out of 39 nations in Moldova's first time to enter the Eurovision Song Contest hosted in Kiev, Ukraine. Their winning entry was "Boonika Bate Doda" (meaning "Grandmama is beating da drum-a"). Moldovan cuisine features national dishes like *mamalyga* (polenta with sheep's cheese), *zama* (chicken noodle soup) and *placinte* (pastry with curd cheese). The traditional beverage of choice is always wine, as most families produce and consume their own home brews.

Moldova's economic indicators are good news and bad news (Dogaru, 2005). An Ernst & Young report on doing business in Moldova (2005) reveals an economic paradox: while consumption increases, incomes stay low. According to a 2004 study on assessing competitiveness in Moldova's economy by Bizpro Moldova and Development Alternatives, Inc., the country is at a crossroads. The legacy of the "old Moldova" still may dominate much of the economy, but transition toward a free market system advances. A 2005 World Bank report on Moldova's opportunities for accelerated growth reveals that, since 2000, Moldova's strong growth performance reversed a decade of economic decline and rising poverty. Between 2000 and 2004, real GDP increased by more than 30 percent and poverty was reduced by more than half.

The period immediately following independence was characterized by accelerating inflation, declines in production and trade, and shortages and high prices of key goods, especially energy products. Moldovans were unable to freely collect their savings from state-owned banks, and most of the population lost much of what little they accumulated during the Soviet era. Things stabilized toward the end of 1993, with the introduction of the national currency, the Moldovan lei (MDL). Monetary policy in 1995 sharply reduced inflation. In 1997, Moldova experienced the first year of growth of output since independence; however, the economy was hit hard in 1998 by a regional crisis starting with Russia's default on its treasury bills. GDP declined by nearly 9 percent that year, but over the next three years, the economy improved. GDP growth remained stable several years beyond 2000, though unemployment remained high.

A sticky problem remained: Moldova lagged behind on structural reforms and on facilitating a business-friendly legal and tax environment (Spanu, 2004). According to a

World Bank survey (2005), Moldova is among the top 10 nations worldwide in achieving significant results in reforming the business environment in 2004, after several tough years, yet the role of government has been questioned. An old Moldovan saying reads: "The fish starts rotting from the head, while the economy starts from the government." Still, privatization launched in 1993 meant progress in selling some state enterprises (but not all), liberalizing prices, phasing out subsidies on consumer goods, and streamlining the banking system. In 2005, proceeds from state property sales totaled $13 million USD.

According to the Ministry of Economy, imports in 2004 totaled $1,774.2 million USD, 21 percent more than in 2003. Imports from former Soviet states increased 48.4 percent and from Eastern Europe 30.1 percent, followed by EU nations (21.5 percent). Major exporters to Moldova were Ukraine, Russia, Romania, Germany, Italy and Turkey (PricewaterhouseCoopers, 2005). In 2004, exports totaled $986.3 million USD, a 26.2 percent increase over 2003. Leading destination nations were former Soviet states, the European Union and Romania. Leading receivers of Moldovan goods were Russia, Italy, Romania, Germany and Ukraine.

Three Moldovan entities facilitate import-export negotiations and transactions. The Moldovan Export Promotion Organization (MEPO) supports exporters and importers, and helps foreign investors on international trade and Moldova's business climate. MoldPro, an NGO that facilitates trade, promotes collaboration between private and public sectors, helping to identify costly issues and develop measures to eliminate barriers to fruitful external trade. MoldExpo is the leading international exhibition center in Moldova offering specialized trade shows promoting Moldova and Moldovan goods and services. Activities include food and drink, cosmetics, tourism, sport, construction materials, medicine and agricultural equipment categories. An exhibit of advertising agency products, technologies, equipment and materials was scheduled for November 2006. In February 2006, the third annual national "Made in Moldova" exhibition was held, attracting more than 70 Moldovan companies, culminating with the announcement of the "Commercial Brand of the Year" contest winner. Poliproject helps to organize international exhibitions, national fairs and specialized programs.

Moldova is working to adopt European standards relating to fighting corruption and organized crime. Several legal acts have passed targeting corruption but are not effectively enforced because of corruption at different levels of government. A Criminal Code enacted in 2003 says offering and accepting bribes are criminal acts, with stiff fines and penalties including imprisonment for violators. International and local organizations also try to counter the problem, but Moldova's ranking in Transparency International's Corruption Index remained relatively low (in 2005, its ranking improved to 95th place out of 159 countries). According to informal surveys, though, about one third of Moldovan firms admitted they occasionally paid bribes.

A government report described a communications campaign developed by the state to inform the public of the importance of citizen participation in advancing the *Economic Growth and Poverty Reduction Strategy Paper* project (2004), meaning proposed country assistance to Moldova for 2005–2008. The objective was to get citizens across Moldova involved in promoting the idea. A national essay contest called "A solution for my country" resulted in 560 student submissions, mobilizing an estimated 2,500–3,000 parents, fellow pupils and teachers. Radio and TV spots aired, including a spot on Moldova 1 for three months, and 10,000 leaflets and 3,000 posters were distributed during organized events and through direct mail.

Moldova had a registered population of 3,968,071, most Eastern Orthodox by faith, according to the national October 2004 census. Urban and rural divisions are 59 percent and 41 percent, respectively. Ethnically, Moldovans/Romanians constituted 78.2 percent, while Ukrainians (8.4 percent), Russians (5.8 percent), Gagauzians (4.4 percent) and Bulgarians (1.9 percent) were other notable groups. Adult male literacy is 95 percent while adult female literacy is 81.3 percent, according to the Department of Statistical and Sociological Analysis, or DSSA (2005).

Some sources say 38 percent of Moldovans live on less than $2 USD daily, while others say 80 percent earn less than $1 USD daily. Understandably, price is the key product purchase determinant. Spanu (2004) claims that income is unevenly distributed among different social and ethnic groups and regions. Official average monthly wages in Moldova remain low in US dollar terms (Prohnitchi, 2005), about $60 for public officials, yet a PricewaterhouseCoopers business guide to Moldova (2005) claims the average monthly salary in the first half of 2005 was $97 USD, estimated to increase to about $110 USD in 2006 (DSSA, 2005). As consumer prices increased almost 11 percent in 2004, household expenses in 2004 were 56 percent for food products, 12 percent for housing, 8 percent for clothes and footwear, and 6 percent for transportation and communications. Smaller percentages accounted for health, alcohol and tobacco, leisure and education, according to the DSSA (2005). Interestingly, alcohol and tobacco expenses were almost double that of education in cities yet almost five-fold education in villages. More than 40 percent of Moldovans are thought to live in poverty, and more than 70 percent of the poor live in rural areas. In some villages, half the population migrated out of the country and, in a survey, over 60 percent of households considered themselves poor, according to the DSSA (2005). Since 1996, estimates are that 1 million citizens have left Moldova. Most emigrants are young, educated and skilled, so Moldova is short about half its labor force.

An opinion poll conducted by the Institute of Marketing and Surveys in Chisinau in November 2004 revealed that 56 percent of the population thinks the economy is moving in the wrong direction (a similar survey from May 2004 showed 48.5 percent). Many believe that the "shadow economy" of business restrictions left over from the Soviet era makes it difficult for many to run successful businesses, ultimately forcing them to "go underground." OPINIA Independent Sociological and Informational Service in Chisinau polled online 834 Moldovan adults in December 2005 and January 2006. Demographically, respondents were heavily skewed in two categories: 91.2 percent were university degreed and 68.1 percent were female. Almost half were 18–30, while 41.8 percent were 31–50 (less than 10 percent were 51+). It revealed more subjects (42 percent) thought the "social-economic situation" in 2005 had been "bad," while 28 percent said "very bad" and 21 percent "average." For the near-term future "direction of the nation," 46 percent said "right" and 44 percent "wrong." More subjects (41 percent) felt that 2006 would be "probably good" compared to 2005, while an equal mix (33 percent) thought in looking back that change from 2004 to 2005 was either "good" or "bad." Such results indicate the harsh realities of the past, yet hope for the future.

In 2003, the state's Department of Tourism Development created an image campaign for Moldova themed: "Feel at home in the heart of nature." According to Stanislav Rusu (2005), head of the department's International Relations and Marketing Division, marketing Moldova as a "positive and attractive tourism destination" is a big task because little is known about the country abroad and because a national awareness effort is needed to encourage Moldovans to enjoy and appreciate their own national heritage. In the 1990s, area nation visitation declined and tourism was not effectively marketed due to Moldova's struggling socio-economic environment. Rusu's staff identified deficiencies like weak national image and branding, lack of financial resources, and underutilization of existing promotional channels. They also recognized the need to stimulate wider use of the Moldova tourism logo and branding by businesses providing tourism services, and to develop tourism promotion programs in embassies, trade organizations and transportation facilities. Finally, thanks to annual tourism fairs at MoldExpo, explained Irina Bulat (2005), tourism manager at Solei Turism in Chisinau, they learned that improving access to tourism information was vital, including creating databases of tourism products and services and securing state funding commitments to permanent annual tourism marketing, according to an internal Department of Tourism Development report (2005).

Agriculture represents about 35 percent of Moldova's GDP, with wine-making and tobacco production two primary industries. The crown jewel of Moldovan agribusiness is 5,000-year-old wine making, accounting for almost half of the nation's total export earnings. Its share of the GDP is about 25 percent. In 2005, Moldova exported $313 million USD in wine, up $38 million over 2004. Of 180 wine making plants and 29 wineries in a nation ranked 7th among the top wine global exporters and where 10 percent of land is covered by vineyards, a handful of names are notable, topped by Cricova, the largest wine cellar in the world, which advertises: "We have what we aspire to and we do this with enthusiasm," according to Ekaterina Robu (2005), Cricova public relations manager. Brands like Milestii Mici, Nisporeni, Stauceni, Hincesti and Vismos also command respect. Moldova celebrates a National Wine Holiday in October, while the government touts optional itineraries for "the wine road tour" (2005). Also, "ExpoVin Moldova 2006," the 15th annual international wine fair held in February at MoldExpo, attracted a record 180 companies, according to organizer Poliproject. Only 50 percent were Moldovan firms.

Moldova used to produce more than half of all tobacco in the Soviet Union. In the 1980s, about one-fourth of Moldova's population earned some income from this sector, as tobacco provided almost 20 percent of government revenue. The industry, however, lost ground later in the decade, even as Moldova became the leading tobacco producer in Eastern Europe. Since 2000, tobacco production leaders have competed in a market saturated by cheap, bootleg versions of famous American brands. Dominant state-owned enterprise Tutun-CTC proclaims in ads that it is "Moldova's Regional Tobacco Leader," selling nearly 4 billion cigarettes domestically and exporting almost 5 billion, mainly to Russia and Ukraine, including its own "American blend" brands recently introduced. It estimates that almost all imports are smuggled. Director General Gheorghe Nafornita admitted that counterfeited brands like "Temp," "Astra" and "Doina" are a big problem. Private tobacco producers play a minor role in Moldova, such as Imperial Tobacco, according to Victoria Manole (2005), Imperial marketing executive. In 1997, Parliament adopted a law limiting tobacco advertising. Article 12 prohibits radio, private and state TV, and outdoor ads, but allows point-of-sale, cable TV, international print media and kiosk ads. Also, local print media and cinema ads are partially restricted, according to a 2003 amendment. No restrictions exist on product placement in TV or film, sponsored events with tobacco brand names, direct mail giveaways or promotional discounts.

One person seems to be a driving force behind the emergence of advertising as a profession in Moldova, Ion Macari, generally considered the "father of Moldovan advertising." He was in the business more than 50 years, mostly in the Soviet Union. In the 1940s, with no marketing or advertising training, because it was prohibited, the Moldova native dared to contact Moscow authorities personally about the potential for advertising in Moldova. A Soviet Vice Minister of Culture approved and told Macari to open the first official Moldovan ad agency. Because space could not be rented for such an undertaking, "Mold Reklama" occupied a room at the state university in Chisinau. Though security agents allegedly spied on "Mold Reklama," Macari's enterprise successfully planned two programs, a chemical herbicide exhibition and an exhibition of French sportswear. This sparked keen interest among others in Moldova to follow his lead, given the right moment: failure of the Soviet state (Macari, 2005). According to Wells (1994), beginning in 1985, Western advertising concepts created a conflict of values among Soviet ad professionals. They were torn between holding on to their social and cultural values and advancing *perestroika* initiatives. Domestic firms wanted to advertise, ad agencies needed to grow as an industry, and media needed other income sources to become less dependent on government subsidies (Grow-Van Dorn and Akimova, 1988).

Communication holding companies became leaders in 2004, uniting diverse ad agencies and allowing advertisers access to professionally produced promotional campaigns, although business-to-business remained lesser developed than consumer advertising. A key to marketing success has been having Western consulting and ad agencies operating in-country, according to the US Department of State's "FY Country Commercial Guide on Moldova" (2001). Three categories of ad agencies in Moldova are: 1) full-service shops offering above-the-line (ATL) strategic planning, creative, media planning and buying services, plus below-the-line (BTL) direct marketing, sales promotion and public relations services; 2) specialized shops providing one type of service, such as design, event planning or Internet service; and 3) media shops specializing in media ad placement (Andronic et al., 2005). Few advertise their own services.

According to the 2006 *Yellow Pages of Moldova*, 123 ad agencies operated early in 2006, although only 16 were full-service. More than 40 offered media planning and placement, while more than 30 provided specialty expertise (souvenirs, accessories, T-shirts, etc.). Additionally, 23 firms provided strategic planning and branding to clients, and nine specialized in outdoor advertising. Video and audio production services were offered by 41 and 22 companies, respectively, while 16 provided BTL services. The average staff size was 12, ranging from a low of two to a high of 40. An estimated 63 agencies were formed after 2000. Interestingly, the oldest still in existence, established in 1973, is Mold Reklama, specializing in outdoor, design and production services. Only six agencies are located outside Chisinau.

The most prominent international agencies in Moldova have included McCann Erickson Moldova, Grey Worldwide Moldova, Ogilvy & Mather, Target Leo Burnett, BBDO, FCB and Lowe Chisinau. Local experts agree that McCann Erickson, which entered the market in 2002, has been most successful to date, though Grey was the most prominent in 1999, according to Media Manager Gheorghe Braileanu (2005). With 18 staff members, McCann's client roster includes Coca-Cola, Goodyear, Glaxo Smith Kline, ExxonMobil, Vimex, and Acasa Medica. Exemplary works include image campaigns for Moldcell, Alba dairy products, Gura Cainarului mineral water and Oriflame cosmetics. The agency also launched Nescafé Gold coffee in 2004 and Winston cigarettes in 2003, according to Natalia Puhleakova, Managing Director (2005).

Alina Fortunatova (2005), Client Services Director, said McCann is the only true full-service shop in Moldova, though the market is ripe for more multinational agencies. Most competitors are media, creative, planning or production houses, "and outside of Chisinau, few small agencies exist, typically with one or two clients often only because of personal connections between agency and company executives." McCann does public service pro bono work, notably for UNICEF (on child abuse, headlined: "Looking for help?"), AMICUL, a non-governmental organization (NGO) offering free counseling and assistance to at-risk children (titled: "All children have a right to protection!"), and an anti-trafficking campaign (features this billboard headline: "YOU are not for sale!").

Though Ogilvy opened in 1998, providing media, BTL, market research and creative services to clients like Lucky Strike and Kent cigarettes, its notable campaign effort was pro bono work presented to the European Commission in 2003 bringing attention to the problem of trafficking of young girls from Moldova. A headline shouted: "Say 'no' to trafficking of women!" Ogilvy closed a few years later (Cenusa, 2005).

Suninform, founded in 1998, is the best known private full-service Moldovan agency, listing clients like Voxtel, Moldcell, Air Moldova, Lukoil, Sun Communications (including SunTV), Agroindbank and Eximbank. Its rate card for 60-second TV spots ranges from $25 to $200 USD per spot, while 30-second radio spots range from $6 to $27 USD per spot, both depending on time slot and not considering discounts. Flat rates for advertising on the state-run Moldova 1 TV channel are significantly higher: from $300 to $500 USD per 60-second spot. Rates vary by day-part and weekday. Sergey Starush, Star Communication Group general manager (2005), admitted that mobile traffic advertising like sides of trolley buses and maxi-taxis is the least costly media option.

Notable private shops include: Star, offering full services to clients like Kraft, Coca-Cola and Riscom computers; Diver Studio, serving clients like Accent Electronics (distributor of HP, Compaq and IBM), Banca de Economii, Banca Sociala, Fidesco food store chain, Air Moldova and Moldavian Airlines, Moldcell, Moldova 1, Moldexpo, Sun TV, Victoriabank, Vitanta beer and Voxtel; Galartmedia, a media planning and buying agency serving clients like Wrigley, Kraft foods, Franzuleta, Zikkurat and Biblion; P&P Studio, specializing in broadcast and print production, and listing clients in banking, food services and television media; Metiba Design, specializing in outdoor advertising, particularly signs and billboards for clients like Moldinconbank, Multievo and Orhei Vit; Ponti Media, serving clients like Cricova, Grand Hall shopping mall, Teodor ballet attire and Hotel Dedeman Grand Chisinau; and Rogers, whose expertise is large format printed products for outdoor ads with clients including ExpoVin 2005, Maximum, Sun TV and Metro Cash & Carry, plus auto brands Renault, Skoda and Peugeot.

Varo-Inform is the best-known Moldovan advertising company responsible for outdoor and transportation signage. Founded in 1990, it employs 40, making it the single largest employer in the agency sector. It has even designed vehicles for transporting Vitanta beer and mail delivery cars for Posta Moldovei. Popular outdoor clients include Voxtel, Moldcell, Benetton, Avon, Panasonic, Philip Morris, Samsung, Toshiba and Union Fenosa.

Few Moldovan agencies to date have entered creative work in international advertising competitions, but local experts believe more will soon submit work. Some shops for the first time entered the annual International Advertising Festival in Kiev, Ukraine, the International TV and Cinema Forum in Yalta, Ukraine, and the Russian Association for Stimulation of Sales program in Moscow, but won no awards. A couple of agencies were recognized for entries judged at the Moldexpo Design and Advertising Contest. Some contacts indicated future interest in the Moscow International Advertising Festival, the Golden Drum International Advertising Festival of the New Europe in Slovenia, and the Cannes Lions in France. Also, to date, no official advertising associations exist in Moldova because "no spirit of cooperation exists yet," Fortunatova (2005) said. Starush (2005) agreed that the need exists "in order to unite all advertising people here."

According to AGB Moldova's Managing Director, Sergey Monul (2005), four of the top 10 television advertisers in Moldova were mobile communications operators and large foreign companies or their local distributors. For 2004, they were Voxtel, Procter & Gamble, Moldcell, Patria Cinema, Efes Vitanta Moldova Brewery, Nestlé, Kraft foods, Evyap body care products, Flacara Cinema and Dr Theiss medicinal preparations. For example, Vitanta claims in its self-promotions that the best employees, superior products and long-standing tradition of constant improvement help it to satisfy increasing market demands. The first brewery in Moldova founded in 1873, Vitanta features seven beer brands and offers six soft drink brands. Its beer advertising proclaims in Romanian: "Tradition in the art of beer!" Voxtel's Tempo calling card declares in Romanian: "On your rhythm" when explaining the voice mail feature in one ad, while another ad declares "Be my favorite." Both ads run the tagline: "Thinking about you." Natalia Cogalniceanu (2005), Moldcell marketing communications associate, said their company's "Friends and Family" promotions feature the "Your connection with your world" message. The Moldovan, Turkish and Finnish joint venture celebrated its fifth anniversary in Moldova in 2005 with the theme: "Moldcell—5 years a part of your life." The company has run more than 70 promotional programs and personalized offers and supported over 50 social and cultural events, including a readership fair with some 6,000 village children who received free fairy tale and poetry books. The festival was tagged "Two Twin Hearts."

Retail advertising appears vibrant in Chisinau, evidenced by samples of four-color, high-quality fliers, circulars, brochures and specialized literature offered at or near the point of sale: Bomba electronics supermarkets declare in Russian, "Seasonal gifts" or "Spring sensations." Green Hills food supermarkets state in Russian and Romanian: "You're invited!" while key competitor Nr. 1 food supermarkets in Russian say "Share the holiday action." McDonald's, which buys 80 percent of its supplies locally and agreed to build more restaurants in Moldova, continues its global "I'm Lovin' It" campaign, featuring the face of Ronald with this message in Romanian: "Learn something from behind the scenes at McDonald's!" Major local economy giants conduct sporadic, smaller-scale ad campaigns compared to market leaders. Bucuria, the largest confectionary plant in Moldova, promotes that "Life is sweeter with us!" as it sells more than 200 products made from natural ingredients in 60 shops. Franzeluta, the largest Moldovan bakery, Guivaer, the largest jewelry factory, and Sherut, the largest floor covering shop, also advertise on a limited basis. Many smaller Moldovan firms do not advertise because they lack knowledge of marketing, branding and message development.

Some enterprises, such as beekeeping and its honey industry, lack much-needed advertising exposure. The National Association of Beekeepers suggested that an ad campaign be launched in Moldova to promote honey production and consumption, but none has yet been developed. At its peak, an estimated 200,000 families in-country were engaged in beekeeping with apiaries on former collective or state, as well as private, farms (Popushoi, 2004).

Moldova's banking system underwent significant changes since being set up in 1991. Commercial banks act under authorization of the National Bank of Moldova, the country's central bank. Local banks are consolidating while preparing to compete with foreign banks entering the market, such as Romania's Banca Comerciala, Austria's Raiffeisen Bank and Russia's Vneshtorgbank. Of the 16 commercial banks in Moldova, the most successful are Agroindbank, advertised as "Your best partner in Moldova"; Victoriabank, "The best bank of Moldova"; Banca Sociala, "The reliable business partner"; Moldinconbank, promoting "Whoever you are, we are working for you!"; and Banca de Economii, boasting "The presence in each square meter," depicting all locations on a national map. Other popular banks with promotional themes are Mobiasbank ("It's Your Bank!"), Fincombank ("Together throughout your life"), Eurocreditbank ("Reflecting a possible you"), Eximbank ("Proud to serve all your needs") and Comertbank ("For your success!").

Nine political parties active in Moldova used advertising during the March 2005 parliamentary elections, including the Communist Party (PCRM), Democratic Bloc of Moldova (BMD), Christian Democratic People's Party (CCDP) and Partidul Democrat din Moldova (PDM). Key winners were the pro-Western PCRM with 46.1 percent of the country, BMD with 28.4 percent and CCDP with 9.1 percent. Formerly allied with Russia, the PCRM expected to win 39 percent, but earned less than the 50 percent they gained in the 2001 elections. Their candidate, Moldovan President Vladimir Voronin and party chair, was barely re-elected to a second term. The centrist BMD, seeking closer ties to Russia, expected to take only 13 percent, while the center-right Romanian-oriented PPCD was predicted to win 15 percent. Only these three parties won seats in the 101-member parliament.

Each party's slogan played a prominent role in the campaign. PCRM proclaimed: "Together we will transform Moldova into a rich country, with wealthy people. With us, Moldova will win!," based on a platform of a new quality of life, economic modernization, European integration, and consolidation of the society. In November 2005, Voronin indicated possibly changing the name of the party to reflect new Western-oriented values, but said: "We are not going to run ahead of the locomotive." About 35 percent of members were in the past members of the Communist Party of the Soviet Union (CPSU). BMD promoted: "We are coming to do good! European integration will be possible only with a new governing! The future is with Democratic Moldova! Together for a better life!" CDPP simply stated: "YES for people. YES for Moldova." PDM proclaimed "Solidaritate, Libertate, Dreptate!"

The Electoral Code regulates conditions where state radio and TV offer advertising time to candidates. Maximum time permitted is two hours over the entire campaign period, including no more than two minutes daily for each sponsor. Private broadcasters may organize debates, and each candidate receives equal time. Candidates may advertise on private broadcasts if they do not exceed three minutes daily per candidate at each station.

In the absence of self-regulation measures, general principles of advertising and the process of producing, placing and broadcasting ads are regulated by the state's Law on Advertising (no. 1227-XII from June 27, 1997). It defines dishonest, false, deceptive and immoral advertising, regulates ads in various media (including radio, TV, newspapers, theatres and videotapes), and regulates ads using specific technologies (telephone, telegraph and telex). It also establishes rights and obligations of ad agents and rights of professional ad organizations.

By law, duration of advertising for state-sponsored (but not private) broadcast media must not exceed 15 percent of time for radio or TV channels during 24 hours, and 20 percent of any one hour of broadcasting. It is prohibited to interrupt youth or religious programs with ads. Ads in state-financed periodicals should not exceed 30 percent of total space in one issue. Also, amoral advertising is prohibited, including discrediting state symbols (like the flag, coat of arms and anthem), religious symbols and the national currency.

The law also establishes restrictions for advertising goods like alcohol, tobacco, medicine and guns. For instance, ads for alcohol or tobacco products must not be broadcast on TV between 7 a.m. and 10 p.m. but when allowed must carry a warning of damages of use. Gun advertising is prohibited from 6 a.m. to 10 p.m. Interestingly, all outdoor advertising must be in Romanian. A state council regulating aspects of radio programming law mandated that at least 65 percent of radio programming be in Romanian. Furthermore, in Chisinau only, foreign advertisers must pay twice as much for outdoor ads because of a city council rule. It is hard to say whether such rules are respected, especially on radio and TV, because inefficient monitoring of programs has existed, despite the presence of measurement firms, according to some sources.

The state Law on the Press from October 1994 regulates relations between print media, government and society through recognizing rights and identifying responsibilities of the media. Article 13 defines requirements for periodical circulation data, yet local publications do not yet have circulation verified by audit companies, said Natalia Angheli-Zaicenco (2005), Independent Journalism Center (IJC) senior consultant. At the same time, some imported publications sold and distributed in Moldova certify circulation volume. Local experts believe some newspapers and magazines exaggerate circulation data to attract advertisers. The IJC is coordinating a proposal to initiate an Audit Bureau of Circulation(s) in Moldova.

Since advertising is a major income source for many periodicals, taxation issues are important. Part of the Tax Code, approved in 1997, says that advertising services are considered value-added taxable (VAT), despite that some media and NGOs tried unsuccessfully to gain exemption from the 20 percent VAT for specific periodicals. Local duties also have been imposed on advertising services in print media. In 2005, the Chisinau Municipal Council adopted a resolution providing for duties on broadcast, print media, and outdoor and transit ads in Chisinau. The duty grew to 5 percent of the service price before VAT, causing an uproar and at least temporary suspension. The concept of state support and incentives for mass media has been on hold since approval by parliament in 1999. In fact, the Law on State Support for Mass Media has not yet been adopted (Marciuk, 2005).

Telecommunications and mail service are important national services to the industry. Reforms in 1993 created two state enterprises, Moldtelecom and Posta Moldovei (Stratan, 2000), modern monopolies paid up to 45 percent of the production costs for their services. Moldtelecom is the national provider of telecommunications services, despite that this market was liberalized on January 1, 2004. Promoted as "Leading Moldova into the Information Age" in ads, it employs 7,800 staff and competes primarily with independent Internet services. Posta Moldovei is the national press distribution company representing 240 Moldovan titles and some 2,400 newspapers and magazines overall. It issued more than 500 postal stamps reflecting important social and political events, such as the 10th anniversary of Moldova's independence, 130 years of Moldovan railways, and the 570th birthday celebration of patron saint Stefan cel Mare.

An estimated 17 percent of Moldovans have Internet access, according to the IREX Media Sustainability Index (2005). Several Internet service providers (ISP) are connected to Moldtelecom's Internet point of presence. Providers include Moldova Online, Moldtelecom, Arax-Impex, Riscom, StarNet, Transcor, MoldInfoNet, Moldpac, Globnet, Telemedia Group, Megadat, NeoNet and DNT, according to Bogasieru (2004). Most users are corporate clients, yet ISPs also offer services for individual clients. By March 2004, 186 Internet cafés were registered. One ISP, Voxtel, registered 100,000 users of its Internet Mobil Online (IMO) service as of December 2005. An estimated 6,000 subscribers were identified in 1999.

Print media advertising in 2005 was estimated to be about $3.5 million USD (IREX Media Sustainability Index, 2005). Media share of advertising spending by medium estimates are: TV 67 percent, outdoor 12 percent, press 11 percent and radio 10 percent. US Ambassador to Moldova Heather Hodges (2004), speaking to Moldova university students, cited a poll claiming almost half of all Moldovans read a newspaper several times weekly, nearly 60 percent listen to radio, and almost 80 percent watch TV daily. The independent press is diverse, with titles appealing to men, women and youth in terms of socio-political, economic, entertainment or cultural interests. Most are headquartered in Chisinau. According to the IREX Media Sustainability Index (2005), 28 national Romanian-language newspapers are published in Moldova. Two are dailies, two bi-weeklies and the rest weeklies. Also, 34 Russian-language newspapers are published, including four dailies, two published in Moscow, and one biweekly. Additionally, about 40 local and regional publications are produced, not including Transniestria. Though numerous magazines are available, few are Moldovan titles.

Most media managers claim that retail and subscription sales, plus advertising, cover about two thirds of publication costs, while "sponsorships" cover the balance. It is hard to determine what "sponsorship" means because purported "secret owners" do not want information to become public. In some instances, sources of media revenues are not identified and disclosures of company accounts are not made. Only owners and shareholders of main independent organizations are identified (Ciubasenco, 2004).

Periodicals are divided along language lines: Romanian and Russian daily and weekly newspapers and magazines, typically with separate readerships. Russian-language titles are preferred in the business community because most urban readers are Russian-language speakers or ethnic Russians or because ad companies prefer Russian-language print media (Stefirta, 2005). An estimated 22 print media in Romanian and 18 in Russian are published in Chisinau. Most Romanian-language titles attract lesser attention from advertisers, explaining why some publish in both languages. No major English-language titles exist in Moldova.

According to Natalia Sineavskaya (2005), Advertising Director of *Komsomolskaya Pravda*, the largest circulation daily newspaper in Moldova, advertising is the largest department. It runs only display ads but plans to add classified ads. Major advertisers include Voxtel, Bomba, Bosch, Nistru Lada (auto) and Lara (real estate). Ads are only in Romanian, despite that the paper is part of a large Russian enterprise. Assistant Advertising Director Yuri Grushev (2005) said that, despite its start in Moldova during an economic crisis, it increased circulation and pages. Though it lost money, the Friday issue began to grow significantly in circulation. Its key competitor is the popular weekly Russian-language television guide, *Antena*. Also, *Makler*, the first and largest newspaper of ads, to date the only major title in Moldova with classified ads, is published in Russian. Together with *Komsomolskaya Pravda*, they are among the few profitable publications in the nation.

Weeklies have enjoyed popularity and larger circulations since the mid-1990s. Key independent weeklies include: *Flux, Saptamina, Novoye Vremya, Timpul de Dimineata, Literatura si Arta, Jurnal de Chisinau, Ekonomicheskoye Obozreniye, Kishiniovskie Novosti, Delovaya Gazeta, Moldavskie Vedemosti, Ziarul de Garda, Kommersant Plus* and *Megapolis*. This category includes party titles such as *Kommunist*, founded by the Party of Communists, and *Democratia*, founded by the Social-Liberal Party.

Though 15 magazines are published in Moldova, their print market share is minor. Commercial titles have a shorter history and are led by *Chef, Siesta, Banca si Finante, Aquarelle, VIP Magazin, Capitala-magazin* (Harabara, 2002) and a new title, *Ost & Co. Chef* and *Siesta* are supported primarily through advertising. Non-commercial specialty titles include *Alunelel* (children), *Contabilitate si Audit* (accounting) and *Sud-Est* (culture and civilization). Though advertising is not their main source of income, they carry ads.

According to Bogasieru (2004), print ad rates run $1.60USD per square centimeter in newspapers, depending on circulation, print quality and page. Seldom is color used, and often paper quality (and image reproduction) is poor. Ad costs range from 40 cents to $1 USD per square centimeter in *Ekonomicheskoye Obozrenie*. *Makler* classified ads cost Moldovans 60 cents and foreign residents $1 USD per square meter. Newspaper rate cards from 2005 showed a range of flat costs for ad space, excluding frequency discounts, taxes, etc. In *Komsomolskaya Pravda*, the smallest and least costly ad (1/128 page) was 42 MDL, while the most expensive full-page ad was 12,075 MDL. *Jurnal de Chisinau* asked 100 MDL for a 1/48-page ad and 4,940 MDL for a full-page ad. *Timpul* charged $50USD for an inside full page. Similarly, 2005 magazine rate cards also indicated a range of flat fees for advertising. In *Aquarelle*, the lowest cost 1/4-page ad was 220 Euros, the lowest cost full-page ad 620 Euros, and the back cover position 1,150 Euros. Additionally, *VIP Magazin* charged 200 Euros for a 1/4 page or 500 Euros for an inside page, and *Chef* asked 250 Euros for an inside full page.

Of 167 television stations in Moldova, 51 private and 116 cable options were available in 2005, but few offered primarily locally-produced content. Most channels rebroadcast programming from Russia or Romania. Also, most television growth has been in Chisinau. Most Moldovans, urban and rural, watch some television. Of an estimated 1.5 million households averaging 2.8 persons, the largest viewing segment by age is 15–24 (18.2 percent), followed by 35–44 (15.3 percent), 25–34 (13.6 percent) and 45–54 (12.8 percent). Smallest viewing segments are 55–64 and 65+, according to the DSSA (2005). A new channel, TV-7, began broadcasting in early 2006, with Russian rebroadcasts and limited original programming.

Russia's state Channel 1 or ORT (Obshchestvyennoye Rossiskoye Televidyeniye) is the most popular channel in Moldova, covering most of the capital and the country, according to AGB Moldova. It rebroadcasts Russian programs, mainly news and movies, and is 51 percent owned by the Russian government. Another major nationwide channel is the public Moldova 1, operated mostly in Romanian by state-run Teleradio-Moldova. It features diverse programming and attracts major advertisers like Moldcell and international brands. With plans to expand beyond the Chisinau urban area, privately-owned ProTV primarily rebroadcasts Romanian content, with daily local newscasts in Romanian and Russian. It is popular with younger viewing audiences, while ORT is popular with older skews, according to an *Observator Economic* (2000) report. Nata Albot (2005), Director of ProFM radio and ProTV announcer, said television makes more money than radio. Russian radio broadcasts dominate the market, while the most popular format is all music and less talk. Most local TV offerings are rebroadcasts from Romania. She said the station continually strives to experiment with content to attract listeners and advertisers. Regarding language, she said Russians do not listen to Romanian or Moldovan, though Moldovans listen to either Moldovan/Romanian or Russian.

Other nationally-available channels are CTC (a Russian channel run by the Russian State Television and Radio Broadcasting Company) and NTV (a Russian national network owned by state-run energy firm Gazprom). A popular alternative among Chisinau viewers is NIT (controlled by a business group linked to Moldova's ruling Communist Party, rebroadcasting Russian and Romanian programming and music, covering 87 percent of Chisinau). Other available channels are Ren TV (a Moscow-based commercial station with strong regional networks in different nations), Euro TV Chisinau (also known as "the mayor's channel"), TVC 21, RIF (TV-1000), TVR-1 (Romanian rebroadcasts), MY3 TV (Russian music channel), RTF, Noviy Kanal, TV-26, Eurosport, Discovery and Euronews. Television advertising blocks are introduced either as "Reklama" (Russian for advertising) or "Publicitate" (Romanian for advertising). Scheduling, based on the legal limit of 12 minutes per hour, includes Moldova 1, typically with 2-minute blocks comprised of shorter spots (30 and 15 seconds), and ProTV, typically with 5-minute blocks comprised of longer spots (60 seconds), according to Bogasieru (2004). On average in 2005, a spot cost $345 USD in prime time. It is estimated that inflation of TV spot costs about 25 percent annually (2004–2005).

Sun Cable, a joint Moldovan-American venture and the largest cable TV firm in the country, featured more than 50 channels for subscribers in 2005. In addition to previously mentioned channels, Sun also offered another 18 Russian channels (including news, sports, reality entertainment, history and nostalgia, business and religious programs) and 10 Romanian channels, plus CNN International, BBC World, ESPN and MTV. Additionally, channels representing Ukraine, Germany, Turkey, France, Italy, Spain and Adjaria were available.

In 2004, the top 10 advertising categories were mobile communications, shops, washing liquids, entertainment, shampoos and soaps, beer, television, insurance, soft drinks and banks. Other important categories were cultural activities, printing services and coffee. Top 10 advertisers were Procter & Gamble, Voxtel, Moldcell, Vitanta, Nestlé, Hayat Kimya, Wrigley, Patria Cinema, Flacara Cinema and Lukoil Cinema. Other important advertisers were Maximum, National Palace, Bosch, Supraten, Camelia and Alina Electronics, said Oleg Sliusarenco (2005), regional research director of TNS-Ukraine in Chisinau.

An estimated 87.5 percent of Moldovans listen at least occasionally to some 40 radio stations. More than 20 stations, including private FM and national AM stations, served Chisinau in 2004 with Moldovan and Russian news, music and other programming. Most popular stations are HIT-FM (featuring Russian music) with an estimated 70 percent reach, Russkoye Radio PoliDisc (65 percent reach), KISS-FM (55 percent reach) and Antena C (city-owned music with some original programming). Radio Moldova, also operated by state-run Teleradio-Moldova, is broadcast across the country. Several stations simply rebroadcast Russian programming. Radio Nova is a private enterprise offering original programs, international news and talk, while ProFM is the local office of the Romanian ProFM station. Others include Russian stations Europa Plus, Radio Monte Carlo, Radio Nostalgie, Nashe Radio, Radio d'Or and Serebriannii Dojdi. Additionally, Dinamit FM, Radio Sanatatea, Radio Contact and Info Radio serve this market.

According to station rate cards, Antena C charges from 19 to 45 Moldovan lei (MDL) per spot, while Russkoye Radio PoliDisc charges from $9 to $27 USD, depending on the time slot and not considering frequencies, discounts, taxes, etc. Cenusa (2004) claims the average cost of a 30-second spot, considering five stations, was 8.33 Euros. Cost per minute was 10 Euros for Dinamit FM and 15 Euros for Radio Moldova and other stations.

Three marketing and media organizations arrived in 2004 in Moldova: TNS Ukraine, AGB Moldova and TV Monitoring. With headquarters in London, TNS Ukraine began collecting, analyzing and interpreting market research data collected by interviewers assigned to Moldova, according to Sliusarenco (2005). In 2004, the firm assessed print publication readership and audiences for leading radio stations. TV Monitoring reports station audience share nationally and in Chisinau by time slots and geographic audiences and maintains logs of commercial spots by channel, length of spot, time slot, sponsor, language and brand name, according to Tatyana Cheban (2005), Director. It also provides information about advertisers in Chisinau based on weekly measures. The company expected to begin offering print and outdoor measurements in late 2005. ABG Moldova, part of the Nielsen Media Research network, also monitors TV and measures audiences. It started delivering Peoplemeter data in January 2004 with 150 households in Chisinau. The next six months, the panel increased to 350, covering urban areas and socioeconomic classes. According to Monul (2005) and Liubovi Cociug (2005), Client Service Director, key clients are television stations (RTR in Moldova, NIT and TVC 21), media buyers, and advertising agencies (including McCann Erickson).

In September 2004, AGB concluded from a TV audience study that Moldovan viewers spent an average of three hours a day watching TV. A January 2005 nationwide audience survey analyzed station share. Research also revealed women watched TV more than men, viewers 55+ concentrated on TV more than other demographic groups, and more educated viewers watched TV more than lesser educated viewers. The largest TV advertisers like Moldcell, Voxtel and Procter & Gamble reduced budgets for this period but maintained their leading positions. According to Starush (2005), some who ignore AGB Moldova data doubt its accuracy, also claiming high and non-negotiable prices. He said the first media sales house in Moldova, Media Communications Group (MCG), tried but failed to gain exclusive rights from TV channels. The problem was that MCG did not work with television channel leader ORT.

As Wells (1994) described, successful advertising in former Soviet republics, like Moldova, is possible if Western influences are encouraged, even as each nation attempts to define its own national identity while addressing unique economic, political and cultural issues affecting the needs of its people. Survival may depend on Moldova's ability to combine Western ways with Moldovan cultural sensibilities within its own business framework, proving Lenin wrong when he purportedly described ad people as "the leeches of capitalism." Indeed, things have changed dramatically since then, though crucial challenges await in dealing with poverty, debt, emigration, trade, business practice, economic concerns and governmental policy.

It seems fitting, given the nation's long, hard struggle from principality to republic, that Moldova's flag bears the band of red, signifying the blood spilled in its defense. Long serving as a focal point for border disputes and expansionist policies, Moldova has been overrun, split up, reunited, conquered, annexed, renamed and repeatedly taken back. This tiny country with old world charm seems to be an enigma, rising from the ruins of Soviet socialism to travel the road toward free market democracy. Though it is not yet there, most experts concur that Moldova is well on the way—a nation in transition from its dubious past to a promising future. Another Moldovan saying comes to mind: "Eating makes me sleepy. When I awaken, I'm always hungry." Again, a duality: cynicism and hope.

References

Albot, Nata, personal interview, March 1, 2005.
Andronic, Liudmila, Dmitrii Baltatu, Oleg Kolechko and Elena Onica (2005). Advertising market in Moldova. In *Prospects of Creating an Audit Bureau of Circulations in the Republic of Moldova* (pp. 215–21). Chisinau: Independent Journalism Center.
Angheli-Zaicenco, Natalia, personal interview, May 25, 2005.
Bizpro Moldova and Development Alternatives, Inc. (2004, July). *Assessing competitiveness in Moldova's economy*. Bethesda, MD: Development Alternatives, Inc.
Bogasieru, Iulian (2004, November). *Opening an Office in Chisinau, Moldova*. Chisinau: Business Information Service for the Newly Independent States (BISNIS).
Braileanu, Gheorghe, personal interview, May 18, 2005.
Bulat, Irina, personal interview, April 17, 2005.
Business Consulting Institute (2004, August). *Final Report for Chisinau Economic Growth Area*. Chisinau: Business Consulting Institute.
Cenusa, Maria, personal interview, February 25, 2005.
Cheban, Tatyana, personal interview, March 2, 2005.
Ciubasenco, Dmitri (2004, July). Corruption in the media of Moldova. *Analytical Bulletin*, Independent Journalism Center, Chisinau, pp. 13–14.
Cociug, Liubovi, personal interview, March 3, 2005.
Cogalniceanu, Natalia, personal interview, January 27, 2005.
Department of Statistical and Sociological Analysis (DSSA) (2005). *Statistical Yearbook of the Republic of Moldova, 2005*. Chisinau: Republic of Moldova.
Department of Tourism Development (2005). *Sustainable Tourism Development Strategy of the Republic of Moldova 2003–2015*. Chisinau: Republic of Moldova.
Dodonu, Veaceslav (2000, April). *Advertising in Moldova*. Chisinau: Business Information Service for the Newly Independent States (BISNIS).
Dogaru, Vitalie (2005, January 21). Moldova's curious growth. *Transitions Online*. [Online.] http://www.tol.org/client/article/13367-moldovas-curious-growth.html (retrieved 2005).
Economic Growth and Poverty Reduction Strategy Paper (2004–2006) (2004, June). Chisinau: Government of the Republic of Moldova.
Ernst & Young Moldova (2005). *Doing Business in Moldova*. Chisinau: Ernst & Young Moldova.
Fortunatova, Alina, personal interview, May 11, 2005.
FY 2001 Country Commercial Guide: Moldova (2000). US Department of State.

Grow-Van Dorn, Jean M. and Irina Akimova (1988, May). Advertising in Ukraine: cultural perspectives. *International Journal of Advertising*, 7(3).

Grushev, Yuri, personal interview, February 23, 2005.

Harabara, Nelly (ed.) (2002). *Ghid Mass-Media 2002 Media Guide*. Chisinau: Independent Journalism Center.

Hodges, Heather M. (2004). The media's role in ensuring an informed public. Paper presented at Moldova State University, February 25, 2004.

Horton, Nancy I. (2003). *The Essential Guide to Moldova*. International Women's Club.

International Research and Exchanges Board (IREX) (2005). *Media Sustainability Index 2005: Moldova* (pp. 169–81). Washington, DC: IREX.

Macari, Ion, personal interview, May 18, 2005.

Manole, Victoria, personal interview, May 23, 2005.

Marciuk, Aleksei (2005). Legal framework for the media. In *Prospects of Creating an Audit Bureau of Circulations in the Republic of Moldova* (pp. 196–204). Chisinau: Independent Journalism Center.

Monul, Sergey, personal interview, March 3, 2005.

Observator Economic (2000, April). With a look to the East and to the West. *Observator Economic*, 4: 54.

Popushoi, Vlada (2004, September). Moldova may forget the taste of honey. *Welcome*, 9(187): 6–7.

PricewaterhouseCoopers Chisinau (2005). *Business Guide to Moldova*. Chisinau: PricewaterhouseCoopers Chisinau.

Prohnitchi, Valeriu (2005). Economic context of mass media development in Moldova. In *Prospects of Creating an Audit Bureau of Circulations in the Republic of Moldova* (pp. 189–95). Chisinau: Independent Journalism Center.

Puhleakova, Natalia, personal interview, May 11, 2005.

Robu, Ekaterina, personal interview, March 16, 2005.

Rusu, Stanislav, personal interview, May 26, 2005.

Sineavskaya, Natalia, personal interview, February 23, 2005.

Sliusarenco, Oleg, personal interview, March 2, 2005.

Spanu, Vlad (2004). Why is Moldova poor and economically volatile? In *The EU and Moldova: On a Fault-line of Europe*. London: Federal Trust for Education.

Starush, Sergey, personal interview, May 17, 2005.

Stefirta, Sorina (2005). Mass media market in Moldova. In *Prospects of Creating an Audit Bureau of Circulations in the Republic of Moldova* (pp. 205–14). Chisinau: Independent Journalism Center.

Stratan, Aurel (2000). Mobile telephony market: it takes two to tangle? *Exclusive Chisinau*, 2: 20–22.

The Wine Road in Moldova (2005). Department of Tourism Development, Republic of Moldova.

Wells, Ludmilla G. (1994, March). Western concepts, Russian perspectives: meanings of advertising in the former Soviet Union. *Journal of Advertising*, 23(1).

World Bank (2005, September 9). *Moldova: Opportunities for Accelerated Growth*. Report No. 32876-MD.

Yellow Pages of Moldova (2006). Chisinau: Varo-Inform S.R.L.

12 Developments in Advertising in a Post-Socialist Environment: Longitudinal Analysis of Polish Print Ads

ELZBIETA LEPKOWSKA-WHITE AND THOMAS G. BRASHEAR

Introduction

After 1989, when Poland decided to adopt a free market economy, political, cultural and economic transformations began to pave a way for new developments in business. A new, more modern consumer society began to emerge, facilitated by the abundance of products and services unheard of during socialism. In this climate Polish advertising is being reshaped to satisfy constantly evolving consumer expectations and demands.

Research in the area of advertising in Eastern Europe is still scarce (Herpen, Pieters, Fidrmucova and Roosenboom, 2000; Lepkowska-White, Brashear and Weinberger, 2003). Not surprisingly, a meta-analysis of 60 studies that examined advertising content in numerous countries did not include any articles that focused on Eastern Europe (Abernethy and Franke, 1996). Many point out that more work is needed on advertising in environments that undergo profound political and economic transformations (Abernethy and Franke, 1996; Herpen, Pieters, Fidrmucova and Roosenboom, 2000; Lepkowska-White, 2004).

This chapter investigates changes in print advertising in Poland after 1989. Using the Western theory of advertising evolution developed by Leiss, Kline and Jhally (1986) and the information about the historical developments of advertising in Poland as the background, the objective is to investigate longitudinal changes in Polish print ads following 1989.

THEORETICAL FRAMEWORK

According to Leiss et al. (1986) developments in advertising over time depend on a number of factors such as political climate (for example democracy vs. autocracy), economic characteristics (for example income, leisure time and unemployment level) and culture (for example individualism and power distance) in a country. In the United States, for instance, over time "The dramatic rise in real incomes, discretionary spending, and leisure time also meant that a far greater proportion of the marketing effort could be devoted to human wants not directly tied to basic necessities. More precisely, messages about necessities could be incorporated within broader 'transformational' message formats ..." (Leiss et al., 1986, p. 49). Over time, in response to changes in the country, the content of ads changed from being focused on products and their characteristics to being centered on symbolic images, people, their personalities and lifestyles (Leiss et al., 1986).

Leiss et al. (1986) divide the advertising evolution in the United States into four stages. In the first stage called *the product information stage* persuasive and rational information about product functional characteristics is prevalent in advertising. In the *product image stage* ads present product pictures and symbolic relationships between goods and consumers where the goods relate to consumer values and ideas. In the *personalized stage* "people are explicitly and directly interpreted in their relationship to the world of the product. Social admiration, pride of ownership, anxiety about lack of use, or satisfaction in consumption become important humanizing dimensions of products ... The product does more than refer to the world of human interaction: it enters and acts in that world and resonates with its qualities" (Leiss et al., 1986, p. 194). Finally, in the *lifestyle stage* products are linked into consumer consumption styles by being an indispensable part of activities in which consumers engage. In summary, the early stages of advertising evolution feature ads that contain a high degree of text to describe functional product features. In the later stages, more visual representation of meaning is used with symbolic messages that intertwine products with the world of consumers.

Advertising in Poland: Historical Perspective

It is expected that similar changes have been occurring in advertising in Poland during the economic, political and cultural transformations which have been taking place since 1989. To describe these developments the economic, political and cultural changes are briefly discussed and the most recent developments in the advertising industry are described.

The economic environment in Poland has been improving significantly. From 1992 through 1998, the country enjoyed uninterrupted growth of 6 percent in Gross Domestic Product (European Advertising and Media Forecast, 2005/2006). Between 1989 and 2002, the economy slowed down but the predictions for 2007 are very optimistic and show that GDP will reach $338.36 US billions (Business Forecast Report, 2004). Inflation declined from 586 percent in 1990 to 3.6 percent in 2001 and has not exceeded this level since (Gulyás, 2003). Political changes leading to democracy are under way, although problems such as corruption and bureaucracy have slowed down this process. In regards to culture, Poles are increasingly more individualistic and focused on themselves and their careers (Kolman et al., 2003). In this political, economic and cultural environment, advertising in Poland is being reborn.

BIRTH OF ADVERTISING IN POLAND

Before 1989, advertising in Poland was rare; the supply of goods was limited and consumer demands unfulfilled. The socialist regime allowed for very few commercials. These were "amateurish," "lengthy," "unprofessional," and featured a narrow range of products such as appliances, steel and domestic cars such as the tiny Fiat 126p (Aleman, 1996). At the end of the socialist rule very few consumer brands (like Baltona, Pewex and Prusakolep) were advertised (Lubelska, 2001).

Just after 1989, advertising became popular as companies that were entering Poland were trying to build awareness and demand for their products. In 1993 ad spending increased by 241 percent, reaching $356.7 million in 1994. In 1998, the process slowed down with ad spending increasing by a more modest 70 percent (Lepkowska-White, 2004). In more recent years, many companies have reduced their advertising expenditures. Some have already established their brands (Lepkowska-White, 2004); the majority, however, has become concerned with the economic slowdown in Poland (Kocinska, 2001). Ad expenditures were about $2.22 billion in 2003 and are forecasted to reach $2.54 billion in 2005 (European Advertising and Media Forecast, 2005/2006).

Advertising Media and Ad Agencies in Poland

In 1990, Poland had only one TV station with 90 percent of the Polish audience (Wrobel, 2001). In the mid 1990s TV remained to be the most popular advertising media, followed by retail storefront displays, shelf space and packaging, magazines and billboards (Nowacki, 1997). Less popular were radio spots, newspaper ads, bus stop advertisements, transit ads and posters, followed by direct mail, catalogs, videotapes and telemarketing. Currently there are 179 television broadcast station in Poland and TV is still the leader with expenditures of $1.36 billion in 2003 and forecasted ad sales of $1.534 billion in 2005 (European Advertising and Media Forecast, 2005/2006). Ad spending in magazines was $322 million in 2003 and is forecasted to reach $369 million in 2005 (European Advertising and Media Forecast, 2005/2006). Advertising in newspapers amounted to $261 million in 2003 and is forecasted to be equal to $300 in 2005 (European Advertising and Media Forecast, 2005/2006). Other advertising media still popular in Poland include billboards, directories and cinema advertising (European Advertising and Media Forecast, 2005/2006).

Currently there are about 800 advertising agencies in Poland, but only 50 provide a full range of advertising services. The major international advertising firms include McCann Erickson Polska, Corporate Profiles DDB Group, Leo Burnett, Grupa NOS/ BBDO, Young & Rubicam Poland and Publicis (European Advertising and Media Forecast, 2005/2006). Among the most important laws that govern advertising practices are those that involve consumer protection, the press, broadcasting, food advertising, alcohol and tobacco, and the pharmaceutical industry (Lepkowska-White, 2004).

Hypotheses

Given the growth in the advertising industry, the influx of well-established international ad agencies after 1989, and growing expenditures on advertising, it is predicted that advertisers in Poland will increasingly use more creative approaches including humor, surprise, celebrities and more eye-catching and interesting ads. Using Leiss et al. (1986) as a framework, it can also be hypothesized that as Polish consumers become more sophisticated, ads in Poland are increasingly more image-based.

H1: Over time, more creative approaches will be used in advertising in Poland. Ads will become more interesting, humorous, surprising, and more likely to feature celebrity endorsers.

H2: Over time, more visual images (and less text) will be present in Polish ads.

According to Leiss et al. (1986), more visual images that intertwine products with the world of consumers were used in US ads over time. It is expected that similar changes have been occurring in Poland with a growing use of consumer and product images in ads. Over time, similarly to the United States, this emphasis should shift from images of products to the images of consumers as the country's situation improves and consumers become more self-centered and individualistic. Therefore, the following relationships are predicted:

H3: Over time, the number of ads with visual representations of products will go up and then decrease.

H4: Over time, an increasing number of ads will contain visual images of consumers.

The Leiss et al. (1986) framework shows that in the first stage of advertising evolution ads are focused mainly on functional product characteristics. Additional research also suggests that in times of transition or difficult economic situations consumers use this information more frequently (Bierzynski, 2001; Heyder, Musiol and Peters, 1992; Jeannet and Hennessey, 1995). Bowes, Ruzicka and Mussey (1990) found that a majority of Polish ads presented basic product information. The Leiss et al. (1986) framework also suggests that as standards of living improve and consumers adopt more individualistic values, ads that focus on consumers, their personalities, lifestyles, needs and demands appear more frequently. Therefore, it is predicted that:

H5: The number of ads focused on product characteristics will increase and then decrease over time.

H6: The number of ads focused on consumers will increase over time.

Past studies suggest that Poles have rather limited purchasing power and, therefore, are likely to be price conscious and look for price-related information (Herpen et al., 2000; Lepkowska-White, 2004). Applying Leiss et al. (1986), it may be inferred that information about price may lose its strong appeal when the economic situation in Poland improves and consumers become more focused on their needs rather than prices. Therefore, it is predicted that:

H7: The number of ads containing information about prices and sales promotions will increase and then decrease over time.

Finally, many new businesses that entered the Polish market in the early 1990s had to advertise their location since they were new to the Polish buyers. Place of purchase might also have been important to the buyers as many stores did not carry a broad range of different brands (Herpen et al., 2000). Since under socialism and during turbulent transformations in Poland consumer rights were often violated (Kozminski, 1992), businesses also had to assure consumers of good product quality to gain their trust. It is hypothesized that as consumers become more familiar with new brands, information on product availability and assurances of good product quality will become less important to the buyers and, therefore, appear less frequently in ads.

H8: The number of ads containing information on product availability will increase and then decrease over time.

H9: The number of ads containing assurances of product quality (reputation of the business, warranty, research about the product) will increase and then decrease over time.

Method

To address the objectives of this study, a total of 822 ads collected in 1988 (26 ads), 1993 (165 ads), 1998 (228 ads) and in 2002 (403 ads) underwent content analysis. Only full page or larger ads were analyzed and duplicates were omitted from the final analysis. The ads were taken from the four most popular Polish magazines (*Polityka, Przekroj, Przyjaciolka* and *Motor*) that target both males and females from upper and lower classes with varied educational background.

Coding categories were developed using Davis' (1997) guidelines and described in a codebook that was created to guide two independent Polish judges in coding. A short description of the coding categories is presented in Table 12.1. The two judges first learned how to use the coding categories and then coded 30 ads to gain experience in coding. More training was provided as needed. In the final analysis, inter-coder agreement was 96 percent.

Data Analysis and Results

The data were tested using chi-square tests. It is important to mention that the analyzed ads most frequently featured cosmetics, cars and car-related products, banking services, telephone, appliances, drugs and food products.

The results show that Hypothesis 1, which stated that more creative approaches are used in advertising in Poland over time, was not supported (Table 12.2).

The second hypothesis, which stated that Over time more visual images and less text are present in the Polish ads, is supported (Table 12.3). In 1988, 73.1 percent of ads contained text *in the entire ad* and only 15.4 percent contained text *in less than half of the ad*. Similarly in 1993, the majority (72.2 percent) of ads contained text in *more than*

Table 12.1   Content analysis—definition of categories (part 1)

Category	Short definition
Interesting	It is interesting and eye-catching
Humor	It is funny
Surprising	It intentionally surprises the reader
Celebrity endorsement	Presents or refers to an actor or a famous person
Picture of the product	Contains product picture
Picture of people	Contains picture of a woman, man, child, family and groups of people
Product focused	Contains information about product functional characteristics such as quality, variety, style, components, packaging, safety, nutrition, performance and new ideas
Consumer focused	Contains information about consumer characteristics such as pursuing a career, well-being, self-improvement, independence, social interactions and relationships with others
Promotions	Contains information about sales promotions such as contests, sweepstakes, rebates, deals and frequency programs
Prices	Contains price(s) of the product(s)
Available	Spells out where the product can be bought
Reputation	Contains information about reputation and opinion about the product and/or the business
Warranty	Contains information about product warranty
Research	Contains information about research results regarding the product from the firm, independent sources or unknown sources

half of an ad (including text on an entire ad) and only 12.7 percent of ads contained *little or no text.* Almost the reverse is true for 1998 and 2002 in which over 50 percent of ads contained text *in less than half of the ad* and only about 20 percent of ads contained text *in more than half of the ad.* These results show that over time less text and more visual images are being used in print ads.

Hypothesis 3, which stated that over time the number of ads with visual representations of products will go up and then decrease, was supported (chi-square = 23.62, p<0.01) and H4, which predicted that over time an increasing number of ads will contain visual images of consumers, was only partially supported as the number of ads containing pictures of people increased and then dropped over time. H5 stated that the number of ads focused on product characteristics will increase and then decrease over time. H5 was only partially supported as the number of product focused ads increased but did not drop over time (chi-square = 283.71, p<0.01). Hypothesis 6 was supported as the number of ads

Table 12.2   Content analysis—number of ads with specific content: Frequencies and chi-square analysis (part 2)

Year	1988	1993	1998	2002	Pearson chi-square
Interesting	0 0%	6 3.6%	31 13.6%	4 1.0%	51.93 p<.01
Humor	0 0%	0 0%	1 0.4%	14 3.5%	12.11 p<.01
Surprising	0 0%	0 0%	6 2.6%	13 3.2%	n.s.
Celebrity endorsement	0 0%	0 0%	6 2.6%	12 3.0%	n.s.
Picture of the product	8 30.8%	70 42.4%	134 58.8%	257 63.8%	29.40 p<.01
Picture of people	0 0%	18 10.9%	63 27.6%	103 25.7%	666.20 p<.01
Product focused	22 95.7%	153 94.4.0%	205 85.8%	372 92.0%	283.70 p<.01
Consumer focused	0 0%	6 3.7%	41 14.1%	82 21.0%	26.40 p<.01
Promotions	0 0%	48 29.1%	20 8.8%	96 24.1%	56.45 p<.01
Prices	3 11.5%	56 33.9%	40 17.5%	72 18.2%	27.93 p<.01
Available	19 73.1%	151 91.5%	154 67.5%	225 (56.1%)	73.75 p<.01
Reputation	1 3.8%	12 7.3%	33 14.5%	18 4.5%	21.01 p<.01
Warranty	8 30.8%	20 12.1%	23 10.1%	19 5.1%	33.96 p<.01
Research	0 0%	7 4.0%	8 3.0 %	17 4.1%	26.90 p<.01

focused on consumers has increased over time (chi-square = 26.40, p<0.01). Hypothesis 7 stated that the number of ads with information about prices will increase and then decrease over time. H7 was partially supported. The predicted trend was observed for ads with price information (chi-square = 19.65, p<0.01), however, the number of ads with information about promotions varied and actually went up in 2002 (chi-square = 34.23,

Table 12.3 Content analysis—number of ads with text versus image: Frequencies and chi-square analysis*

Year	1988	1993	1998	2002	Total
No text	0 0%	2 1.2%	7 3.1%	6 1.5%	15 1.8%
Text on less than half of an ad	4 15.4%	19 11.5%	112 48.9%	198 48.9%	333 41.0%
Text on half of an ad	3 11.5%	25 15.2%	68 29.8%	97 24.1%	193 24.5%
Text on more than half of an ad	0 0%	59 35.8%	21 9.2%	52 12.8%	132 16.0%
Text on the entire ad	19 73.1%	60 36.4%	20 8.8%	52 12.8%	151 18.3%
Total number of ads	*26*	*165*	*228*	*403*	*822* *100.0%*

Note: * significant at p<0.01.

p<0.01). H8 stated that the number of ads containing information on product availability will increase and then decrease over time. H8 was supported (chi-square = 31.46, p<0.01). Finally, Hypothesis 9, which stated that the number of ads containing assurances of product quality (reputation of the business, warranty, research about the product) will increase and then decrease over time, was partially supported. H9 was supported for reputation (chi-square = 9.10, p<0.05) and warranty (chi-square = 15.74, p<0.01), but no significant differences were observed for research. It is important to note that the overall number of ads with this informational cue was very low.

Limitations

It is important to look at this study in the light of its limitations. Only print ads from four Polish magazines were analyzed. Despite the popularity of these magazines and their large readership, this sample may not be representative. Two judges analyzed a large number of print ads, which might have caused fatigue and, therefore, some mistakes in the analysis. Finally, only selected advertising messages were investigated and, therefore, other studies should look at other developments in the content of ads.

Conclusions

The results of the study show that the theory of advertising evolution proposed by Leiss et al. (1986) is useful in predicting major changes in advertising content in Poland. Specifically, Polish print ads are becoming more visual and less based on text over time. Interestingly, however, the number of ads with pictures of products and/or people went up and then decreased. This indicates that other visual images are being used. The use of visual images is most likely a response to preferences of Polish consumers. Past studies show that Poles like ads with big color pictures or a mixture of big pictures and functional information about products (Nowacki, 1997).

This study also shows that the number of ads containing product characteristics remained high even in 2002. This confirms prior findings that in times of transition or economic hardship consumers may have stronger inclination for factual product information (Bierzynski, 2001; Heyder et al., 1992; Jeannet and Hennessey, 1995). Indeed, past literature suggests that Polish consumers prefer specific information about products' functional characteristics (in addition to visual images) over any other information in ads (Nowacki, 1997).

The study shows that information about consumers is increasingly used in the Polish ads from 1989 to 2002. It may be a result of Polish consumers becoming more individualistic and self-centered and, therefore, advertising becoming more consumer focused (Kolman et al., 2003; Leiss et al., 1986). However, it is important to keep in mind that the number of ads with product characteristics is still much higher than ads with any other information.

This research also shows that information about product availability and assurances of quality was increasingly important between 1989 and 1998 when new businesses were gaining market share and developing trust among new buyers in Poland. By 2002, fewer ads contained this type of information perhaps because most of these companies had already established themselves in the Polish market.

Price information was most popular in the early 1990s. Since then its use has dropped. Interestingly, information about sales promotions became more popular again in 2002. It seems that advertisers decided to use sales promotions in response to the economic slowdown lasting from 1998 until 2002, which past studies show forces consumers to be more price sensitive.

Finally, this study also shows that print ads in Poland have not become more creative over time (at least using the categories tested in this study). The use of humor, surprise and celebrity endorsers is infrequent and has not changed between 1989 and 2002. This suggests that Polish ads are rather tedious and dull (the highest number of interesting ads in the analyzed period was equal to only 13.6 percent in 1998) and partially explains why attitudes toward advertising in Poland are mixed. To improve these perceptions more creative approaches should be used in the future.

In summary, the study shows that some advertising themes in Poland continue to be frequently used and others have gained or lost popularity. Information about products functional characteristics is the most popular and used increasingly over time. Print ads in Poland also have become more visual and consumer oriented. In the most recent years they did not contain much information about product availability, prices and assurances of quality, which was important and frequently used when businesses were entering the Polish market. Finally, Polish ads are rather dull which may explain some negative perceptions toward ads.

References

Abernethy, A.M. and Franke, G.R. (1996). The information content of advertising: meta analysis. *Journal of Advertising*, 25(2): 1–17.

Aleman, A. (1996, September). Poland struggles to develop advertising identity. *Warsaw*, 25.

Bierzynski, J. (2001, July 31). Witamy w ciezkich czasach. *Rzeczypospolita*, 10.

Bowes, E., Milan Ruzicka and Dagmar Mussey (1990, October 8). Eastern Europe: lifestyle ads irk East Europeans. *Advertising Age*, 1–2.

Davis, J.J. (1997). *Advertising Research: Theory and Practice* (pp. 392–416). Upper Saddle River, NJ: Prentice Hall.

European Advertising and Media Forecast (October 2005 and July 2006), 20(5). Henley-on-Thames: World Advertising Research Center.

Gulyás, Ágnes (2003). Print media in post-Communist East Central Europe. *European Journal of Communication*, 18(1): 81–106.

Herpen, E., R. Pieters, J. Fidrmucova and P. Roosenboom (2000). The information content of magazine advertising in market and transition economies. *Journal of Consumer Policy*, 23: 257–83.

Heyder, H., K.G. Musiol and K. Peters (1992). Advertising in Europe: attitudes towards advertising in certain key East and West European countries. *Marketing and Research Today*, 20: 58–67.

Jeannet, J. and H.D. Hennessey (1995). *Global Marketing Strategies*. Boston, MA: Houghton Mifflin.

Kocinska, A. (2001, October 29). Ad nauseam Warsaw awash in free dailies as newcomers enter market. *Financial Times*.

Kolman, L., N.G. Noorderhaven, G. Hofstede and E. Dienes (2003). Cross-cultural differences in Central Europe. *Journal of Managerial Psychology*, 18(1): 76–88.

Kozminski, A.K. (1992). Consumers in transition from centrally planned economy to the market economy. *Journal of Consumer Policy*, 14: 351–69.

Leiss, W., S. Kline and S. Jhally (1986). *Social Communication in Advertising: Persons, Products and Images of Well Being*. Toronto: Nelson Canada.

Lepkowska-White, E. (2004). Polish and American print ads: functional individualistic, collectivist and experiential appeals. *Journal of Global Marketing*, 17(4): 75–92.

Lepkowska-White, E., T.G. Brashear and M. Weinberger (2003). A test of ad appeal effectiveness in Poland and the US: the interplay of appeal, product and culture. *Journal of Advertising*, 32(3): 57–68.

Lubelska, K. (2001). Ojciec, Frugo! *Polityka*, 36: 78–81.

Nowacki, R. (1997). Preferencje nabywcow w zakresie form reklamy jako podstawa dzialalnosci reklamowej. *Marketing i Rynek*, 5: 24–9.

Poland macroeconomic data and forecasts (2004, 4th Quarter). *Poland Business Forecast Report*, 2.

Wrobel, J. (2001). Watch this space: advertising and media, 1–3. [Online.] www.cia.gov (retrieved January 29, 2001).

CHAPTER 13

Advertising in Slovenia: Eastern European Spirit, Western European Style

MICHAEL H. MCBRIDE AND JANEZ DAMJAN

In Slovenia, the most progressive of all the nations that were once part of Yugoslavia, advertising has grown though it has not yet prospered. Labeled in tourism campaigns as "The Green Piece of Europe" or "The Sunny Side of the Alps," Slovenia has come a long way in a short time economically and politically, and advertising (termed "oglaševanje" or "reklama" locally) as an industry has followed. Advertising in the emerging democracies of Eastern and Central Europe has been in transition just as individual nations have arrived at different points in their evolution from socialist to market-driven economies. But few countries in this region can match the growth and development of advertising in Slovenia. For instance, the gross volume of advertising per Slovenian citizen rose by nearly five times from 1994 to 1999 and is estimated to be rising multifold well into the new century.

Before detailing the advertising industry in Slovenia, it is important to describe the setting and the conditions that largely account for the current state of advertising in Slovenia, termed "the country at the crossroads ... both rich and diverse ... facing the future with know-how, innovativeness, and dynamism" (Chamber of Commerce and Industry of Slovenia, 2005).

Slovenia: The Culture

Slovenia is a nation whose national hero is a poet. According to Apih (1996), a notable Slovenian advertising specialist, native poets and writers awakened a national consciousness and gave it its identity for all citizens, portraying their version of the Slovenian world as the prominent female image said to reflect among other things a degree of male misery. It is not surprising that a common visual theme in many Slovenian advertising campaigns utilizes the feminine form or a model. Further, the first woman in the life of every man is considered to be his mother. Perhaps the greatest Slovenian writer, Ivan Cankar, erected a monument to his mother that burdened generations of Slovenian males with guilt. Analysis of Slovenian advertising also commonly reveals humorous or tongue-in-cheek messages incorporating both males and females with some notion of the female "coming out ahead."

Perhaps more importantly, crossing gender boundaries, according to Debeljak (1997), the persistence of commonality and community is a powerful, traditional phenomenon in Slovenian life. The shared quality of all Slovenians, their common identity, contributes greatly to their unity as a people that distinguishes them from their neighbors and from Western cultures. In fact, cross-cultural experts studied 19 European nations on the basis of cultural homogeneity (and heterogeneity), finding that Slovenia ranked high (5th) in the company of three of the four Scandinavian nations on similarity of cultural value orientations, or "cultural cohesiveness" (de Mooij, 2005). Further, Slovenians' self-conscious preoccupation with how small they are as a nation is also unique. Just as a government promotional campaign proclaimed, "Slovenia: Small but Beautiful," Slovenians remain fixated on the magic number of their estimated population (two million), which exerts a real influence on their daily lives, over choices they make, and over how they view themselves in the context of Europe and the world. These characteristics are often reflected in Slovenian advertising.

Slovenia: The Country and Its People

Described as a "varied mosaic" whose landscape stretches between the Adriatic Sea and the Alps (Slovenia in brief, 2003), Slovenia is the least populous nation of 120-million-strong Eastern and Central Europe (CIA World Factbook, 2006). Slovenia (formally Republika Slovenije) is also physically the smallest nation in the region, comparable to New Jersey, and shares borders with Austria, Hungary, Croatia and Italy. When Slovenia and several other countries joined the EU (and NATO) before 2005, it became part of a new "Mega-Europe" of 25 states and more than 450 million consumers (Mueller, 2004). Its largest city and capital is Ljubljana, numbering about 276,000 (Eastern flair, 2006). About 70 percent of the population of Slovenia is 15–64 years old, while 16 percent is 14 or younger and 14 percent 65 or older. Regarding approximately 650,000 households, ethnically, 9 of 10 citizens are Slovenian (with traces of Croat, Serb and Muslim). Though most business people speak at least one foreign language, all speak Slovenian, the common, official language similar to Croatian and Serbian, though German is widely understood by elders and English is preferred by youth (US Department of State, 2004). The nation is mostly Catholic (70 percent) and maintains a 99 percent literacy rate (with 30 percent of the population having completed basic education, 43 percent vocational/middle school, 9 percent higher education, and 18 percent not completing basic education).

Surveys of Slovenians reveal insights into their culture. More than a third of 776 citizens surveyed expected 2006 to be generally like 2005, with nearly 35 percent anticipating a better year and nearly 25 percent a worse year, according to the daily newspaper *Delo*. Economically, only 20 percent expected improvements while almost 45 percent said the economy would be worse (Survey: Slovenians only moderately optimistic, 2006). According to one survey, Slovenia has more in common with 14 Western European nations than with the former Yugoslavian countries or post-socialist Eastern European nations regarding values. Specifically, Slovenian values are more similar to those of Germans and Scandinavians in terms of attitudes toward civil society, family, religion, politics and democracy (Slovenian values, 2005). A 2005 survey on consumer confidence about the future revealed that confidence was highest among the 16–29 demographic but lowest among 50–64. As expected, confidence was significantly higher in wealthier households and among employed persons (Statistical Office of the Republic of Slovenia, 2006, January 24). A household budget survey of 3,794 households in 2003 indicated that the largest allocation was food and non-alcoholic beverages (20.3 percent), followed by transportation/vehicles (16.4 percent) and housing/utilities (11.9 percent) (Statistical Office of the Republic of Slovenia, 2005, September 12). Of interest, more than 80 percent of Slovenians 15 and older own and regularly use one or more credit or debit cards. Most frequent users are in the 40–49 demographic. Slovenia leads the Eastern and Central European region in card use. An average Slovenian purchased SIT 482,000 in goods and services in 2004 (Slovenians fond, 2005).

Regarding Slovenian families, the number of families is increasing but they are smaller, the typical family unit is a married couple with children (average family with children has 3.4 members), in almost half of lone parent families the mother or father is 50+, and almost a quarter of families are childless or children no longer live with their parents (Statistical Office of the Republic of Slovenia, 2005, May 12). Women account for almost half of all employed persons, are better educated, and work longer hours than men but earn 9 percent less (Women work longer hours than men, 2006). As for children, more than half of them have a sibling, the share of children will continue falling in the general population, 84 percent are living with both parents, and in their spare time they like to watch TV (Statistical Office of the Republic of Slovenia, 2005, October 4).

Slovenia is the most prosperous country of transition Europe, with a generally healthy economy. It has been described as belonging to the high-marketization, high-Westernization cluster of European countries (unlike its fellow former Yugoslavia nations belonging to the low-marketization group) (Nowak 1996). According to the World Economic Outlook, Slovenia's economy is expected to expand annually by 4 percent in 2006 and 2007 (IMF anticipates, 2006), driven largely by international trade. Its economy was considered the 32nd most competitive in the world in 2005, according to the World Economic Forum. Among EU members, it was the second most competitive economy among new EU members and fared much better than the other former Yugoslavia countries (Report: Slovenian economy, 2005). On the Index of Economic Freedom for 2006, Slovenia gained seven places to place 38th of 157 nations surveyed by the Heritage Foundation (Slovenia advances, 2006). Slovenia was the 14th most innovative country among the 25 EU member states, according to the European Innovation Scoreboard (EIS) for 2005 (Slovenia 14th, 2006). The unit of currency is the tolar (SIT), with an average exchange rate of about 190 to the US dollar, as of June 2006 (Statistical Office of the Republic of Slovenia, 2006).

While annual GDP growth averaged 2.7 percent, 4.2 percent and 4.2 percent for 2003, 2004, and 2005 respectively, GDP grew 5.1 percent from the first quarter of 2005 to early 2006, one of the highest rates in years. Annual export growth for these same years was 3.1 percent, 12.5 percent and 8.3 percent, and import growth 6.7 percent, 13.2 percent and 7.2 percent, respectively, yet import growth in early 2006 was double digit thanks in part to soaring domestic expenditures (GDP growth, 2006). Major import/export partner nations are Germany and Italy. Annual inflation ranged from 5.6 percent in 2003 to 2.6 percent in 2005 and was expected to be 2.5 percent in 2006 and 2.4 percent in 2007. Unemployment has annually been about 6+ percent but was decreasing at a record pace in 2006, already lower than any time in 15 years (Unemployment in Slovenia hits record low, 2006). Yet patterns of high monthly consumer price increases continued well into 2006, largely affected by higher prices of housing, utilities, food and petroleum products (Statistical Office of the Republic of Slovenia, 2006, May 31).

Historical Context

Slovenia gained independence from Yugoslavia on June 25, 1991 and adopted a parliamentary democratic government. It liberalized the economy and oriented toward the West. Despite substantial economic growth and other positive developments, Slovenia has not been spared typical transition problems, such as unemployment, financial instability, slow privatization and public disappointment. Foreign investment activity has been substantial, but so has the importing of foreign products. Major multinational brands quickly gained market share in many consumer product categories. Such development caused difficulties for domestic companies, which also lost important markets in other former Yugoslavia republics.

Advertising in Slovenia is older than the country's independence, as print ads were found in newspapers as early as the late eighteenth century, but the modern form is drastically different. After World War II, under the Yugoslav socialist regime, commercial activities were stifled. For years, promotions agencies served exporters, then when television arrived in the late 1950s early forms of commercials were developed. During the 1960s, national television was the sole producer of commercials, just as leading newspapers designed most print ads. In the early 1970s, the first Slovenian agency, Studio Marketing, was established. It played a key role for more than a decade, producing award-winning television advertising and other promotions. In the 1980s, the entrepreneurial spirit in advertising emerged; thus, many new agencies appeared and hundreds of freelancers offered design and related services. As in all socialist nations, advertising was practically non-existent the first two decades after World War II, though in the mid 1960s liberal economic reforms, increased competition, and higher living standards strengthened the case for advertising.

To further understand advertising in Slovenia before 1990, one must realize that for almost three decades Slovenian consumers had free access to foreign media (Italian and Austrian television, and foreign newspapers and journals sold in large cities) and markets (strong foreign tourism and no travel restrictions existed before 1968), forcing Slovenian advertisers to keep up with the latest developments. After 1991, a market economy began to emerge.

Free enterprise continues to develop as capitalism has taken root in countries like Slovenia that have moved to privatize state-owned enterprises, establish free prices, relax import controls, secure investments and joint-ventures with multinational companies and wrestle with inflation. No region of the world experienced as much change following the fall of the Berlin Wall in 1989 as Eastern and Central Europe. Many nations still have much in common (foods, accommodation facilities, entertainment and public transport) and share, to varying degrees, similar political and legal bureaucracies, yet some have more effectively developed economic systems. From the Baltic to the Balkans, this volatile region, the source of much of our Western culture, was where both world wars began and was the primary battlefield in the Cold War.

Advertising Media Boom

Gross estimates of advertising media spending in Slovenia were 300 million Euros for 2006, according to the Institute for Market and Media Research, Mediana. TV advertising's share was 60 percent, followed by magazines (17 percent), newspapers (11 percent), radio (7 percent) and outdoor (5 percent) (Country by country, 2006). Cinema advertising was negligible, and Internet advertising was not measured.

Advertising media space boomed, thanks largely to political turnover and privatization over several years. The number of Slovenian media constantly grew in the 1990s from 859 in 1998 to 955 at the end of the twentieth century (573 were print media), 43 new media in 1999 alone. All media have seen decreased ratings in terms of readership or audience attention because of the influence of the Internet.

Media wars fought in the Balkans may best be described as one Eastern European put it: "Imagine two bald men fighting over a comb." With the communist propaganda machine all but non-existent, numerous trans-border television and FM radio stations, as well as newspapers and magazines, have competed to capture a largely unresponsive audience. Earlier in the 1990s, old media disappeared, with some evolving and adapting, and many more new media emerged. For instance, Slovenia acquired three new national television stations, three new national daily newspapers and dozens of local radio stations. Across Eastern and Central Europe, print media's share of total advertising expenditures dropped from more than 80 percent to around 50 percent, more comparable to developed countries, while television's share grew from as low as 10 percent to almost 50 percent. In absolute terms, however, the press also increased advertising income resulting in an overall significant increase in media usage.

Major Media Choices

Due to the unique language of Slovenia, which has always been a key cultural element, print media in Slovenia have been traditionally well developed. Though foreign media were readily available, they have not played a significant role, with the exception of Croatian sports dailies. In each media class, considerable competition exists.

According to media reports in the Slovenian publication *Marketing Magazin* and the *Statistical Yearbook of the Republic of Slovenia*, annual turnover of Slovenian mass media from advertising increased more than 17-fold, despite that in terms of US dollar equivalents that growth was substantially less (under two-fold). As a percentage of GDP, almost a three-fold increase occurred. Further, media shares in annual advertising turnover illustrated the greatest increase for newspapers other than dailies and magazines, with slight increases for radio and outdoor media. Television, however, dropped more than 12 percentage points.

Regarding broadcast media in Slovenia, five television channels (two state and three commercial) cover the country, with considerable nationwide penetration by cable TV (in some locales over 50 percent). State-owned media are only public radio and television, subsidized by the state that sell advertising and collect license fees (Mocnik and Petkovic, 2000). There are 38 commercial radio stations, 32 local and regional non-commercial stations, 15 stations for minorities, eight public stations and two student stations. Most (95 percent) Slovenian households had television sets and 49 percent of TV households had VCRs and cable. There was a 20 percent+ increase in color TV ownership in the recent past. Kanal A, Slovenia's original commercial TV station, established in 1992, achieved 20 percent prime-time market share and their own data estimated coverage at about 85 percent. Among TV stations, the largest is POP TV with a yearly frequency of advertising totaling 35,000 minutes, which generated 12 billion SIT of gross value. Kanal A was second with 20,000 minutes, while both Slovenian National TV channels (SLO 1 and SLO 2) combined broadcast just under 20,000 minutes of advertising. TV advertising amounted to 56 percent of the gross value of advertising, totaling 15.5 billion SIT. Radio's gross share totaled 2.8 billion SIT. The government raised its contribution for national radio and TV, as of March 2000, to a 3 percent increase. In almost six years since the government started controlling radio and TV subscription, the latter was raised by an average of 61 percent, slightly affecting growth in consumer prices and inflation. Most TV commercials advertised cars (9 percent), followed by casinos and lotteries (7 percent), hair care preparations (6 percent), washing powder (5 percent) and office electronics (4 percent). The prevailing product advertised on radio has been automobiles (17 percent).

About 70 percent of all media and more than 67 percent of print media are based in the Ljubljana region. There are more than 500 different publications devoted to niche market sectors, and almost 1,000 print media in the country with a total circulation of some 5.8 million copies, though precise circulation data is not known as print media is not obliged (by law or otherwise) to publish circulation figures (Milosavljevi, 2002). There are five daily newspapers and several hundred magazines of all types. For example, an estimated 210 monthlies in Slovenia maintain an overall circulation of 2.5 million, including 88 quarterlies, 72 bi-monthlies, 56 annuals, 35 publications published twice annually and 34 weeklies. Among daily newspapers, the daily tabloid *Slovenski Novice* and the weekly *Nedeljski Dnevnik*, a separate tabloid-style edition of the daily *Dnevnik*, were the most widely read Slovenian periodicals in 2005 and the first quarter of 2006. Since early 2005, around 90,000 copies of *Slovenski Novice* were sold quarterly, reaching over 91,000 in early 2006. The leading hard journalism newspaper, *Delo* (the largest newspaper company in Slovenia), followed circulation-wise. Sold copies dropped from around 75,000 in early 2005 to 70,000 in early 2006. *Dnevnik* and *Vecer* follow, with *Dnevnik* selling around 49,000 early in 2006 and *Vecer* experiencing a drop from 50,000 to 47,000 from 2005 to 2006. The business daily *Finance* rose from 11,000 to 12,000 copies, while the sports daily *Ekipa* dropped from 7,600 to 7,000. *Nedeljski Dnevnik* led among weeklies with 130,000 sold per quarter, followed by the tabloid *Lady* (54,000), *Nedelo*, the Sunday edition of *Delo* (52,000), and the religious paper *Druzina* (48,000).

Additionally, a national readership survey showed that *Cosmopolitan* was the most popular monthly, while *Zurnal* topped the list of free weeklies (Two tabloids, 2006). Other magazines have included *Mladin*, a weekly political title with full-page, four-color ads, *Manager Zasebno*, a monthly four-color business title with display ads, *Jana*, a weekly women's and family title with full-page ads, and *Mag*, a weekly political title with full-page, four-color ads. The 200th anniversary of the first Slovenian newspaper was celebrated in 1997 with reproduction of its first print ad. Most commonly advertised products in print are cars (16 percent), publishing (8 percent), finances (7 percent), events (5 percent) and office electronics (5 percent).

Regarding telecommunications in Slovenia, 93.7 percent of Slovenians used a mobile phone in 2004, above the 89.6 average in the EU (Slovenia ahead, 2006) and a whopping 4,500 percent more than in 1996. Over several years, Telekom Slovenije has introduced new telecommunications networks and more competitive services, and is digitalizing services in order to remain the leading telecommunications service provider in the nation.

In terms of outdoor advertising, Metropolis Media was set up in 1992 and started developing giant poster panels, first in Ljubljana. Now, the company boasts more than

2,270 sites across Slovenia and remains the sole marketer of "metrolights" (night-lit, double-sided boards) near bus stops in Ljubljana and throughout the country. Automobiles (25 percent), office electronics (16 percent), finances (6 percent) and non-alcoholic beverages (6 percent) were the most popular products or services advertised via outdoor.

Cyber cafés offering Internet service to the public and the number of Internet service providers has continued growing, resulting in a critical mass of consumers and firms participating in the global online marketplace. Rapid adoption of the Internet as a commercial medium has caused firms to experiment with innovative ways of marketing to consumers in computer-mediated environments. A survey conducted by the Faculty of Social Science at the University of Ljubljana found that most respondents recognized graphic banner ads for products or services and knew they could reach an advertiser's webpage by clicking on the banner, and those often using the Internet remembered different ads more often than those rarely using it. Researchers also found that 30 percent of Slovenian companies had Internet access and that more than half those surveyed said they liked Internet ads that led them to interesting sites.

A 2006 survey of 700 citizens found that a third of Slovenians have made online purchases, more than half making three or more purchases in 2005. More than 40 percent of Slovenian Internet users spent over 50,000 SIT on online purchases, with books being the most popular item followed by computer equipment, event tickets, clothing and airline tickets. Also, a 2005 survey of 3,300 Slovenians revealed that almost half used the Internet several times daily, mainly at home, with men the most frequent users. It confirmed that the Internet influences shopping habits, with half searching for information online before making purchases and 10 percent opting for net shopping at least once monthly. In early 2005, 48 percent of all Slovenian households had Internet access, with 50 percent aged 10–74 regularly using the Internet. Leading Slovenia DSL Internet providers are Voljatel, Siol and Arnes and cable Internet providers are Telemach, Arnes and KRS Tabor. In 2005, the number of broadband connections was three times higher than in 2004, more than the EU average. An estimated 371,000 Internet connections exist in the country. As many as 55 percent are phone connections, followed by DSL with 28 percent and cable with 16 percent.

Consumer Media Habits

A recent survey commissioned by the European parent of Slovenian cable operator UPC Telemach found a large generational gap, with young Europeans saying they use TV for entertainment while older citizens use it as a source of information. In Slovenia, 33 percent of 6,000 polled in 2005 over the Internet, by telephone, and by questionnaire placed more trust in broadcasts by public television while 18 percent favored commercial TV stations. Content-wise, young Slovenians were strongly against religious programs and most were not interested in foreign or domestic politics as a broadcast subject. In 2002, a nationwide survey of 7,732 phone respondents and another 1,903 personally interviewed revealed that the average Slovenian spends 16 hours weekly watching TV and 19 hours weekly listening to the radio. Watching TV was not considered a socially desirable activity, though more than two-thirds watched TV at least one hour daily. Readership of auto magazines decreased substantially. TV guides, women's titles, special supplements, weeklies and monthlies were deemed less popular. Over 15 percent saw a movie at the cinema at least once monthly, though only 2 percent were considered avid moviegoers. The Internet was gaining in popularity, with 13.5 percent using it daily. Another 26 percent used it once weekly, and 30.9 percent once monthly (Slovenians keen movie-goers, 2002).

A survey on attention paid to mass media in Slovenia concluded that the average attention to media fell in 1999, a trend noticed for several years. Average Slovenian attention to media amounted to four hours daily in 1999. On average, Slovenians listened to radio for 194 minutes, watched 151 minutes of television, and read the daily newspaper for 15 minutes and magazines for six minutes daily. A trend indicated that radio was heard mostly in the mornings and television viewed after 6 p.m., while newspapers and magazines were read equally throughout the day. Also, over 80 percent of more than 8,000 surveyed regularly watched television, listened to radio, and read newspapers and magazines. Three quarters of the population regularly read at least one monthly magazine, about 50 percent one weekly publication and 47 percent a daily newspaper. Regular daily newspaper readers devoted 30 minutes on average, regular radio listeners four hours daily and regular TV viewers three hours.

Austrian media experts recently analyzed Slovenian markets and determined them to be small for profitable media buying. Several experiments have been tested, for instance: agency pools where one purchases media space for all others and receives larger discounts. At the moment, a notable price war exists among media, each offering large discounts (up to 30 percent) to agencies but also to large advertisers.

Notable Advertising Regulations

The Code of Journalists of the Republic of Slovenia, adopted in 1993, states in Principle 7 that "advertising messages and advertisements must be clearly and undoubtedly separated from journalistic messages." Principle 7.1 reads: "Advertisements and paid advertising messages must be distinguished from the messages in the spirit of this code in their form, contents, and approach. In case of any doubt, it is necessary to add a note and thus point out that a message is a paid advertisement" (Journalists of the Republic of Slovenia, 1993). Regarding television, Slovenia permits up to 12 minutes of advertising per hour, except during prime time (18:00–23:00) when the maximum is 9 minutes. It also limits total advertising to 15 percent of the broadcast day, or an effective average of 9 minutes per hour. Slovenia also prohibits ad breaks during films broadcast by public television. Further, the law limits advertising to 30–35 percent of the public broadcaster's total budget, with subscription fees accounting for 40–45 percent and direct state support providing the remainder (Gillette, 2001).

Also, surreptitious advertising is prohibited, according to the Mass Media Act enacted in June 2001. Advertising may not prejudice respect for human dignity, incite discrimination on the grounds of race, sex or ethnicity, or political or religious intolerance, encourage behavior damaging to public health or safety or to the protection of the environment and the cultural heritage (Article 47/1,2). Further, ads targeting primarily children or in which children appear may not contain scenes of violence, pornography or any content that could damage their health or mental and physical development or otherwise have a negative effect on the impressionability of children (Article 49/1) (Rovsek, 2004).

Incidentally, changes to the anti-smoking act extending a ban on advertising all tobacco products eliminated the possibility of any advertising of new tobacco products, effective November 2005. Government-sponsored changes were backed in a 65 to 1 parliamentary vote. The only advertising of tobacco products allowed in Slovenia is logos on smoking accessories, on commercial premises and at tobacco stores. Additionally, according to Jancic (1996), important self-regulatory activity occurred in 1994 with organization of the Slovenian Advertising Association that adopted a Code of Slovenian Advertising Practice and established an Honorary Arbitration Court comprised mostly of advertising industry members. Since then, this court gained significant respect not only from the advertising community but also from the public.

Major Advertisers in Market

Of the top ten global marketers in Slovenia for 2005 (Table 13.1), US-based Procter & Gamble (1st) and Wm. Wrigley (10th) were joined by German-based household cleaning giant Reckitt Benckiser (2nd), home and personal care leader Henkel (6th), and family-owned Tchibo Holding (8th); France's consumer and professional products and cosmetics leader L'Oréal (5th) and food industry power Danone Groupe (9th); and Austria's Telekom Austria (7th). Two Slovenian advertisers ranked high: household products distributor Pejo Trading (3rd) and Telekom Slovenije (4th). The top six advertisers exceeded $11 million USD in media expenditures, while Pejo Trading experienced a one-year increase exceeding 400 percent. Danone Group spent almost 127 percent more than the year before, as other advertisers also achieved marked increases. Only two advertisers decreased spending from 2003 to 2004: the mobile industries.

Compared to 2002–2003 data (*Advertising Age's Global Marketing Special Report, 2004 edition*), notably, Procter & Gamble also held the top position, while Pejo Trading, Danone

Table 13.1   2005 top global marketer media expenditure by country: Slovenia

Advertiser	2004 (USD)	2003 (USD)	% change
Procter & Gamble	19.0	15.8	20.2
Reckitt Benckiser	17.4	10.1	71.4
Pejo Trading	15.6	3.1	400.2
Telekom Slovenije (+Mobitel)	12.1	12.4	-2.4
L'Oréal	11.3	11.2	0.2
Henkel	11.0	6.9	60.2
Telekom Austria (+Simobil)	9.6	11.2	-14.3
Tchibo Holding (+Beiersdorf)	9.3	8.5	10.0
Danone Group	6.0	2.7	126.9
Wm. Wrigley Jr.	6.0	3.9	53.9

Source: Advertising Age's 19th Annual Global Marketing Special Report, November 14, 2005, 12.

Group and Wrigley made the list. L'Oréal dropped from 2nd, Telekom Austria dropped from 3rd and Tchibo Holding dropped from 6th. Netherlands-based consumer goods leader Unilever (8th), automaker PSA Peugeot Citroen (9th), and automaker Renault (10th) dropped out of the top ten. Also, Mobitel alone was 4th (not part of Telekom Slovenije), Henkel climbed one place and Reckitt Benckiser three places.

Major Western companies such as Procter & Gamble (P&G), Henkel and Unilever started saturating the packaged-goods market in Eastern and Central Europe in the mid 1990s as the countries continued their shifts toward market-driven economies and consumers continued stratifying into different levels of affluence. Agency experts in the region admitted that Western companies were fighting a competitive battle there, reorganizing opportunities and trying to reduce the possibility of consumer backlash against a flood of Western products. Research indicated that some consumers felt many Western products were still too expensive and consequently out of reach, partly explaining why marketers responded by looking for a range of pricing opportunities to address portions of society resenting the charge of Western companies on their home turf.

Interestingly, multinationals were sparsely represented in top-ten lists of advertisers beginning in 1992; today, it is the opposite. For example, in 1992, only Henkel Zlatorog was listed (ranked 10th), and in 1993, Henkel was 3rd and P&G 9th. The following year, Master Foods appeared 2nd and Renault-Revoz 10th, and in 1995 Daewoo-Comedus ranked 9th. Further, except for the State Lottery, no other Slovenian companies on the 1992 top list are ranked today (Krka pharmaceutical, Mladinska Knjiga publisher, Emona chain store, Tobacco Ljubljana, Lek pharmaceutical, Mercator chain store, SKB bank and Delo media). Generally speaking, automobiles and telecommunications are the most advertised items, according to Slovenian media research sources.

Other interesting findings include the most advertised item on radio being automobiles and the most prominent trademark appearing on posters being the telephone company Simobil with a large lead over rival Mobitel, as well as Peugeot, Telekom Slovenije, Kia, Probanka, Triglav insurance, Mercator, McDonald's, Citroen, Toyota, Fiat and the Perutnina Ptuj meat company. Additionally, advertisers are appearing on websites, particularly those associated with Slovenian business, such as DHL Worldwide Express and Mobitel.

Two multinational representatives in Slovenia have been in the news, one reported to do what is necessary to stay in the country and another that continues to enhance its presence in the country. Coca-Cola Beverages Slovenia and Vino Brezice reached an agreement to cooperate in producing Coca-Cola products designed for the Slovenian market, following the decision by the Slovenian branch of the US multinational to transfer its bottling factory from Slovenia to Bosnia as part of corporate restructuring. The accord indicates the company's determination to stay in the Slovenian market. Set up in December 1993, McDonald's Slovenia invested 2.8 billion SIT into fast-food restaurants. While four were run as franchises, four were managed directly by McDonald's Slovenia. Slovenia opened its fourteenth restaurant near Ljubljana just before the turn of the century and since has opened additional franchises, attracting more than five million guests.

Damjan (2005) describes how brands in Slovenia developed across seven periods: 1) before World War I, 2) between both wars, 3) state socialism (before economic reforms in 1965), 4) liberalization of the economy (1966–75), 5) self-management socialism (1976–88), 6) transition (1989–2003) and 7) after entry into the EU (2004–present). For instance, the first brands appeared as the names of known inns and hotels, exposing their names in communications with customers perhaps as early as the late 1700s. Later, brand names like Radenska, Union (beer), Kolinska and Zlatorog become those celebrating century-long anniversaries.

Today, Milka (chocolate), a Kraft product, is considered the most recognized brand in former Yugoslav nations, including Slovenia. It scored highest on the Brand Potential Index (BPI) in a 2005 survey measuring visibility, consumer experience, choice and consumption in this region. The next three places, in order, went to Coca-Cola, fabric conditioner Lenor, and spice and herb mixture Vegeta. The highest-ranked Slovenian brands were fruit juice Fructal (35th), soft drink Cockta (50th) and mineral water Radenska (63rd). Mercator remained the largest Slovenian company in 2005, while Krka was ranked as the best Slovenian company, according to the "101 Biggest and Best Slovenian Companies" survey in business daily *Finance*.

Slovenia itself approved major advertising spending in 2006 for tourism. The Slovenian Tourist Board (STO) set a promotional budget of 1.28 billion SIT for a campaign under the slogan: "Slovenia—a diversity to discover," highlighting the Slovenian coast, vineyards, world-famous Lipizzaner horses and other attractions. Versions were prepared in Slovenian, German, Italian and French. A one-minute TV spot ran on CNN International several times daily in May presenting the nation as a tourist destination. Thirty- and fifteen-second versions also ran several times daily in June and again in September and October. It cost 180,000 SIT (Slovenian tourism ad, 2006). An estimated 2.4 million tourists (including 1.55 million foreigners) spent 1.45 billion Euros in Slovenia in 2005, a 10 percent increase over 2004, led by Italians, Germans, Austrians, Croats and Britons, respectively (Tourism revenues up, 2006).

Growing Agency Business

The entrepreneurial spirit among Slovenian advertising specialists has been strong, according to several Slovenian agency contacts. Most designers, researchers and copywriters started their own businesses, resulting in almost 200 "registered" agencies last year alone, though from 1991 to 1997 the number of full-service agencies in Slovenia grew from 23 to 63. Over this time, annual revenue in millions of US dollars increased more than four-fold. Yet, market conditions forced many to join forces, despite that a variety of advertising services has been available. In terms of the largest agencies, many roughly retain their positions in the marketplace and their client rosters. Because the market in Slovenia is comparatively small, the average size of an agency here also is small and ties with international agencies are less formal.

According to *Advertising Age*'s Agency Report (2000), the top 13 agencies in Slovenia all are headquartered in Ljubljana. Most top agency business volume grew from 1998 to 1999, however, the clear leaders were McCann Erickson Slovenia (increasing 44 percent) and Pristop & Grey (increasing 42 percent). Lowe Avanta Ljubljana and Futura DDB also grew at a high rate (28 percent), though most other agencies either recorded single-digit percentage increases or no increase. Only Studio Marketing International JWT, which led the country's list in 1998, lost a double-digit percentage of business. Other major shops include Futura DDB, Formitas BBDO, S. Team Saatchi & Saatchi, Publicis, Mayer & Co., Lowe Avanta Ljubljana, Votan Leo Burnett, Bates Slovenia, Ogilvy & Mather and TBWA Ljubljana.

Creative Controversies

Western advertising critics claim that Eastern and Central Europe (including Slovenia) has struggled to find its creative resonance. For example, *Advertising Age* columnist and critic Bob Garfield (1998) wrote of the Golden Drum International Advertising Festival of the "New Europe," held in Slovenia: "Just when you think eastern and central Europe are nearly fully integrated into the West, with all the economic benefits and cultural dilution that implies, something happens to remind you that the so-called New Europe is exactly the clumsy adolescent it imagines itself to be." He cited ads spoofing, alluding to, or focusing upon symbols of communism (the color red) and Marxist ideals or exaggerations, conflict and war, privatization and social rules, for instance. Not all agree with Garfield, but few argue against the notion that the industry here is at a creative crossroads. The best advertising is of an international standard, though some suffers from an apparent lack of understanding of what constitutes effective advertising (Creativity as the fundamental mission, 1998).

At the Golden Drum, which annually draws the top creative work from throughout Eastern and Central Europe and former Soviet Union countries, simple, strong conceptual ideas and top-notch executions have marked show winners with a style that has developed, in part, from the influence of neighboring regions. Jurors have cautiously avoided criticizing the region's creative sensibility because the industry is so new (Thoughts of the jury members, 1997), yet they acknowledged that production quality was becoming so uniformly slick that ads risk losing their national flavor, resulting in a "New Europe" seemingly less focused on what dreams lie ahead than on the oddly cherished nightmare left behind. They said Eastern European creatives often stop before telling the memorable, original, absorbing idea, revealing a lack of discipline (Tilles, 1997). Though language barriers cannot stop good work, earlier during transition, multinational clients simply adapted ("translated") Western ads for Eastern and Central European audiences. Schulberg (1997) claims that, as the world gets smaller, ideas must get more focused and speak to a broad audience within a narrow strategy. Award-winning and compelling advertising increasingly comes from new centers of creativity around the world, which harbors hope for Slovenia and this region. Many advertising leaders in the region believe that the "New Europe's" creativity has a comparative advantage but only if it is wrestled out of the hands of its Western teachers and yields to its inspiration and potential. Local experts tend to agree that focus should be as much on ideas that draw from history, cultural heritage and values as on product and service benefits (Ivanov, 1998).

Zavri (1996) describes the development of a typical Slovenian campaign: "Let's Have Fun." In May 1996, the Slovenian Ministry for Economic Affairs budgeted for a campaign to promote Slovenian tourism to the domestic market. Several Slovenian agencies vied for the account. The Ministry's goals were to retain share of native guests in Slovenian tourist destinations, increase the national budget for communications, and increase use of the visual identity of Slovenian tourism. Competing agencies realized that the low budget (270,000 DEM, German marks) meant a traditional mix of advertising tools would not work, but an integrated marketing plan to include advertising, public relations and direct marketing could. Publics were segmented and special communications designed for each. The project was announced at a news conference followed by meetings with journalists. Editors of national and local media were informed about campaign progress and feature stories on less known Slovenian sites of interest. Project presentations were made for members of a parliamentary committee for economics, and a letter describing the project was sent to then President of Slovenia, Milan Kucan. The project also was presented to members of Slovenian tourist associations and to representatives of large tourist resorts. Responses to direct mail were put into a database of potential customers sent to Slovenian tourist companies. The primary objective was to increase citizen interest in discovering Slovenian tourist services. TV, radio and print ads appeared in national media, with 50 percent discounts via media sponsorships. Direct mail went to 600,000 Slovenian households, with a reply card featuring a short questionnaire addressing where and how respondents would like to spend their holidays and which activities they would pursue. The Slovenian tourist board received 60,000 responses resulting in a database of more than 100,000 addresses of potential tourists. Public opinion surveys were conducted before, during and after the campaign to measure its effectiveness and enable tools to be adapted to different audiences.

Festivals and Special Recognition

The Slovenian Advertising Association was formed to bring together professionals working in all aspects of the industry. This organization has solved many problems in its short existence and has encouraged participation at important festivals held in the country. The annual Golden Drum International Advertising Festival of the "New Europe," held in Slovenia and organized by Slovenian advertising specialists, is prestigious among advertising industry professionals in Eastern and Central European nations, Russia, and former Soviet Union countries. Under the slogan "New Vision," the 12th Golden Drum festival in October 2005 attracted a record 2,483 ads from 40 countries in television, print, radio, direct marketing and web categories at the six-day event, organized by the Slovenian Advertising Chamber (Slovenia's largest advertising festival, 2005). Top agency winners were from Romania, Latvia and the Czech Republic. Comparatively, the 6th Golden Drum festival in 1999 attracted less than half that number. Key Slovenia winners then included a "Golden Mouse" for best website, a special prize for artistic achievement in advertising, and "Golden Drumsticks" to two agencies for print ads for Mercedes and Renault (Damjan, 1996). The 7th Golden Drum in October 2000 for the first time presented participants as organizers from beyond the borders of the "New Europe." The President of Slovenia typically presents the "Golden Rose" to the agency of the year (Damjan, 1997). The 2006 festival slogan was "Magic Touch."

Festival director Jure Apih claimed that advertising in Slovenia faces great challenges because of new media, globalization and a new attitude toward consumers. "Slovenian advertising started with a major advantage over others in the region, but this advantage is gone today. Others started developing intensively, and the West invested heavily into it. Now, the requirements of Slovenian advertising are determined by the market much more than by the creative potential," he said. "We must realize that advertising is what promotes an economy. It really acts as the flag carrier in new markets. Slovenian advertising is certainly capable of such campaigns" (Preseren, 2002). In short, he admitted that the festival would continue to try erasing gaps between East and West, rich and poor, and developed and developing cultures.

In related news, Slovenia's Mediamix Advertising Agency won a second Cannes Lion, a bronze award, at the 53rd Cannes Lions International Advertising Festival in France in

2006 (its first Lion, a gold, was awarded in 2001). To date, Mediamix is the lone Slovenian shop to garner a Cannes award. The agency was also a top winner at the 15th Festival of Slovenian Advertising (SOF), also in 2006, which recognized Futura DDB as "Best Agency" for the third year in a row. Meanwhile, the "Advertiser of the Year" award went to Simobil, Slovenia's second largest mobile operator, for its long-term awareness of the importance of trademark management. Other top agency winners included Mayer McCann, Saatchi & Saatchi, Formitas BBDO and Mediamix. A record 800 competing ads were judged. By comparison, the 12th SOF recognized Pristop as the top agency (followed by Luna/ BWTA and Publicis Studio PET) and Mobitel as the top advertiser and the 9th Slovenian Advertising Festival in 2000 attracted 512 entries, a 40 percent increase over 1998. Futura DDB was named agency of the year (and recognized for best television commercial and overall campaign), while Pivovarna Lasko (brewery) was named advertiser of the year. Also, the Slovenian Association of Advertising Agencies (SZOA) sponsors Slovenian ad entries in the EURO EFFIE awards program honoring effective communications in two or more countries within Europe.

The first and now premiere global university student advertising competition, "Inter-Ad," sponsored by the International Advertising Association (Giges, 1998), got its start in Slovenia. Formerly "MESAC," the pilot Mid-European Student Advertising Competition was held in conjunction with the Golden Drum during the 1994–95 academic year. Annually, a major client sponsor has requested that teams develop complete campaign proposals and submit them in plans book format. Earlier, universities sent presentation teams to the on-site competition as well. It attracted university teams from several Eastern and Central European nations, including Hungary, Slovenia, Croatia and Bulgaria. Though student teams from Hungary and Croatia dominated early competitions, teams from Slovenia placed consistently.

Future Perspectives

Though the growth of advertising in Slovenia has slowed, due largely to a general economic recession, this industry has made significant progress in the few years that the country has been free. Privatization efforts have continued while financial markets have been liberalized and enterprises have been restructured and reformed, helping to create conditions conducive to foreign investment and maintenance of a stable tolar. Still, barriers exist to further development. According to Slovenian advertising experts, enhanced competition has meant greater opportunity for the industry. Also, advertisers have created pressure to lower the prices of creative work, which could mean lowering quality standards in some cases. On the other hand, the younger generation has more marketing education, and competition is keener among service providers. Many critics would agree that the average quality of advertising in Slovenia is higher, but there appear to be fewer excellent commercials. This trend may continue, with domestic companies lowering their budgets. More agencies are becoming translators and adapters, rather than true creative shops. In short, advertising is said to be "a tough business" in Slovenia although still an attractive career goal for the next generation of Slovenian advertising specialists in this nation described by Lenarcic (2004) as "beautiful and sturdy, an old country determined to thrive in a modern world."

References

Advertising Age's 19th Annual Global Marketing Special Report (2005, November 14), p. 12.

Advertising Age's Global Marketing Special Report, 2004 Edition (2004, November 8), p. 11.

Agency report (2000, April 24). *Advertising Age*, s36.

Apih, Jure (1996). Women in Slovenian advertising. *GD Forum*, 32–5.

Chamber of Commerce and Industry of Slovenia (2005, October). *Slovenia Your Business Partner 2005–2006*.

CIA World Factbook (2006). Slovenia.

Country by country advertising spending (2006). *European Advertising and Media Forecast*.

Creativity as the fundamental mission of advertising (1998, November). *Golden Drum Magazine*, 10: 6.

Damjan, Janez (ed.) (1996). *Golden Drum 1996 Forum: Proceedings of the Seminar on Marketing Communications at the 3rd International Advertising Festival of the New Europe, Portoroz*. Slovenia: Slovenian Advertising Association.

Damjan, Janez (ed.) (1997). *Golden Drum 1997 Forum: Proceedings of the Seminar on Marketing Communications at the 4th International Advertising Festival of the New Europe, Portoroz*. Slovenia: Slovenian Advertising Association.

Damjan, Janez (2005, November). The older are the best: on development of Slovenian brands. *Place Branding*, 1(4): 363–72.

Debeljak, Erica (1997, May). The persistence of community in Slovenia. *MM—Marketing Magazin Slovenia*, 14: 34–7.

deMooij, Marieke (2005). *Global Marketing and Advertising: Understanding Cultural Paradoxes*. 2nd ed. Thousand Oaks, CA: Sage.

Eastern flair (2006, May/June). *National Geographic Traveler*, 23(4).

Garfield, Bob (1998, October 19). Ad review. *Advertising Age*, 71.

GDP growth at 5.1% in the first quarter (2006, June 12). *Slovenia Business Weekly*, 23.

Giges, Nancy (ed.) (1998). *Open Communications in the 21st Century*. London: International Advertising Association and Atalink Ltd.

Gillette, Robert (2001, August 1). Advertising on public television: current policy in Western, Central, and Eastern Europe. *IREX (International Research and Exchanges Board)*.

IMF anticipates 4% economic growth in Slovenia (2006, April 24). *Slovenia Business Weekly*, 17.

Ivanov, Dimitri (1998). Image conscious Eastern Europe. *New Moment*.

Jancic, Zlatko (1996). Advertising self-regulation in Slovenia. *GD Forum*, 66–9.

Journalists of the Republic of Slovenia (1993). *Code of Journalists of the Republic of Slovenia*.

Lenarcic, Ed (2004). *Slovenia: A Travel Guide to the Sunny Side of the Alps*. Toronto: Interlog.

Marketing Magazin, 1992–98.

Milosavljevi, Marko (2002). The Slovenian media landscape. European Journalism Centre.

Mocnik, Rastko and Brankica Petkovic (2000, May 9). Country reports on media. *Education and Media in Southeast Europe*, pp. 41–3.

Mueller, Barbara (2004). *Dynamics of International Advertising: Theoretical and Practical Perspectives*. New York: Peter Lang.

Nowak, Jan (ed.) (1996). *Marketing in Central and Eastern Europe*. Binghamton, NY: International Business Press.

Preseren, Pologna (2002, October 15). Jure Apih: Golden Drum Festival has its image. *Slovenia News*, 42.

Report: Slovenian economy 32nd most competitive in the world (2005, October 3). *Slovenia Business Weekly*, 40.

Rovsek, Jernej (2004, March). *Media System of Slovenia*. Task Force on Coordination of Media Affairs, Hans-Bredon-Institut, Hamburg, Germany.

Schulberg, Jay (1997, June 30). Successful global ads need simplicity, clarity. *Advertising Age*, 17.

Slovenia 14th most innovative country in the EU (2006, January 16). *Slovenia Business Weekly*, 3.

Slovenia advances 7 places on economic freedom index (2006, January 9). *Slovenia Business Weekly*, 2.

Slovenia ahead of EU average in mobile phone use (2006, March 13). *Slovenia Business Weekly*, 11.

Slovenia in brief (2003, April 23). *Slovenia News*, 16.

Slovenian tourism ad shown on CNN (2006, May 15). *Slovenia Business Weekly*, 19.

Slovenian values prototypical of European ones (2005, October 17). *Slovenia Business Weekly*, 42.

Slovenians fond of their credit or debit cards, survey shows (2005, October 3). *Slovenia Business Weekly*, 40.

Slovenians keen movie-goers, prefer radio to TV (2002, October 15). *Slovenia News*, 42.

Slovenia's largest advertising festival takes place in Portoroz (2005, October 3). *Slovenia Business Weekly*, 40.

Statistical Office of the Republic of Slovenia (1997). *Statistical Yearbook of the Republic of Slovenia, 1997*, vol. 36. Ljubljana: Statistical Office of the Republic of Slovenia.

Statistical Office of the Republic of Slovenia (2005, May 12). *Families in Slovenia*. Ljubljana: Statistical Office of the Republic of Slovenia.

Statistical Office of the Republic of Slovenia (2005, September 12). *Household Budget Survey, Slovenia, 2003*. Ljubljana: Statistical Office of the Republic of Slovenia.

Statistical Office of the Republic of Slovenia (2005, October 4). *Children in Slovenia*. Ljubljana: Statistical Office of the Republic of Slovenia.

Statistical Office of the Republic of Slovenia (2006). *Slovenia in Figures*. Ljubljana: Statistical Office of the Republic of Slovenia.

Statistical Office of the Republic of Slovenia (2006, January 24). *Consumer Survey, Slovenia, July 2005*. Ljubljana: Statistical Office of the Republic of Slovenia.

Statistical Office of the Republic of Slovenia (2006, May 31). *Consumer price indices, Slovenia, May 2006*. Ljubljana: Statistical Office of the Republic of Slovenia.

Survey: Slovenians only moderately optimistic about 2006 (2006, January 2). *Slovenia Business Weekly*, 1.

Thoughts of the jury members (1997). *Golden Drum*, 5: 4.

Tilles, Daniel (1997, December 8). New Europe, new outlook. *Adweek*, 33–6.

Tourism revenues up 10% in 2005 (2006, June 19). *Slovenia Business Weekly*, 24.

Two tabloids Slovenia's top periodicals (2006, June 12). *Slovenia Business Weekly*, 23.

Unemployment in Slovenia hits record low (2006, June 12). *Slovenia Business Weekly*, 23.

US Department of State (2004). *Doing Business in Slovenia: A Country Commercial Guide for US Companies*. US and Foreign Service and US Department of State.

Women work longer hours than men, but earn less (2006, March 13). *Slovenia Business Weekly*, 11.

Zavri, Franci (1996), "Let's have fun" campaign. *GD Forum*, 91–3.

IV South America

14 *Multinational Advertising Agencies in Latin America: From Historical Development to Present Practices*

GLADYS TORRES-BAUMGARTEN

Globalization has left its imprint on markets the world over, and its effects on the economies and business environment in Latin America are no exception. While the region has succeeded in attracting the interest of international business researchers, their focus has largely been on issues such as trade, foreign direct investment and inflationary pressures in the region. Seventeen years after Martínez, Quelch and Ganitsky (1992) wrote an article exhorting marketing academicians not to forget Latin America, it appears that their pleas may have largely fallen on deaf ears—despite some exceptions. The expansion of the advertising industry in Latin America is the area that has attracted the greatest attention on the part of international marketing researchers to date. However, beyond the industry's internationalization, there is a dearth of international marketing research on Latin America seeking to understand advertising practices in the region. For example, little is known about the degree to which advertising is standardized (or adapted) within the region. This issue is likely to be of interest to marketing and advertising researchers and practitioners, given the industry's penetration and sophistication in the region today. Yet, Latin America has failed to attract the attention that other emerging markets have garnered—most notably Asia. While the interest in Asia is understandable, the formidable rise in Latin America's advertising industry, the size of its markets, and the significant presence of multinational clients and agencies warrants increased attention.

The first part of this chapter reviews the extant literature on the historical development and drivers of internationalization in the advertising industry in the region throughout the twentieth century. The second half of the chapter focuses on current advertising practices within Latin America, utilizing the extant literature as a foundation, that when combined with a recent empirical study (presented here) on advertising practices in the region, seeks to contribute by drawing managerial implications of interest to academics and practitioners alike.

Internationalization of the Advertising Industry in Latin America

EARLY HISTORY

The internationalization of the advertising industry in Latin America predates the accelerated patterns of international trade and investment that occurred worldwide during the 1980s and 1990s, and in fact, can be traced as far back as the 1920s and 1930s when global expansion of the advertising industry was spearheaded by the New York-based advertising agencies of J. Walter Thompson, N.W. Ayer and McCann Erickson.

J. Walter Thompson began offering advertising services to its US clients in 1864, and by 1899 had opened its first international office in London. J. Walter Thompson continued its international expansion throughout the 1920s and 1930s, by which time its network extended to all world regions: Africa, Asia, Europe and Latin America. The agency opened its first Latin American office in 1929 in Sao Paulo, Brazil and within that same year opened additional Latin American subsidiaries in the capital cities of Argentina, Chile and Uruguay. A second Brazilian office was opened as early as 1931 in Rio de Janeiro (http://library.duke.edu/digitalcollections/rbmscl/jwtinternationalads/inv/). Growth of J. Walter Thompson's global web accelerated quickly during this time because of a pivotal agreement between the agency and General Motors (GM). Shortly after commercialization of the automobile and following attempts by GM to handle its advertising in-house, J. Walter Thompson and GM reached an agreement whereby the agency would pursue the same international expansion as their client and be assured of their business worldwide (Scanlon, 2003). The GM/J. Walter Thompson arrangement was mutually beneficial as it guaranteed GM access to advertising professionals wherever production facilities were established and it also fueled J. Walter Thompson's worldwide success. At the time, however, J. Walter Thompson followed an ethnocentric staffing policy at its Latin American subsidiaries, where, according to Scanlon (2003), key management positions were reserved for US expatriates. Despite this approach and initial ties to the home office, the subsidiaries were expected by J. Walter Thompson to become self-sufficient and profitable in a relatively short, two-year time frame (Scanlon, 2003). J. Walter Thompson's global reach and international experience soon became attractive to other US-based manufacturers whose international expansion had brought them to Latin America and which sought to develop a relationship with an advertising agency that could handle their accounts in multiple geographic markets.

J. Walter Thompson's presence in Latin America and in other international markets made its subsidiary managers aware of the need for market research to guide the development of effective advertising. Market research capabilities had evolved into the core competency that differentiated many of the larger, international advertising agencies from their smaller—and often more local—counterparts. While in Argentina, J. Walter Thompson conducted market research aiming to understand local consumers' decision-making and purchasing behavior. J. Walter Thompson described their unique selling proposition at the time as creativity based on facts, where "facts" were uncovered through their competitive advantage, i.e., market research. The multinational advertising agencies' progress in Latin America was also fueled by growth in local media, such as newspapers and magazines that experienced unparalleled growth in the 1920s (Hower, 1949); as did radio in the 1930s (Fejes, 1980).

Another prominent US advertising agency, N.W. Ayer extended its reach into South America at about the same time that J. Walter Thompson entered the region. N.W. Ayer opened two offices in 1931 in Sao Paulo, Brazil and Buenos Aires, Argentina. As was the case for J. Walter Thompson, N.W. Ayer's southward expansion was motivated by its primary client's (i.e., Ford's) progress in the region (Hower, 1949). The agency very quickly established its competitive position in South America and came to be known for its management training initiatives, research capabilities, its attempts to adapt advertisements to local market conditions and in general, for its sound business practices.

McCann Erickson opened offices in Buenos Aires, Argentina and Rio de Janeiro in Brazil in 1935 (http://www.mccann.com/) to serve another multinational client, Standard Oil. The affiliate made history in the region because it was the first to be headed by a Brazilian (as compared to the other multinational affiliates in the region that were largely headed by US expatriates).

Thompson, Ayer and McCann continued extending their global (and Latin American) reach throughout the 1930s and often succeeded in attracting additional business from other US-based multinational firms. J. Walter Thompson's client roster in the 1930s included consumer packaged goods companies such as Pond's, durable goods companies such as Frigidaire and communications companies such as International Telephone and Telegraph (Scanlon, 2003). J. Walter Thompson, and its multinational advertising agency counterparts at Ayer and McCann capitalized upon their international reach and promoted it as their differential advantage (*vis-à-vis* the local firms) in seeking new business. However, the multinational agency subsidiaries were not the only agencies in the region to gain renown. The local advertising industry began to flourish in countries such as Brazil and Argentina, and some of the local agencies began to rival the multinational advertising agency subsidiaries in the region.

Between 1915 and 1959, the 15 largest US-based advertising agencies opened or acquired a total of 50 offices overseas (Fejes, 1980). At the end of World War II, most of US advertising activity was domestic: the United States' ad spending of $5.7 billion accounted for approximately 75 percent of the world's $7.4 billion advertising expenditures.

CHALLENGES IN LATIN AMERICA DURING THE EARLY YEARS

While Latin America proved to be a highly profitable market region for J. Walter Thompson in the early half of the twentieth century, US advertising expatriates based in Latin America did not appear to fully (or even partially) understand the cultures for which they were developing advertising (Hower, 1949; Scanlon, 2003). Scanlon suggests that senior managers/US expatriates at J. Walter Thompson's subsidiary in Argentina, for example, often lacked a basic understanding of the country's history, geography and its consumers, along with its implications for advertising development. It is conceivable that that could have been a source of conflict within the organization. It is unclear, however, the extent to which senior managers' cultural misconceptions were countered by host country nationals (generally in lower ranked positions). Local country managers' unwillingness to address cultural misconceptions may have been complicated by the staffing policies that J. Walter Thompson pursued at the time. It is certainly plausible that the organizational structure (with US expatriates at the helm, and host country nationals in lower managerial levels) could have led to disagreements between senior managers and local staff on issues dealing with strategic or executional choices in advertising development. If, for example, it is true that culture is slow to change, then it may be fair to assume that the cultural foundations that Hofstede was to find several decades later about Argentine culture were already present during J. Walter Thompson's and N.W. Ayer's early years in Argentina. Specifically, Hofstede found that Argentines scored fairly high on power distance and on uncertainty avoidance (in McFarlin and Sweeney, 2006, pp. 125–6). These two characteristics would have meant that Argentine staff may have been hesitant to point out disagreements to their US supervisors. It is not known how often cultural differences and its implications for advertising development in Argentina would have surfaced. Therefore, it remains unclear whether disagreements in advertising development were actually discussed, or if the ethnocentric views of US senior management prevailed.

Sentiments that advertising executives were out of touch with the advertising's intended audiences began to surface (Scanlon, 2003). On the one hand, the expatriate advertising managers had often fine-tuned their advertising and copywriting skills in country markets that culturally were vastly different from Latin American markets, and on the other hand, local advertising personnel also found it challenging to write advertising messages for those in economic classes that differed markedly from their own. Advertising executives grappled with the question of how best to develop global advertising that would concomitantly be meaningful to differing markets. Often, the agency's home country provided the direction and creative that would ultimately be implemented across markets with minor variations.

THE LATTER HALF OF THE TWENTIETH CENTURY

As the pace of international expansion began to increase in the 1960s, other advertising agencies saw the opportunity to go abroad while their clients (or potential clients) did the same. International expansion of clients and their agencies meant that they too might reap the benefits that J. Walter Thompson/General Motors and N.W. Ayer/Ford had obtained in the early part of the century. As US manufacturing firms increased their foreign direct investments, including many in Latin America, the US-based advertising firms followed them, foreseeing the need for communication services in new markets (Weinstein, 1977; Fejes, 1980).

An international presence gave agencies several advantages over more nationally-oriented ones: 1) broad reach, enabling them to service multinational clients more effectively; 2) an increased source of revenues (and often, healthier margins due to lower operating costs) from new markets; and 3) less reliance upon the performance of one (the US) economy, particularly at a time when ad spending in the United States was beginning to taper off and international growth prospects were more promising. Local agencies— and in particular, the larger, more prominent local agencies—often desired the affiliation with a large multinational agency to gain access to the advertising and general marketing knowledge and skill that these agencies possessed.

Fejes' study (1980) of US-based multinational advertising agencies indicated that in the period from 1915 to 1959, the agencies opened or acquired 50 overseas branch offices. This contrasts with the following decade (1960 to 1971) in which a total of 210 overseas branch offices were opened or acquired. In Latin America specifically, there were 18 subsidiaries of multinational agencies in 1960, with billings totaling nearly $19 million. These figures were due largely to the presence of some of the multinational agencies that had established their presence early on in the region (i.e., J. Walter Thompson, N.W. Ayer and McCann Erickson).

1970s

Consolidation altered the face of the advertising industry in the 1970s worldwide. The large multinational agencies continued to grow, and their international expansion into Europe, Asia and Latin America deepened. Some major industry players merged or acquired existing firms in an effort to compete more effectively in the increasingly global business environment. Smaller multinational agencies, however, were forced to reduce their international presence. One indication of the wave of consolidation that occurred in the industry during this decade was that in 1970, the industry trade journal *Advertising Age* showed 56 agencies having international billings, versus 36 agencies with international billings in 1977. By 1977, multinational agency billings outside the United States totaled $5.8 billion, and accounted for approximately 30 percent of total US agency billings.

While the majority of non-US billings in the 1970s were derived from advertising business in developed nations (Western Europe, Canada, Australia and Japan), the business generated in developing countries was growing as well. Latin American billings in 1970 totaled $258 million, or roughly a 13 1/2-times increase versus a decade earlier (Fejes, 1980, p. 41).

The international marketing environment began to change during the 1970s as well, with consumerism and stricter advertising legislation on the rise. While in the United States stricter advertising legislation took the form of bans on cigarette advertising on television (1971); in Latin America, multinational advertising agencies were growing increasingly concerned over the wave of nationalization that had affected many other international businesses, and that was about to affect them more directly. During this time, for example, legislative changes in Argentina called for close to 80 percent local ownership of advertising agencies. This meant that the international advertising webs that had developed many years earlier would have to sell a large portion of their subsidiaries to nationals within a three year period (International Advertising Association, 1974). This threat to multinational advertising agencies was halted in 1976 when a political coup in Argentina led to the creation of a government that was more favorable to international investment.

1980s

Inward foreign direct investment in the advertising industry transformed the US sector during this decade. The face of US advertising was changed after several US-based multinational advertising firms (Dancer-Fitzgerald-Sample, Backer & Spielvogel and Ted Bates Worldwide) were acquired by UK's Saatchi & Saatchi. In 1987, another British company, the WPP Group, acquired J. Walter Thompson, and followed that with the acquisition of another US gem, Ogilvy & Mather two years later (West, 1996). The mergers and acquisitions within the industry during this decade fine-tuned the role of the advertising holding company. Multinational client firms wanted to capitalize upon the cost efficiencies that arose when dealing with a single worldwide media-buying agency. As a result, multinational agencies continued to grow into mega-agencies, through increases in foreign direct investment aimed at establishing a competitive advantage in media buying efficiencies. In general the larger the holding company, the greater its competitive advantage in the media-buying area. As holding companies grew through foreign direct investments, so too did the individual multinational agencies that formed the holding company.

Advertising investment in Latin America at the time, however, was much more cautious. Agencies strengthened their presence in Latin America through strategic alliances—that may or may not have involved ownership—with large, local firms in the region. The guarded undertakings reflected the difficult times in Latin America during this decade: the region's average GDP growth rate during the 1980s declined to 1.1 percent from a 6.2 percent rate in the 1970s (Martínez, Quelch and Ganitsky, 1992), and real wages actually declined in many Latin American nations. In countries such as Argentina, Mexico and Peru, the real value of the minimum wage actually declined by 50 percent over the ten year period. Governments were also increasingly concerned over the growth of their international debt, and policy-making at the time was influenced by it (Guell and Richards, 1998).

Despite the economic decline, advertising spending in the region continued to increase, albeit at a slower rate than in earlier years. While ad spending increased, there was also growing concern over American economic imperialism in Latin America, palpable through its increasing presence and dominance of the advertising industry in the region. Meanwhile, others saw the penetration of the advertising industry by US firms in Latin America as an unavoidable part of the globalization process (Kim, 1995).

1990s–PRESENT

The 1990s were marked by swift changes in the political economy of many Latin American nations as many of them embraced democratic ideals. This led to more favorable attitudes and conditions toward international businesses. Countries such as Mexico and Chile underwent widespread political and economic reforms. With more democratic governments and greater moves toward privatization, the profile of the advertising industry within Latin America was altered once again. It could be argued that the winds of political reforms in Latin America of the late 1980s and early 1990s were merely representative of the tides that were sweeping the world over.

The profile of the advertising industry worldwide—and in Latin America—was not expected to change significantly since the mid 1990s when the industry experienced a renaissance of sorts, expanded into new markets and increased penetration into existing ones. In Latin America, many of the multinationally recognized names in the advertising industry either acquired or formed additional partnerships with the larger domestic agencies in Latin America, and penetrated some of the new, smaller advertising markets in the region.

Why is Latin America of Interest Today?

Latin America is—or should be—of interest to marketers for several reasons:

STRENGTHENING INWARD FOREIGN DIRECT INVESTMENT

Latin America has succeeded in attracting annual foreign direct investment (FDI) averaging approximately $70 billion per year during the FDI boom of 1996 to 2001 (see Appendix), with Brazil arising as the leader in inward FDI in the region (UNCTAD, 1998).

Much of the inward FDI at that time was fueled by large privatization efforts undertaken by several Latin American nations in key sectors. Since then, FDI in the region has declined, and in 2004, Latin America attracted $56 billion in FDI, or a 44 percent increase over the prior year's sum of $39 billion. This marked the first time that the region experienced an increase in FDI from year to year since 1999, and suggests that a new investment boom in the region may be occurring (ECLAC, 2005). Current levels of FDI in Latin America may be viewed as a barometer of growth in the region; but also as an indicator of the need for advertising services in the future.

KEY FDI MARKETS ARE STRONG ADVERTISING MARKETS

Some of the Latin American nations that experienced the largest increases in FDI in 2004 have also historically been strong advertising markets. In 2004, Brazil, Mexico, Chile, Colombia, Trinidad and Tobago and El Salvador experienced significant increases in FDI versus the prior year, and Brazil, Mexico and Chile have traditionally been leading advertising markets from a spending viewpoint, as well as from a creative standpoint. Furthermore, Brazil, Mexico and Chile accounted for three out of four Latin American nations that attracted significant FDI between 1996 and 2001. Brazil's inward FDI (and to a lesser extent, Mexico and Chile's FDI) has been categorized as largely market-seeking FDI in services (*vis-à-vis* the manufacturing-oriented FDI that typified investment in the 1970s) (ECLAC, 2005). The market-seeking nature of this FDI suggests that advertising growth prospects are favorable in the region.

LARGE CONSUMER MARKETS AND STRENGTHENING CONSUMER CONFIDENCE

Latin America's 15 largest markets consist of nearly 520 million people as of the middle of 2005, yet consumer confidence varies across markets (see Table 14.1). The highest consumer confidence levels as of 2004 could be found in Chile, Colombia, El Salvador, Peru and Mexico with slightly lower levels in Brazil and Argentina, and some of these markets are also showing increased private sector consumption from 2004 to 2005. Chile, for example, increased its private sector consumption by 7.4 percent, Argentina by 7.0 percent, Mexico by 6.6 percent and Brazil by 4.0 percent from 2004 to 2005. These are signs that portend growth in Latin America's advertising industry.

ECONOMIES HAVE STABILIZED

The United Nation's ECLAC (Economic Commission for Latin America and the Caribbean) foresees a positive economic outlook for Latin America in the near future. The region's overall growth rate of 4 percent in 2005, and more robust growth in 2006 of 5.3 percent fuel confidence in the region (ECLAC, 2005)—however, 2007 projected GDP growth in the region is expected to be less than in 2006 and is expected to be more in line with the 4 percent growth seen in 2005. The economies have stabilized as evidenced by the relatively calm inflation rates and low unemployment rates in individual countries (see Table 14.2).

Table 14.1 Latin American consumer confidence and consumption growth from 2004 to 2005

Consumer confidence		Consumption growth	
Nations ranked in descending order of consumer confidence, with 1 being the lowest and 10 the highest.		Chart shows estimated year-on-year variation in private sector consumption from 2004 to 2005 as a percentage.	
Nation	**Confidence**	**Nation**	**% Change**
Chile	7	Chile	7.4
Colombia	7	Argentina	7.0
El Salvador	7	Mexico	6.6
Peru	7	Venezuela	5.7
Mexico	7	Peru	5.7
Brazil	6	Ecuador	5.1
Argentina	6	Colombia	4.4
Ecuador	5	Brazil	4.0
Nicaragua	5	El Salvador	4.0
Venezuela	5	Nicaragua	3.9
Guatemala	4	Guatemala	3.4
Honduras	4	Honduras	3.0
Dominican Republic	4	Dominican Republic	2.7
Bolivia	1	Bolivia	2.1
Paraguay	1	Paraguay	2.0

Source: Market Statistical Analysis with support data from the Central Intelligence Agency and the International Monetary Fund.

Advertising in Latin America Today (2000 to Present)

ADVERTISING SPENDING

The start of the twenty-first century was marked by an exceptional year for the multinational advertising agencies in Latin America. Advertising billings in key Latin American markets, such as Brazil, Argentina and Mexico increased versus the previous year due to new business and increased spending by existing clients. New business was largely the result of the boom in the dot-com and telecommunications industries in Latin America (Penteado, 2001). However, advertising expenditures then fell sharply the following year, after the technology and dot-com bubble burst (Business: consumer republic; advertising, 2005, p. 83). While the cutbacks in advertising expenditures affected all world regions, the technology bubble burst occurred at the same time that several

Table 14.2 Human development indices for 2004

Country	Population (in millions)	Average population growth/ year (%)	Infant mortality/ 1,000 births (by deaths)	Life expectancy (years)	Adult literacy rate (%)	Real GDP/ capita (US$)	Unemployment rate (US$)	Inflation rate/year (US$)
Argentina	39.5	0.98	15	75	97	13,600	11	11
Bolivia	8.8	1.49	53	65	87	2,700	8	5
Brazil	186.1	1.06	29	71	86	8,500	10	7
Chile	15.9	0.97	8	76	96	11,300	7	4
Colombia	42.9	1.49	20	71	92	7,100	12	5
Costa Rica	4.0	1.48	9	76	96	10,000	7	18
Ecuador	13.3	1.24	23	76	92	3,900	11	2
Mexico	106.2	1.17	20	75	92	10,000	4	4
Paraguay	6.3	2.48	25	74	94	4,900	16	7
Peru	27.9	1.36	31	69	88	6,000	9	2
Uruguay	3.4	0.47	11	76	98	10,000	12	5
Venezuela	25.3	1.40	22	74	93	6,400	12	16

Source: United Nations Development Program, Human Development Report for 2006 http://hdr.undp.org/en/statistics/data/.

notable advertising markets in Latin America were also experiencing an extended period of hyperinflation (most notably, Argentina).

In general, the environment for international advertising agencies in Latin America can be a challenging one. While prospects for growth in the region are excellent, advertising agencies must continue to monitor individual countries in the region for signs of weakness. Billings often fluctuate from year to year, due to exchange rate fluctuations (or devaluations of local currency) and this leads to reductions in reported billings. In addition, the advertising firms are also susceptible to economic downturns in individual countries, as in the case of Argentina in 2001–2002, or changing political environments that appear to be growing increasingly critical of multinational companies' presence (and in particular, that of US firms) in countries like Venezuela, Bolivia and Peru.

Global advertising expenditures in 2006 were expected to total $599.5 billion (+5.3 percent over 2005), according to Robert Coen's December 2006 advertising expenditures report issued by McCann Erickson (http://www.mccannworldgroup.com). While US ad spending for 2006 was expected to total $285.1 billion, representing a 5.2 percent increase over the previous year, ad spending outside the United States was expected to increase by 5.5 percent to $314.4 billion. Projected growth rates for global spending, however, mask the reality of projected growth in emerging markets *vis-à-vis* the industrialized nations. While the Coen Report only includes data on advertising outlook for two Latin American countries, the data reveal that Mexico and Brazil are expected to increase their ad spending faster than most other industrialized markets. However, the growth projected for the two prominent Latin American nations is significantly lower than that predicted for key Asian nations; specifically, Indonesia, China, S. Korea and India (see Table 14.3).

A more optimistic outlook on advertising spending rates in Latin America can be gauged by looking at the top advertisers in each country as published in *Advertising Age* (Endicott, 2006). In 2005, Mexico and Brazil's ten leading advertisers each spent approximately $770 million and $745 million, respectively. More importantly, Brazil's top ten advertisers increased their spending in 2005 by 52 percent versus the prior year, while Mexico's top advertisers increased their spending by 17 percent versus 2004 levels. In the same period, the ten leading advertisers in Argentina increased their spending by 39 percent, Chile's by 20 percent, Peru's by 38 percent, etc. The double-digit increases suggest that international marketers need to gain a deeper understanding of the advertising industry and its practices in Latin America in order to compete more effectively in the region, and in turn, possibly even to strengthen their global competitiveness.

KEY ADVERTISING PLAYERS

The key advertising markets in Latin America continue to be Brazil, Mexico, Argentina and Chile. In recent years, the advertising industry has gained prominence in Puerto Rico and ad spending there has increased. Puerto Rico attracts advertising dollars from many US-based clients such as Procter & Gamble, Sears, Pfizer, Yum Brands, financial services and telecommunication services (Verizon) companies. Key advertisers throughout Latin America can be grouped by industry: consumer packaged goods companies (such as Unilever, Danone Group, Procter & Gamble, Colgate-Palmolive, S.C. Johnson), automotive companies (e.g., GM, Ford, Fiat) and telecommunications and oil companies.

Table 14.3 2006 ad outlook in key industrialized and other selected countries

Country	2005	2006	2007 (proj.)
Japan	+1.3%	+2.2%	+4.3%
Germany	+1.2	+2.5	+1.4
United Kingdom	+3.8	+3.8	+5.3
France	+3.0	+3.1	+3.4
Italy	+3.7	+4.1	+8.2
Spain	+7.6	+5.8	+4.8
Canada	+4.5	+4.4	+3.3
Mexico	+5.0	+9.0	+7.5
Australia	+6.0	+4.3	+4.6
Netherlands	+2.1	+3.4	+3.0
Brazil	+14.7	+10.0	+9.0
Indonesia	+16.5	+15.0	+15.0
China	+20.7	+23.6	+28.0
South Korea	+10.0	+8.0	+7.5
India	+11.0	+13.0	+14.0

Note: Percent change over prior year in nominal currencies.

Source: Robert Coen 2006 Insider's Report; Universal McCann, global media services operation of McCann Worldgroup. http://www.mccannworldgroup.com/news/pdfs/Insider1206.pdf.

ADVERTISING CREATIVITY

Several Latin American markets have earned world renown for their advertising creativity and production quality. This expertise has developed over the years as advertising and several advertising-related industries, such as film and television production, have long flourished in countries such as Brazil, Argentina and Mexico. 2004 marked a significant year for the Latin American advertising industry in that the top winner in the Gunn Report was Almap BBDO, a Brazilian-based agency. (The Gunn Report recognizes creativity in advertising each year by compiling and tallying up winners of all major advertising competitions worldwide.) This recognition marked the first time that a Brazilian (or for that matter a Latin American) agency had won the top spot. (Wentz, 2004). In December 2005, Brazilian agencies once again showed the world that they could successfully compete in new media when they won two of the coveted Grand Awards at the New York Festivals' interactive and alternate media awards (Anderson, 2005, p. 23).

Despite recent accolades accruing to Brazilian agencies, they have also been criticized for failing to effectively reach the lower income segment of the population (Montoya, 2005). Montoya states that the challenge is particularly acute because of the large economic disparity between the advertising executives and this market segment, making this reminiscent of some of the criticisms that had been lodged against some of the earliest advertising executives in the region.

ADVERTISING REGULATION IN LATIN AMERICA

Advertising regulation is one of the areas that stands out as differing markedly across Latin American markets (Zbar and Hoag, 1996). While some nations may have highly restrictive laws toward advertising (e.g., Venezuela), particularly with regards to products such as alcoholic beverages and cigarettes, others rely more heavily upon industry self-regulation (e.g., Chile, Mexico, Brazil).

Advertising Development Practices

The previous sections underscore the fact that key differences still exist with regards to advertising across the various Latin American markets, possibly impeding the use of global—or even regional—advertising. Disparities exist in advertising regulations, the scope of development of the industry, spending allocations by media and projected ad spending across different countries. Yet, the continuing presence and broadening scope of multinationals within Latin America may tempt some firms to consider the financial and marketing efficiencies of standardized advertising within the region. This dichotomy is yet another representation of the age-old "standardization versus localization" debate.

Advertising practitioners and academicians have long debated the extent to which advertising within a region or the world can (or should) be standardized (Elinder, 1961; Agrawal, 1995; Onkvisit and Shaw, 1999). It has been argued that advertising standardization offers two distinct advantages: cost advantages arising from efficiencies and economies of scale achieved in advertising production, and more importantly, marketing advantages arising from a unified brand image that often leads to instant recognition across international markets that, in turn, may lead to increased revenues in the long term.

Advertising standardization research, however, has largely focused on Europe and, more recently, on Asia (Tai and Wong, 1998; Samiee, Jeong, Pae and Tai, 2003; Chao, Samiee and Yip, 2003). Rarely has Latin America been the subject of such an investigation. The first notable exception was a study conducted in 1991 by Grosse and Zinn. (The majority of research studies on advertising in Latin America consist of cross-cultural studies using content analysis to analyze message content in finished commercials.) The Grosse and Zinn study can be viewed as a seminal paper in the area of marketing standardization in developing markets, and in particular, Latin America; yet, it had several limitations: its goals were broad, aiming to measure not only advertising standardization, but standardization in all marketing mix variables. As a result, advertising was viewed as a single-item measure. Perhaps if advertising had been defined in terms of its various components, then a better understanding of *what* is standardized and *what* is adapted might have been gained. More importantly, respondents in the Grosse and Zinn study were Latin American directors of client firms. This is seen as problematic in one key respect: senior level managers may not be as familiar (as middle level managers) with the day-to-day operations, and therefore, may not be the best qualified to gauge the standardization or adaptation of a company's marketing mix. In addition, if advertising practices in the region were to be identified, it was preferable to obtain this information from advertising professionals in the region. These limitations were addressed in a more recent exploratory study that this author conducted on advertising practices in Latin America and that is summarized in the next section. However, one additional study that addressed the standardization versus adaptation issue in Latin America should also be referenced here. Chhabra (1996) sought to identify the extent to which multinational firms with a presence in South America adapted various elements of the marketing mix. Chhabra's empirical work uncovered that multinationals tended to adapt the promotion and pricing more often; but less so for the product and distribution elements. Chhabra's work, like Grosse and Zinn's, looked broadly at various elements of the marketing mix, and queried the managers from multinational firms, complicating the implications of their work strictly from an advertising perspective. However, the finding in both studies that promotion in the region was at times localized and at times standardized led to a more detailed empirical study focusing on one of promotion's subcomponents, advertising. A description of that study follows.

Adaptation or Standardization in Latin America? Some Exploratory Evidence

A study[1] was undertaken in 2000 in an effort to comprehend one specific part of the marketing mix, i.e., the current advertising practices in Latin America. This research was conducted at a point when multinational advertising agencies were well entrenched in the region, often with multiple offices in the principal advertising countries. As suggested previously, it was deemed important to gather *advertising* information from *advertising* professionals within Latin America. As a result, questionnaires were sent to account executives at the Latin American subsidiaries of the top 11 US-based multinational advertising agency brands at the time (e.g., J. Walter Thompson, Ogilvy & Mather, etc.) as identified in the trade journal, *Advertising Age* (April 24, 2000). Five countries were selected: Argentina, Brazil, Chile, Mexico and Peru. The first four markets were selected due to their size and prominence in the advertising industry, and Peru was selected as representative of a less developed advertising market so that comparisons might be made between it and the aforementioned developed advertising markets.

The primary research objective was to establish what aspects of the advertising development process are standardized or adapted in Latin America. A secondary research objective was to identify the role that the subsidiary (versus the home country office) plays in advertising development for their multinational clients in Latin America.

To address the first research question, advertising services were broken down into its various sub-components, heeding Michael Porter's call to "disaggregate firms into the fundamental activities they perform to do business" (1986, p. 17).

Porter's value chain of activities framework was used to break down the advertising development process into its various components/activities. Seventeen activities were identified (in consultation with advertising executives):

1   A version of this study was presented at the American Marketing Association 2003 meeting. Complete reference can be found at the end of this chapter.

- target market analysis
- competitive analysis
- marketing objectives
- marketing strategy
- advertising objective
- advertising strategy
- copywriting
- pre-production testing
- media planning
- media buying
- television production
- radio production
- magazine production
- newspaper production
- post-production testing
- direct response advertising
- event sponsorship

Respondents (advertising account executives at the Latin American subsidiaries of the largest US-based multinational advertising agencies) were asked to evaluate whether each activity was handled on a global, regional or local basis for their multinational client(s). A total of 60[2] usable responses were received (see Table 14.4). While the respondent base was small, responses likely reflected the general practices in the region since personnel from 10 out of the 11 targeted agencies responded and the country-by-country distribution of respondents was also widespread, as shown below:

Table 14.4 Respondent distribution

Country	Number of respondents	% of total
Argentina	8	13%
Brazil	18	30%
Chile	10	17%
Mexico	19	32%
Peru	5	8%
Total	60	100%

Responses indicated the following:

- Strategic activities (those earlier in the value chain of activities) tend to be coordinated across a broader geographic area (namely globally or regionally) than some of the more execution-related elements of advertising service production. This was consistent with

---

2   Sixty questionnaires did not yield a sufficient number from Peru in order to compare an underdeveloped advertising market to the other four, more developed advertising markets in Latin America.

the aforementioned works on advertising standardization in Latin America, notably the Grosse and Zinn and Chhabra studies, as well as another case that focused on the Goodyear Tire Company's advertising strategies in multiple markets, including Brazil and Mexico (Peebles, Ryans and Vernon, 1977).

- Several activities—such as media planning and media buying—that stand to gain from greater coordination at the regional level—are still performed on a country-by-country basis.
- Radio and newspapers, traditionally deemed to be "local" advertising vehicles, are in fact coordinated on a local level, while the broader reach media vehicles, television and magazines, are coordinated on a more regional, and even global level.

These findings suggest that despite the scope of investment by manufacturing and service firms throughout Latin America and the concomitant growth of the advertising industry, that advertising development is largely the responsibility of the individual subsidiary. Most of the advertising activities were handled individually by each of the Latin American subsidiaries included in this latest study, with little apparent input or coordination from either the home office or a pan-regional integrating subsidiary. This means that attitudes toward the management of multinational advertising agency subsidiaries in Latin America may have come full circle. Whereas early on in their history subsidiaries were reliant upon the direction they received from the home office, home country management now appears to have embraced more of an arm's length approach to managing its subsidiaries in Latin America and subsidiaries are allowed significantly more autonomy than in prior years.

The second question sought to identify the locus of decision-making in the Latin American subsidiaries of the largest US-based multinational advertising agencies. Respondents were asked to identify *where* final decisions were made for each of the value chain of advertising activities. The objective here was to identify if decisions were made by the home office, or alternatively, if there was a subsidiary within the region that coordinated advertising activities for Latin America overall. The findings revealed that:

- Latin American ad agency subsidiaries operate largely as autonomous units when developing advertising for their respective countries. The subsidiaries are generally the sole decision makers for each of the activities of the advertising value chain. Joint decision-making is rare, but when it does occur, the second country is generally the United States, i.e., the home country office.
- Limited joint decision-making suggests that there is relatively little coordination among the various subsidiaries in the region. None of the Latin American subsidiaries stood out as a regional coordinator, despite the fact that some key markets are more readily recognized for their advertising expertise than others.

This study indicated that advertising development in Latin America today is largely performed on a multi-domestic basis. Depending upon the activity, this may be due to country-specific factors such as: legal/regulatory issues, cultural differences or lack of availability of regional media. The subsidiaries may look to the home country office for some guidance, however, most decisions are made by the individual Latin American subsidiaries. Many respondents felt that their level of autonomy in decision making had actually increased over the previous five years. This suggests that while the multinational advertising agencies' presence in Latin America is significant, advertising development is largely adapted for each individual market. This may be indicative of a need for better coordination mechanisms within Latin America before pan-regional efforts can be implemented; or alternatively, it may suggest that the multi-domestic approach in the region may lead to development of more locally responsive advertising for the markets they serve. This issue merits further investigation, particularly since regional coordination may not be done at the account executive (i.e., respondent) level, but rather at higher managerial ranks within the subsidiary. Future research may consider collecting this type of information from several or all levels of management at the Latin American subsidiaries.

Conclusion

Latin America is a region that merits greater attention and understanding on the part of advertisers if advertising communications are to be effective there. The region continues to attract international retailers, consumer packaged goods firms, consumer durable manufacturers and service firms, fueling the competitive environment as firms vie for a larger slice of Latin American consumers' "pesos." There are many country-related factors that present a challenge to advertisers: varying regulations, differences in advertising vehicle usage across markets, as well as demographic, cultural and language differences. These country-specific factors may dictate the use of multi-domestic advertising. The empirical study reported here indicates that multinational advertisers are currently localizing advertising in the region, more than they are standardizing its various elements. It remains unclear, however, if the preponderance of multi-domestic advertising is due to the advertisers' commitment to local responsiveness, or if it is due to a failure on the part of individual country subsidiaries to establish coordination mechanisms within the region. Greater coordination of advertising activities could potentially result in more effective advertising programs in the region. A pan-Latin American approach to advertising might not only offer cost-saving opportunities to multinational advertisers, but more importantly, the unified advertising communications across the region may aid in building a stronger brand image through coordinated advertising and marketing messages within the region. Additional research is needed to identify the underlying reasons that may explain the prevalence of multi-domestic advertising in the region. In addition, the relationship between the US-based headquarters and its Latin American subsidiaries must be investigated more closely in future research. One possible explanation for the autonomy given to Latin American subsidiaries today is that the US office may now be more willing to yield to host country decisions. This may reflect increased confidence in the advertising professionals in the region, and would also represent a significant shift in attitude on the part of the US headquarters from the way Latin American subsidiaries were initially viewed and managed in the early to late part of the twentieth century.

Changing political tides in Latin America could have a negative impact on the business climate and investment in several key markets in the region, and this in turn could affect the prospects for advertising industry growth in the region. Leaders in Venezuela, Bolivia and Ecuador, who have recently increased their socialist rhetoric, favor more nationalistic views toward FDI and additionally, frown upon US investment. If FDI into Latin America is curtailed, or if US-based multinationals are made to feel less welcome, then the Latin American advertising agency subsidiaries may experience budget reductions if multinational clients curtail advertising spending in specific markets. The increased political risk is limited to a few markets, and these are not significant advertising markets (from a spending standpoint). Prospects for the ad industry in Latin America remain optimistic, underscoring the need to more readily understand effective advertising practices in the region.

References

Advertising Age (2000, April 24). The 56th Annual Agency Report. *Advertising Age* (Midwest region edition). 71(18): S16.

Agrawal, M. (1995). Review of a 40-year debate in international advertising. *International Marketing Review*, 12(1): 26–48.

Anderson, M. (2005, December 12). Brazil, Germany top NYF show. *Adweek*, 46(48): 23.

Business: consumer republic, advertising (2005, March 19). *The Economist*, 374(8418): 83.

Chao, P., S. Samiee and L. Sai-Chung Yip (2003). International marketing and the Asia-Pacific region. *International Marketing Review*, 20(5): 480–93.

Chhabra, S.S. (1996). Marketing adaptations by American multinational corporations in South America. *Journal of Global Marketing*, 9(4): 57–74.

ECLAC (2005, April). *Statistical Yearbook for Latin America and the Caribbean, 2004*. [Online.] http://www.eclac.org/cgi-bin/getProd.asp?xml=/publicaciones/xml/0/21230/P21230.xml&xsl=/deype/tpl/p9f.xsl&base=/tpl/top-bottom.xslt (accessed March 28, 2011).

Elinder, E. (1961, December). How international can advertising be? *International Advertiser*, 6–12.

Endicott, C.R. (2006, November 20). Global spending at top 100: $98 billion. *Advertising Age* (Midwest region edition), 77(47): S6–8.

Fejes, F. (1980). The growth of multinational advertising agencies in Latin America. *Journal of Communication (pre-1986)*, 30(4): 36–49.

Grosse, R. and W. Zinn (1991). Standardization in international marketing: the Latin American case. *Journal of Global Marketing*, 4(1): 53–78.

Guell, R.C. and D.G. Richards (1998, May). Regional integration and intra-industry trade in Latin America 1980–90. *International Review of Applied Economics*, 12(2): 283–301.

Hower, R.M. (1949). *The History of an Advertising Agency*. 1st ed. Cambridge, MA: Harvard University Press.

http://library.duke.edu/digitalcollections/rbmscl/jwtinternationalads/inv/ (accessed March 31, 2011).

http://www.mccann.com/ (accessed March 31, 2011).

http://www.mccannworldgroup.com/news/pdfs/Insider1206.pdf.

International Advertising Association (multiple unnamed authors) (1974). The global challenge to advertising. *Journal of Advertising*, 3(1): 21–5.

Kim, K.K. (1995). Spreading the net: the consolidation process of large transnational advertising agencies in the 1980s and early 1990s. *International Journal of Advertising*, 14(3): 195–217.

Martínez, J., J. Quelch and J. Ganitsky (1992, Winter). Don't forget Latin America. *Sloan Management Review*, 33(2): 78–92.

McFarlin, D. and P. Sweeney (2006). *International Management: Strategic Opportunities and Cultural Challenges*. 3rd ed. Boston, MA: Houghton Mifflin.

Montoya, M. (2005, September 16). Insider's view: Brazil. *Campaign*, 19.

Onkvisit, S. and J. Shaw (1999). Standardized international advertising: some research issues and implications. *Journal of Advertising Research*, 39(6): 19–24.

Peebles, D., J.K. Ryans and I.R. Vernon (1977). A new perspective on advertising standardization. *European Journal of Marketing*, 11(8): 569–76.

Penteado, C. (2001, August). A big year for LatAm. *Ad Age Global*, 1(12): 13–16.

Porter, M.E. (1986). The strategic role of international marketing. *The Journal of Consumer Marketing*, 3(2): 17–21.

Samiee, S., I. Jeong, J.H. Pae and S. Tai (2003). Advertising standardization in multinational corporations: the subsidiary perspective. *Journal of Business Research*, 56: 613–26.

Scanlon, J. (2003, Autumn). Mediators in the international marketplace: US advertising in Latin America in the early twentieth century. *Business History Review*, 77(3): 387–415.

Tai, S. and Y.H. Wong (1998). Advertising decision making in Asia: "Glocal" versus "regcal" approach. *Journal of Managerial Issues*, 10(3): 318–25.

Torres-Baumgarten, G. (2003). Degree of advertising standardization in Latin America. *American Marketing Association Conference Proceedings*, 14: 211.

UNCTAD (1998, November 2). Foreign investment into Latin America soars—new records set; Brazil emerges as the champion in attracting foreign direct investment according to UNCTAD's World Investment Report 1998 [Online.] http://www.unctad.org/Templates/webflyer.asp?docid=3145& intItemID=1465&lang=1 (accessed March 28, 2011).

United Nations Development Programme. *Human Development Report*. [Online.] http://hdr.undp.org/en/statistics/data/ (accessed March 28, 2011).

Weinstein, A.K. (1977, Spring). Foreign investments by service firms: the case of multinational advertising agencies. *Journal of International Business Studies*, 8(000001): 83–91.

Wentz, L. (2004, November 15). Omnicom shops dominate Gunn's worldwide ranking. *Advertising Age* (Midwest regional edition, Chicago), 75(46): 14.

West, D.C. (1996). The determinants and consequences of multinational advertising agencies. *International Journal of Advertising*, 15(2): 128–39.

Zbar, J.D. and C. Hoag (1996, October) Latin America cracking down. *Advertising Age* (Midwest region edition, Chicago), I16.

Appendix—Latin America Net FDI Flows, by Country, 1990–2004[a]

	1990–1995[b]	1996–2000[b]	2001	2002	2003	2004[c]
			Millions of dollars			
1. South America	10,684.3	53,173.6	38,566.3	27,421.3	23,418.7	34,103.8
a) Chile	1,498.7	5,667.0	4,199.8	2,549.9	4,385.4	7,602.8
b) Mercosur	5,923.4	36,760.0	24,978.7	17,867.1	11,529.3	20,275.6
Argentina	3,457.2	11,561.1	2,166.1	1,093.0	1,020.4	1,800.0
Brazil	2,229.3	24,823.6	22,457.4	16,590.2	10,143.5	18,165.6
Paraguay	99.3	188.0	84.2	9.3	90.8	80.0
Uruguay	137.5	187.2	271.0	174.6	274.6	230.0
c) Andean Community	3,262.1	10,746.7	9,387.8	7,004.3	7,504.1	6,225.5
Bolivia	136.5	780.2	705.8	676.6	166.8	137.0
Colombia	843.3	3,081.1	2,524.9	2,114.5	1,746.2	2,352.0
Ecuador	327.8	692.4	1,329.8	1,275.3	1,554.7	1,200.0
Peru	1,093.6	2,000.8	1,144.3	2,155.8	1,377.3	1,392.5
Venezuela	861.0	4,192.2	3,683.0	782.0	2,659.0	1,144.0
2. Mexico and Caribbean Basin	7,628.1	17,421.4	32,229.4	19,620.9	15,707.8	22,273.9
a) Mexico	6,112.8	12,873.1	27,634.7	15,129.1	11,372.7	16,601.9
b) Central America	633.5	2,340.2	1,932.3	1,699.9	1,987.1	2,022.0
Costa Rica	241.4	495.2	453.6	662.0	576.8	585.0
El Salvador	19.4	309.5	278.9	470.0	103.7	389.0
Guatemala	85.9	243.7	455.5	110.6	115.8	125.0
Honduras	42.5	166.1	189.5	175.5	198.0	195.0
Nicaragua	47.4	229.2	150.2	203.9	201.3	261.0
Panama	197.1	896.5	404.6	77.9	791.5	467.0
c) Caribbean	881.8	2,208.0	2,662.4	2,792.0	2,348.0	3,650.1
Jamaica	128.1	349.6	613.9	481.1	720.7	605.2
Dominican Republic	211.3	701.5	1,079.1	916.8	309.9	463.0
Trinidad and Tobago	275.2	681.5	834.9	790.7	616.0	1,826.0
Others	267.2	475.4	134.5	603.4	701.4	755.9
Latin America and Caribbean	**18,312.4**	**70,595.0**	**70,795.7**	**41,042.2**	**39,126.6**	**56,377.8**

Notes: [a] Net FDI inflows are defined as FDI inflows to the reporting economy minus capital outflows generated by the same foreign companies. Does not include financial centers; [b] Annual average; [c] ECLAC estimates, except in the cases of Venezuela, Brazil, Chile and Mexico.

Source: Economic Commission for Latin America and the Caribbean (ECLAC) on the basis of information from the International Monetary Fund (IMF) Balance of Payments Statistics, November 2004, and official information as of March 1, 2005.

15 *An Overview of Advertising Trends and Strategies in Latin America: A Colombian Case*

JAIME S. GOMEZ

Introduction

This chapter provides an overview of the advertising industry structure in Latin America and some of the factors that are driving changes in the way companies market their products. We will focus our attention on three main points. First, the clarification of the geographical and cultural definition of Latin America as a significant factor for the proper design of advertising strategies; second, multinational advertising trends in general in Latin America; and third, some specifics about the advertising industry in one of the medium-sized markets of the region, Colombia.

During the last two decades, the Latin American markets landscape has been greatly affected by a process of both globalization and liberalization of international trade. The former is reflected in the privatization and deregulation of the public sector enterprises mainly into the hands of multinational companies (a business enterprise in a home country with foreign subsidiaries). The latter is characterized by a large flow of goods and services across national borders, and foreign direct investment. This process has been carried out by multinational corporations seeking to expand their markets, and governments' national policies seeking to provide a better scenario in which to achieve their economic objectives and improve the quality of life of their population. It is important to note, however, that the social and economic imbalances, and in particular, the increase in poverty levels in most Latin American countries are frequently attributed to globalization. This has been a cause of political and social unrest reflected in massive protests mainly by manufacturing and industrial workers and educators unions.

All of the above issues describe the political, social and cultural environment in which commercial enterprises, especially multinational ones, must design their marketing strategies in order to enter these highly volatile yet highly profitable marketplaces. If products or services are to be sold across national borders, the survival of these companies will depend largely on the extent to which they give serious consideration to regional particularities. In addition, characteristics of individual countries such as laws, values and beliefs, and national identity must also be taken into account before any marketing strategy is created or any advertising campaigns implemented. In summary, multinational marketers must be acutely aware of, and carefully weigh both the socio-economic and cultural factors of a particular environment. These factors must be confronted by the foreign subsidiary even though they may contrast with those values of the home country (Bogart, 1959).

What is Latin America?

In order to clarify the concept of Latin America we must start by looking into the lexical meaning of the word America. The use of the word *America* as a synonym for the United States, although a common and culturally accepted term in the United States, Europe and Asia, is in fact a misrepresentation of its true geographical association. The following two considerations address these issues.

First, America is a continent that is subdivided into three subcontinents: North, Central, and South America (in many instances Central America is considered as part of North America). (See Figure 15.1.) Canada, the United States and Mexico make up North America. Recently, the term *The Americas* has been used to refer to the whole continent and avoid the ambiguous interpretation of the word America as meaning the United States. This ambiguity in the lexical meaning of the word America is one example of how international marketers and advertisers using the word America or American in an advertising campaign in the United States market would have to alter the ad or campaign when adapting it for South or Central American markets. Failure to do so risks the possibility of harmful, unintended consequences because of these audiences finding the term offensive, for it excludes them from what they perceive as their natural geographic continental association.

Second, the word Latin refers to a person or country where the language spoken is derived originally from Latin. The Romance languages spoken in the Roman Empire include Spanish, French, Portuguese and Italian among others. (English is a Germanic language.)

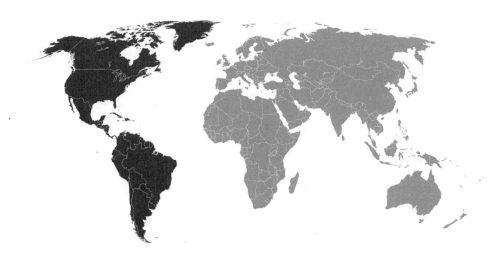

Figure 15.1 The Americas

Based on the above consideration, it should become clear what the lexical meaning of Latin America is and what countries are included in the American continent: The Americas. However, the term Latin America has been defined in several ways depending on the perspective—geographical, lexical or cultural—from which the definition is coming. Lexically, the Oxford American Dictionary defines the word America as the "parts of Central and South America where Spanish and Portuguese is the main language." (Portuguese is spoken in Brazil.) (See Figure 15.2.)

The Strategic Research Corporation (SRC), an international marketing and business development consultancy firm, excludes Cuba and all the Caribbean non-Spanish speaking countries from its definition of Latin America. For the most part in this chapter, we shall adhere to this definition since it is the one most commonly used for the purposes of designing business strategies in Latin America consumer markets. However, we shall also take into consideration the Latin market in the United States because of the size of its population, estimated at 35 million (about 12 percent of the US population) and its buying power, estimated to be between 300 to 400 billion dollars in

Figure 15.2 Latin American countries

2002 (Robles, Simon and Haar, 2003). This buying power reached $798 billion in 2006 and is expected to reach $863 billion in 2007, making it the largest minority market in the United States (Dodson, 2007).

One final aspect of the Latin American definition to be considered in this section is the issue of national identity. SRC's definition of Latin American comprises 19 countries. Although under certain circumstances they can be clustered in a large single market, each of the countries has a well defined cultural identity that must be taken into account when developing marketing strategies. Each nation has different ethnic and cultural subgroups that must also be entered into the list of considerations of a well researched and planned strategy. Furthermore, even in the Latino market in the United States these differences remain significant. Marketers are now segmenting the Latino (Hispanic) population in the United States by nationality, length of stay in the United States, and population size in the target area. This is not to say that there are not instances in which strong, common binding grounds such as language (Spanish) or national sports (soccer, except in Venezuela, Puerto Rico and Dominican Republic) exist, but merely highlights the importance of considering differentiated approaches when planning for the Latin American market as a whole. Regarding this last point, there is also the view within some advertising circles that the global market has homogenized the needs and desires of consumers, making the difference between the regional and national very superficial. The debate between the goods and evils of standardized versus specialized multinational advertising is an old one among marketing specialists (Mueller, 1991).

Trends and Strategies in Latin American Advertising

For this section we will begin by considering the size of the Latin American consumer market. Following this, we will present an overview of the present trends and evolution of the industry in Latin America.

SIZE OF THE LATIN AMERICAN MARKET

Latin America has a population of over 520 million, as compared to the 335 millions combined of Canada and the United States. Approximately 52 million are in the 15–19 year old bracket, more than are found in Canada, the United States and Western Europe combined. Latin America has an economically active population of 270 million, also more than the 179 million in Canada and the United States combined. In addition, the annual population growth in Latin America is around 3.5–4 percent. This, once again, is more than the 2.7 percent in the United States and 2.3 percent in Canada. Although the total buying power of Latin America is less than the United States and Canada, the figures above represent an enormous and dynamic market base from which a wide range of industries and business may accrue the benefits of massive economies of scale.

The performance of the advertising industry is closely linked to the overall state of national economies and the size of the marketplace in which it performs. David Ogilvy once said that advertising budgets would always be a true reflection of the economic performance of markets and national economies.

The past ten years in Latin American economies seem to support Ogilvy's statement. The better the economies perform the larger the advertising budgets. When there are strong economic growth conditions, advertising budgets have periods of great revenues and profits as they bring product information to customers, thus stimulating and facilitating consumption and satisfaction of needs.

Consumer buying power is generally considered a leading indicator of economic growth. All business enterprises, especially multinational corporations, design their marketing strategies based, to a great degree, on their target markets' consumer buying power. As part of the marketing strategy, companies must decide what part of their total marketing budget should be spent in advertising. Most likely, unless other exceptional circumstances exist, the greater the consumer buying power the greater the amount of resources they will assign to carry out their advertising efforts.

The largest buying power of Latin America is concentrated in Brazil, Mexico and Argentina. The three of them comprise 72.2 percent of the total Latin American consumer buying power. Table 15.1 shows Latin America buying power for the year 2000.

The three largest Latin American markets, Brazil, Mexico and Argentina, experienced severe financial crises during the 1990s and early 2000s. Even though their economies are now experiencing moderate growth, there are still many areas of their economies, such as unemployment rates and distribution of wealth, that need to be improved. The rest of the Latin American countries have also gone through periods of economic recession, compression and stagnation. Globalization and its ideological foundation, the neoliberal economic model, has been blamed for many of these crises and for the grave social and economic inequalities that permeate most of the Latin American countries. As a consequence, voters have become disillusioned with the traditional parties for their failure to deliver prosperity. The political arena has been transformed and leftist political movements promising to fulfill the needs of the majority by ending corruption and redistributing wealth have now come to power in many of the Latin America countries (Forero, 2006). However, the economic outlook for Latin America shows great potential for global marketing. Most market analysts predict a healthy economic recovery in the near future.

Foreign direct investment (FDI), the long-term investment of a parent enterprise in a foreign affiliate, is another economic indicator of a nation's potential for economic growth,

Table 15.1   2000 Latin American consumer buying power in billions of dollars

Country	Amount
Brazil	386.5
Mexico	383.1
Argentina	207.0
Venezuela	73.7
Colombia	54.9
Chile	47.2
Peru	41.9
Puerto Rico	24.5
Guatemala	16.4
Uruguay	15.8
Dominican Republic	13.6
El Salvador	11.0
Ecuador	8.8
Paraguay	6.8
Bolivia	6.2
Costa Rica	6.1
Panama	5.7
Honduras	3.9
Nicaragua	2.2
Total	1,315.3

Source: Strategy Research Corporation 2001 market report.

Table 15.2 Main recipients of FDI in Latin America in billions of dollars

	2004	2005
Mexico	18.24	17.80
Brazil	18.14	15.06
Colombia	3.11	10.19
Chile	7.17	7.20
Argentina	4.27	4.66
Venezuela	1.51	2.95
Peru	1.81	2.51
Ecuador	1.16	1.53

Source: Inter-American Development Bank.

rendering it very useful for international and local marketers. The flow of direct investment to Latin America by multinational corporations has declined in comparison with the high volumes of the late 1990s when it surpassed $70 billion. FDI in 2005 was $62 billion. Table 15.2 shows the main recipients of FDI in Latin America in years 2004 and 2005.

TRENDS AND EVOLUTION OF THE ADVERTISING INDUSTRY IN LATIN AMERICA

One of the factors that determines trends and costs of the marketing mix is the value chain process linking the content designers with the end consumers. Typically, this value chain consists of three stages: media development, production and packaging, and distribution. Each of these stages entails different activities requiring human, technical and financial resources. The success or failure of any advertising enterprise will depend, essentially, on how each one of these components are incorporated into their strategic planning.

A definition

There are many definitions of advertising all of which embody a single theme. Advertising is the means by which enterprises inform consumers about their products and services and try to persuade them to use those products or services.

Traditional way

Conventionally, the Latin American advertising industry has been modeled after the United States' and Europe's. The traditional advertising industry consists primarily of advertising agencies that provide clients with both the creative work and media planning and buying. The creative work involves research, copywriting, and the production of art, audio and video. The media planning and buying is the tactical placement of the advertising product in media outlets such as magazines, television, newspapers, radio, Internet or film (product placement), among others. These agencies are designated full-service advertising agencies and have long been predominant in the industry. Traditionally, an advertising agency was required by a client to perform the advertising services and the agency would be paid a percentage, usually 15 percent, of the media billings. Agencies are now using a labor-based compensation, in which they charge the client for hours spent on their accounts plus a profit margin. In addition, advertising agencies, both large and small, are performing the creative tasks and are outsourcing the media buying to specialized companies, known as media shops. These media shops came about because of the proliferation of media outlets, including television networks, cable channels, satellite and most recently the Internet.

Advertising expenditure

Advertising expenditure in Latin America has been increasing steadily for the past decade, with the exception of 1999 in which there was a slight decline caused by the economic recessions suffered by several countries in the region. Figure 15.3 shows the increase from 1995 to 2004. Figure 15.4 shows the ten countries with the most expenditure in advertising.

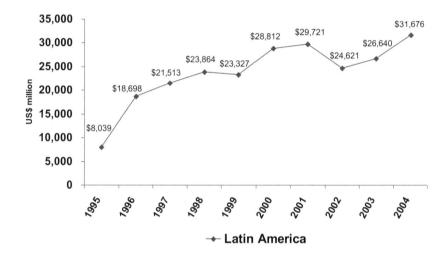

Figure 15.3 Advertising expenditures in Latin America 1995–2004

Source: World Advertising Trends, 2005.

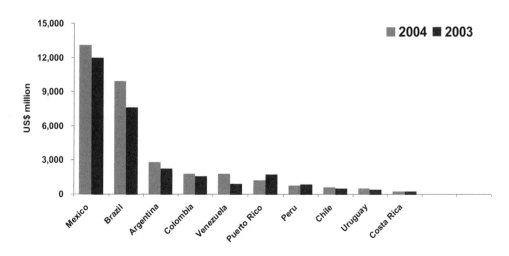

Figure 15.4 Advertising expenditure by country 2003–2004

Source: World Advertising Trends, 2005.

The trends

The basic trends that altered the structure of many industries around the world also affected the advertising industry. Advertising enterprises have been part of the wave of expansion, diversification and internationalization brought about by the open market policies adopted by most nations during the early 1990s. Trends and tendencies in the industry crossed international borders. As clients, aware of the possibilities of global presence through digital technologies, became conscious of the new forms of marketing communications their target audiences were consuming, advertising agencies were forced to adapt to this changing environment. Adaptation to this new environment demanded a modification of the use of traditional media mix (television, radio, printed media, cinema and outdoors) to reflect major changes in media consumption habits, especially in the 18–34 age bracket. There is a consensus among the advertising industry players that the greatest change in consumer habits in the last five years has been the Internet.

Major advertisers throughout the world, including Latin America, have made adjustments to their traditional media mix and have reduced their use in favor of new channels such as Internet, public relations and cellular media, among others. Figure 15.5 shows the reduction in traditional media worldwide in 2006.

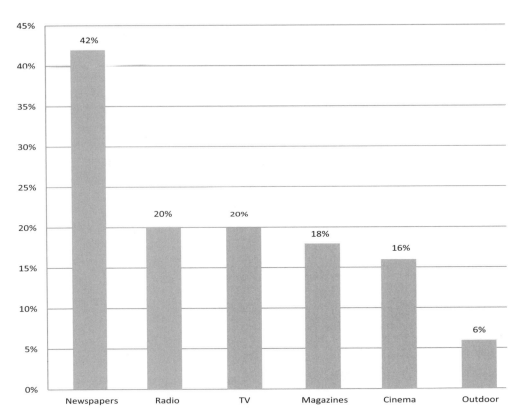

Figure 15.5 Worldwide reduction in traditional mix, 2006

Source: ICOM, 2006.

Despite, however, the global tendency by companies to reduce advertising expenditures in the traditional mix, Latin American companies are still allocating the majority of their ad spending to television, printed media and radio (see Figure 15.6):

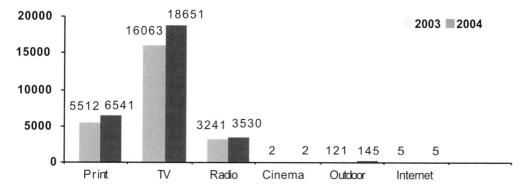

Figure 15.6 Advertising expenditure by medium in Latin America
Source: World Advertising Trends, 2005.

Television is still the leading recipient of most of the advertising expenditure. Data in Figure 15.7, advertising expenditure by medium in the month of September 2006 in Colombia, seems to confirm that the traditional media is still the preferred media mix.

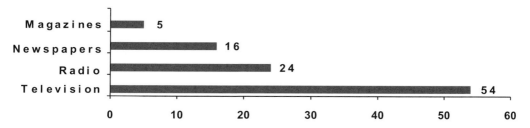

Figure 15.7 Advertising expenditure by medium in Colombia during September 2006
Source: IBOPE Colombia, 2006.

Online advertising in Latin America has increased steadily but it is still a very small portion of the total advertising spending (see Table 15.3).

The Internet penetration in Latin America continues to rise exponentially. Even though the region is still behind most regions of the world in the number of Internet subscribers and users, broadband adoption certainly surpasses any other region in the world (see Figure 15.8).

This surge in broadband adoption greatly expands the potential for advertisers to reach a highly desirable target in Latin America: the younger generations. Video and audio are no longer the sole purview of broadcasters. Streaming and rich interactive media are now pervasive throughout the Internet. The Internet has become a complementary and supplementary tool for advertising campaigns that offers the

Table 15.3   Online advertising spending versus total spending in Latin America in billions of dollars

Year	Total	Online
2001	25.1	0.8
2002	27.6	1.1
2003	30.3	1.5

Source: Merrill Lynch, IDC, WEFA, press reports.

opportunity to maximize the rate of exposure of a target audience. For instance, traditional media now have websites that serve as an added value to their regular features. Television news and other programming are placed on websites to be downloaded on demand. Newspapers upload their daily editions, seeking to reach not only national or international audiences but a very specific and captive audience: the members of diasporic communities. It is simple for an immigrant to enter the website of a newspaper or radio station and get real-time information of events in her native country, and for an airline or tourism agency to target that immigrant using a "buzz" or "viral" marketing technique.

The advent of Internet Protocol Television (IPTV) will certainly open another marketing channel that will create another source of competition to the now popular multi-channel broadcasters. At the end, the technological convergence and the trans-latinization of advertising enterprises will undoubtedly keep advertisers constantly readapting and experimenting in order to find the appropriate mix to reach their audience.

Last of all, below-the-line tactics and channel planning are two methodologies that are being used extensively throughout Latin America and have become important alternatives to the traditional mix. Below-the-line refers to advertising campaigns carried out through means different from the traditional mix, such as sponsorships, events, direct mail, trade shows and word-of-mouth among others. Channel planning is based on the premise that advertisers can optimize the effectiveness of a message if they can match the communication objective with the communication channel. In order to achieve this, the marketer first seeks data about what channels best communicate detailed information to the target audience about the quality, price and other particularities of the product. Then, the marketer uses that data to select the channel or channels (traditional or below-the-line) that could best achieve the objective.

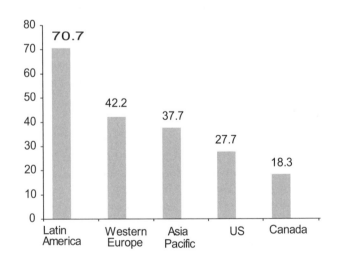

Figure 15.8 Broadband subscriber growth from 2004 to 2005

Source: eMarketer, 2006.

A Colombian Case: Juan Valdez and the Colombian National Federation of Coffee Growers

This section is divided in two parts. The first part provides the reader with a brief description of Colombia. The second part describes a successful campaign of product and brand recognition carried out by the National Federation of Coffee Growers that positioned Colombian Coffee at the top level of global coffee markets.

COLOMBIA

The República de Colombia (Republic of Colombia) is located in the northern tip of South America, bordering the Caribbean Sea between Venezuela and Panama. In addition, it also has borders with the Pacific Ocean, Ecuador, Peru and Brazil (see Figure 15.9).

Colombia has a population of approximately 45 million. It has an area of 1,138,000 square kilometers (almost twice the size of Texas). The labor force composition is as follows: 22.7 percent in agriculture, 18.7 percent in industry and 58.5 percent in services. Coffee is a major agricultural export for Colombia and an essential component in the national income distribution scheme. Most coffee tree crops are grown in small parcels, by over 500,000 families, on rough and steep terrain on the Andean slopes which makes its harvesting a very labor-intensive process.

Figure 15.9 Geographical position of Colombia

JUAN VALDEZ

In September 2005, the Juan Valdez character won the "Advertising Icon of the Year" award of *Advertising Week* organized in New York (see Figure 15.10). This section tells the story about one of the most successful advertising campaigns in Latin America: the Juan Valdez advertising campaign by the Colombian National Federation of Coffee Growers. (The Federation is one of the largest non-profit organizations in the world and is made up of individual coffee farmers—the *cafeteros*). Federation representatives are elected in all provinces (*departamentos*) where coffee is produced, making Juan Valdez an authentic symbol that represents all coffee growers in Colombia.

Café de Colombia

Figure 15.10   The Juan Valdez logo

Source: With kind permission from Federación Nacional de Cafeteros de Colombia.

The campaign and the Juan Valdez character were created in 1959 by the Doyle Dane Bernbach (DDB) of New York advertising agency. DDB merged later with Needham Harper Steers of Chicago to become DDB Needham Worldwide Advertising and BBDO Worldwide, all three under the ownership of Omnicom; currently the campaign is managed by Weber Shandwick worldwide, which belongs to the Interpublic Group.

The original Juan Valdez campaign, geared to promote Colombian Coffee consumption and one of the first ingredient brand campaigns in history, was two-pronged: educational and image campaigns. The Juan Valdez campaign was successful because it gave the product a good image and consumers wanted to be associated with it. It also created the perception of superior quality. Most of all, however, it inspired millions of people to demand and start drinking Colombian coffee. During the more than 45 years since its inception the campaign has gone through different stages, including some of financial constraints and some of refocusing target audiences due to generational accommodations. These accommodations or adjustments saw the setting for Juan Valdez moving from the rich coffee fields of the Colombian mountains through cruise liners and airplanes during the 1980s and then through skiing and fishing scenes, and even at the opera, since the early 1990s.

The campaign focused on illustrations of extreme demand in humorous, sophisticated settings. Planes, trains and automobiles would make 180 degree turns in order to get Colombian coffee. This campaign, which won numerous industry awards including Effies, CLIOs and ADDYs, portrayed Colombian Coffee in a very positive light and built high awareness for the brand as it enhanced its image (Advertising Colombian Coffee: Café de Colombia, 2006).

Initially, Juan Valdez was introduced in television commercials as a typical Colombian coffee grower roaming the coffee fields of the Colombian mountains with "Conchita," his donkey, hand-picking the ripe coffee beans under excellent climactic and soil conditions. This was intended to educate the audience about the growing and harvesting conditions so they could almost "taste" the quality of a coffee coming from such an exceptional environment. This stage took place from the inception to the early 1980s. Starting in the mid 1980s, once the high quality factor had been addressed the campaign moved to show people where to find Colombian Coffee and how to identify it. To accomplish this, the ads turned to portray Juan Valdez and Conchita walking through the aisles in the supermarkets and picking coffee brands with the Juan Valdez logo. The logo, featuring

Valdez, his mule and the coffee mountains in the background, was introduced in 1981 by the Federation of Coffee Growers to serve as a seal to guarantee consumers that the product is truly 100 percent Colombian coffee. The ads were not directed to identify or differentiate a brand, but rather to point to the origin, 100 percent Colombian coffee, of different brands of the product.

The Federation created two logos. One for the United States and Canada that reads "*100%* Colombian Coffee" and another one for the rest of the world that reads "Café de Colombia." In 1995 the Federation decided to globalize the product and phased out the English version because "current advertising programs, including multinational media buys and sports sponsorships with global reach, suggests that a common logo across borders will generate the highest awareness while minimizing consumer confusion" (World Best Logos and Brands, 2007). However, even though the logo is currently used in all advertising and promotional campaigns, the North American marketers are still allowed to use "100% Colombian Coffee" on their packages. The recognition of the logo has reached its maximum level in Spain and the United States, the largest advertising markets for Colombian coffee. In the United States almost 85 percent of people surveyed associated the logo, without any legend underneath, with coffee; and about 50 percent identify it as the Colombian coffee logo. The Juan Valdez campaign is a good example of how an effective marketing strategy can promote the image of a product and affect

Figure 15.11   The new face of Juan Valdez

Source: With kind permission from Federación Nacional de Cafeteros de Colombia.

consumers' attitudes towards other national values and, in many cases, to perceive an advertising icon as a stereotyped image of national identity. Juan Valdez became in the eyes of many a symbol, just like the flag or the national anthem, of Colombian identity. Furthermore, "for a country so closely allied in the global mind with drug traffickers and terrorists, Colombians have been grateful to Valdez for presenting another side to their country" ("Juan Valdez" is hanging up his poncho, 2006).

In April 2006, after more than 40 years as the Colombian Coffee icon, Carlos Sánchez, the fictitious (he never grew a coffee bean in his life), mustache-bearing coffee grower announced his retirement from his role as Juan Valdez. In June of 2006 the Federation introduced its "new" Juan Valdez after a two-year process in which thousands of candidates were auditioned (see Figure 15.11).

The "society debut" of the new Juan Valdez gave the Federation an opportunity to re-launch the campaign, reminding consumers of the positive values of Colombian coffee growers that are associated with the product. In addition, the campaign introduced new product dimensions, which included the Juan Valdez Coffee Shops. Today's campaign is more media oriented and directed to younger consumers that are interested in new coffee mixes. The Juan Valdez campaign is in itself one of the great examples of how a producers' association of a developing country can join forces to create an advertising icon, making it one of the most successful product recognition campaigns in the history of advertising.

Bibliography

Advertising Colombian Coffee: Café de Colombia (2006). [Online.] www.juanvaldez.com/menu/ advertising/index.html (retrieved October 30, 2006).

B2B Marketing Online: Trends and Tactics (2006). [Online.] www.emarketer.com/Reports/All/Em_ b2b_mktg_nov06.aspx (retrieved November 9, 2006).

Belcher, J. (2006). Is old-media influence really declining? *eMarketer*. [Online.] www.emarketer.com/ articles/print.asxp?1004229&src=print_print_article_graybar_article (retrieved November 29, 2006).

Bogart, L. (1959). Changing markets and media in Latin America. *The Public Opinion Quarterly*, 23(2): 159–67.

Cross-media advertising in Latin America (2005). [Online.] www.zonalatina.com/Zldata93.htm (retrieved October 17, 2006).

Demers, D.P. (1994). Relative constancy hypothesis, structural pluralism, and national advertising expenditures. *Journal of Media Economics*, 7(4): 31–48.

Dodson, D. (2007). Minority groups' share of $10 trillion US consumer market is growing steadily, according to annual buying power study from Terry College's Selig Center for Economic Growth. [Online.] http://www.terry.uga.edu/news/releases/2007/minority_buying_power_report.html (retrieved March 29, 2011).

Forero, J. (2006, April 20). Latin America's populist shift. *New York Times*.

Horsky, S. (2006). The changing architecture of advertising agencies. *Business and Management Practices*, 25(4): 367–83.

IBOPE Colombia (2006). Inversión publicitaria para cada medio. Septiembre 2006. Instituto Brasilero de Opinion Publica y Estadistica.

"Juan Valdez" is hanging up his poncho (2006, May, 31). *USA Today*.

Latin America Focus: growth years ahead for emerging Latin American markets (2002). *FIPP Magazine World*.

Mueller, B. (1991). An analysis of information content in standardize vs. specialized multinational advertisements. *Journal of International Business Studies*, 22(1): 23–39.

Robles, F., F. Simon and J. Haar (2003). *Winning Strategies for the New Latin Markets*. New York: Financial Times, Prentice Hall Books.

Silk, M. (2001). Beyond a boundary? Sport, transnational advertising and the reimaging of national culture. *Journal of Sports and Social Issues*, 25(2): 180–201.

Suarez, J.I. (1995). Advertising in Latin America. *Studies in Latin America Popular Culture*, 14: 245–52.

World Advertising Research Center (2002). *World Advertising Trends 2005*. Henley-on-Thames: World Advertising Research Center.

World Best Logos and Brands (2007, December 7). Café de Colombia Logo. [Online.] http://worldsbestlogos.blogspot.com/2007/12/caf-de-colombia-logo.html (retrieved March 29, 2011).

PART V

Cross-Cultural Exploration: North America and Others

16 *Gender Role and Social Power in African and North American Advertisements*

BRUCE A. HUHMANN AND JENNIFER J. ARGO

Introduction

In developing advertisements, advertisers must be cognizant of cultural conventions. Among the most basic cultural conventions are the roles that are considered suitable for each gender (Maynard and Taylor, 1999; Wiles, Wiles and Tjernlund, 1995). Many studies have been conducted in North America that investigated gender roles (i.e., the occupations, settings and product categories associated with each gender) in both television commercials and magazine advertisements (e.g., Bretl and Cantor, 1988; Courtney and Lockeretz, 1971; Courtney and Whipple, 1983; Dilevko and Harris, 1997; McArthur and Resko, 1975). In addition, there have been a number of cross-cultural studies that looked at gender roles in advertising, but the entire continent of Africa has been overlooked with one exception (Mwangi, 1996). The need to understand the depiction of the genders in African advertising is great as the emerging economies of Africa continue to grow in importance to world trade.

While it is important to understand cross-cultural differences in gender roles, it is also necessary to understand the social power afforded to each gender to gain a fuller appreciation for the treatment of each gender within a society. While studies in North America have shown increasingly less stereotypical portrayals of women in terms of their gender roles, women are still portrayed as possessing less social power than men (Bretl and Cantor, 1988; Courtney and Whipple, 1983; Klassen, Jasper and Schwartz, 1993). While there have been changes, equality is not represented in the more subtle visual cues of social power as often as it is with the more obvious gender role variables. For example, 75 percent of women in advertisements from three US magazines from 1984 to 1989 were depicted as having less social power than males, compared to 87 percent from 1972 to 1977 (Klassen, Jasper and Schwartz, 1993). In general, the gender roles and social power that advertisers depict is a reflection of what they believe the target market desires or will accept.

The general lack of research on advertising in the emerging economies of Africa has important consequences. As Africa's standing in the world economy grows, it is becoming increasingly more important to understand its cultural conventions and current advertising practices. Western nations, such as the United States, are beginning to recognize the potential for international trade with African nations (Katzenellenbogen, 2004). For example, exports from the United States to Africa are rising by 8 percent a year and the overall value of goods shipped to Africa totals 45 percent more than US exports to all the former Soviet Bloc countries (USA ready to launch, 1999). In addition, Africa has growing upper and middle classes that are, unlike in the colonial past, becoming more ethnically diverse (Belk, 2000; Dreyer, 1989; Rowlands, 1994). These emerging upper and middle classes rely on advertisements to assist them in their purchase decisions and are an important consumer market. Finally, many multinational corporations are currently selling, or are considering selling, their products in Africa making it an increasingly important market to understand. Therefore, determining the content of African ads is needed to facilitate marketers' communication with this growing consumer market. To begin this investigation, this study focuses on the depiction of gender, which if done incorrectly can lead consumers to reject an ad before they even process its message (Kilbourne, 1986; Whipple and Courtney, 1985).

The purpose of the current study is to compare advertisements from Africa against advertisements from North America on this important aspect of advertising—gender roles and social power. The comparison of gender roles and social power in advertising is needed to know whether gender depictions in African ads mirror those in North American ads, which would allow multinational corporations to standardize that portion of their advertising in these markets.

To control for colonial background differences, only ads from former English and French colonies in Africa and North America were considered. Advertisements were selected from six emerging African economies. Five of these countries had British colonial backgrounds—Egypt, Kenya, Nigeria, South Africa and Uganda. One African nation had a French colonial background—Morocco. For comparison purposes, advertisements were also selected from the North American nations of the United States of America and Canada, with both French and English colonial backgrounds. These countries were also selected because they are all actively involved in, or moving toward increasing, global business.

Gender Roles in North America

Previous research in Canada and the United States found that males and females are depicted in stereotypical roles in advertising. Many studies found that females are under-represented in advertisements and, when they are depicted, they are often portrayed as a homemaker and/or a parent, in home settings, and as promoters of feminine products including household products, clothing and food. Males, in contrast, are over-represented, often found in business and outdoor settings, in professional occupations, and promoting masculine products and big-ticket items such as cars, tools and financial services (see Courtney and Whipple, 1983 for a review). In addition, males are more likely to promote technology-based products than are females (Dilevko and Harris, 1997). More recent studies suggested that, while gender role stereotyping continues to be prevalent, the inequality may be becoming less severe (Bretl and Cantor, 1988).

Gender Roles in Africa

Unlike research conducted using North American advertisements, gender role portrayals in African advertising are not well documented. Mwangi (1996) was the only study found to specifically examine gender role portrayals in African advertisements. In her content analysis of Kenyan television commercials, Mwangi analyzed the representation of males and females as a central character or providing a voiceover, as well as the products, settings and occupation associated with each gender. Using commercials from two Kenyan networks, her results mirrored much of the research conducted with North American advertisements. Specifically, females were more often depicted in home settings and in commercials for household, personal and baby products. Males were portrayed more often in workplace and outdoor settings, as well as in commercials for automobiles, hardware, alcohol and financial services. Further, the distribution of the occupations was consistent with findings in North American research. Males were represented in all occupations studied except domestic, office/secretarial and teaching, whereas females were present in only four of 13 occupations (domestic, teaching, office/secretarial and sports). Most females were depicted in the domestic category. One result found in later (e.g., Bretl and Cantor, 1988), but not earlier (e.g., Courtney and Lockeretz, 1971; McArthur and Resko, 1975) North American research was that Kenyan commercials depicted females as often as males as the central character. Thus, certain gender role stereotypes may not be unique to North American ads; they may appear in African ads as well. Therefore, we hypothesize that:

H1: Traditional gender role stereotypes exist in both North American and African advertisements.

Social Power in North America

Another variable that is used in the study of gender depictions is social power. Social power focuses less on one's job as defining an individual and more on verbal and nonverbal (e.g., body language) communication between an individual and other characters in the ad or the reader as indicative of the status and respect afforded to that individual. One taxonomy, which includes some aspects of social power, based on a sample of North American print ads was developed by Goffman (1979). He believed that one could better understand inequality in a society by examining the images produced by that society, such as in commercials and advertisements. He suggested that one's body position, size, gestures, facial expression and behaviors were indicative of one's social status. According to Goffman (1979), social status is displayed by having height superiority (e.g., standing over a seated person, being physically taller, etc.), leading or instructing others, being in superior positions (e.g., standing, walking upright, etc.), displaying dominance, actively engaging other people in the ad or the reader through eye contact with the camera, and engaging in a utilitarian contact with the product. A lack of social status is portrayed by being physically lower, receiving help from others, being in inferior body positions (e.g., being prone, prostrate, sitting or lying down), displaying deference, withdrawing from social situations, and engaging in self-touch or gentle touch (e.g., cradling or caressing an object). For example, Goffman (1979) showed that males were regularly portrayed as larger, higher or taller than females, who were often portrayed as physically prostrating themselves by lying down or sitting on the floor or furniture. Further, females were portrayed with their eyes downcast or their faces hidden behind an object, which indicates lower status, whereas males looked directly into the camera as if confronting the reader of an ad eye-to-eye, which implies a higher status. Goffman believed that the depiction of each gender in regard to height superiority, function ranking, body position, deference or dominance, licensed withdrawal and contact represented societal inferiority on the part of females and societal superiority on the part of males. Several researchers found consistent results using Goffman's taxonomy (e.g., Belknap and Leonard, 1991; Browne, 1998; Klassen et al., 1993).

In addition to nonverbal communication variables included in Goffman's taxonomy, an analysis of the verbal communication associated with each gender serves to measure social power. Previous research has examined the type of arguments attributed to each gender in ads as indicative of social power (e.g., Brentl and Cantor, 1988; McArthur and Resko, 1975). Higher social power is associated with the ability to provide factual or scientific information, whereas lower social power is associated with the ability to provide only personal opinions as the type of persuasive argument. In North America, the ability to provide useful information has traditionally been associated with males in advertisements. For example, while Bretl and Cantor (1988) found that each gender appeared about as often as central characters, 90 percent of all TV commercial narrators were male.

Social Power in Africa

The previous discussion of social power focuses specifically on research conducted using primarily North American ads. No previous research examined the social power of each gender in African media. However, it is expected that females will be depicted with superior social power in more advertisements from Africa than from North America for three reasons. First, there still exist remnants of the pre-colonial matriarchal culture among some of the African tribes (Amadiume, 1997). Even in non-matriarchal cultures, pre-colonial African women held substantial rights, which Western cultures traditionally did not afford women. Pre-colonial African women, while considered subordinate to their husbands, had important familial rights as sisters and daughters (Ufomata, 2000). These pre-colonial woman also possessed political power and resisted relinquishing it, which was demonstrated in Nigeria in 1929 when the women of the Igbo tribes had enough political power to fight the appointment of new chiefs by the British (Howard, 1984). Even in post-colonial Africa, women continue to play major roles in various political struggles and civil wars, such as the one that brought Yoweri Mauseveni to power in Uganda in 1985 (Byanyima, 1992).

In many modern African societies, women's associations play an important role and there is better representation of women in African than in North American democracies. For example, 27 percent of the representatives to South Africa's National Assembly and 18 percent of the representatives to Uganda's National Assembly are female (Goetz, 1998). In comparison, 2001 saw an all-time high in the proportion of women in the US Congress with women comprising 13 percent of senators and 14 percent of representatives. Also, some African nations have governmental bodies charged with ensuring women's rights, such as South Africa's Commission on Gender Equality (Tripp, 2003).

Women have substantial economic rights in some African societies. For example, the majority of traders in the marketplaces in African urban areas are women (Afonja and Aina, 1995). Among the Yoruba people of Nigeria, women maintain independent economic activity throughout their lives. Their economic activity is so prevalent that women dominate the markets of southwestern Nigeria (Falola, 1995). African women tend either to have formal work outside the home or to be involved in agriculture, trading at the marketplaces or the production of crafts (Ufomata, 2000).

Finally, women play an important role in traditional African religious activities and ceremonies. For example, traditional African religion regards the mother or wife as the most important member of the family and reveres her as the center of familyhood (Mbiti, 1988). Spirit mediums, who contact the world of spirits to interpret dreams, provide guidance, and function as traditional healers, are primarily women. Traditional African religious practices, including the use of spirit mediums, are common even among educated Christian and Muslim Africans (Moreover: the spirits, 2000). Because of the traditional and continuing political and religious status of women in many African societies, we hypothesize that:

H2: Females will be depicted as possessing superior social power in more advertisements from Africa than from North America.

Method

A content analysis of print advertisements from former English or French colonies in Africa (Egypt, Kenya, Morocco, Nigeria, South Africa and Uganda) and North America (Canada and the United States) was conducted. From each country, an issue of a popular consumer magazine representing each of the four following types—general interest, women's, news and business—was randomly selected (Egypt: *Horreyati, Kalam An-Nas, Al Mussawar, Al Ahram Iktisadi*; Kenya: *The Post on Sunday, Parents, East African Alternatives, The Weekly Review*; Morocco: *Parade, Citaine, Le Temps du Maroc, Maroc Expansion*; Nigeria: *Nigerian Link, Cosmos, Crystal, Ecowas International*; South Africa: *You, Femina, Huis Genoot, Business in Africa*; Uganda: *Guardian Magazine, Relate, The Link, Success*; Canada: *Reader's Digest (Canada), Châtelaine, Maclean's, Canadian Business*; United States: *Reader's Digest (US), Ladies Home Journal, Newsweek, Business Week*). Because ads reflect target market values, selecting ads from these four types of magazines provided a wide range of target markets. In total, 32 different magazines from 1999 were examined resulting in a total of 961 advertisements.

This study examines magazines because print advertisements account for 44.8 percent of advertising spending in Africa (Africa and the Middle East, 1998) and 40 percent of advertising spending in North America (Magazine Publishers of America, 2003; *TV Basics*, 2004). Thus, print advertising is one of the main vehicles for marketing communication in both African and North American societies. It is important to examine the content of these advertisements in order to analyze the messages that are being communicated to and are reflective of that society.

The sample included all advertisements that were a quarter of a page or larger, regardless of whether or not the advertisement contained a human depiction. To avoid ads with crowd scenes or large groups from mitigating the pattern of results, no more than four of the largest figures were randomly selected for coding from any one advertisement. All human depictions were considered in the analysis, regardless of whether they were photographed or drawn.

This study examined four variables associated with differences in gender roles: 1) the gender of the central character(s), 2) the setting in which the character(s) appear, 3) the occupation of the character(s), and 4) the product category advertised. Settings included home, work, outdoor and other. Occupations included professional occupations (e.g., white-collar business person, teacher, reporter, lawyer, doctor, dentist), nonprofessional occupations (e.g., stewardess, blue-collar worker, secretary, clerical aide, cook, maid, servant), homemaker/parent and other. Following previous gender role research (Courtney and Lockeretz, 1971; Dilevko and Harris, 1997; Wiles et al., 1995), product categories were collapsed into gender-neutral and gender-typed products, either masculine or feminine, as well as technology-based and non-technology-based products. The gender-neutral products were related to pet food and supplies, entertainment, retail stores and restaurants, healthcare equipment and services, alcohol, tobacco, mail-order and direct marketing, travel destinations and services, and advertisements for governments, non-profits or trade associations. Of the gender-typed products, the masculine products were those related to automobiles and automobile accessories, tools and home repair, industrial and business equipment, financial services and distribution services. The feminine products were those related to food, cleaning, clothing and accessories, jewelry, home furnishings and appliances, personal grooming and cosmetics. Technology-based products involved healthcare equipment and services, distribution services, automobiles and automobile accessories, tools, industrial and business equipment, and financial services. Non-technology-based products included home furnishings, jewelry, clothing, food, alcoholic and nonalcoholic beverages, tobacco, personal grooming, cosmetics, retail stores and restaurants, pet food and supplies, and cleaning products.

Table 16.1 describes the variables that were used to study social power. Social power included variables based on the work of Goffman (1979): 1) height superiority or inferiority, 2) function ranking, 3) deference or dominance behaviors, 4) body position, 5) licensed withdrawal, and 6) the type of contact the character(s) made with the product, as well as one variable based on the work of Brentl and Cantor (1988) and McArthur and Resko (1975): the argument type associated with the character(s). All social power variable coding included the option of not applicable. Height superiority and inferiority were measured only in ads that included more than one person.

Two pretests were conducted prior to data collection. One of the authors conducted the first pretest by content analyzing a selection of advertisements in order to refine the coding instrument before it was given to the coders. Two coders conducted the second pretest after they were instructed and trained by the authors. Training for the more subtle social power variables required that the coders familiarize themselves with Goffman (1979). During this pretest, the coders practiced on a small set of advertisements from both African and North American magazines not included in the final sample. Once the coders clearly understood the coding categories and instructions, they each coded all of the advertisements included in the sample, working independently of each other and the authors.

To reduce bias in the final results, coders were selected to represent both continents and both genders. One coder was a male from an African country (Morocco) and the other was a female from a North American country (Canada). Both coders were fluent in

Table 16.1 Social power variable descriptions

Variable	Categories
Height	1. Inferiority—another person is taller or positioned above this person. 2. Superiority—this person is taller or positioned above all others. 3. Equal height or positioned to be eye-to-eye with others in ad.
Function ranking	1. Person is leading, giving orders or instructions, and/or pointing something out to others. 2. Person is receiving instructions/help and/or is being shown how to do something, hand fed, pushed or guided.
Deference/ Dominance	1. Shows deference through subordination behaviors (e.g., head, knee or body cant, child-like postures, displays of appeasement or mock fear, bowing). 2. Shows dominance—control or authority (e.g., holding, carrying, supporting or restraining someone, chasing someone, throwing something or someone, putting arm across another person's shoulders, trying to occupy extra space).
Body position	1. Superior (e.g., standing upright, arm extended around another). 2. Inferior (e.g., sitting, laying down, etc.).
Licensed withdrawal	1. Withdrawn—he/she is psychologically removed from the social situation, not oriented to situation, or in need of protection (e.g., looks shy, giggles nervously, covers part of face with hands, fidgeting, finger(s) in mouth, averts head or eyes, hides or peeks out from behind an object, looks into space with an unfocused gaze, snuggles or nuzzles person/object). 2. Engaged—he/she confronts or engages others in the ad or the reader.
Contact	1. Utilitarian—manipulating or grasping objects, causing object to work or operate. 2. Gentle—caress, cradle, stroke or gently touch an object with hands/face. 3. Self-touch—hands touch face/neck/body (not just dangling at sides or resting on lap).
Argument type	1. Factual—includes statements containing facts about the product or findings of research and/or statistics. 2. Opinion—refers to the personal feelings of the person in the ad and statements regarding the effects of the product according to the person giving the argument.

French and English—the two principal languages of the sample of ads; however, the text of the ads from the Egyptian magazines were translated from Arabic and the ads from one of the South African magazines (i.e., *Huis Genoot*) were translated from Afrikaans by native speakers of those languages living in North America. Inter-coder reliability was calculated using Rust and Cooil's (1994) proportional reduction in loss technique, which corrects for chance coding agreements. Reliability ranged from 0.82 for deference/dominance behaviors to 0.94 for character gender. The average agreement across judges was 0.89. Coders discussed and resolved disagreements.

Results

Analysis of the gender role portrayals in African and North American magazine advertisements revealed a number of similarities and a few differences that exist between the two continents (see Table 16.2). Partial support was found for Hypothesis 1. Consistent with the hypothesis, in advertisements from both continents, males were portrayed more often than females in work settings, in professional occupations and with masculine products. The association of males rather than females with technology-based products approached, but did not attain significance for both African and North American ads.

Some additional support for Hypothesis 1 was found in regard to female role portrayals. Ads from both continents portrayed females more often than males in nonprofessional occupations, with feminine products, and with non-technology-based products.

As indicated previously, role stereotypes for gender-typed products were upheld in ads from both continents as males were associated with traditionally masculine products and females were associated with traditionally feminine products. Further, in ads from both Africa and North America, males and females were equally likely to be shown in advertisements for gender-neutral products.

Contrary to Hypothesis 1, there was no difference in the number of male and female portrayals in North American ads, but, as expected, males were more likely to appear than females in African ads. Neither African nor North American ads showed any significant difference between male and female portrayals in outdoor settings or at home. Not surprisingly, the lack of stereotypical depictions in home settings was concomitant with no gender difference in the number of portrayals as homemakers or parents in African or North American ads.

Support was found for Hypothesis 2, which stated that females would possess superior social power in more ads from Africa than from North America (see Table 16.3). Of the social power variables in which a difference was observed between genders, all four variables with differences in North American ads reflected traditional male social power superiority; however, five variables with differences in the African ads reflected female social power superiority, whereas four reflected male superiority. Interestingly, the same four variables reflected male superiority/female inferiority in social power as shown in ads from both continents: 1) males were more likely to be shown engaging in utilitarian contact, whereas 2) females engaged in more deference behaviors, 3) more gentle contact, and 4) more self-touch.

In five variables, gender equality was observed in North American ads, but female superiority/male inferiority in social power was observed in African ads. These five variables depicted a greater propensity for males to be depicted with 1) height inferiority, 2) inferior body positions, and 3) withdrawn from social contact, whereas females in African ads were more likely than males to be shown, 4) engaged in social contact, and 5) providing more factual arguments for the brand.

Gender equality was observed in ads from both continents for the six remaining social power variables. Males and females were equally likely to 1) have height superiority, 2) lead others, 3) receive their help, 4) display dominance behaviors, 5) have superior body positions, and 6) use opinion arguments in persuading the reader.

Table 16.2 Gender role findings for North American and African ads

	North America			Africa		
	Male % (N)	Female % (N)	Chi² value	Male % (N)	Female % (N)	Chi² value
Number of portrayals	48.7% (240)	51.3% (253)	0.171	59.1% (482)	40.9% (333)	5.930*
Setting						
Work	83.3% (10)	16.7% (2)	5.333*	90.9% (10)	9.1% (1)	7.363*
Home	52.4% (11)	47.6% (10)	0.048	20.0% (1)	80.0% (4)	1.800
Outdoor	55.4% (36)	44.6% (29)	0.754	54.3% (25)	45.7% (21)	0.348
Occupation						
Professional	76.2% (48)	23.8% (15)	17.286*	85.7% (42)	14.3% (7)	25.000*
Nonprofessional	12.2% (6)	87.8% (43)	27.939*	31.4% (16)	68.6% (35)	7.078*
Parent/homemaker	36.8% (7)	63.2% (12)	1.316	35.7% (5)	64.3% (9)	1.143
Products						
Masculine	74.6% (53)	25.4% (18)	17.254*	68.9% (31)	31.1% (14)	6.422*
Feminine	23.9% (16)	76.1% (51)	18.284*	17.6% (13)	82.4% (61)	31.135*
Gender-neutral	42.7% (32)	57.3% (43)	1.613	46.0% (29)	54.0% (34)	0.397
Technology-based	57.7% (64)	42.3% (47)	2.604**	60.3% (38)	39.7% (25)	2.683**
Nontechnology-based	25.4% (18)	74.7% (53)	17.254*	21.2% (18)	78.8% (67)	28.247*

Notes: * p ≤ 0.05, ** p < 0.10.

Table 16.3 Social power findings for each gender in North American and African ads

	North America			Africa		
	Male % (N)	Female % (N)	Chi² value	Male % (N)	Female % (N)	Chi² value
Height						
Superiority	56.8% (50)	43.2% (38)	1.636	56.5% (52)	43.5% (40)	1.565
Inferiority	43.7% (66)	56.3% (85)	2.391	57.4% (112)	42.6% (83)	4.313*
Function ranking						
Leading others	58.3% (14)	41.7% (10)	0.667	66.7% (8)	33.3% (4)	1.333
Receiving help	52.2% (12)	47.8% (11)	0.043	28.6% (2)	71.4% (5)	1.286
Behavior						
Dominance	44.7% (17)	55.3% (21)	0.421	57.9% (11)	42.1% (8)	0.474
Deference	31.7% (53)	68.3% (114)	22.281*	38.8% (66)	61.2% (104)	8.419*
Body position						
Superior	51.6% (99)	48.4% (93)	0.188	50.8% (97)	49.2% (94)	0.047
Inferior	50.0% (51)	50.0% (51)	0.000	61.3% (49)	38.7% (31)	4.050*
Licensed withdrawal						
Engaged with reader/others	46.1% (47)	53.9% (55)	0.627	39.3% (55)	60.7% (85)	6.429*
Withdrawn	52.1% (134)	47.9% (123)	0.471	55.9% (143)	44.1% (113)	3.515**
Contact						
Utilitarian	60.3% (82)	39.7% (54)	5.765*	62.5% (80)	37.5% (48)	8.000*
Gentle	37.3% (19)	62.7% (32)	3.314**	25.8% (8)	74.2% (23)	7.2881*
Self-touch	32.1% (18)	67.9% (38)	7.143*	33.9% (21)	66.1% (41)	6.452*
Arguments						
Factual	46.2% (66)	53.8% (77)	0.846	39.8% (49)	60.2% (74)	5.0813*
Opinion	35.3% (6)	64.7% (11)	1.471	28.6% (2)	71.4% (5)	1.2857

Notes: * p ≤ 0.05, ** p < 0.10.

Discussion

The current study analyzed the gender roles and social power in ads from African and North American magazines. In terms of gender roles, males are portrayed more often than females in ads from African but not North American magazines. Also, the results demonstrate that traditional gender role stereotypes persist in seven out of 11 setting, occupation and product variables measured for ads from both continents. More males are shown in work settings, professional occupations and ads for traditionally masculine and technology-based products. In contrast, more females are shown in nonprofessional occupations and in advertisements for traditionally feminine and non-technology-based products. The basic similarity in gender role portrayals between African and North American ads is logical given the influence of English and French culture on the economies of all these nations as well as the emulation of Western employment and consumption patterns. In Africa, the emulation of Western consumption patterns is particularly strong among the growing middle and upper classes who are the likely target audience of the African magazines analyzed. Moreover, working-class Africans frequently watch Western television programs or films and seek to model some aspects of the observed behavior and consumption patterns (Belk, 2000; Monga, 2000).

Advertisers mirror the cultures' values to enhance the acceptance of their ad messages. Despite a call for equal rights for women from some in North America, North American advertisers showed gender parity on less than half of the gender role variables measured. While this represents a move toward greater gender role parity since the 1970s (e.g., Courtney and Lockeretz, 1971; McArthur and Resko, 1975), it is obvious that males are still depicted in settings and occupations and with products that North American society considers more prestigious, technologically complex, or substantial. Gender role stereotypes as portrayed in North American ads are very similar to those in ads from the emerging economies of Africa, which is promising for marketers wishing to standardize messages across the two continents.

In regard to social power, females are depicted as possessing superior social power in more ads from Africa than from North America. In North American ads, gender parity was observed in 11 comparisons and male superiority was observed in four comparisons. In African ads, gender parity was observed in six comparisons, female superiority in five comparisons, and male superiority in four comparisons. Superior social power for females in more African than North American ads was found even though fewer females than males appeared in the African ads, whereas almost equal numbers of males and females appeared in the North American ads. While females in African ads do not necessarily display more social power than males, they are depicted with more social power than females in North American ads. The differences in social power between the two continents that this study uncovered are consistent with the unique roles of African females in traditional African religion and society, as well as modern politics.

Specifically, African ads depicted more males than females with height inferiority and inferior body positions. For example, a Postbank wire money transfer ad (Kenya) shows a taller female with cash standing next to a shorter male. Also, in a Compu-Slim computer ad from South Africa, a female medic stands above her reclining patient. African ads also depicted males as more withdrawn from social interactions than females. For example, a Daewoo Motor Egypt ad shows a professional man in an office looking down at his desk rather than at the camera or another person. In contrast, another Egyptian ad for Banha electronics stores shows a woman making direct eye contact with the camera. Females in African ads were more engaged in social interactions than males. For example, a CelTel Cellular ad (Uganda) shows two women talking at a restaurant. Finally, more factual arguments are relayed by females than by males in African ads. For example, a Nivea moisturizer ad (Morocco) shows one woman explaining the product benefits to another. A woman also explains college degrees available from Damelin in an ad from South Africa. Considering these results in tandem with results for the gender role variables, it appears that Shields' (1990) observation that "men act," whereas "women appear" seems to hold true across both continents. Even the areas in which African women exhibit more social power were primarily related to their self-presentation, or appearance (e.g., height, body position and social contact with the reader or others in the ad), not to their actions in the professional occupations, using technology or even operating or using the advertised product through utilitarian contact.

Contribution

The current study contributes to the understanding of gender roles and social power in a continent that advertising researchers have previously neglected. To date, only one study, Mwangi's (1996) study of Kenyan television commercials, had examined gender role portrayals in African advertising. This study replicates many of Mwangi's findings of traditional gender role stereotypes in product categories, settings and occupations in print ads from six African countries with English and French colonial backgrounds. These results are compared with gender roles from two North American countries that also had English and French colonial backgrounds. The current study expands the understanding of similarities in gender role portrayals between Africa and North America and uncovers the superior social power of women in African ads in comparison to women in North American ads.

The current study should assist multinational corporations in developing advertisements that will fit the gender roles and social power acceptable in Africa. Research has demonstrated that gender role portrayals that violate or transgress a culture's preferences can negatively influence attitudes toward the ad, whereas more positive ad attitudes are generated when gender role portrayals are in line with cultural preferences (Kilbourne, 1986; Whipple and Courtney, 1985). The good news for practitioners is that similarity exists between African and North American ads in their portrayal of gender roles. This should facilitate standardization of advertisements or ad campaign themes between the two continents. However, practitioners should be aware of the superior female social power in African ads contrary to traditional Western gender stereotypes.

The results demonstrate the importance of examining the behaviors indicative of social power, in addition to the variables typically included in gender role research, such as the occupations, settings and products associated with each gender. The results appear to indicate that, while ads from both Africa and North America favor portrayals of men in professional occupations, the work place, or ads for traditionally male and technology-related products, women in Africa are shown as possessing a certain degree of social power in comparison to men. In comparison, North American ads show gender equality or male superiority in social power variables. Inclusion of variables measuring social power provides a much fuller understanding of gender differences in a culture.

In some societies, women may perform traditional tasks, yet be afforded greater respect or social status. A study that did not include variables to measure social power would not have uncovered this interesting difference in advertising's depiction of gender between the two continents.

Limitations and Future Research

There are several limitations to this research that provide possible avenues for future research. First, advertisements from only one media were examined. Future research should investigate gender roles and social power in African broadcast and Internet advertising.

Second, although this study controlled for cultural variations to a degree by only selecting ads from countries with English and French colonial backgrounds, the examination of gender roles was at the continental level. Comparing the two continents illuminated the remarkable differences and similarities in gender depictions at this level of analysis. However, both Africa and North America are comprised of many subcultures, some of which would likely find the continent-level gender roles and social power uncovered by this study too conservative or too liberal. While the current study strived to give an overview of the comparisons between gender roles and social power in African and North American ads, future research could investigate specific countries, regions or subcultures to compare the gender roles or social power at those levels of analyses with the results of the current study.

Third, the data provide a snapshot of current advertising depictions of gender roles and social power. Comparison with previous research on gender roles in North America indicates that changes have occurred since the 1970s, as gender role portrayals in advertisements appear to be slowly moving toward more equality. Change likely has and will continue to occur in gender role portrayals in African media, as well as in the depictions of social power for each gender within both continents. Thus, this is not a definitive study of this topic, but rather a beginning. Hopefully, future research will determine what, if any, changes have taken place to help understand the trend in advertising depictions of gender roles and social power in Africa.

Conclusion

This study compared advertising depictions of gender roles and social power between African and North American magazines. The findings indicate that a basic similarity in gender roles exists between countries with English and French colonial backgrounds on the two continents; however, the ads in Africa, unlike those in North America, are more likely to show women as possessing superior social power. In North American advertising, women are presented as inferior to men in the spheres of work, technology and social situations. While African women are not presented as the equals to men in the spheres of work or technology, they have more power in the social sphere. This underscores an important difference in advertising's depiction of gender between Africa and North America.

References

Afonja, S. and O. Aina (1995). *Nigerian Women in Social Change*. Ile-Ife: University of Ife Press.

Africa and the Middle East: focus on the smaller adspend regions (1998). *International Journal of Advertising*, 17: 515–20.

Amadiume, I. (1997). *Reinventing Africa: Matriarchy, Religion, Culture*. London: Zed Books.

Belk, R. (2000, October). Consumption lifestyles of the new elite in Zimbabwe. Paper presented at the annual conference for the Association for Consumer Research, Salt Lake City, UT.

Belknap, P. and W.M. Leonard II (1991). A conceptual replication and extension of Erving Goffman's study of gender advertisements. *Sex Roles*, 25: 103–18.

Bretl, D.J. and J. Cantor (1988). The portrayal of men and women in US television commercials: a recent content analysis and trends over 15 years. *Sex Roles*, 18: 595–609.

Browne, B.A. (1998). Gender stereotypes in advertising on children's television in the 1990s: a cross-national analysis. *Journal of Advertising*, 27: 81–96.

Byanyima, K.W. (1992). Women in political struggle in Uganda. In J.M. Bystydzienski (ed.), *Women Transforming Politics: Worldwide Strategies for Empowerment* (pp. 129–42). Bloomington, IN: Indiana University Press.

Courtney, A.E. and S.W. Lockeretz (1971). A woman's place: an analysis of the roles portrayed by women in magazine advertisements. *Journal of Marketing Research*, 8: 92–5.

Courtney, A.E. and T.W. Whipple (1983). *Sex Stereotyping in Advertising*. Lexington, MA: Lexington Books.

Dilevko, J. and R.M. Harris (1997). Information technology and social relations: portrayals of gender roles in high tech product advertisements. *Journal of the American Society for Information Science*, 48: 718–27.

Dreyer, L. (1989). *The Modern African Elite of South Africa*. New York: St. Martin's Press.

Falola, T. (1995). Gender, business, and space control: Yoruba market women and power. In B. House-Midamba and F.K. Ekechi (eds), *African Market Women and Economic Power: The Role of Women in African Economic Development* (pp. 23–40). London: Greenwood Press.

Goetz, A.M. (1998). Women in politics and gender equity in policy: South Africa and Uganda. *Review of African Political Economy*, 25: 241–62.

Goffman, E. (1979). *Gender Advertisements*. Cambridge, MA: Harvard University Press.

Howard, R. (1984). Women's rights in English-speaking Sub-Saharan Africa. In C.E. Welch, Jr. and R.I. Meltzer (eds), *Human Rights and Development in Africa* (pp. 46–74). Albany, NY: State University of New York Press.

Katzenellenbogen, J. (2004, November). Africa in for more US attention. *Business Day*, 11.

Kilbourne, W.E. (1986). An exploratory study of the effect of sex role stereotyping on attitudes toward magazine advertisements. *Journal of the Academy of Marketing Science*, 14: 43–6.

Klassen, M.L., C.R. Jasper and A.M. Schwartz (1993). Men and women: images of their relationships in magazine advertisements. *Journal of Advertising Research*, 33: 30–39.

Magazine Publishers of America (2003). *The Magazine Handbook: A Comprehensive Guide for Advertisers, Advertising Agencies, and Consumer Magazine Marketers 2003/4*. New York: Magazine Publishers of America.

Maynard, M.L. and C.R. Taylor (1999). Girlish images across cultures: analyzing Japanese versus US *Seventeen* magazine ads. *Journal of Advertising*, 28: 39–48.

Mbiti, J. (1988). The role of women in African traditional religion. *Cahiers des Religions Africaines*, 22: 69–82.

McArthur, L.Z. and B.G. Resko (1975). The portrayal of men and women in American television commercials. *Journal of Social Psychology*, 97: 209–20.

Monga, Y.D. (2000). Dollars and lipstick: the United States through the eyes of African women. *Africa*, 70: 192–208.

Moreover: the spirits that move Africa (2000, February 5). *The Economist*, 78.

Mwangi, M.W. (1996). Gender roles portrayed in Kenyan television commercials. *Sex Roles*, 34: 205–14.

Rowlands, M. (1994). The material culture of success: ideals and life cycles in Cameroon. In J. Friedman (ed.), *Consumption and Identity* (pp. 239–52). Chur: Harwood.

Rust, R.T. and B. Cooil (1994). Reliability measures for qualitative data: theory and implications. *Journal of Marketing Research*, 31: 1–14.

Shields, V.R. (1990). Advertising visual images: gendered ways of seeing and looking. *Journal of Communication Inquiry*, 14: 25–39.

Tripp, A.M. (2003). Women in movement: transformations in African political landscapes. *International Feminist Journal of Politics*, 5: 233–55.

TV Basics 2004–2005 (2004). Toronto: Television Bureau of Canada.

Ufomata, T. (2000). Women in Africa: their socio-political and economic roles. *West Africa Review*, 2. [Online.] http://www.africaknowledgeproject.org/index.php/war/article/view/431 (retrieved March 31, 2011).

USA ready to launch investment invasion (1999, June). *African Business*, 8–10.

Whipple, T.W. and A.E. Courtney (1985). Female role portrayals in advertising and communication effectiveness: a review. *Journal of Advertising*, 14: 4–8, 17.

Wiles, J.A., C.R. Wiles and A. Tjernlund (1995). A comparison of gender role portrayals in magazine advertising: the Netherlands, Sweden, and the USA. *European Journal of Marketing*, 29(11): 35–49.

17 Exporting American Advertising Strategies: A Comparative Case Study of the United States, Japan and New Zealand

JOSEPH P. HELGERT AND ANNE ZAHRADNIK

Introduction

The comparison of direct-to-consumer advertising (DTCA) between the United States and New Zealand hinges on two basic concerns: economic and social. The economic concerns are foremost in the minds of the corporate executives of pharmaceutical companies who see DTCA as a way to generate demand and increase sales for high-stakes, prescription-only pharmaceutical products. In the US, this has taken the form of an increase in DTCA in 1988 (US$25 million) to 1999 (US$3.6 billion). In New Zealand, DTCA increased 41.7 percent from 1999 (NZ$28 million) to 2000 (NZ$48 million) (Association of New Zealand Advertisers, ACNielsen, Hunter Research as reported in *Direct-to-Consumer Advertising of Prescription Medicines in New Zealand: A Discussion Paper*, 2000).

For government prescription support (PHARMAC in New Zealand, several bills are pending in US), the economic concern has been multi-faceted. Parties for and against allowing DTCA want a definitive answer as to whether or not it increases the costs of providing prescription drug services. They also want to know, as some DTCA supporters contend, if increased prescription drug use has an overall net positive effect for government-supported healthcare by preventing hospitalizations. As for social benefits, does DTCA advertising produce a better-informed consumer of pharmaceuticals who is more empowered to interact positively with his or her healthcare provider? Or, does it damage the provider/patient relationship by providing only partial, biased information. How can the quantity and quality of information be balanced to best serve consumers of healthcare? What are the costs of medicalizing health services and thus creating patients who insist on advertised drugs from their physicians with little knowledge of diagnosis and potential side effects? The findings on the direct costs to government support (and third-party payers in the US) and benefits to the consumer have been mixed (see Coney, 2002; Lexchin, 1999; Rosenthal, Berndt, and Donahue, 2002; Sheffet and Kopp, 1990; Weissman, Blumenthal, Silk, and Zapert, 2003).

Taking that complex set of factors into account, the broader question is how does this scenario fit into the globalization of American-style marketing? Does the resistance to the spread of DTCA signal a change in the influence the US has had over marketing consumerism of all kinds?

GENERAL STATEMENT OF PROBLEM

The specific problem to be addressed in this chapter is whether or not the comparison of New Zealand and US DTCA signals an end to America exporting marketing tactics and the culture of capitalism to the rest of the world. Is this the beginning of the end; is it another step in an ongoing process, or just a bump in the road?

This chapter reviews the accusations that the American free enterprise system exports marketing tactics, and the underlying cultural values, from which they spring, to developed and developing countries around the world without invitation. The chapter examines the cases of two countries, Japan and New Zealand.

In Japan, pioneering advertisements by American firms General Motors and Pepsi-Cola lead to the legalization and use of comparative advertising. Comparative advertising is a type of marketing communication that involves factual and argumentative advertisements to contrast competitive product features with superior features of the sponsor's product. Comparative advertising in Japan was banned until large American corporations disregarded the law and broke the cultural taboos against direct comparison in the Japanese marketplace.

New Zealand is one of only two countries in the world that allow large-scale DTCA of prescription drugs. DTCA bypasses medical providers in order to influence directly the patient/consumer. The only other country that allows this type of indirect advertising to such an extent is the United States. Canada now permits limited DTC advertising of medicines, but is not expected to allow the trend to develop further. It is also under consideration in the UK and the European Union (EU). Those situations will be covered in more detail later. Two other countries, South Africa and Australia, have considered it, but ultimately both decided against it (Joncheere, 2002).

The change of legislation, loosening of regulation, and subsequent specific guidelines needed to allow and control such advertising in New Zealand pre-date similar actions in the United States and may well serve as a model for other countries.

Pharmaceutical marketing practices are related to freedom of commercial speech. In the US, the extent to which the First Amendment guarantees freedom of speech to commercial entities advertising legal products is under debate. In 1942, the US Supreme Court said that the free speech rights of individuals are different than the commercial free speech rights of corporations. This became known as the commercial speech doctrine. The court said corporations were not in the mind of the founding fathers when protecting speech rights. But starting in 1975, court cases have set precedents that have successfully protected commercial speech from interference by the federal government for the advertising of legal products (Overbeck, 1992).

In New Zealand, free speech rights are attributed to the 1990 Bill of Rights Act, which, in common with many countries, is held to provide the legal basis of the right to advertise (Eagle, 2002).

United States corporations are increasingly invoking the First Amendment to the US Constitution to defend controversial speech. US courts have come to afford corporations most of the same protection for political speech as are provided to individuals. The courts are also providing ever-increasing levels of protection for commercial speech, gradually approaching the peak protection guaranteed for political debate (Weissman, 1998).

In fact, Northwestern University Law School Professor Martin Redish told a congressional committee, "There can be no constitutionally acceptable justification for the suppression or widespread disruption of the truthful advertising of a lawful product" (Weissman, 1998). This chapter seeks to determine whether a change in the origin of new marketing practices signals the decline or continuance of the American marketing system as a model for the rest of the world.

SIGNIFICANCE

New Zealand and the US are the only two developed nations that permit DTCA of prescription drugs to such an extent. Canada is experimenting with limited advertising and the EU is debating whether to follow their example. Which country started DTCA is part of the exploration of this chapter. Both the US and New Zealand permit DTCA by omission rather than by design, since both countries have strong constitutional reasons for not prohibiting DTCA of prescription drugs (Hoek and Gendall, 2002). As referred to earlier, DTCA has become a US$3 billion plus market in the years since US federal law opened up DTCA to drug companies (Shields, 2003). Even more rapid growth has occurred in New Zealand.

RATIONALE

For government administrators, the primary economic concern at issue is what role DTCA has played in healthcare costs. Such political influence could be instrumental in other countries that are considering allowing DTCA (Coney, 2002). Secondarily, the economic impact of banning DTCA now has some significance for the economy of both countries.

PURPOSE

The purpose of this chapter is to determine, if possible, the impact that American marketing practices have had on the development of DTCA in New Zealand and vice versa. Permitting by omission causes a mixed time line of DTCA development between the two countries.

LITERATURE REVIEW

Theoretical foundation

For the purposes of this chapter, a theory of American imperialism will be accepted, and seen whether fallout from such a perspective has affected the development of DTCA in New Zealand and worldwide. The competing theoretical framework is the unconditional promotion of American cultural values through exports, cultural products and managerial practices.

Previous research

Besides mixed research signals as to the ultimate costs and benefits of DTCA in both the US and New Zealand, there is consensus that there are "considerable gaps" in the current knowledge about DTCA (Cohen, 2002).

Questions/hypotheses

In the literature, questions include: What are the costs and benefits of DTCA? How do consumers view and use the information available in DTCA? How does such information change patient expectations and their relationship with their healthcare provider? What physician attitudes support and do not support DTCA? What is DTCA's effect on drug subsidies? How does DTCA affect new prescription volume? What is the relationship between risk statement completeness and perceptions of DTCA? How is regulatory policy evaluated in the US and New Zealand?

Overview

TERMS

Direct-to-consumer advertising

DTCA is directly targeted to the ultimate consumer, even though there may be an intermediary such as a doctor, nurse practitioner, physician assistant or original equipment manufacturer.

DTCA is allowed in the US and New Zealand by permissive, constitutionally-based speech freedoms, but it is also driven by the highly competitive pharmaceutical market. Marketing directly to healthcare providers is an old, well-worn strategy that every pharmaceutical company invests large sums in. With the changing expectations for patient/provider relations, however, patients, potential patients and people who influence potential patients became viable targets for marketing. Where once the physician alone made the prescribing decision, now healthcare payers, pharmacists and patients themselves are now increasingly involved. Reaching those "influencers" with relevant massages is becoming ever more complex and expensive. As if this were not challenging enough, competition between prescription drugs—from decreasing periods of exclusivity and from patent expirations and as well as competitive advertising—is intensifying (David, 2001).

David (2001) also states that healthcare professionals and payers will continue to play a role. However, the balance between customers will change; where once the consumer played a minimal role in the equation, in the future she will stand center stage.

Comparative advertising

Comparative advertising is a type of marketing communication that involves two types of selling messages: 1) factual advertisements, which contrast competitive product features with superior features of the sponsor's product, and 2) argumentative advertisements, which use reasoning or emotional appeals to distinguish the sponsor's product from competitors.

Medicalization

This term describes the increasing tendency for people to seek pharmacological treatment for a growing number of conditions (Direct-to-Consumer Advertising of Prescription Medicines in New Zealand: A Discussion Paper, 2000) that were not previously considered candidates for "cures." Conditions such as male pattern baldness and impotency used to be thought of a part of the normal aging process. Now healthcare consumers see them as disease states to be taken care of with medical assistance.

Consumers now have a broader outlook and see pharmaceuticals not merely as medicines to cure illness, but as a means to prevent illness and enhance wellness. Baby boomers, who tend to have a higher amount of disposable income than their parents and less time in which to spend it, have the strongest tendency toward medicalization. In healthcare marketing they are known as the target market of "worried well." They tend to question medical authority, self-medicate and look for alternative/complimentary medicine solutions when conventional treatments fail. This generation is growing older and per capita spending on healthcare for people aged 65-plus is already more than double that for those in mid life (David, 2001).

Learned intermediary

The learned intermediary doctrine is a legal term that applies when a manufacturer provides adequate information about a certain drug's composition and effects to the prescribing physician, thus limiting its product liability (Matter, 2002).

Perceptions of cultural imperialism

Founded in Marxist thought, this term sees culture as based upon the means of production and is used to support the status quo of a capitalist system—including private property, the pooling of private capital to fund business enterprises, consumerism and materialism.

Marketing

Traditionally, marketing has provided products or services for consumers as described through the four Ps: price, promotion (including advertising), place (the means of distribution of the product) and the product itself.

Political influence

Political influence may come in the form of domestic economic policy, lobbyist efforts, special interests and legislative initiatives.

Self-regulation

In most industrial segments, the practice of self-policing of industry members to a code of practice is an effort to forestall or weaken government regulation.

QUESTIONS/HYPOTHESIS

How have new strategies in international marketing by parent pharmaceutical companies affected the adoption of DTCA in New Zealand? Is the marketing of pharmaceuticals the medical equivalent of the marketing of computer software, an industry dominated by the US? How have industry profit averages driven the strategies of international pharmaceutical marketing? How has the adoption of free speech initiatives, clearly stimulated by the US model, provided the philosophical basis for DTCA? How has the absence of strong consumer lobbyists affected DTCA in New Zealand? How have differences in domestic economic policy affected the development of DTCA? How have differences in regulatory policy affected DTCA?

COMPARATIVE CASE STUDY

Case analysis is a technique used extensively in the professional disciplines with situations of great complexity, managerial/administrative decision-making and political/legislative change. Comparative and direct-to-consumer advertising are such situations. Cases provide background to the situation, a statement of problem, critical factors, alternatives, recommendations and finally, cautions and/or benefits of any recommendations.

DATA

The data for this analysis includes primary reports from the New Zealand Ministry of Health, US House and Senate reports and testimony, Food and Drug Administration documents, and secondary analysis from scholars, practitioners and industry watchers.

Limitations

The current data lacks the insight gained from a review of internal documents of agencies and ministries involved that could focus the affect of US practice in the development of DTCA in New Zealand.

SOURCE

Documents, as illustrated in the attached bibliography, come from a variety of sources including official government publications, scholarly articles, industry trade articles and independent research organizations.

Limits

Each and every data source has accompanying biases. Utilizing a cross section of sources and reconciling conclusions between each will help minimize the effect.

Analysis

COMPARATIVE ADVERTISING

Introduction in Japan (Helgert, 2001)

Comparative advertising is a type of marketing communication that involves two types of selling messages: 1) factual advertisements, which contrast competitive product features with superior features of the sponsor's product, and 2) argumentative advertisements, which use reasoning or emotional appeals to distinguish the sponsor's product from competitors. Until very recently, Japanese companies avoided comparative advertising, considering it taboo. This avoidance stems from the cultural caveat that Japanese companies should try to maintain "harmony." In fact, before 1986, comparative advertising was illegal in Japan. The Japan Fair Trade Commission prohibited comparative advertising, viewing it as similar to slander.

This aversion to comparative advertising presented a difficult situation for American companies wishing to enter the Japanese markets. Since comparative ads played a major role in American advertising, they were considered a necessary ingredient for advertising in Japan as well. So, despite the Japanese cultural ban on comparative advertising, American advertising agencies moved into Japanese markets and gradually introduced comparative ads. As a result, the American advertisers gradually altered the Japanese advertising environment by making comparative advertising acceptable.

Pepsi-Cola, the first soft drink product to position itself competitively against Coca-Cola, launched the first Japanese competitive ads. In 1991, Pepsi extended its "Pepsi Challenge" advertising campaign into Japan with the intention of raiding Coca-Cola market share. Japanese supermarkets held "taste comparisons" similar to those implemented so successfully in the United States. These events heralded the beginning of Japanesestyle "challenge advertising." This section describes the process of bringing about this rather dramatic change to a cultural value.

Historical perspective: "Harmony" doctrine

Crown Prince Shotoku Taishishi (Prince of Sagely Virtue, 574–622), who had significant impact on Japanese culture during his time, continues to influence Japanese society even today through his ideas about contemporary marketing, and commerce and advertising practice (Hiromichi, 1983; Lu, 1974; Sansom, 1958; Tsunoda, DeBary and Keene, 1958). As a regent for empress Suiko (593–628), Prince Shotoku promoted the growth of Buddhism, improved relations with China, and promoted learning as a way of understanding the world. He also used his personal religious beliefs as a basis for political reform in Japan (Sansom, 1958).

Shotoku sought to imbue politics with the civilizing influence of his religion. In the year 604, at just 21 years of age, Prince Shotoku championed a document known as the *Constitution of Seventeen Articles*. The document, although not accepted as the prince's own work, is a set of moral precepts, political principles and normative injunctions. The *Constitution* provided a basis for the political reform sought at the time. It also paved the way for the eventual success of subsequent reforms (Lu, 1974). Within this document are clues to the values under which Japanese business operates.

The *Constitution*'s first article most captures the business conduct sentiment that still influences behavior today. That article is summarized as noting that harmony is to be valued and cherished, and opposition for opposition sake must be avoided as a matter of principle. All men are influenced by partisanship, and there are few that are intelligent or sagacious. If those above are harmonious and those below are friendly and cordial, there is concord in the discussion of business, reason will prevail, and there will be nothing that cannot be accomplished (Aston, 1972).

Advertising regulations respond to market pressure

This section of the work is the basis for the Japanese avoidance of comparative advertising. The document presents the historical, cultural caveat that Japanese companies should try to maintain "harmony." The Constitution also prescribes the general values of kenkyo (modesty) and omoiyari (being considerate) (Hasegawa, 1995). Because of these principles, Japanese companies avoided comparative advertising and considered it taboo. In fact, until 1986, comparative advertising was illegal. The Japan Fair Trade Commission (JFTC) prohibited comparative advertising, viewing it as similar to slander.

However in 1986, the JFTC altered course, for two reasons: 1) the JFTC was concerned about the staggering trade surplus with the United States, and 2) foreign firms complained that the ban hampered effective advertising efforts.

Seeman (1986) adds that foreign corporations, American in particular, had long complained that the ban on comparative advertising made selling products in Japan difficult. During the summer of 1985, the Japanese government responded to these foreign (especially American) complaints by advancing a "market-opening package." The package included a series of trade and tariff changes that allowed foreign companies more access to Japanese markets.

While the Japanese government prepared its marketopening package, foreign companies repeatedly complained that restrictions on comparative advertising constituted a trade barrier. In September 1986, the JFTC dispatched members of affiliated foundations to the United States. Here they studied how United States firms practiced comparative advertising (Seeman, 1986). Later, the JFTC prepared guidelines for suitable comparative advertising, based on factual data. The guidelines banned ads that denigrated competitive products.

However, in its 1986 ruling, the JFTC lifted the ban and created guidelines for comparative advertising. The guidelines required factual proof to support comparisons in ads. Thus firms received permission to make advertisements showing where their products were superior to competitors.

Birth and development of Japanese competitive ads

Among foreign competitors, Pepsi was the first soft drink product to position itself competitively against Coke. CooperChen (1997) reports on the PepsiCola effort to raid market share from Coca-Cola. In 1991, Pepsi introduced its "Pepsi Challenge" advertising campaign into Japan. Japanese supermarkets held "taste comparisons" similar to those implemented so successfully in the United States.

A shortlived joint venture between United States ad agency McCann Erickson and Japanese agency Hakuhodo developed the "Pepsi Challenge" concept. Initially, television stations rejected the television ads, in which Diet Pepsi "challenges" Diet Coke. However, Japanese consumers loved the ads. Meanwhile, the JFTC stated that the ads were legal. The JFTC reasoned that the ads were factual, and did not slander Coke (Barranger, 1993).

In one ad, popular American rapper MC Hammer regains his dance rhythm after selecting Pepsi instead of Coke. Consumers watched these ads as if they were viewing a baseball game and the ads became a favorite pastime. Viewers requested the spots and television stations sent them copies.

Maskery (1992) reports on a 1995 GM ad depicting a Cadillac Seville with a headline asking consumers to "compare our Seville's fuel efficiency with Infiniti's." A Nissan Infiniti Q45 lurks in the background of the newspaper photograph.

Not to be outdone by GM, Ford ran its own comparative ad that posed a rhetorical question to Ford's chief rival Volkswagen: "Why is the Volkswagen Golf so expensive in Japan?" Volkswagen immediately protested, but by then, the advertising industry had turned a corner. The "Japanesestyle comparative ads" had become less factual and more argumentative in nature.

In 1993, comparative advertising spread from cars to computers. Barrager (1993) reports on the rivalry of personal computer manufacturers NEC and Compaq. American computer manufacturer Compaq entered the Japanese market with a lowprice strategy. NEC responded by promoting its feature of Japaneselanguage software.

Conclusion

In spite of Prince Shotoku's precepts, Japan adapted to open conflict in the marketplace. Inoue (1996) asserts that advertising industry deregulation was a major influence. He cites the 1986 Japan Fair Trade Association ruling as the beginning of deregulation.

However, deregulation played a minor role. The true prime mover was the introduction of American-style comparative advertising messages. These messages represent a cultural force. Implicit in the messages were competitive market values that impacted Japanese society in two ways: the new messages not only persuaded consumers to buy, but also enhanced the marketing process.

Over time, the new messages bypassed earlier cultural taboos against comparative advertising. Where the market went, the marketing rules followed. Thus the strongest motivator of the change was culture, rather than politics or economics.

DIRECT-TO-CONSUMER ADVERTISING

United States

Competition is a part of the democratic capitalist value system. Competition is seen as a component in many of the marketing activities in the US and in US overseas activities, as seen earlier. In addition to comparative advertising, DTCA has been a growing technique used by marketers to curry favor with a consuming public, even for products that are not sold directly to the public (Wolfe, 2001).

Because of the strong First Amendment in the US Constitution, there is no way that DTC prescription drug advertising could ever be banned in this country. Having said that, however, there is an urgent need for more fine-tuned, better-staffed and much tougher government regulation of its content. There is little doubt that false and misleading advertising to patients and physicians can result in prescriptions being written for drugs that are more dangerous and/or less effective than perceived by either the doctor or the patient. This can then lead to a subsequent toll of deaths and injuries that would not have occurred had safer, more effective drugs been prescribed.

Overview—primary demand advertising

Advertising scholars relate direct-to-consumer or by-pass advertising as a form of primary demand or "pull" advertising. In this type of advertising, manufacturers or growers advertise to the consumer public even though they sell exclusively to original equipment manufacturers or other redistributors who may or may not include the product or commodity inside another product or as part of their sales inventory. Many times this type of advertising is sponsored by grower or industry associations whose purpose is to keep the commodity foremost in the consuming public's mind and thus generate sales along the trade channel.

Intel Ò

Intel Corporation's promotion of computer microprocessors is an exception to the general commodity type of primary demand advertising. In this case, Intel wants the end user of personal computers to favor the inclusion of the Intel-brand microprocessor inside an original manufacturer's computer. Instead of promoting microprocessors in general, it is a promotion of the Intel-branded microprocessor in contrast to its competitors such as Applied Micro Devices. Intel spends upwards of half a billion dollars a year advertising to computer end-users to buy a computer that has an Intel microprocessor inside. Hence the familiar tagline for this campaign: "Intel Inside."

ORANGE JUICE

The Florida Department of Citrus receives money from orange growers to promote the idea of Florida orange juice rather than individual brands such as Tropicana or Minute Maid. This is an effort to position a mature product in the mind of the consumers so that demand increases for Florida orange juice in contrast to orange juice from other domestic and international sources. Agricultural commodity producers often band together in the US to pool resources and develop a larger campaign for their products than they could afford individually.

MILK

The National Fluid Milk Processor Promotion Board has successfully spent over a US$1 billion for their campaign "Got Milk" to combat the slowing of interest in and demand for milk. The campaign features celebrity endorsers promoting the health benefits of drinking milk. No specific brand of milk is mentioned.

OTHERS

In addition to the above high-profile campaigns, the cotton growers industry and carpeting industries in the US have each tried to stimulate primary demand for their product category over individual brands of manufactured cotton and carpeting.

Pharmaceutical advertising

Considering all the commercial and legislative forces pushing to allow DTCA in countries around the world, it is interesting that only the United States and New Zealand have DTCA (Cohen, 2002). As stated earlier, both countries allowed DTCA of pharmaceuticals by omission rather than authorization. In the United States, there is no legislation prohibiting DTCA, although several such bills are being proposed at this time. The Federal Drug Administration regulated most aspects of pharmaceutical use and promotion through 1962, with its specific authority over DTCA as part and parcel of its authority over prescription drug advertising generally (Levitt, 1995). The Kefauver-Hayes Amendment to the Food, Drug and Cosmetic Act required advertising to meet four goals:

1. ads could not be false or misleading;
2. ads should provide balanced information on risks and benefits;
3. ads should contain all the facts that are material to the drug's use;
4. ads should include a brief summary that includes every known risk of use (*Direct-to-Consumer Advertising of Prescription Medicines in New Zealand: A Discussion Paper*, 2000).

Direct-to-consumer advertising first surfaced in the US in the early 1980s (Levitt, 1995). Initially pharmaceutical executives were opposed to DTCA citing fear of liability, exorbitant cost and lower profits (*Direct-to-Consumer Advertising of Prescription Medicines in New Zealand: A Discussion Paper*, 2000). The partial relaxation of promotional provisions allowed drug category advertising rather than specific product or brand promotion (Eagle, 2002). This was similar to the approach DTCA had taken in primary demand stimulation up to that point. Immediately following several tentative ventures by pharmaceutical marketers, the FDA saw two drawbacks to DTCA: the lack of ability on the part of consumers to understand the information provided, and the increased pressure on physicians to prescribe demanded medicines (Levitt, 1995). The cautions led to a voluntary moratorium from 1983 to 1985. In 1985, the FDA lifted its moratorium but re-affirmed that DTC advertisements must meet the same standards as those aimed at professionals. It was at this time that the FDA evaluated more fully the impact of DTCA. Based on pioneering campaigns, the FDA saw three types of DTCA:

1. see your doctor ads that focused on doctor and disease (no drug promotion);
2. reminder advertising that focused on disease and condition (named drug with no required brief summary including every known risk);
3. specific drug for specific condition (a heightened sales intensity).

After reviewing the effect of these basic types of DTCA, the FDA decided in 1997 to loosen the restrictions on the consumer advertising of prescription medicines (Goetzel, 2001). An additional concern arose from the advent of the third type of specific DTCA. By going beyond reminder advertising, manufacturers removed the physician from an active role and thus lost a valuable "learned intermediary" defense to product liability for pharmaceuticals (Matter, 2002).

Once the provisions against DTCA were loosened, manufacturers quickly found that DTCA provided increased sales (Shields, 2003). Between 1999 and 2000, 50 of the most directly advertised drugs showed sales 2.3 times sales of other drugs, and prescriptions grew six times prescriptions of other drugs (Coney, 2002). DTCA spending increased 35 percent and has doubled since 1997. Table 17.1 summarizes US annual spending on DTC pharmaceutical advertising.

Table 17.1 US spending on direct-to-consumer pharmaceutical advertising (US$ millions)

1989	1991	1993	1994	1995	1996	1997	1998	1999	2000	2001	2002
12	55	150	250	350	791	1,070	1,320	1,850	2,500	2,679	3,616e

Source: Mintzes (2002), Calfee (2002) and IMS Health Data (2003).

PATIENT/DOCTOR RELATIONSHIP

In its initial stages, DTCA was seen to allow patients greater involvement in decisions regarding health management and medication. Many patients rejected a paternalistic approach by doctors (Eagle, 2002). Even the American Medical Association thought that, if used appropriately, DTCA would have the potential to increase patient awareness about treatment options and enhance patient–physician communication (*Direct-to-Consumer Advertising of Prescription Drugs*, 2000).

Matthews (2001) maintains the US healthcare system is transitioning from a physician-directed system to a patient-directed one, primarily because of the growing availability of healthcare information, but that DTCA is simply a response to the transition, not the cause of it.

The overwhelming presence of DTCA, especially on television, has had unanticipated effects. For example, traditionally, pharmaceutical manufacturers were protected from product liability by the learned intermediary doctrine. This gave them an exception to the duty to warn customers directly. The exception imposes the duty to warn, not to the foreseeable user of the product (the patient) but rather to the prescribing physician (Matter, 2002). But with increasing amounts of DTCA in the US, the learned intermediary doctrine no longer absolves pharmaceutical manufacturers from liability to warn consumers. There have been cases where pharmaceutical manufacturers have been held liable for failure to warn physicians adequately. The FDA describes this as over-promotion of products (*Stevens vs. Parke*). In these cases, courts pointed out that vigorous sales programs had the effect of persuading doctors to disregard medicinal warnings (Matter, 2002).

Possible damage to the provider/patient relationship is another example. Research has indicated patients' requests for medicines are a powerful driver of prescribing decisions. Physicians often prescribe the requested medicines, even when they are ambivalent about the choice of treatment. Because of that, concerns about opening up the regulatory environment to permit direct to consumer advertising in the EU and Canada seem well justified (Mintzes et al., 2002).

There is even controversy over just how much consumers are actually taking control of their own healthcare. Tu and Hargreaves (2003) state that, contrary to popular images of American consumers actively researching personal health concerns, only 38 percent of adults, or 72 million people, sought health information in the previous year from a source other than their doctor. In contrast, nearly two thirds of American adults (62 percent) failed to seek any health information. Tu and Hargreaves' implications for policy makers show that. Healthcare information can be a double-edged sword, and much depends on the credibility and purpose of the information.

Policy makers in Canada, the UK and the rest of the EU are keeping a close eye on such research. Health Action International Europe states:

> Consumer advocates and public health experts stated strongly that the proposal's likely outcome would be US-style spiraling health costs and irrational drug use. They also emphasized that the Commission's proposal to allow industry to supply advertising about medicines available for treatment of diabetes, asthma, and HIV/AIDS failed to follow the EU's own precautionary principle of "first, do no harm." The symposium's presentations and discussion revealed an obvious need for better independent information about medicines for consumers. (Joncheere, 2002)

In Canada, according to Chepesiuk (2002), self-regulation is well-entrenched and far ahead of the US. The PAAB and Rx&D have actively enforced their codes with respect to many of these problems.

In the UK, a group of regulations covers DTCA:

- The Medicines Act 1968
- Directive 92/28/EEC on the Advertising of Medicinal Products for Human Use
- The Medicines (Advertising) Regulations 1994 SI 1994/1932
- The Medicines (Monitoring of Advertising) Regulations 1994 SI 1994/1933
- The Medicines for Human Use (Marketing Authorisations etc.) Regulations 1994 SI 1994/3144
- The Medicines (Advertising) Amendment Regulations 1996 SI 1996/267
- The Medicines (Advertising and Monitoring of Advertising) Amendment Regulations 1999 SI 199/267
- The Control of Misleading Advertising Regulations 1988 SI 1988/915: Regulation of the Promotion of Medicines (2003)

Also as part of the Health Action International Europe report, Medawar (2001) voices strong opinions against allowing DTCA in the EU and specifically argues against US-style advertising.

> What the US decides to do about direct-to-consumer advertising is that country's own business and own choice. But there cannot be many countries whose people would gain by embracing the American way of life. It is unaffordable to any national community. European health systems tend to prioritize general health needs. The American model makes a sharp distinction between "health winners" and "health losers" and is hard driven by market imperatives and needs. Let's not forget that three-quarters of a million people declare bankruptcy each year in the US because of catastrophic illness—and that more than 40 million have no health insurance at all. The EU's health care systems need protection from the ravages of uncontrollable demand that direct-to-consumer advertising would bring. It is also worth keeping in mind that no other country in the world has the regulatory capacity of the US Food and Drug Administration. Indeed, two-thirds of the world's countries "still do not have laws to regulate pharmaceutical promotion or do not enforce the ones they have." What the EU decides about direct-to-consumer marketing will greatly influence what happens in candidate countries and in other areas of the world.

Giving the World Health Organization perspective, Joncheere (2002), found that definitions of drug promotion and information varied by country. Because of that, WHO decided regulatory implementation at the national level is quite difficult to enforce, and has led to substantially different enforcement regimes, including different ways of regulating and controlling promotion than neighboring states, and different priorities. Many lack resources for applying existing laws governing promotion and advertising. And, Joncheere reports, "Considerable difficulties were reported in dealing with the often 'hidden' advertising (disease-symptom-oriented material, TV news programs, etc.) and the targeting of areas of 'under treatment' of certain diseases." Concerning actions in the UK on DTCA, Meek (2002) explains the Medicines Control Agency justifies the regulation of drug industry advertising in order to protect the public from false and misleading claims: "In order to protect public health it is essential that advertising and promotion of medicines should be subject to effective monitoring and control at all times." Control has been established through several Acts of Parliament to underpin a complex system of industry self-regulation (Meek, 2002).

The EC's involvement is explained partly by the rapid growth of the Internet—law enforcement has become extremely complicated. One problem is the blurring of the traditional dividing line between "promotion" and "information": how can you control one but not the other? And enforcing national laws becomes virtually impossible because Internet traffic is global (Medawar, 2001).

MARKETING MIX

Based on lax federal government regulations, a small group of US pharmaceutical companies experimented with prescription drug advertisements in the early 1980s (Calfee, 2002). Values central to the American system of capitalism became the springboard for the experiments. A central tenet of the free market system is that providing product information to consumers—as long as that information is truthful and non-misleading—is good for competition and consumers. But the value of a free and unfettered information flow became secondary when making marketing decisions—

these decisions are made on the basis of the likely returns on investment. Pharmaceutical giant and aggressive marketer Merck reported profits of 30 percent for the year 2000 (Socolar and Sager, 2001). Supporting critics of the capitalist system also say that intense advertising of prescription drugs may create a demand for a product when there is no essential need. The most controversial example of this type of promotion was the marketing campaign for Viagra, the male potency drug from Pfizer. Here unprecedented amounts of money were spent including a breakthrough endorsement by past Senator Robert Dole, who, in an interview with CNN correspondent Larry King, inadvertently mentioned he used the drug. Pharmaceutical marketers quickly followed up and signed the senator as a product endorser.

Pharmaceutical executives are quick to point to what they describe as excessive research and development costs to bring a new product to the market when politicians and consumers lament the apparent high cost of medicines. Executives ignore the fact that revenues spent on research and development are one half to one third the amount spent on marketing, advertising and administration combined (Socolar and Sager, 2001). Much of these costs are incurred in hiring of marketing personnel. Between 1995 and 2000 the number of people employed in marketing rose more than 30,000 or 59 percent, with the vast majority being sales people (Socolar and Sager, 2001). Advertising costs, another component of the promotional "P" for giant GlaxoSmith Kline were US$239 million and Pfizer/Pharmacia US$176 million. After acquiring Warner Lambert, Pfizer became the 9th largest US advertiser in 2001 with spending of US$624 million (Goetzel, 2001). Citing its advertising success, the advertising trade magazine *Advertising Age* selected pharmaceutical marketer Pfizer as its marketer of the year (Goetzel, 2001). Pfizer divides its advertising across several agencies including Donny Deutsch (Lipitor, Bextra), Cline Davis, Mann (Viagra), WPP's J. Walter Thompson (Celebrex), Aegis Group's Carat USA and Darcy, Mascius Benton and Bowles (Relpax) (Goetzel, 2001).

Television, because of its relatively low cost per contact and extensive reach, is the pharmaceutical advertisers' medium of choice. The ad category receives over US$1.6 billion in pharmaceutical ads each year. A breakout of ad spending by company is given in Table 17.2.

Table 17.2   Direct-to-consumer pharmaceutical television advertising (US$ millions)

GlaxoSmith Kline	Pfizer	Merck	Johnson & Johnson	Astrazeneca
202.8	166.8	126.6	116.9	110.4

Source: Nielsen Monitor Plus (as cited in Bittar, 2000).

LEGISLATIVE ACTIVITIES

It is important to re-state that there are very few regulations regarding DTCA in the United States. Critics of the Federal Drug Administration's oversight of DTCA point out that FDA regulations and resources are dangerously inadequate (Wolfe, 2001). Combined with consumer perception that there is far more oversight than actually exists, the FDA is scrambling to shore up its regulatory coverage and enforcement. The primary First Amendment support quoted by pharmaceutical marketers has allowed them to win several lawsuits over the last few years. The FDA is hoping to reduce the number of successful lawsuits and tighten control (Vence, 2003).

Foley (2000) suggests options for strengthening FDA oversight of DTCA by: requiring prior approval by the FDA of advertising content; requiring all DTC advertisements to included standardized warning messages, comparable to requirements for cigarette advertising; developing and refining standards for information dissemination; and imposing sanctions for false or misleading DTC advertisements (Foley and Gross, 2000).

Meanwhile, political pressure to curtail or eliminate DTCA is growing in the US on several fronts. As state and federal governments take on more and more of the burden of paying for prescription drugs, legislative response to perceived high drug prices is increasing. From special interest groups to sitting legislators to presidential candidates, calls are coming for reducing the price of prescriptions and advertising costs is named as a primary driver. For example, this press release appeared on the PRNewswire:

> AIDS Healthcare Foundation (AHF), the nation's largest specialized provider of HIV/AIDS medical care today applauded the US Government's call yesterday to ban pharmaceutical companies from certain widespread—and often illegal or unethical—industry marketing practices. AHF went one step further by also calling upon the government and industry to implement policy to lower drug prices to reflect the expected decreased marketing costs the pharmaceutical industry will incur as a result of these new regulations. The Foundation was concerned enough about the impact of excessive marketing costs on drug prices that it sponsored legislation (AB 686, Koretz, West Hollywood 2002) earlier this year in California to slash the taxpayers' tab for such drug marketing costs (US Government bars unfair drug marketing practices, 2002). [The bill died in committee before reaching Governor Davis' desk.]

Assemblyman Paul Koretz, also in California, has introduced a bill to reign in drug marketing costs so the savings can be passed on to California taxpayers. The bill—Assembly Bill 686—would prohibit the State of California from paying for pharmaceutical manufacturer's costs for the marketing of drugs that are prescribed for life-threatening chronic conditions, except those costs that are associated with the necessary and appropriate education of patients and physicians (US Government bars unfair drug marketing practices, 2002).

Sitting legislators, responding to pressure from constituent groups such as senior citizens and those suffering from chronic health conditions, are introducing legislation to control DTCA and physician detailing as a means to bring down the price of prescription drugs.

In a nation-wide radio address, Michigan Senator Debbie Stabenow said,

> We have also introduced legislation to rein in the excessive amounts of money drug companies spend on advertising and promotions. When you're watching television, doesn't it seem like every other ad, if not EVERY ad is for some new prescription drug? Well, that's because the Fortune 500 drug companies spend two and a half times more money on advertising and administration than on research and development of new life-saving drugs. And the cost of all this advertising is subsidized by American taxpayers through tax breaks. We need to encourage drug companies to spend more on medical research than market research. To do this, Senator Carnahan and I and several of our colleagues have sponsored legislation that would allow the drug companies to deduct advertising expenses from their taxes only up to the amount they spend on research and development. (Stabenow and Carnahan, 2002)

Democratic presidential candidates are voicing opinions as well. Every one has a prescription drug benefit plan proposal. As part of their suggestions for federal government drug subsidies, they include cost cutting measure that almost always blame DTCA, at least in part, for the high cost of prescriptions. Edwards (2003), for example, includes this message on his campaign website.

Pharmaceutical ads have become a multi-billion dollar industry, with many drug makers spending more on marketing, advertising and administration than on research and development. Edwards believes we must ensure that advertising does not wrongly drive up costs for consumers. Edwards' plan would require new restrictions on drug advertisements to ensure that they provide the whole truth to the public about drug side effects and efficacy compared to placebos and cheaper alternatives. Edwards would also double FDA resources dedicated to enforcing DTC advertisement rules; repeal President Bush's rule that unnecessarily slows down action on misleading drug advertisements; grant FDA authority to levy civil fines after due process for violation of federal advertising rules; and require drug companies to perform greater head-to-head testing of drugs as a condition of FDA approval. (Edwards, 2003)

Legislative action against DTCA in countries outside the US and New Zealand aren't as restricted by constitutional protection of commercial free speech. As early as 1999, Brown described legislative action as, "The Government is in the legislative process of granting to the Medicines Control Agency (MCA) its new requested and draconian power" (Brown, 1999).

In 2003, the Association of the British Pharmaceutical Industry declared for self-regulation as the most appropriate way to manage pharmaceutical company's product information and the Internet. The research-based pharmaceutical industry has a long tradition and experience of self-regulation. UK-based pharmaceutical companies comply with the ABPI Code of Practice and pharmaceutical companies worldwide are bound by the IFPMA Code of Pharmaceutical Marketing Practices.

On their website, the Association of the British Pharmaceutical Industry (ABPI, 2003) lists existing relevant legislation.

- Council Directive 92/28/EEC of March 31, 1992 on the advertising of medicinal products for human use. This, in essence, forbids advertising to the general public for prescription-only products and allows such advertising for over-the-counter (OTC) products.
- Council Directive 92/27/EEC of March 31, 1992 on the labeling of medicinal products for human use and on package leaflets. This sets out requirements for the labeling of products and for package leaflets.
- Council Directive 92/26/EEC of March 31, 1992 concerning the classification for the supply of medicinal products for human use. This harmonizes (on a European level) the criteria which determine whether a product should be OTC or prescription-only.

To reduce the pressure for more regulation, advertising agencies and medical publications have funded the Coalition for Healthcare Communication, which dutifully reports that consumer attitudes are positive and DTCA is a valued source of information. In the Coalition's view consumers feel the additional information has a favorable impact on patient/physician discussions. One cannot ignore the biased source of this research.

New Zealand

In New Zealand, the same permissive regulatory environment, spearheaded by the 1981 New Zealand Medicines Act, permitted the emergence of DTCA. International pharmaceutical executives and their advertising agencies saw the growth of DTCA in the United States and attempted the same experiments that tested the regulatory waters. It is important to note that even though the US and New Zealand are the only countries that allow DTCA, the size of the markets is vastly different. Australia has a pharmaceutical market one-fortieth the size of the US pharmaceutical market (Socolar and Sager, 2001; IMS Health Data cited from PHARMA Pharmaceutical Industry Profile, July 2001, ch. 7, fig. 7-2). In proportion, the amount of spending on DTCA in New Zealand is smaller, but annual growth rates are comparable. (35 percent US and 24 percent New Zealand). DTCA spending for recent years is shown in Table 17.3.

Table 17.3   New Zealand direct-to-consumer pharmaceutical advertising (NZ$ millions)

1999	2000
14.3	17.9

Source: Association of New Zealand Advertisers as reported by the Ministry of Health, *Direct-to-Consumer Advertising of Prescription Medicines in New Zealand: A Discussion Paper* (2000).

In June 2003 the New Zealand Medical Association issued a statement calling for the ban of DTCA.

The NZMA is calling on the Government to prohibit Direct to Consumer Advertising (DTVA) of prescription medicines in New Zealand. "The NZMA has been reviewing its position on DTCA of prescription medicines and has now decided that the disadvantages outweigh the benefits," says NZMA Chairman Dr Tricia Briscoe. "We believe it is time for the Government to move into line with most other countries in prohibiting DTCA." "This is a change in our positions, but our previous reluctant acceptance of DTCA was always based on the need for stronger self-regulation and the principle that pharmaceutical companies must not test the boundaries of self-regulation." "We no longer have confidence that self-regulation is sufficient to protect the interests of either patient or doctors, nor do we feel that greater government regulation would provide adequate protection. We have therefore come to the conclusion that DTCA or prescription medicines should be prohibited." (NZMA calls for ban on DTCA, 2003)

Kaye (2003) also report that the New Zealand pharmaceutical industry will be forced to curb its direct to consumer advertising after a review by the Ministry of Health found tighter regulation was necessary. Suggested changes from the review included banning branded sponsorship of events, banning brand name drugs on vehicles and only allowing drug companies to advertise in broadcast and print media, refusing them access to consumers directly through direct mail or allowing the running of competitions. Increased fines for non-compliance and mandatory voice-overs of risk information could also be implemented in the next 12 months through amendments to the Medicines Act 1981 or in relation to work being done on a new Therapeutic Products Act. The New Zealand

Health Minister Annette King said concerns about a range of issues led to the review, including submissions from consumer groups and medical and advertising organizations, but the result was that the principle of industry self regulation would continue.

Pharmaceutical advertising

Many of the issues identified in DTCA in New Zealand are the same as those in the US case. Health industry watchers cite the access to quality information, profit pressures on pharmaceutical companies, the effect on doctor/patient relationships and the medicalization of the consumer population (*Direct-to-Consumer Advertising of Prescription Medicines in New Zealand: A Discussion Paper*, 2000). Although DTCA in New Zealand was permissible with the Medicines Act of 1981 and the Medicines Regulation Act of 1984, it was not until the mid 1990s that pharmaceutical companies began advertising directly to end consumers (Hoek and Gendall, 2002). It is still unclear why DTCA in New Zealand did not emerge until ten years after it was permissible under New Zealand regulations. Some industry analysts suggest that DTCA arose from omission and the emergence of DTCA in the US (Hoek and Gendall, 2002). Others have postulated that DTCA began in response to the New Zealand Bill of Rights in 1990. It was at this time that the legislation passed specifically protected freedom of speech. Commercial freedom of speech guaranteed by the US Bill of Rights has been used by US pharmaceutical manufacturers to protect DTCA.

The first attempts at DTCA in New Zealand did not conform to legislative requirements. Campaigns by SmithKline French, Wellcome and Edinburgh Pharmaceutical Industries were in violation of the minimal requirements for DTCA (Coney, 2002). Significant DTCA advertising campaigns in New Zealand did not occur until the 1997 US Federal Drug Administration law change that clarified the acceptable forms. This time period also allowed the comparison of international marketing techniques by parent pharmaceutical firms. Even with this clarifying example from the US on what was acceptable for DTCA, the New Zealand system of DTCA control was entirely based on self-regulation as coordinated by the Association of New Zealand Advertisers. Merck Sharp Dohme initiated the first aggressive campaign for ProscarÒ (finasteride), a heart medication not concurrently subsidized by PHARMAC (Coney, 2002).

PATIENT/DOCTOR RELATIONSHIP

Critics of the New Zealand health industry initially chided doctors for their resistance to DTCA. The resistance was blamed on paternalism—the doctor–patient relationship developed in the middle of the twentieth century. The active role of the patient was seen as being modeled in the US where escalating costs had put pressure on the relationship. Active patients self-diagnose, suggest diagnoses or advocate treatment options—knowledge of which may come from DTCA campaigns.

However, "evidence-based medicine" that focuses on evidence of effectiveness alone as the basis for clinical choices is incomplete. A more complete approach is "economics-based medicine," which requires evaluation of both the costs and the benefits of healthcare. Where healthcare resources are scarce, decisions based on effectiveness alone do not maximize health benefits for a population and can result in inefficiency and inequity. Economic evaluation may improve healthcare by including opportunity costs in decisions. Economic frameworks are increasingly having an effect on public reimbursement of pharmaceuticals, particularly in Australasia and Europe (Maynard and Bloor, 2003).

Demand for drugs by patients in Europe had been influenced primarily by user charges. However, recently, the over-the-counter (OTC) market has been developing, and there have been moves toward direct-to-consumer (DTC) advertising. Both influence patients' behavior and require regulation (Maynard and Bloor, 2003).

DTC ADVERTISING

Advertising of drugs directly to consumers is well established and a matter of continuing dispute in the United States. However, the European Commission is moving slowly to allow it (Marketing plans for medicinal products available on prescription only, 2001). DTC advertising has been banned in Australia, but such efforts may be limited in the current global economy with wide access to information.

MARKETING MIX

Just as in the US, pharmaceutical executives overcame their initial resistance to the prospect of DTCA, by one of its positive outcomes for marketers—the contribution to profits. Most research on advertising poses mixed results for sales or even volume. The connection between advertising and profit was made over two decades ago (Farris and Moore, 2004). Many marketers go further in comparing the profit range (average of 18 percent) for pharmaceuticals as being comparable to new economy/knowledge economy industries such as computer software with heavy investment in high-tech intellectual property (Eagle, 2002).

LEGISLATIVE ACTIVITIES

The other contribution that advertising makes to pharmaceutical products is branding. This is important since, in New Zealand, where many prescription medicines are subsidized by the government through PHARMAC, there is considerable pressure to replace brand name prescription products with generic products because they cost less. Failure to obtain subsidies through PHARMAC had been another reason drug companies decide to promote their branded products directly to end consumers (Hoek and Gendall, 2002).

With expanding volume for more expensive, branded products, it is no wonder that the New Zealand regulatory framework for DTCA could not keep up either in more directive regulations and legislation or in the amount of money needed for personnel to draft and administer such tightened regulations. In contrast, it relies on the Association of New Zealand Advertisers, whose dues are paid directly by the advertisers to self-regulate the practice. The only other fallback that the New Zealand regulatory framework has is judicial action in the case of non-compliance. This might also prove to be unsuccessful based on the successful commercial speech lawsuits in the US.

POLITICAL PRESSURE

PHARMAC was originally opposed to DTCA thinking that it would increase New Zealand's drug bill by creating artificial needs for expensive branded medicines (Wenley, 2000). The other side of this argument may be that DTCA puts pressure on PHARMAC and the New Zealand government for subsidizing drugs as more people become aware of treatment options. PHARMAC continues to insist that the current system of voluntary review is unsatisfactory. In its present self-regulatory mode, the Association of New Zealand Advertisers (ANZA), as pre-emptive judge and jury for DTCA ads, may be woefully inadequate to protect consumers.

In the past, after a high-profile Xenical campaign, ANZA created the Therapeutic Advertising Advisory Service (TAAS), which became a voluntary, non-binding reviewer of advertisements at the concept and storyboard stages. The ads were reviewed and breaches of the code or statutes were identified. Along with ANZA and TAAS, the Advertising Standard Authority (ASA) introduced a code for DTCA hoping to avert more stringent government regulation. The code was revised in February of 1999 (Hoek and Gendall, 2002). Amidst the conflicts of interest between advertisers, the media and the government, the last resort would be for the government to prohibit all DTCA as most countries throughout the world have done. Australia, Canada, the UK and the US all have strong lobbyists against DTCA (Coney, 2002). Just as pharmaceutical marketing practices have leaked across the globe these grassroots lobbyists may also make advances in the New Zealand. The most formidable stumbling block to complete prohibition is the protection afforded through speech freedoms. The New Zealand Bill of Rights of 1990 states "everyone has the right to freedom of expression to seek, receive and impart information and/or opinions of any kind in any form" (Section 14). If this type of open-ended guarantee can be adequately defended in court, New Zealand pharmaceutical companies will have plenty of ammunition to fight a complete prohibition.

One difference between the New Zealand and US implementation of self-regulated DTCA is the economic policy that surrounds the healthcare system. In contrast to the previous Democratic Party initiatives to develop a market-based approach to healthcare delivery, the National Party government has been successful (Coney, 2002) and PHARMAC's push for more regulation may supersede private protection based on free speech concerns.

Results

DIFFERENCES

Commentators on DTCA policy have fundamental differences of opinion. Calfee (2002) suggests the United States should take advantage of the New Zealand experience in that New Zealand has demonstrated that self-regulation for DTCA can work. Others, including Coney (2002), do not see New Zealand as offering a model that other nations would be wise to follow.

SIMILARITIES

The United States and New Zealand share a commitment to free speech rights. Whether those free speech rights should be reserved for corporate entities and commercial speech is still in a fluid state in New Zealand as it is in the US. Consequently there will probably be a rise in the public relations efforts, including lobbying in New Zealand to protect such extrapolated rights.

Discussion

EXPECTATIONS

At the onset of this investigation, there seemed to be a trail that would help illuminate the causal connection between DTCA in New Zealand and the United States. The situation in both countries seems to be much more complex and it would take additional research to find key occurrences that may connect the development further.

AGREEMENT WITH PREVIOUS RESEARCH

Since there is much debate and disagreement between the previous research and public discussion, there would seem to be no agreement with the overall thrust of previous research and the current analysis. Many spurious variables as to the relationship between the development histories would need to be explored.

THEORY/PRACTICAL APPLICATIONS

This summary of research and public discussion provides a needed agenda to continued research and discussion but offers no clear answer on the relationship between the international developments of DTCA.

LIMITATIONS

To determine the effect of cross-department or cross-company activities in bringing DTCA to the information marketplace, many more avenues of communications need to be explored (*Prescription Drug Expenditures in 2001: Another Year of Escalating Costs*, 2002). As highly visible as they are, there are still many unknowns about the impact of DTC drug ads—on prescribing trends, the public's health and drug costs. Consensus has emerged in the last year that more research is needed to measure and clarify this impact. Our results do not address the affect of DTC ads on the public's health. But they add to the growing circumstantial evidence that such ads are one element—and perhaps an increasingly important one—in the recent trend to the expanded use of newer prescription drugs and the resultant increased overall spending on pharmaceuticals.

FUTURE DIRECTIONS

Further research into the proactive programs of international pharmaceutical companies, media companies and advertising agencies would need to be completed before a clearer picture of the relationship between international DTCA could be made.

DTCA is motivated by a market concept of the health system in which consumers are shaped by commercial and other pressures to access competing providers of service. In these conditions values of health gain and of a managed and sustainable, publicly funded health system are secondary to those of efficiently clearing markets for health products and services (*Direct to Consumers Advertising of Pharmaceutical Products*, 2001).

Within a publicly funded health system DTCA is likely to have major financial implications (clearly there is an impact in privately funded systems, but a public system is more tightly budget-limited). Firstly the intention of DTCA is to lift patient demand for advertised products. Where visits to the doctor and prescriptions are either fully funded or subsidized from the public purse—as they are in New Zealand—then DTCA is likely to have a major impact on the health budget (*Direct to Consumers Advertising of Pharmaceutical Products*, 2001).

In 1997 the FDA clarified that television advertisements could refer consumers to a physician, a 1-800 number, a manufacturer website and a magazine article that provides the full description of the drugs as required by labeling regulations (Rosenthal, Ernst, Donohue, Epstein and Frank, 2003).

References

ABPI (2003). [Online.] http://www.abpi.org.uk/information/industry_positions (retrieved June 9, 2002).

Aston, W.G. (1972). *Nihongi*. Rutland, VT: Tuttle Company.

Barranger, D. (1993, February 22). Japan tiptoes toward comparative ads. *Adweek*, 10.

Bittar, C. (2002, April 21). Prescription drugs. *Adweek*, 44.

Brown, A. (1999). *A Report to ASBOF*. [Online.] http://www.adassoc.org.uk.position/asbof.html (retrieved October 5, 2000).

Calfee, J.E. (2002). Public policy issues in direct-to-consumer advertising of prescription drugs. *Journal of Public Policy and Marketing* (Fall).

Chepesiuk, R. (2002). If you had the choice ... Canadian pharmaceutical marketing. *The Pharmaceutical Advertising Advisory Board Review*, 12–13.

Cohen, J.B. (2002). Introductory comments: direct-to-consumer prescription drug advertising: evaluating regulatory policy in the United States and New Zealand. *Journal of Public Policy and Marketing* (Fall).

Coney, S. (2002). Advertising of prescription pharmaceuticals: a consumer perspective from New Zealand. *Journal of Public Policy and Marketing*, 21(2): 213–23.

Cooper-Chen, A. (1997). *Mass Communication in Japan*. Ames, IA: Iowa State University Press.

David, C. (2001). Marketing to the consumer: perspectives from the pharmaceutical industry. *Marketing Health Services*, 21(1): 4–11.

Direct to Consumers Advertising of Pharmaceutical Products (2001). [Online.] http://www.pha.org.nz/publications/dtca.htm (retrieved June 9, 2003).

Direct-to-Consumer Advertising of Prescription Drugs (2000). Council on Ethical and Judicial Affairs.

Direct-to-Consumer Advertising of Prescription Medicines in New Zealand: A Discussion Paper (2000). Wellington: Ministry of Health.

Eagle, L. (2002). Direct consumer promotion of prescription drugs: a review of the literature and the New Zealand experience. *International Journal of Medical Marketing*, 2(4): 293–310.

Edwards, J. (2003). Senator Edwards' plan to make prescription drugs more affordable. [Online.] http://www.johnedwards.com (retrieved June 6, 2003).

Farris, P.W. and M.J. Moore (2004). *The Profit Impact of the Marketing Strategy Project: Retrospect and Prospects*. Cambridge: Cambridge University Press.

Foley, L. and D. Gross (2000). *Are Consumers Well Informed about Prescription Drugs? The Impact of Direct-to-Consumer Advertising*. Washington, DC: Public Policy Group of the American Association of Retired Persons.

Goetzel, D. (2001, December 10). Ad Age Marketer of the Year: Pfizer. *Advertising Age*.

Hasegawa, K. (1995). Does the US comparative advertising TV practice work abroad? The case of Japan and the United States. Paper presented at the International Communication Association, Albuquerque, New Mexico.

Helgert, J. (2001). From harmony to confrontation in Japanese advertising. *Japan Studies Association Journal*, 3.

Hiromichi, M. (1983). *Kodansha Encyclopedia of Japan*. Tokyo: Kodansha.

Hoek, J. and P. Gendall (2002). Direct-to-consumer advertising down under: an alternative perspective and regulatory framework. *Journal of Public Policy and Marketing* (Fall).

IMS Health Data (2003). Total US promotional spending by type. [Online.] http://www.imshealth.com/ims/portal/front/articleC/O,2777,6599_41551570_41718516,00.html (retrieved May 19, 2003).

Inoue, O. (1996). Advertising in Japan: changing times for an economic giant. In K.T. Firth (ed.), *Advertising in Asia: Communication, Culture and Consumption*. Ames, IA: Iowa State University Press.

Joncheere, K. de (2002). Providing prescription medicine information to consumers: is there a role for direct-to-consumer promotion? Paper presented at the Health Action International Europe Symposium, the Netherlands.

Kaye, L. (2003). Tighter controls for NZ pharmaceutical ads. [Online.] http://www.bandy.com/auarticles/21/)c006721.asp (retrieved June 9, 2003).

Levitt, G. (1995). Advertising prescription drugs directly to the consumer: can FDA stop worrying and learn to love direct-to-consumer advertising? [Online.] http://www.venable.com/tools/elecmarket/dirtocom.htm (retrieved October 5, 2000).

Lexchin, J. (1999). Direct-to-consumer advertising: impact on patient expectations regarding disease management. *Disease Management and Health Outcomes*, 5(5): 273–83.

Lu, D. (1974). *Sources of Japanese History*. New York: McGraw-Hill.

Marketing plans for medicinal products available on prescription only (2001). [Online.] http://www.healthyskepticism.org (retrieved June 5, 2003).

Maskery, M.A. (1992, March 30). In Japan, Detroit dares to compare. *Advertising Age*, 63: S521.

Matter, M.R. (2002). Emerging direct-to-consumer advertising of prescription drugs and the learned intermediary doctrine. *Defense Council Journal*, 79–87.

Matthews, M. (2001). *Who's Afraid of Pharmaceutical Advertising? A Response to a Changing Health Care System Policy Report 155*. Lewisville, TX: Institute for Policy Innovation.

Maynard, A. and K. Bloor (2003). Dilemmas in Regulation of the Market for Pharmaceuticals. *Health Affairs*, 22(3).

Medawar, C. (2001). Because you're worth it. *Health Matters*, 43(Winter).

Meek, C. (2002). *Direct-to-Consumer Advertising of Prescription Medicines: A Review of International Policy and Evidence*. London: Royal Pharmaceutical Society of Great Britain.

Mintzes, B. (2002). For and against: direct-to-consumer advertising is medicalising normal human experience. *British Medical Journal*, 324(7342): 908–9.

Mintzes, B., L. Morris, R.L. Kravitz, A. Kazanjian, K. Bassett, J. Lexchin et al. (2002). Influence of direct to consumer pharmaceutical advertising and patients' requests on prescribing decisions: two site cross sectional survey. *British Medical Journal*, 324: 278–9.

NZMA calls for ban on DTCA (2003). [Online.] http://www.scoop.co/nz/mason/stories/GE0304/S)))11/htm (retrieved April 9, 2003).

Overbeck, W. (1992). *Major Principles of Media Law*. New York: Harcourt Brace Jovanovich.

Prescription Drug Expenditures in 2001: Another Year of Escalating Costs (2002). Washington, DC: National Institute for Health Care Management Research and Educational Foundation.

Rosenthal, B., B. Ernst, J. Donohue, A. Epstein and R. Frank (2003). *Demand Effects of Recent Changes in Prescription Drug Promotion*. Washington, DC: The Henry J. Kaiser Family Foundation.

Rosenthal, M.B., E.R. Berndt and J. Donahue (2002). Promotion of prescription drugs to consumers. *New England Journal of Medicine*, 346: 498–505.

Sansom, G. (1958). *A History of Japan to 1334*. Stanford, CA: Stanford University Press.

Seeman, R. (1986). Comparative adversiting restriction to be eased. *The Japan Law Letter*.

Sheffet, M.J. and S. Kopp (1990). Advertising prescription drugs to the public: headache or relief? *Journal of Public Policy and Marketing*, 9(1): 42–6.

Shields, T. (2003, January 27). Drug-ad fight looms in Congress. *Adweek*.

Socolar, D. and A. Sager (2001, October 2). Pharmaceutical marketing and research spending: the evidence does not support PHARMA's claims. Paper presented at the American Public Health Association Annual Meeting, Atlanta, Georgia.

Stabenow, D. and J. Carnahan (2002). Weekly radio response on the cost of prescription drugs.

Tsunoda, R., W. DeBary and D. Keene (1958). *Sources of Japanese Tradition*. New York: Columbia University Press.

Tu, H. and J. Hargraves (2003). *Seeking Health Care Information: Most Consumers Still on Sidelines*. Washington, DC: Center for Studying Health System Change.

US Government bars unfair drug marketing practices: AIDS healthcare foundation urges lower drug prices to reflect reduced marketing costs (2002). [Online.] http://www.aegis.com/news/pr/2002/PR021007.html (retrieved May 7, 2003).

Vence, D. (2003, March 3). FDA seeks to clarify rules for pharmaceutical advertisements. *Marketing News*, 37: 6.

Weissman, J., D. Blumenthal, A.J. Silk and K. Zapert (2003). The effects of direct-to-consumer drug advertising. *Health Affairs*, 22(2): 14.

Weissman, R. (1998). First Amendment follies: expanding corporate speech rights. *Multinational Monitor*, 19(3).

Wenley, S. (2000, February 9). Minister puts DTC ads under gun. *New Zealand GP*, 1–2.

Wolfe, S. (2001). Testimony before the Subcommittee on Consumer Affairs Hearing, Senate Commerce Committee Hearing on direct-to-consumer advertising [Online.] http://www.citizen.org/publications/release.cfm?ID=6785 (retrieved April 23, 2002).

Epilogue:
Is There a Common Thread in International Advertising?

EMMANUEL U. ONYEDIKE

We have come to accept advertising as a paid, non-personal communication through various media by organizations and individuals who are in some way identified in the advertising message. We have also seen advertising as a form of persuasive communication. O'Guinn, Allen and Semenik (2009) see international advertising as the preparation and placement of advertising in different national and cultural markets.

The common thread I found among the chapters of this book is the concern over the values and context that advertising messages convey. Transnational corporations produce advertisements that are shown locally in Africa, the Middle East, Asia, Europe and Latin America. Alozie points out advertisements convey specific ideological and contextual values and have the capability of undermining the cultural values of recipient countries. Dakroury argues that advertising must represent the audience's taste, values and popular culture for it to achieve its goal in the Arab world. Hetsroni laments the displacement of Israel's traditional national symbols in advertisements by global Western values.

Quarles cautions companies itching to advertise in Cambodia to consider the country's cultural environment. O'Connor and Casper discuss how multinational tobacco companies use indirect advertising strategies in China to keep their brands in consumers' minds. They sponsor events and programming, product tie-ins, and product placement in films or other media venues. The authors state the companies seek to develop linkages with other companies that possess desired legitimacy. In reality, the companies want to associate themselves with social norms without changing their core businesses. Also, the authors state the companies rely on traditional forms of advertising to present a desired corporate image. Fortunately for the multinational companies, Asian consumers have a deep-seated craving for Western products.

On the other hand, Venkateswaran analyzes how the Indonesian government plays a balancing act between preserving indigenous value systems and encouraging growth, media convergence and consumerism. The author advises multinational advertisers that using nonverbal messages, face-saving tactics and building long-term relationships may appeal to their intended consumers in Indonesia. Meanwhile, Bhatia and Bhargava examine the marketing, linguistic and advertising challenges facing those who want to reach and persuade the emerging markets of rural India. They point out that advertisers will have to rely on a complex mix and manipulation of conventional media to get their messages across. Still in Asia, Xue looks at advertising's communication styles in

China, Japan and South Korea. He points out their advertising appeals are related to group consensus, veneration of the elderly or tradition, and status. On a comparative note, the author states US commercials use more individualistic appeals than those in Korea or China. He also describes the East Asian advertising techniques as a soft-sell approach as opposed to the hard-sell, direct approach of the US where product qualities and virtues are emphasized. He underscores the importance of choosing appropriate advertising appeals that match consumers' interests, needs and cultural beliefs in order to persuade them.

As for Europe, McBride describes Moldova's ambivalent attitude toward advertising. On one hand, advertising is allowed, but on the other hand it is heavily regulated. There are rules limiting political ad-time for candidates during election campaigns. Ads for alcohol or tobacco products are not allowed on TV between 7 a.m. and 10 p.m. When allowed, such ads must carry a warning about potential damage to consumers. On the other hand, Amos Owen Thomas evaluates advertising practices and improvisations that businesses use in Kazakhstan. This resource-rich economy made an uneasy transition from communism to capitalism after the dissolution of the Soviet Union in 1991. According to Thomas, multinational advertising corporations introduced advertising in the country and contributed a third of all advertising expenditure. He also points out that television rating research is considered unreliable. Therefore, advertisers in Kazakhstan rely on their instincts in choosing programs in which to advertise their products. Thomas thinks media and advertising in the country are less developed than in the rest of Europe. Meanwhile, McBride and Damjan describe advertising in the emerging democracies of Eastern and Central Europe as transitional. They cite Slovenia as a country that has more in common with West European nations than other former Yugoslavian countries in terms of values and attitudes toward civil society, family, religion, politics and democracy. They conclude that advertising in Slovenia reflects Western values.

With respect to Latin America, Torres-Baumgarten explains that as a result of disparities in advertising regulations, scope of development of the industry, spending budgets and spending allocation by media, it may be difficult to use global or regional advertising across various markets. The author notes that on strategic activities, the multinational companies use standardized approaches across the regions. However, their subsidiary agencies operate as country-specific and autonomous units. Meanwhile, Gomez states the Latin American advertising industry has been modeled after that of the United States and Europe. The author cautions that the laws, values, beliefs and national identities of countries must be considered before any marketing strategy or advertising campaign is created or implemented.

Comparative looks at advertising indicate that for gender roles and social power, advertisers portray what they think is acceptable to the target markets. Huhmann and Argo compared magazine advertisements from Africa against those from North America and found some similarities and a few differences. In ads from both continents, males were portrayed more often than females in work settings, in professional occupations, and with masculine products. They found no difference in the number of male and female portrayals in North American ads. However, there were fewer females than males in African ads. They also found that females possess superior social power in more ads from Africa than from North America. On another angle, the American free enterprise system is often accused of exporting marketing tactics and the underlying cultural values to most countries without invitation.

Helgart and Zahradnik did a comparative analysis of direct-to-consumer advertising strategies used in the United States, Japan and New Zealand. They looked at comparative advertising as a type of marketing communication involving two types of selling messages: factual ads which contrast comparative product features with superior features of the sponsor's product and argumentative ads, which use reasoning or emotional appeals to distinguish the sponsor's product from that of the competitor. Prior to 1986, comparative advertising was illegal in Japan. Harmony and being considerate to others are highly regarded in Japan's culture. Comparative and competitive ads were initially seen as threats to those two values. According to the authors, American advertisers gradually altered the Japanese advertising environment by making comparative advertising acceptable. The authors also state that because of free speech rights, United States and New Zealand are the only two developed countries that permit robust direct-to-consumer advertising of drugs.

Advertising has its foundation in culture. In recognition and respect of the critical role culture plays in everybody's life, the Ibos of Nigeria say it is the firewood found in each locality that is used to cook local meals. How come, then, that international advertising insists on a one-size-fits-all approach to preparing and disseminating persuasive messages? Advertising must reflect and respect diverse cultures.

What could be done in light of all the new forms of advertising and marketing, media expansion, technological advances and globalization? I think that advertisers, as persuasive communicators, should let ethical principles guide whatever they do. Why? The indirect effects of advertising have raised ethical concerns. Advertisements seem to attack value systems when they glamorize certain lifestyles, such as smoking and alcohol consumption, and promote acceptance of stereotypes. Cohen (2000) states cigarette advertising is rich in imagery and symbolic associations, such as exciting lifestyles, masculinity, femininity, success and sophistication.

As Patterson and Wilkins (2008, p. 69) argue, ethical thinking must have equal weight as market research and strategic communication in the advertising process, if advertising practitioners want to be trusted. They further assert (2011) that the ethical goal of advertising "should be the empowerment of multiple stakeholders" (p. 59). The stakeholders, in this case, include potential buyers and sellers, and other citizens.

I recommend to all international advertisers Patterson and Wilkins's (2011, pp. 59–63) amplified TARES test of ethical persuasion, which expanded Baker and Martinson's (2001) TARES test. Practitioners who take the test will know whether their advertisements are ethically worthy. They have to answer five questions: Are the ad claims truthful? Is the claim an authentic one? Does the ad treat the receiver with respect? Is there equity between the sender and the receiver? Is the ad socially responsible? The authors elaborated on respect by calling on advertising practitioners to ask themselves this question, "Am I willing to take full, open and personal responsibility for the content of this ad?" (2011, p. 62). On equity, they want practitioners to answer the question, "Is the recipient of the message on the same level playing field as the ad's creator?" (p. 62). On being socially responsible, they state there must be ways to protect those who could be significantly harmed by using the advertised products (p. 63). They also want practitioners to answer the question, "Does this ad increase or decrease the trust the average person has for persuasive messages?" (p. 63).

Though standardization is prevalent in international advertising, studies in this book indicate that in some places partnership between transnational and local companies is flourishing. Multinational advertisers are localizing advertising in Latin America more than they are standardizing various elements. Development of a global economy has ushered in a number of changes as far as values and lifestyles are concerned. These changes are also reflected in advertising. Let us hope that with globalization people are capable of understanding, and are willing to accept and respect different cultures.

References

Baker, S. and D. Martinson (2001). The TARES test: five principles of ethical persuasion. *Journal of Mass Media Ethics*, 16(2 and 3). As discussed in Patterson, P. and L. Wilkins (2011). *Media Ethics: Issues and Cases*. 7th ed. New York: McGraw-Hill.

Cohen, J. (2000). Playing to win: marketing and public policy at odds over Joe Camel. *Journal of Public Policy and Marketing*, 18(Fall): 155–67.

O'Guinn, T., C. Allen and R. Semenik (2009). *Advertising and Integrated Brand Promotion*. 5th ed. Boston, MA: South Western Publishing.

Patterson, P. and L. Wilkins (2008). *Media Ethics: Issues and Cases*. 6th ed. New York: McGraw-Hill.

Patterson, P. and L. Wilkins (2011). *Media Ethics: Issues and Cases*. 7th ed. New York: McGraw-Hill.

Index

If you have found this book useful you may be interested in other titles from Gower

The Psychology of Marketing:
Cross-Cultural Perspectives
Gerhard Raab, G. Jason Goddard, Riad A. Ajami and Alexander Unger
Hardback: 978-0-566-08903-9
Ebook: 978-0-566-08904-6

Memorable Customer Experiences:
A Research Anthology
Edited by Adam Lindgreen, Joëlle Vanhamme and Michael B. Beverland
Hardback: 978-0-566-08868-1
Ebook: 978-0-566-09207-7

Project Success:
Critical Factors and Behaviours
Emanuel Camilleri
Hardback: 978-0-566-09228-2
Ebook: 978-0-566-09229-9

Talent Management in the Developing World:
Adopting a Global Perspective
Joel Alemibola Elegbe
Hardback: 978-1-4094-1813-9
Ebook: 978-1-4094-1814-6

Visit **www.gowerpublishing.com** and

- search the entire catalogue of Gower books in print
- order titles online at 10% discount
- take advantage of special offers
- sign up for our monthly e-mail update service
- download free sample chapters from all recent titles
- download or order our catalogue